COMPARATIVE STUDIES IN RELIGION AND SOCIETY
Mark Juergensmeyer, Editor

1. *Redemptive Encounters: Three Modern Styles*
   in the Hindu Tradition
   Lawrence A. Babb

2. *Saints and Virtues*
   Edited by John Stratton Hawley

Saints
and
Virtues

Saints
and
Virtues

Edited by
John Stratton Hawley

UNIVERSITY OF CALIFORNIA PRESS
Berkeley • Los Angeles • London

UNIVERSITY OF CALIFORNIA PRESS
Berkeley and Los Angeles, California

University of California Press, Ltd.
London, England

© 1987 by
The Regents of the University of California

1 2 3 4 5 6 7 8 9

Library of Congress Cataloging-in-Publication Data

Saints and virtues.

Bibliography: p.
Includes index.
1. Saints — Comparative studies. 2. Virtues.
3. Religious ethics — Comparative studies. I. Hawley,
John Stratton, 1941 –
BL488.S35 1987 291.6 86-24993
ISBN 0-520-05984-0 (alk. paper)

Printed in the United States of America

CONTENTS

PART II • SAINTS OF THE MODERN WORLD

ACKNOWLEDGMENTS

Most of the essays presented here were formulated and first discussed in the context of a multiyear, comparative study of social values that was cooperatively undertaken by the Graduate Theological Union in Berkeley and the Center for the Study of World Religions at Harvard University. The project was directed by Mark Juergensmeyer and John Carman, and was supported by generous grants from the National Endowment for the Humanities and the Eli Lilly Foundation, to whom all participants — many from other institutions — are greatly indebted.

The editor would like to thank a number of friends and colleagues who have commented critically on various aspects of this volume, chief among them Caroline Bynum, Paul Courtright, Barbara Metcalf, Kevin Reinhart, and Laura Shapiro. Walton van Winkle, Steven Hopkins, and Andrew Davis have considerably eased the task of readying the manuscript for publication, and Naomi Schneider of the University of California Press has been staunch in its support. Two sets of students and colleagues — first on the West Coast, then in the East — gave life to this book by participating in comparative seminars on sainthood that were conducted as it began to be and as it neared completion. The earlier course — at the Graduate Theological Union in 1982 — was co-taught with Mark Juergensmeyer, and the later one — at Columbia University in 1986 — with Robert Somerville. To both men the editor is grateful for measures of confidence and encouragement that have made it possible to contemplate the preparation of this volume with some equanimity, and so many other things as well.

NOTE ON TRANSLITERATION

Standard, internally consistent systems of transliteration have been adopted for terms not normally written in roman script. Certain words, however, have achieved sufficient currency in English that their usual spelling has been preserved, even if it is at variance with what a more rigorous policy of transliteration would require. Examples are such familiar terms as Sufi, Shiva, Krishna, and Confucius, when they occur independently in a sentence. If such terms are found in sequences of foreign words or as elements in compounds, however, they appear in the form that integrates them into the larger whole (*ṣūfī, śiva,* etc.).

INTRODUCTION: SAINTS AND VIRTUES

John Stratton Hawley

Here in the West our notion of both religion and morality tends toward the didactic: teachings and precepts seem to buttress the lives of those we call good. The religious person is pictured as someone who has internalized what is often termed a "system of beliefs," and the moral person is one who lives up to his or her principles. The world's great religious traditions are hedged about with articles of faith and codes of conduct — commandments great and small — that enhance this way of seeing things; and today, when people are more ready than ever to question their traditions, these commandments loom especially large in the popular view of religious life. But the great religions did not gain their hold on us by precepts alone. Within each religion a powerful body of tradition emphasizes not codes but stories, not precepts but personalities, not lectures but lives.

This literature of lives is widespread and deeply influential. Christendom has its vast corps of saints: their individual stories were already being strung into hagiographical garlands in the fourth century, and papal legislation about the canonization process was still being formulated in the nineteenth. Jewry has its righteous ones (*tsaddiqim*), patriarchs, and prophets. Muslims, too, have stories of the prophets (*qiṣaṣ al anbiyā'*) — though what is meant by the term is rather different — and anecdotes about the life of the "seal of the prophets," Muhammad, and a range of lesser figures. Stories of spiritual guides and about the righteous and still potent dead (*walīs, shaykhs, ṣūfīs, pīrs*) also flourish. Hindu hagiographical collections sometimes begin high, at the level of divinity, but soon descend to the still remarkable but distinctly human lives of their devotees. Sacred biographies in Buddhism concern not only the life of the Buddha but those of his immediate followers as well; tales of other notable personages such as *bodhisattvas* and world-renouncers have also been carefully preserved. In China, Buddhist accounts were paralleled by and sometimes integrated into an enormous body of Confucian and especially Taoist hagiography, the latter dealing with everything from local adepts to heads of therapeutic lineages to divine agents who carried the force of Lao Tzu; and often a distinctly didactic note was sounded as a life was told.

These collections of extraordinary and exemplary lives differ significantly from one religious community to another, and from subgroup to subgroup and period to period; but they bear family resemblances that are often striking. Indeed these various hagiographical traditions might be threads drawn from a single skein of yarn: the weavers of the larger fabric of tradition had different ideas about where a thread should go and how often it should be used, but once one knows what color to look for, one will almost always find it. And this worldwide attention to "the lives of the saints" has by no means been neglected in our own time. On the way to the airport from downtown Seattle, freeway drivers pass a huge concrete retaining wall on which a devotee has spray-painted a latter-day postscript to the Chinese hagiographical tradition. "Chiang Ching," it announces: "Live like her."

When this reminder went up, Jiang Qing was on trial in the People's Republic as the leading member of the Gang of Four, who had been spearheads of the subsequently discredited Cultural Revolution. Like so many Christian saints, particularly the earliest, she seemed to be preparing herself for martyrdom. Like the Christian martyrs, she refused to recant, displaying exemplary adherence to the cause for which her followers thought she had lived, even when others fell away in discouraging numbers. Like them, she participated in a select fellowship of the just to which she was tied, as many of them were, by bonds of personal friendship and cooperation. And, like them, she lent her name as an amulet for the succor and aid of those who never knew her, but believe. The American revolutionaries who inscribed her name must have felt that its very letters were enough to call forth an image sufficient to guide correct behavior. Their exhortation, even in old-style imperialist transliteration, tells us much about the persistent moral force of saintly lives.

It seems unlikely that the bishops at the Second Vatican Council had Jiang Qing on their minds when they issued their authoritative pronouncement on "the authentic cult of the saints," but the factors that lifted her name to such prominence might have come straight from the council's own words:

> Let the faithful be taught, therefore, that the authentic cult of the saints consists not so much in the multiplying of external acts, but rather in the intensity of our active love. By such love, for our own greater good and that of the Church, we seek from the saints "example in their way of life, fellowship in their communion, and aid in their intercession."[1]

---

1. Walter M. Abbot, S.J., gen. ed., *The Documents of Vatican II* (New York: Herder and Herder/Association Press, 1966), 84. The quotation is from the preface granted for use in various dioceses.

With this pronouncement the council drew attention to three areas in which the lives of remarkable persons could serve to enrich and empower the lives of ordinary individuals: example, fellowship, and aid. While the bishops, of course, assumed only one community of faith tying saint to commoner — the Christian Church — these three aspects of veneration go a long way toward explaining the power of saintliness in a wide spectrum of religious and cultural traditions, and suggest a context within which all saints exert their moral force.

EXAMPLE

The key term is *example,* a word whose meanings diverge in two directions that are only distantly related. In one sense an example is an instance, an illustration, a case in point. In the other, an example is not a subset of something larger but a paradigm that sets the shape for a series of imitative phenomena that follow in its wake. It is a model, a prototype, not merely an example but an exemplar. Both these usages help us to state the moral impetus so often present in hagiographical traditions. On the one hand, saints can be examples *of* something, or even of someone; on the other, they can be examples *to* someone. Often, of course, they are both — and sometimes, one must admit, neither.

In the first instance one finds saints portrayed so as to exemplify virtues already known to those who hear their stories. What is remarkable about a life, then, is the purity with which it reflects a particular mode of character. In Butler's *Lives of the Fathers, Martyrs, and other Principal Saints* the narrator's eye in story after story is trained on the way in which the saints gave away their earthly wealth and abjured all luxuries of the body. Many of these accounts center around great donations — made all at once or staggered according to some rational program — and the adoption of a regimen of bread and pulse. If they are read as a group, the stories seem a single lesson in self-abnegation told over and over again.

Other hagiographical collections strike a slightly different note. Rather than instantiating a single well-known virtue or a small set of interrelated virtues in a multiplicity of lives, they choose lives to represent each virtue, thereby displaying the range of virtues that life ideally ought to comprehend. The tales of the charismatic *tsaddiqim* in Hasidic Jewry since the eighteenth century frequently illustrate this principle — stressing the fervent devotion of one master, the charity of another, the humility of a third, the unshakable trust of a fourth — and some collections of Buddhist *avadānas* do the same. Several of the earliest of these collections highlight particular virtues exemplified by the Buddha's disciples: Ānanda's compassion, Sāriputta's wisdom, and Moggallāna's magical power. These virtues could be replicated in similar hagiographical anthologies that were created for later generations. The "eminent monks" described in the *Kao-seng-chuan* of sixth-century China remind one of the Buddha's own disciples and the virtues they exemplify, and accounts of *bodhisattvas* also served as emblems of cardinal Buddhist virtues: in particular Avalokiteśvara stood for compassion and Mañjuśrī for wisdom.

In *jātaka* tales, which related the praiseworthy actions of the Buddha Śākyamuni in past lives, a whole series of virtues that had theretofore been taught in ethical fables were made a part of the biography of the One whose life comprehended all virtues. And it is charming to see that Aesop, who seems ultimately responsible for having framed a number of these moral tales, found his own way into hagiographical literature. In certain Muslim lists of prophets he appears as a man named Luqmān, and as one of the prophets his lineage was fulfilled by a figure with a range of personal virtues as comprehensive as the Buddha's own: Muhammad. In accord with the general centralizing urge of Muslim faith and with the conviction that Muhammad was the unique prophet of the present age, official Islam had little impetus to disperse his virtues among several hypostatizations, but in compensation the literature of early Islamic tradition (*ḥadīth*) has an overwhelmingly influential collection of tales concerning his own life. Both individually and collectively, quite a number of these tales can be read as preaching certain virtues — generosity, truthfulness, submission to God — and they, like other, seemingly incidental features of Muhammad's life, have served to give shape to the imitation of the Prophet in Muslim piety.

In such ways virtues that were expounded as principles took on flesh and blood. In Buddhism the first treasure of the faith, its teaching (*dharma*), was amplified by a second, the person of the Buddha himself. In Islam it was not only the message of the Prophet but the exemplification of facets of that message in the character of the messenger that built the tradition: The Qur'ān was supplemented by the *ḥadīth*. And in both these traditions, as well as in others, such virtue was also taught in the lives of a panoply of ancillary figures. Strikingly, this exemplification occurred even in traditions such as the Chinese and the Hindu, where the central "secular" virtues were kept at arm's length from the ecstatic realm that served as the home of so many saints. The lives of not a few Taoist luminaries are told in such a way as to proclaim the efficacy of filial piety, a seemingly secular, Confucian virtue; and in India, virtues such as generosity and courage, which have a clear place within the scheme of *dharma*, are sometimes surprisingly exemplified in the lives of *bhakti* saints.

This understanding of saints as persons who attain their status because they exemplify what is generally preached and accepted might from an ethical point of view be called a "deductive" conception of sainthood. Here virtues predate the saints that give them living form. But the exemplary power of the saints can be understood in another way: they can be seen as models, persons from whom one can learn patterns of life for which no principle or code can serve as an adequate representation. This approach would be an "inductive" conception of sainthood, which corresponds to the second sense of the term *example*. And this approach is perhaps even more critical than the first to an appreciation of the centrality of saints.

In the article that begins this book Peter Brown explores this notion of exemplar as it appears in the Christianity of the late Roman Empire — that is, near the generating point of the Christian cult of the saints. He suggests that such saints gathered and exerted their moral force through a process of intimate learning that rendered them "personal classics" from the point of view of Greco-Roman *paideia* and "representations of Christ" against the background of Jewish and Christian thinking about the nature and transmission of "the image of God." These men and women represented Christ and the unblemished humanity he had restored, not as parts of a more complex fabric or as instances of truths generally known, but as whole people who "carried Christ" with such totality as to "re-present" for their generation the luster that had characterized the original. Their personhood was the crux of the morality they taught — often implicitly rather than discursively — and what they sought to imitate and perfect was no specific aspect of the life of Jesus, as in later understandings of the phrase *imitatio Christi*, but the unfallen Adam that waits to be rediscovered within us all. They were not examples typifying aspects of the whole, they *were* convincingly the whole; as exemplars they contrasted markedly to a world of shards and fallen fragments by which they were surrounded. They showed the way through to a level of being so coherent that in contrast to the dimness or at best reflected glory of ordinary existence it seemed able to generate its own light. Hence the language of luminosity pervades descriptions of them. Their impact was registered in "flashes of signal light" and "shining visions," not in what is usually meant by moral instruction.

This sense of virtue as something exuded as light, and of moral learning as something in the nature of seeing or experiencing revelation, is by no means confined to the literature of Christian saints. Such luminosity is a staple of Hindu descriptions of the saintly and divine, and Hindus travel great distances literally to obtain the sight (*darśan*) of those they venerate, often expecting no verbal communication. One focus of such devout journeys is Sathya Sai Baba, a modern saint with a pan-Indian following, who is described in Lawrence Babb's contribution to this collection. Jewish accounts of the *tsaddiqim* often stress a similarly palpable glow in the saintly faces of these sometimes enigmatic teachers — a radiance whose history takes one back to the visage of Moses himself and that confirms the lineage to which they belong, as if it had been transmitted by blood. And adepts in certain Taoist traditions, to cite still another milieu, are also said to manifest this inner luminosity. Such descriptions reveal that human excellence, including moral excellence, cannot fit, ultimately, into discrete categories of words and acts. It is a pervasive quality — a "becoming," as Caroline Bynum says in characterizing the imitation of Christ among medieval women mystics — and one can appropriate it only through an act of absorption. It is not a thing to be mastered.[2]

This returns us to the problem inherent in the two divergent senses of the word *example*. According to the word's first meaning, the saintly example instantiates and thus clarifies general principles of morality and qualities of character that can be articulated as meaningful and understood as possible for all participants in a society or community of faith. When one speaks of one's saintly mother, one is probably pointing in the direction of such perfection in the living out of ordinary morality. In its second sense, by contrast, the saintly exemplar does not always accord so easily with the moral standards that articulate a culture's highest sense of itself. Often saints do not just heighten ordinary morality. They implicitly question it by seeming to embody a strange, higher standard that does not quite fit with the moral system that governs ordinary propriety and often cannot be articulated in normal discourse.

In discussing stories that depict some of the devotional (*bhakti*) saints of north India, I have called this a "morality beyond morality." Because such saints exemplify something deeper than ordinary morality, they cannot always be expected to serve as examples for action in "this world." As Christians have pondered their saints, too, they have recognized that ordinary people should not always be bidden to follow the saints' example. One might wonder at the saints, one might try to imitate the virtues they teach, but one should not necessarily imitate what they themselves do, for their actions are sometimes unpredictable, even outlandish.

Hester Gelber draws our attention to this aspect of things in her essay on St. Francis. She explains the significance of the moment in which Francis insisted on having himself paraded naked before the good people of Assisi and notes the resistance of one of his own disciples to participating in the display and the hesitancy of his chroniclers to let it stand on in its own terms as an example for posterity. For Francis himself, it was probably, as Gelber puts it, a "theater" more than a paradigm, and other saints occasionally sounded a note of overt caution in recommending their acts to their disciples. They sometimes saw that their model might be too seductive, too heady for the ordinary. At times they would urge people to go beyond a concern with rules and works, to trust in the force of love and accept the attraction of union with God; but at other times they would dwell on the importance of humility and obedience in an effort to find a common ground that could relate their extraordinary states and acts to other people's ordinary ones.

One suspects that in the enthusiastic telling of the lives of *bhakti* saints there is also an implicit note of caution. On the one hand, it is a matter for wonder and celebration that the extraordinary virtues of these saints manage

2. Caroline Walker Bynum, "Women Mystics and Eucharistic Devotion in the Thirteenth Century," *Women's Studies* 11 (1984): 201–2.

somehow to generate a confirming, sympathetic response in the wider world. Such moments of response — the saints' miracles — are often called just that in the original: *acaraj* — "surprises," "wonders." But by labelling these moments wondrous, the authors effectively issue a caution to ordinary mortals. The medium in which the saints live is not quite their own and should perhaps be regarded at a certain distance.

This two-sided presentation is a genuine ambivalence. The world of love and ease that such saintliness makes possible is clearly valued as superior to the realm of ordinary interactions, and it exerts a strong attraction on the Hindu and Indian Muslim populace. Followers often appeal to their saints — *sants, bhaktas,* and *pīrs* — for miraculous egress from the difficulties of this world. Yet at the same time both the authors of these hagiographies and the crowds who hear them appear to understand that the attractive, exemplary power of the saints is not exhausted if their extraordinary power cannot be directly assimilated into the workings of life as we normally know it. The saints' lives reveal a supernal standard against the background of which the limitations of ordinary morality are easier to bear, even if nothing visibly changes in the near at hand. Even in that indirect influence the saints' power is being tapped. As Lawrence Babb says in regard to Sathya Sai Baba, a notoriously enigmatic figure, in his article in this collection: "The overarching moral message of his persona . . . seems to be a recipe less for how to lead a virtuous life than for how to lead a life in which virtue has meaning."

In certain settings the two sides of the ambivalence with which religious communities view their saints can be broken apart. Most familiarly, this split follows a division between religious specialists and the general populace: lay audiences are expected to react one way to the example of the saints, clerical or religious audiences in another. One can see this clearly in Stanley Tambiah's essay on the wide and many-layered following of Acharn Man, a forest monk of modern Thai Buddhism. Acharn Man's monastic pupils related to him in a "professional" way, receiving his instruction, emulating his deeds, and, now that he is dead, reading his biography. His lay devotees, by contrast, appropriate his virtue less as moral canon than as charismatic power, which is mediated to them through amulets blessed by his successors. A similar tension exists in the medieval Christian West. When a lay audience is assumed for a hagiographical work, the saint tends to be depicted as extraordinary in a miraculous sense, while the saint will appear as a devotional model if an audience of monks is assumed. And if the audience assumed consists of mystics, the saint is hardly delineated as a model at all.

Religious traditions that resist this bifurcation between religious specialists and the laity are apt to generate images of saintly exemplitude whose correspondence to the patterns just sketched is complex and hard to predict. Two essays in this book particularly illustrate the complexity. Tu Wei-ming's study of the Confucian tradition depicts in the sage a figure whose virtue is ultimately inimitable, not because he stands at a distance from common humanity, but because he identifies with it so totally. It is the humility of learning that makes him sagely — a humility that must be personally learned and cannot be appropriated from a model. The ideal of the "wise pupil" (*talmid ḥakham*) is also one of the great standards in Judaism, as Robert Cohn's essay explains, but it is only one of several ideals that loosely correspond to the notion of "saint." Cohn proposes that Judaism's characteristic refusal to regard any ideal as unattainable by all Jews (at least all Jewish males) has prevented the emergence of a special class of beings such as saints and has played a role in keeping the several ideals of Jewish personhood in tension with one another. At the same time it is fascinating to note how many of the features associated with saints and their virtues — a sense of righteousness beyond the law, an ability to intercede in affliction and transfer merit after death, the power to perform miracles, and last but not least, the familiar tension between exemplitude and inimitability — can be found in the "saints" of Judaism, too.

FELLOWSHIP

The pronouncement of Vatican II about what was authentic in the cult of the Christian saints singled out the saints' fellowship as the second important element. In part the bishops had in mind contacts between ordinary people and this select company, but that the elect do form a company is itself a notable phenomenon. Saints typically come in flocks — even the most unusual have analogues elsewhere in the tradition that make them meaningful — and one of their functions is to provide an image of a divine society, a community that can serve as a nurturant family of faith spanning the seen and unseen realms. This community can be conceived in a number of ways. The prophetic lineage that occupies so important a place in Jewish thinking is one. Another in the Jewish sphere is the notion of an elite core of hidden "righteous ones" (*tsaddiqim*), numbering from two to thirty-six at a time, who link the generations in a moral bond that extends far into the past; it endures and causes history to cohere, whatever the failings of the mass may be.

The closest analogue to this concept in Islamic thought is undoubtedly the idea that there are saints who at any given time form an invisible hierarchy in the world, with the "lodestar" (*quṭb*) saint at the top. But one can make other comparisons too. The succession of God's messengers (*rusul*) bears some resemblance to these *tsaddiqim,* since Allah is said to have distributed them on a regular basis to different generations and communities until he revealed his message in its fullness through Muhammad; and in Sufi traditions, such as those discussed by William Brinner and Lamin Sanneh in this volume, it is typically conceived that there are forty generations' worth of masters (*shaykhs*) extending from the present age back to the Prophet. Christians have adopted the somewhat similar idea of the "fellowship of the saints" (*communio sanctorum*), which is conceptually and historically related to this wider milieu. Though in its earliest meaning the phrase *communio sanctorum* referred to participation in the sacraments, it soon acquired the additional meaning that has become more familiar, since *sanctorum* could be construed not only in the neuter but in the generic masculine, and thus refer not to the sacraments but to members of the church, or specifically to the saints.

One can readily appreciate the impetus toward conceiving of and trusting in such linkages. A sense of comfort is conveyed by the conviction that one is not alone in the struggles of faith but rather accompanied by a "cloud of witnesses" whose spiritual accomplishments far exceed one's own. For all the distance that separates God's saints, prophets, and righteous ones from ordinary human beings, their lives are intertwined with ours: the background scenery and accompanying figures in their stories are recognizable. And so too, sometimes, are their inner motives. Hence their lives are often told not only with awe but with an element of fondness that springs from the knowledge that they shared at least some of the common vicissitudes of humanity. This tone of familiarity can be heard in stories of Hindu saints, particularly those of a *bhakti* stripe, as well as in certain Christian accounts. Not infrequently, moreover, some of the most memorable accounts in the lives of Hindu and Christian saints occur at just those points when one saint meets another. Encounters between the canonized women of Jesus' world are vividly remembered—the meeting of Saints Mary and Elizabeth when both are pregnant, for instance—and the tradition of Vaiṣṇava singer-saints in south India begins with a moment when three of them take shelter together from a storm. St. Athanasius writes a biography of St. Anthony; Periyālvār adopts Āṇṭāl as his daughter; St. Francis gives counsel to St. Anthony of Padua; Mīrā Bāī goes to Ravi Dās for her initiation. And in a way vaguely reminiscent of the Renaissance delight in drawing St. Anne and St. John the Baptist into a common frame with Jesus and Mary, Hindu popular tradition continues to create encounters between saints who are not reported to have met at all in earlier hagiographies.

This desire to create an extended sacred family is very much the rule in the history of religions; Protestantism's insistence that God's family is strictly nuclear remains a definite exception. The Reformers' efforts in the direction of hagiographical birth control have been much studied, but the more prevalent urge to enlarge the family is equally intriguing. It generates a network of familiar spirits—sometimes organized with greater hierarchical precision, sometimes with less—who communicate a sense of the continuity, variety, and amplitude of the community of faith, and who as erstwhile denizens of this world span the gap between the known and the unknown. They mediate between the numbingly quotidian phenomena of this life and the central, sometimes densely mysterious forces that control it. Hence they often serve as apt patrons and protectors to draw particular places—churches, temples, towns, or groves—into a wider and more complex grid of reality.

The existence of such great numbers of saints significantly alters the ethical medium in which actions in this world are conceived to occur. Acts are no longer neutral; they take place in a context charged with family resources and responsibilities. Even in such traditions as the Muslim and the Jain, where the possibility of shared spiritual merit is officially disavowed, there is a popular urge to venerate exemplary guardian figures. Doubtless this stems in part from the plain observation that one is not alone in this world, but surely it may also arise in the hope of mitigating that reality. If there are saints, then the social nexus given by birth or circumstance need not provide the only context determining one's acts and giving them meaning. The community of saints provides a supplement, and many of the lives of individual saints underscore the distances at which members of this special corps stand from the common mass. Theirs is a society apart, hence it significantly enriches the environment within which actions make sense.

Few traditions contend that the only powerful spirits are those that use their power for good, and in the Vodou conception, as Karen Brown makes clear, the ranks of the saints themselves (*lwa*) contain ambivalent possibilities. But even Vodou saints serve to leaven the moral environment of ordinary living, providing an element of depth and enrichment that serves to restore what Haitians call "balance." And this happens, not unexpectedly, in distinctly communal contexts. Most societies that have been drawn into the great historical religions concede that the world is habitually out of balance, fallen into error. Hence the general impetus of hagiological thinking is to weight the scales toward the good — the auspicious and harmonious, the path to salvation — both by providing an image of a familial environment in which good acts can succeed and by giving assurance that members of this sanctified family stand ready to help the weak if but petitioned.

AID

Prayer and petition constitute a major element in any ethnology of religion. Their aim is often not only what we would normally consider greater moral adequacy but greater well-being in general, for the hearers of these prayers are persons, not principles. As living beings they potentially superintend a greater range of behavior than that designated by "ought." Muslim sailors and fisherfolk in Bengal take their appeals for safety at sea to Pīr Badar, and a host of other *pīrs* across the Indian subcontinent — some with backgrounds that seem as much Hindu as Muslim — are responsible for curing diseases, guarding cattle, or restoring fertility. In Buddhist Thailand, talismans conveying the blessings and psychic energy of saintly forest-dwelling monks are used in a variety of worldly pursuits, and the gracious powers associated with relics of the Buddha and those close to him have long played a significant role in stimulating pilgrimage in the Buddhist world. The bones, ash, and memorabilia of Christian saints have been no less potent in attracting the petitions of the faithful, and in Haitian Vodou, as Karen Brown points out, talismans of the saints serve as "condensation points for the complex and contradictory stuff of life," providing help in the orientation of individual personalities and acts. Even the Prophet Muhammad himself, whom one might have thought to be invulnerable to such "popular" usages, is sought for his intercessory powers, and as William Brinner reports in his essay here, a well-known Arabic poem depicting the Prophet's powers is used as an amulet throughout the Islamic world.

The widespread importance of such a petitionary cultus makes it plain that saints are perceived, not merely as exemplars in an abstract sense — images of right living — or as an imaginary family of faith and morality, but as living agents of ethical and even physical change. They are besought not just as models to guide behavior but as purveyors of the power that makes action possible. The achievements of the saints are not all that make them extraordinary; in fact, such miraculous doings are considered in more than a few traditions to be strictly incidental to what makes them saints. Central instead is the saints' power to effect changes in the lives of others; what they possess is intrinsically contagious.

In a curious way this contagious power often seems to stem from the fact that the saints do not ultimately own the force they wield. They are frequently conceived as a second echelon of holy beings, dependent for their own power upon their access through devotion to a more encompassing, higher divinity. They minister to devotees, but they are themselves devotees. This symmetry of roles makes them not only accessible but also effective as conduits of power, for their personalities exemplify the modes in which such power can be received. No wonder, then, that Vatican II stressed the intercessory role that the Church has traditionally attributed to the saints, and laid emphasis as well on the counterpart role assigned to the believer: an attitude of devotion or love.

Not every tradition makes so clear a place for a mediating role in understanding its saints, but in the portraits of exemplary figures that are painted by other communities one often finds a similar sense that the saints' power to elicit submission in others derives from their own submission. To speak of submission is to suggest Islam — the word means precisely that — and the lives of Muslim prophets are told in such a way as to underscore this cardinal virtue. Orthodox Muslim teaching recoils from the notion that prophets or anyone else should exercise an intercessory role, since that would imply a distance between ordinary believers and God. As William Brinner's essay in this volume makes clear, that revulsion has been a significant driving force in purist movements within Islam from the ninth century to our own. Yet as Lamin Sanneh's essay suggests, the Muslim world is densely populated with *walīs, shaykhs, ṣūfīs,* and *pīrs* who seem able to exercise just that function by virtue of the means by which they gain their power: prayer and submission. Many of these personages share with the prophets not only this sense of submission but also the strength provided by lineage, which in their case is enhanced by the devotion of one *pīr* to another in a student-teacher succession. When an ordinary Muslim comes to a *pīr* or *walī* for help, then he or she receives as aid a power doubly transmitted: once through the *pīr*'s submission to God, and a second time through his submission to his own *pīr*, and thereby to God again.

In Judaism, Hasidic lines of charismatic authority roughly approximate the Muslim cult of *ṣūfīs, walīs,* and *pīrs,* and in Judaism too the power of the prophets' words derives from a fundamental displacement of self. Similarly in portraits of Hinduism's *bhakti* saints, one finds an emphasis placed on such "open" virtues as generosity, fearlessness, and selflessness; and their devotion is again the source of the effortless capacity to be of aid to others. Even in Buddhism, where a suspicion of theism blunts directly intercessory ways of speaking about the power of exemplary figures such as the forest-dwelling monks of Thailand, there is the sense that the merits of their sanctity are transferable to the laity. These merits do not inhere in the monks themselves but are essentially shared and sharable. They are a force that flows naturally outward because it is generated by self-abnegation, rather than by any effort on the part of an adept to concentrate strength within himself. Such self-abnegation may not always correspond to our inbred notions of the "saintly," as is made clear by the flamboyant virtuosity of Alourdes in her role as medium and mediator — or, as Karen Brown implies, orchestrator — for the Haitian *lwa* archetypes. But in her case it is perhaps more obvious still that saintliness has crucially to do with an ability to receive and communicate a power that aids others, a power that is learned through the saint's submission to a transcendent and encompassing reality.

It would be hard to imagine a greater contrast between saintly personalities than is revealed by seeing Mohandas Gandhi in as close a proximity to Alourdes Champagne as he is in this volume. But the ability to help others looms as large in any portrait of Gandhi's saintliness as it does in that of Alourdes, or of Sathya Sai Baba, who stands between these two, and coming to the help of others was near the core of Gandhi's own conception of what he was about. Like many other saints, he insisted, as Mark Juergensmeyer explains, that the power he had to offer others was in no way particularly his; but the name he used to describe that source was distinctively new. He said it was truth itself (*satya*), and the aid to be found if one grasped onto it (*satyāgraha*) had much to do with the fact that it was no one's special possession but accessible to all. To seize onto the truth was to reach out toward wider and wider communities — including, pointedly, one's adversaries, people who perceived the truth quite differently. Yet people turned to Gandhi as if the power he communicated was his own, and the man's intense absorption in his "experiments with truth" and determination to achieve control over his baser impulses suggest that the sainthood people attributed to him was something he sought himself. He, however, stoutly denied this, protesting perhaps a bit too loudly and insisting, as with his "experiments," that such sanctity was available to all and could not be had by proxy.

One of the attractions of Gandhi, particularly for his Western followers, was that he appeared to construct his saintly identity *de novo*, rather than accepting any single cultural tradition as a guide. One can see that he adapted to his own ends such trappings of traditional Hindu ascetic practice as the ashram, the place of retreat; *brahmacarya*, the practice of celibacy; and the *dhotī*, his unpretentious garb. But he used each of these in a somewhat unconventional way, and the saintly lineage he embraced for himself was hardly what one would expect in a Hindu. No wandering poets, no world-abjuring fakirs — Gandhi's holy community was activist, international, and strongly Christian: Jesus, St. Francis, and Tolstoy were its great pillars. As a consequence of this mix of traditions, Gandhi appeared somewhat strange to both his constituencies, the Indian and the Western, and to this he may have owed some of his charismatic appeal.

In a certain way Gandhi's eclecticism puts him squarely in the company of many generations of saints, whatever tradition they belonged to, for it sprang out of a mission he felt to break through the unsatisfying commonplaces of ordinary existence. In another sense, however, it is a feature of his life that emerges with particular ease in the modern world and is particularly appropriate to it, since the twentieth century stands out from all others for its heightened capacities of global communication and for the increasingly fragile boundaries that separate its parts. On this account Gandhi may especially serve as the patron saint for this volume, in which we try to see whether there are beings who can recognizably be called "saints" no matter what tradition they come from, and whether the communities they represent have recognized them in those terms.

It is perhaps fortunate that because Gandhi is historically near at hand and because he was such a public personality, we have almost as powerful a sense of his frailties and conceits as of his determined sanctity. In dealing with him, we cannot ignore questions about the difference between a life as it is lived and as it is reported, and our attention is inevitably drawn to the important role played by followers in constructing their saints. Because memories are still relatively fresh and records massive, we can raise the embarrassing question of just how saintly Gandhi was, but we cannot dispute how saintly he felt to the great numbers of people who looked to him for guidance. And because the history of Gandhian movements is still being made, we have a chance to take a new look at the old, perhaps central dilemma that saints present to ethical understanding: to be exemplary, the saint must reveal a deeper morality than the world can seemingly abide; yet in the act of doing so the saint ceases to be a model that people really can — or perhaps should — follow.

Does Gandhi show that sainthood is alive and well in the modern world, or is he an untimely aberration? With questions such as these, John Coleman opens the essay that concludes this book. He finds it hard to deny that the "culture of saints" is gone from the Judeo-Christian West: saints are no longer a significant part of our vocabulary or expectations. But referring to a central tension that persists throughout these essays, he notes that saintly virtue has never been experienced merely as ordinary virtue in perfected form. The saints contravene pious expectations at least as much as they fulfill them, providing a "critical negativity" that has the potential to correct and re-orient ordinary values. In that sense there has always been a measure in which saints are absent from a culture's currency and invisible to its eyes, which suggests to Coleman that one ought to look in other directions than traditional ones — perhaps even to fiction — if one wants to locate the saints of the modern West. He leaves us with the sense that the game of saints is an important one, and that it is not yet over.

PART I

Traditional Visions of Saintliness

ONE

The Saint as Exemplar in Late Antiquity

Peter Brown

In a thoughtful discussion of a recent book (*The Analogical Imagination,* by David Tracy) a reviewer raised the following objection, that its author

> may well have to defend himself against theologians who argue that applying the notion of "classic" to persons has only a limited usefulness. Persons are not works of art, not pieces of literature, not paradigmatic actions. . . . By making them into classics, do we not neglect certain aspects of their lives and remove them from history?[1]

It might be helpful to begin any paper on the saint as an exemplar in Late Antiquity by explaining in some detail why such an eminently commonsensical remark would have impressed Late Antique readers — pagan, Jewish, or Christian — as the tacit abandonment of the rationale of their whole culture. For the classics, a literary tradition, existed for the sole purpose of "making [persons] into classics." Classic books were there to produce classic persons. Any other function was vaguely ridiculous:

> Two things can be acquired from the ancients — wrote Lucian of Samosata, attacking a *parvenu* who had made his money in the book trade — the ability to speak and act as one ought by emulating the best models and shunning the worst; and when a man clearly fails to benefit from them in one way or the

This paper was delivered at the Graduate Theological Union at Berkeley as part of a seminar sponsored by the Berkeley-Harvard Project in Comparative Ethics, and, at Harvard, as part of the same project's conference on "Sacred Persons as the Embodiment of Moral Values." I am grateful for the comments of Charles F. Keyes on the latter occasion. I would wish to refer to his own article, "Charisma: From Social Life to Sacred Biography," that forms the introduction to studies concerned with problems similar to my own, now available in Michael A. Williams, ed., *Charisma and Sacred Biography* (Chico, Calif.: Scholars Press, 1982), 1–22.

1. J. B. Cobb, Jr., "Review of *The Analogical Imagination,*" *Religious Studies Review* 7, no. 4 (1981): 287.

other, what else is he doing but buying haunts for mice and lodgings for worms, and excuses to thrash his servants for negligence?[2]

We find ourselves in a world whose central elites were held together by what Henri-Irenée Marrou has brilliantly characterized as "The Civilization of the *Paideia*."[3] The Greco-Roman world, in which the saints later appeared, was a civilization of *paideia* in the same way as our own is a civilization of advanced technology. It invariably tended to opt for the necessary self-delusion that all its major problems could be both articulated and resolved in terms of its one major resource — in this case, by the paradigmatic behavior of elites groomed by a *paideia* in which the role of ancient exemplars was overwhelming. The tendency to see exemplary *persons* as classics was reinforced by the intensely personal manner in which the culture of *paideia* was passed on from generation to generation. Intensive male bonding between the generations lay at the heart of the "Civilization of *Paideia*." No student ever went, as we do, to a university conceived of as an impersonal institution of learning — to Cal, MIT, or "State" (how much these abbreviations speak of our desire to take the impersonality of learning absolutely for granted!). He would always have gone to a person — to Libanius, to Origen, to Proclus. The most poignantly expressed relation in the ancient and medieval worlds was that between teacher and pupil. From the farewell poem of Paulinus to Ausonius, his old master

> Thee shall I behold, in every fibre woven.
> Shall I behold thee, in my mind embrace thee,
> Instant and present, there, in every place.[4]

to Dante's encounter with Brunetto Latini in the *Inferno*, we are never very far from

> la cara e buona imagine paterna
> di voi, quando nel mondo ad ora ad ora
> m'insegnavate come l'uom s'eterna.[5]

Rather than be surprised by such an intensely personalized system, we should remember how long it survived unchallenged. Exemplars, if carefully sought out, studied, and remembered at appropriate moments, were still thought to add a strand of steel to the frail fiber of eighteenth-century gentlemen: "Fancied myself Burke," wrote Boswell — admittedly one of the frailest — "and drank moderately."[6]

    2. Lucian, *The Ignorant Bookseller*, sec. 17, trans. A. M. Harmon, Loeb Classical Library, vol. 3 (Cambridge, Mass.: Harvard University Press, 1969), 195.

    3. H. I. Marrou, *A History of Education in the Ancient World*, trans. G. Lamb (New York: Sheed and Ward, 1956), 96–101 and 217–26.

    4. Paulinus, "Poem 10," lines 54–56, in *Wandering Scholars*, trans. H. Waddell (London: Constable, 1927), 11.

    5. *Inferno*, canto 15, lines 83–85.

    6. W. Jackson Bates, *Samuel Johnson* (New York: Harcourt Brace, 1975), 361.

If there is reason for surprise, it is twofold. First, we have a culture that believes that the past has become the past only through the remediable accident of neglect, not through any irreversible process of change and unidirectional evolution that would render the moral paradigms of a man of the sixth century B.C. irrelevant to the behavior of a man of the fourth century A.D. Moral exemplars of a thousand years previously had no built-in obsolescence: what was good for them could be good for you.

Second, we confront the very real truth that people *can* "mold" themselves, like clay, "carve and polish" themselves like a statue (I use the current images of education) so as to form themselves through and through according to very rigid and demanding rules of exemplary behavior. Neither distance of time nor the resistant quirks of individual character were regarded as reasons for *not* permeating the men and women of the "Civilization of *Paideia*" with the paradigms offered to them by the exemplary figures of the ancient past. The "ancients," therefore, already enjoyed the status of human classics, molding others by their example.

In Late Antique hagiography we can see how the old-fashioned faith in the capacity of a culture to "make persons into classics" met with ideological and sociological pressures that the "Civilization of *Paideia*" had never faced. Judaism, and later Christianity, brought to this Mediterranean-wide system of human discipline and personal poise the unprecedented weight of a providential monotheism, which, in both cases, placed an exceptional weight on the joining points between God and humanity, and which, in the case of Christianity, proposed as its central figure a being — Christ — in whom human and divine were joined.

The old constellation of exemplars could never look the same. It was not that they were pagan, still less that the moral paradigms of the ancients were deemed totally irrelevant to believers in the new faith. It was rather that in this changed milieu God, and no purely human system of transmission, no totally human *paideia*, played the decisive role in bringing the exemplars of the past alive from age to age. The idea of a "Community of the Righteous," linking Israel to its forebears and through those to God, has been rightly described as "a singular feature in religious history."[7] With this belief the exemplar ceases to be merely a past human paradigm reactivated, by human means, in the present — a mere "good example," if a very venerable one, endowed with great potency. The "man of God," the "righteous man," had a *revelatory* quality about him. The known presence of righteous men in Israel had the effect of bringing God himself back from exile in the hearts of those who doubted his abiding presence in a darkening world.[8] No longer thought of as guiding stars set in a flat and distant sky, the saints of Israel and the Early

7. A. Goldberg, "Der Heilige und die Heiligen: Vorüberlegungen zur Theologie des heiligen Menschen im rabbinischen Judentum," in *Aspekte frühchristlicher Heiligenverehrung*, Oikonomia 6 (Erlangen: Copy Center 2000, 1977), 19.

8. Goldberg, "Der Heilige," 25.

Church are a Milky Way thrown down from heaven to earth[9] by a God who "wishes all men to be saved."[10]

Furthermore, in Christian thought, God himself was proposed to man as the Exemplar behind all exemplars:

> For the first making of man was according to the imitation of God's likeness [wrote Gregory of Nyssa], and the promise of Christianity is that man will be brought back to the original happiness. If, then, original man be God's likeness, our definition will probably not miss the mark if we declare that Christianity is an imitation of the divine nature.[11]

The result of this view was to present human history as containing a sequence of exemplars, each of which made real, at varying times and in varying degrees, the awesome potentiality of the first model of humanity — Adam, human nature created "in the image of God," before the Fall. For "in Moses and men like him the form of that image was kept pure. Now when the beauty of the form has not been obscured, then is made plain the faithfulness of the saying that man is an image of God."[12] In Christ, the original beauty of Adam had blazed forth; for that reason the life of the Christian holy man could be treated as a prolonged and deeply circumstantial "imitation of Christ." But "circumstantial" in what way?

We should begin by making a careful (though inevitably somewhat schematic) distinction between this, the Late Antique form of the Imitation of Christ, and the disciplining of the religious sensibility associated with later Christocentric devotion in the late Middle Ages and Reformation. This latter strand of the Western religious sentiment is so far better known, it stills runs so imperceptibly in the blood of modern Christians, that the Late Antique ideal of the "Christ-carrying man" is frequently not even recognized as such.

To imitate Christ, Gregory of Nyssa — and others less profound and idiosyncratic than himself — scanned the human race as a whole, finding in the righteous of *all* ages that shimmer of the original and future majesty of man. Adam had borne it and Christ had brought it back, evanescent, elusive but reassuringly the same, like the fleeting expression of a face cunningly carved (here Gregory was thinking of the ancient equivalents of those little anamorphic pictures — now available in plastic — which show different scenes

9. Paulinus, "Poem 19," line 18. The image reappears, surprisingly, in the Qasīda Sāsāniyya of Abū Dulaf, line 188: C. E. Bosworth, *The Medieval Islamic Underworld* (Leiden: E. J. Brill, 1976), 213.

10. P. van den Ven, ed., *Vita Symeonis Junioris*, Subsidia Hagiographica 32 (Brussels: Société des Bollandistes, 1962), 1; A. J. Festugière, ed., *Vita Theodori Syceotae*, Subsidia Hagiographica 48 (Brussels: Société des Bollandistes, 1970) i:1 (cf. the editor's remarks, of characteristic learning and somewhat less insight, on this, "le commun bagage de nos auteurs" i, p. vi).

11. Gregory of Nyssa, *De perfectione christiana*, as cited in G. Ladner, *The Idea of Reform* (New York: Harper Torchbooks, 1967), 91.

12. Gregory of Nyssa, *De hominis opificio* 8.

when viewed from different angles) so that from one side the divine quality of man might appear, a sweet light smile playing across the whole face, while from the other all that could be seen was the hard frown of fallen man.[13] The imitation of Christ, therefore, was to bring that elusive touch of the majesty of Adam into the present age. Though the phrase does not, to my knowledge, occur among Late Antique Christian writers in this context, *repraesentatio Christi*, making Christ present by one's own life in one's own age and region, appears to be the aim and effect of the early Christian *imitatio Christi*.

> Indeed, the Christ-bearing man, having become
> forebearing, shines down on all men like the sun,
> showing to all the life of Heaven.[14]

It might be worth our while, therefore, to stop for a moment to consider some of the concrete circumstances that rendered such a belief, in its various forms, eminently adapted to the rise of Christianity in the Late Antique world.

I would like to begin by acknowledging a debt to the recent work of Edward Shils on the nature of charisma itself, but more so on the subtle manner in which it can be seen to be distributed and "reactivated" in complex societies. For Shils, the main concern is how the "central value system" — that is, "the values which are pursued and affirmed by the elites of the constituent sub-systems" of a society[15] — comes to penetrate the cluttered periphery of more sensible, immediate loyalties and preoccupations that make up the day-to-day life of a large society. For only when this "central value system" permeates parts, at least, of its periphery, if at very different levels of intensity, can a society maintain the minimum sense of common purpose and continuity necessary for it to persist as a single whole. Now, writes Shils:

> what sociologists and social anthropologists call the central values or belief system of a society can be lived up to only partially, fragmentarily, intermittently and only in an approximate way. . . . For the rest of the time, the ultimate values of the society, what is sacred to its members, are suspended amidst the distractions of concrete tasks.[16]

Given this view of the largely half-perceived penetration of the larger society by its "central value system," we can view charisma not so much as an eruption, as the *Aussertäglich* breaking through the routine structures of

13. Ibid.; cf.3.

14. Ps.-Athanasius, *De passione et cruce Domini*, in *Patrologiae Graecae Cursus Completus*, edited by J.-P. Migne, vol. 28, col. 237A (Paris: J.-P. Migne, 1857).

15. Edward Shils, *Center and Periphery: Essays in Macrosociology* (Chicago: University of Chicago Press, 1975), 4. I owe much to the further elaboration of Shils's ideas by C. Geertz, "Centers, Kings and Charisma," in *Culture and Its Creators*, eds. J. Ben David and T. N. Clarke (Chicago: University of Chicago Press, 1977), 150–71; now in *Local Knowledge* (New York: Basic Books, 1983), 121–46, but not on the issues on which I touch in this paper.

16. Shils, *Center and Periphery*, 111.

institutional life, but rather as something less dramatic and less highly "personalized." Charisma is seen less in terms of the extraordinary, set aside from society, than as the convincing concentration in a person, an event, an institution, or a discipline of the lingering senses of order and higher purpose on which the cohesion of a society depends. Rather than inevitably marking a moment of breakdown and new departure, "concentrated and intense charismatic authority transfigures the half life into incandescence."[17]

Now if there was ever a society that suffered from a permanent ache of center and periphery, it was the Roman Empire. If ever there was a body committed by its ideology to penetrating a periphery wrapped, in the words of the great *Cherubic Hymn* of the Orthodox Liturgy, in "the cares of this life," with a sense of the "coming of the King of Kings," it was the Christian Church that had developed in the Roman Empire. Furthermore, the culture and concrete institutions of the Church had tended to coagulate in the same locations where the "central value system" of the empire had already existed at its greatest intensity. Before the conversion of Constantine and for centuries after, the Church should never be seen (as it is so often presented in maps) as a single wash of color spreading evenly and inexorably across the *orbis terrarum:* it was an archipelago of little islands of "centrality" scattered across an "unsown sea" of almost total insouciance.

Hence the crucial importance of the holy man as "Christ-carrying" exemplar. In almost all regions of the Mediterranean, from the third century onward, he was far more than an exemplar of a previously well-organized and culturally coherent Christianity: very often, he quite simply *was* Christianity. Looking at Pachomius reading the Gospels in the little, newly-founded church in the deserted village of Tabennisi, noting that he "controlled his eyes as he ought and that his mouth matched his mind," "men of the world, seeing the man of God in their midst, had even greater desire to become Christians and believers."[18] Only we, who can hide behind books and machines for the propagation of the gospel, can afford to underestimate the crucial importance, in the frontier life of the Early Church, of the human exemplar: "I am convinced that God added to the length of their days [wrote the cultivated Constantinopolitan lawyer Sozomen of the holy men of Syria] for the express purpose of furthering the interests of religion."[19]

The idea of the holy man as Christ made accessible adds a rather different shade of color than I had first thought possible to the picture of the holy man, whose "Rise and Function" I had sketched out a decade ago, in more *grisaille* tones. In that study the holy man was presented in terms of his function as a "rural patron" and as a "charismatic Ombudsman" in the villages of the

17. Ibid., 130.

18. *Vita Pachomii Graeca Prima* 29. This crucial text is edited and translated (with a few major errors) by A. A. Athanassakis, Society of Biblical Literature (Missoula, Mont.: Scholars Press, 1975), and is now translated in its Greek and Coptic versions by A. Veilleux, *Pachomian Koinonia* (Kalamazoo, Mich.: Cistercian Publications, 1980).

19. Sozomen, *Historia ecclesiastica* 6: 34.

eastern Mediterranean.[20] If I were now to do more justice to his role as exemplar, the greatest single feature of my portrayal of the holy man that would have to be modified would be his "splendid isolation." I would be concerned to present him less as a deliberately distanced judge, counselor, and arbitrator: more as a moral catalyst *within* a community. I would tend now to ask myself what abiding "identikit" of religious expectations led villagers to recognize in a holy man, however spasmodically, imperfectly, and in however self-interested a manner, a figure who distilled in concrete and accessible form "central" values and expectations (as Shils might define them) that had a lifetime, a viscosity, an inertia, and a resilience that outlived the day-to-day "one-shot" strategies of patronage and arbitration by the holy man as "objective outsider." I would dwell more on the more intangible bonds of love and esteem that bound the holy man, as exemplar, to his disciples and clients.

The remainder of this paper, therefore, aims to explore, as systematically as possible given the shortness of space, a few of the methodological consequences of Shils's revised view of charisma, especially as these have caused me to modify my own views on the use and function of the holy man. How did the Late Antique saint both fulfill in the eyes of others and internalize in himself the double role of "Christ carrier" and representative of a "central value system" wished upon him both by a theologian as adventurous as Gregory of Nyssa and by a sociologist as sane as Edward Shils?

Let us begin with the holy man at his most particular, as the particular disciple of a particular master. Our starting point is a marble plaque discovered in the ruins of a little church in central Anatolia. It is an inscription set up by a certain Lucianus, the disciple of none other than the great martyr, Saint Lucian of Antioch.[21]

> Having lived without conceit,
> Having honored as is due,
> Lucian the martyr,
> He who nurtured you.
> With him Christ made you
> A follower of Himself,
> A carrier of His Cross:
> A Cross dwelt on divinely in the mind,
> And touched by you [the martyr Lucian]
> In concrete pains [of death].

Such language enables us to perceive at once the secret of the vigor of the early phases of the ascetic movement of the fourth century. In this movement the intensity of the master-pupil relationship that had ensured the continuity

20. "The Rise and Function of the Holy Man in Late Antiquity," *Journal of Roman Studies* 61 (1971), now available with updated footnotes in *Society and the Holy* (Berkeley and Los Angeles: University of California Press, 1984), 103–52; see also "Town, Village, and Holy Man," now ibid., 153–65.

21. S. Eyice-J. Noret, "S. Lucien disciple de S. Lucien d'Antioche," *Analecta Bollandiana* 91 (1973): 365.

and the characteristics of the "Civilization of *Paideia*" had been heightened to such an extent that literacy itself, both the medium and the *raison d'être* of traditional *paideia,* was vaporized in the intensity of face-to-face loyalty. Direct force of example was what mattered most; and the imitation of Christ, not mediated by any text or visual aid, was the logical extension to the divine Master of the tangible, almost preverbal adherence of the human pupil to his human model. A little later the Pachomian monasteries had grouped large bodies of men through the same hope of direct contact with a master: "knowing that, in listening to him, we make ourselves servants of Jesus."[22] "Indeed," said the monks to the Patriarch Athanasius, "when we look at you, it is as if we look upon Christ."[23]

Behind this sudden, early fourth-century faith in the availability in their own times, and in widely separate areas, of Christ the Exemplar *par excellence* of the believer, there lies the experience of the Great Persecution. Desultory though these persecutions might be to a modern historian, what brutalities and death did occur in the years between 303 and 320 fitted with perfect precision into the expectations of a preexisting mentality of the *repraesentatio Christi,* as this had grown in resonance and circumstantiality in the course of the third century.[24] Such persecutions found their answer in the heightened confidence that exemplar would rapidly succeed exemplar, as monk succeeded martyr along the Nile. As a result we are left with some of the most vivid examples of a purely personal system of exemplary behavior ever preserved in the Christian Church.

"Go and join a man who fears God [advised Abba Poimen]: just by remaining near him you will gain instruction."[25] He was totally poor and had no goods to leave behind, except the robe he had stood up in and the mat on which he had lain. Even if educated, he was largely (if not totally) deprived of the expensive and time-consuming tools of literary fame. Thus, an Abba really had only one legacy that he could leave to the world — his words and his example. But those were often impressive:

> Abba Or and Abba Athre did not come from the same part of the country yet, until they left their bodies, there was great peace between them. Abba Athre's obedience was great, and great was Abba Or's humility. I spent several days with them, without leaving them for a moment, and I saw a great wonder that Abba Athre did. Someone brought them a little fish and Abba Athre wanted to

22. Theodore, *Catechesis* 3.23 (now trans. A. Veilleux, *Pachomian Koinonia* 3 (Kalamazoo, Mich.: Cistercian Publications, 1982), 107.

23. *V. Pachomii* 144.

24. Careful reading of T. D. Barnes, *Constantine and Eusebius* (Cambridge, Mass.: Harvard University Press, 1981) leaves no doubt as to the confidence of the late third-century Church and the ability of its leaders to impose a preformed perspective on the excitements of their times.

25. *Apophthegmata Patrum:* Poimen 65, cited in P. Rousseau, *Ascetics, Authority and the Church* (Oxford: Oxford University Press, 1978), 21 — by far the most thoughtful treatment of the whole subject.

cook it for the old man. He was holding the knife in the act of cutting up the fish and Abba Or called him. He left the knife in the middle of the fish and did not cut up the rest of it. I admired his great obedience, for he did not say, "Wait till I have cut up the fish." I said to Abba Athre, "Where did you find such obedience?" He said to me, "It is not mine, but the old man's." He took me with him, saying, "Come and see his obedience." He took the fish, intentionally cooked some of it badly, and offered it to the old man, who ate it without saying anything. Then he said to him, "It is good, old man?" He replied, "It is very good." Afterwards he brought him a little that was well cooked and said, "Old man, I have spoiled it," and he replied, "Yes, you have spoiled it a little." Then Abba Athre said to me, "Do you see how obedience is intrinsic to the old man?" I came away from there [concludes Abba Sisoes, our narrator] and what I have told you, I have tried to practice as far as I could.[26]

These anecdotes grip us: "the flash of a signal light, brief, arresting, intense."[27] But the monk's journey moved on from such delightful particularity. It took him out onto a plateau, surrounded by a mountain range of breathtaking immensity. The greatest figures in the long history of the righteous on earth stood beside him. To be a "man of God" was to revive, on the banks of the Nile, all other "men of God" in all other ages. "The ascetic must observe most closely [said Anthony] the life and practice of the great Elijah."[28] Occasionally, the lost countenance of Adam could blaze again among these humbled faces: "Just as Moses, while his face was glorified, took on the glory of Adam, so the face of Abba Pambo shone like lightning, and he was like a king sitting on his throne."[29] It is Adam as we see him on the mosaic pavement of a fifth-century Syrian church: man as monarch of the creation, sitting with imperial serenity amidst the wild beasts in Paradise. His quiet pose, like that of Pambo at his meditations, captures the mighty order of man's first estate.[30] Little wonder that strong millennial hopes flickered around the persons of the holy men and around the walled monasteries of the Nile. For his region, Abba Apollon was "like some new prophet and apostle dwelling in our own generation."[31]

I want to end by suggesting a few avenues for exploring the manner in which men, who were frequently recent arrivals as participants in the "central value system" of the Christian Church, made this "central value system" their own.

By modern standards (at least, by the standards of a generation or so ago), the culture of Pachomius and his monks, for instance, must have been a thing

26. *Apophth: Pistos,* in *The Sayings of the Desert Fathers,* trans. B. Ward (Kalamazoo, Mich.: Cistercian Publications, 1975), 166–67.

27. Rousseau, *Ascetics,* 12.

28. Athanasius, *V. Antonii* 7.

29. *Apophth:* Pambo 12.

30. M. Y. Canivet and P. Canivet, "La mosaique d'Adam dans l'église syriaque de Huärte," *Cahiers archéologiques* 24 (1975): 49–60.

31. *Historia monachorum* vii, 8.

of rags and patches.[32] Only in the course of long, intense discourses on the
meaning of Scripture, which they would all have been reading for the very
first time, did some of the most vivid anecdotes in the life of Pachomius
emerge, and these are arranged in rough biographical sequence. But their
immediate context is an attempt to understand a genuinely alien gospel in the
light of their own recent experiences: Pachomius learned how to remember
the nails of Christ's Passion, when treading barefoot among the terrible
acacia-thorns to gather firewood for his newly founded community.[33] The
idea of the growth of Christ in the soul can so often seem a doctrine veiled in
a golden fog when we read it in the pages of even so exquisite an exponent as
Gregory of Nyssa. It derived its unbroken vigor in early Christian times from
the innumerable, heroic flounderings of men who had to find out what
Christianity was in the act of becoming Christian exemplars.

What resources did these men have to turn to? I would like to suggest the
crucial role of liturgical prayer. Chewing through the Psalms and the exclama-
tory prayers to Jesus that already formed such an important part of ascetic
culture — like the village women whom Abba Macarius remembered as a
child, chewing at mastic to sweeten their breaths[34] — the monk would be
taken instantly out of time into the world of the prophets. For these were
propheticae voces, now heavy and potent in their own mouths. Christ was
eternal, and so could be addressed in all ages and in all places through them.
And so was the devil. The "Prophetic Sound" of the Psalms drove him
away, as Martin, a very newly ordained exorcist could do, as he crossed the
frightening Alps.[35] There were even "spirit-bearing fathers," who opined
that the permanent enemy of the human race had a particular horror of Psalm
67.[36] Such certainties about essentials stood out like rocks in a sea of doubt
and partial ignorance, quite as clear and fully formed, if often as distant, as
the present, warning cry of the muezzin in half-Muslim lands.

Last but not least, a warm and abiding Late Classical sense of the intimacy
and resilience of bonds of invisible friendship with invisible protectors and
with the company of the righteous gave to the "Christ-carrying man" a
sense of resources lodged deep within himself. Your exemplar was close both
to you and to his own Exemplar. As long as we look at the saints only as
distant "good examples" (as moderns tend to do) or merely as effective
"patrons" (as Late Romans frequently tended to do), we will not touch on

32. Hence constant debate on the "orthodoxy" of the Pachomian settlements, raised by
their possible connection with the Gnostic literature discovered near a major monastery, at Nag
Hammadi: H. E. Chadwick, "Pachomius and the Idea of Sanctity," in *The Byzantine Saint,*
University of Birmingham Fourteenth Symposium of Byzantine Studies, ed. S. Hackel, Studies
Supplementary to Sobornost 5 (London: Fellowship of St. Alban and St. Sergius, 1981), 17–19.

33. *V. Pachomii* 11.

34. A. Guillaumont, "Une inscription copte sur la 'Prière de Jésus,'" *Orientalia Christiana
Periodica* 34 (1968): 322.

35. Sulp. Sev., *V. Mart.* 6:162.

36. Ps.-Athanasius, *Quaestiones ad Antiochum ducem,* in *Patrologiae Graecae Cursus Completus,* edited by J.-P. Migne, vol. 28, col. 605B (Paris: J.-P. Migne, 1857).

a layer of the formation of the Christian sensibility that is, in my opinion, as yet insufficiently explored. In a plethora of books on the anthropology and psychology of the various Fathers of the Church, I have yet to find studies that tell me about the Christian believers' map of their own selves, and its capacity for relationships with invisible guides and invisible enemies. Yet few periods in the ancient world devoted such serious and consequential attention to the manner by which the frail essence of the concrete identity could be seen as supported and given consistency through being flanked by hierarchies of protectors thought of as close in their interactions with the believers' souls as if the protectors were aspects of the believers' own selves. If I have moved in any way beyond the rather distant portrayal of the holy man as a patron, arbitrator, and "professional outsider," which characterized my work of the early seventies, it is in the exploration of this difficult theme, especially in Chapter 3 of my *Cult of the Saints*.[37]

As for its implications: most of us still have Christian names — in a Western country at any rate. For a Late Antique man or woman this assignment of name had meant to take at baptism a guide and companion, who could act almost as an ideogram for one's own soul. Thus it was quite normal for a woman, in a partially Christianized family, to recognize the martyr-saint Thecla simply because her little granddaughter, named after and ever protected by the saint, looked just like her![38] It was in this deep manner that Christ was thought to dwell at the root of the self. It was he who revealed himself as the ever-present *boēthos*, the helper, of Anthony, once Anthony had overcome the rival claim of layers of demonic self.[39] The martyrs and saints had carried this Christ "in their very marrow,"[40] to such an extent that the protection of the saint was certain to bring close to the believer the deeper paradigm of Christ himself. It was not merely cultural confusion that caused a shipowner to recount to Paulinus of Nola a miraculous delivery from the storm, in terms of a double vision of Christ and of Saint Felix:

> Yes, the Lord Himself sat at the stern, now with his own shining countenance and gleaming hair, as described in the Apocalypse, now in the revered appearance of his friend and confessor, my lord and our common patron Felix.[41]

In this very visual uncertainty we catch a hint of the resources of the personality, as conceived by Late Antique Christians, when they looked at the "Christ-bearing man," or prayed in his shrine.

37. Brown, *The Making of Late Antiquity*, 69–72, with the articles to which I was most deeply indebted.

38. *Vie et miracles de S. Thècle* 13, ed. G. Dagron, Subsidia Hagiographica 62 (Brussels, 1978), 314.

39. Brown, *The Making of Late Antiquity*, 89–91; Robert C. Gregg and D. Groh, *Early Arianism: A View of Salvation* (Philadelphia: Fortress Press, 1981), 131–59 and *in toto* is now essential.

40. S. Cavallin, ed., *Vita Honorati* 38 (Lund: C. W. K. Gleerup, 1952).

41. Paulinus, "Letter 49," line 3, in *Ancient Christian Writers* 36, trans. P. G. Walsh (New York: Newman Press, 1967), 261.

At death all of this became plain. The great men of the desert were greeted by carefully ordered processions of guides and protectors. Death is, therefore, the final meeting of masters and their pupil, on which the patient "making of persons into classics" had always depended, and also the moment when, in the meeting of Christ and man, the glory of the human self could be glimpsed in its awesome fullness:

> It was said of Abba Sisoes that when he was at the point of death, while the Fathers were sitting beside him, his face shone like the sun. He said to them, "Look, Abba Anthony is coming." A little later, he said, "Look, the choir of prophets is coming." Again his countenance shone with brightness and, lo, he spoke with someone. Then the old men asked him, "With whom are you speaking, Father?" He said, "Look, the angels are coming to fetch me, and I am begging them to let me do a little penance. . . . Truly I do not think I have even made a beginning yet. . . ." Once more his countenance became like the sun and they were all filled with fear. He said to them, "Look, the Lord is coming. . . ." Then there was a flash of lightning and all the house was filled with a sweet odor.[42]

Late Antique Christians lived perched, in this manner, between particularity and grandeur. A culture that produced the most confident and influential metaphysical formulations of the Christian faith—the unflinchingly essentialist nature of which can weigh on many of us like so many crystal girders—was the same culture that had the rigor, the consequentiality, and the human warmth to attempt to link this mighty, transcendent structure with the existential position of the believer in a largely non-Christian world. Until comparatively recently it has been habitual to dismiss Byzantine hagiography as an interesting rubbish-tip to be picked over by historians of social conditions and popular beliefs. I would strongly recommend, however, that an hour spent in the company of a Pachomius, an Abba Sisoes, or a Saint Martin can tell us, more than a whole course in modern dogmatics, how to begin to answer the challenge posed by Dietrich Bonhoeffer almost half a century ago, a challenge that is, for that reason, half a century more pressing: "It is becoming clear every day that the most urgent problem besetting our church is this: how can we live the Christian life in the modern world."[43]

42. *Apophth:* Sisoes 14, in Sayings, trans. Ward, 180.
43. D. Bonhoeffer, *The Cost of Discipleship* (New York: Macmillan, 1963), 60.

TWO

A Theater of Virtue:
The Exemplary World of
St. Francis of Assisi

Hester Goodenough Gelber

When confronting his contemporaries, Francis of Assisi induced them to take an uncomfortable stock of themselves, and for generations afterward he presented a problematic figure — difficult to assimilate into the Western traditions of Christianity and equally difficult, perhaps impossible, to dismiss. Even now, beyond the saccharine safety of his prevailing image as preacher to the birds, Francis's insistence on Christ's poverty lends support to liberation theologians engaged in the political struggles of the Third World. The earliest portraits we have of Francis depict him as an exemplary, if disquieting, saint, and how he came to occupy that status, engage his audience, and produce such powerful effects on his contemporaries rewards exploration.[1]

To teach by example requires an injection of self into one's social context. This is quite a complex matter. Every action develops the potential for ethical interpretation, yet virtues or sets of values may be incompatible with one another, so that attempts to exemplify them result in tension. The relationship between an exemplary person's sense of self and the exemplary role he or she acquires may therefore be troubled. Moreover, to be exemplary is to be exemplary to others; it is to perform for an audience expected to interact with

A shorter version of this paper, entitled "Francis of Assisi: A Psychological Interpretation of an Exemplary Self," was delivered on 28 December 1984 to the American Society of Church History. I wish to thank the commentators at that session, Barbara Newman and Donald Weinstein, for their very helpful suggestions and observations, and I would also like to thank Lee Yearley, Calvin Normore, and Ward and Ruth Goodenough, who read various versions of the essay and gave me the benefit of their quite diverse points of view.

1. *St. Francis of Assisi, Writings and Early Biographies: English Omnibus of the Sources for the Life of St. Francis*, ed. Marion A. Habig, 4th rev. ed. (Chicago: Franciscan Herald Press, 1983), 1669–1760 (hereafter *Omnibus*), contains a convenient research bibliography for works up to 1969, and also references on pp. 1680–82 to other bibliographic tools basic for studying Francis of Assisi.

the exemplary person in what may be a great variety of ways. To grasp the intricacies of teaching by example, we must try to describe the intersection of personality, role, and social context.

We might begin to explore the nature of Francis's exemplarism by examining a conflict between two values in his system of beliefs: the requirement that he nurture others and the requirement that he practice ascetic self-denial. Accounts of his life show him struggling to reconcile these two virtues, and his attempts to give expression to each of them created serious difficulties for him. Yet these two demands seem so firmly rooted in the underlying structure of Francis's personality that it was nearly impossible for him to reject either.

The conflict between these two values is evident in a puzzling story that relates an event of the winter of 1220–21, from the period of Francis's last years.[2] Not yet recovered from a bout with quartan or malarial fever, Francis went to the church of San Rufino for confession. There he took off his tunic and ordered the Minister General of the Order, Pietro di Catanio, on pain of obedience, to tie a cord around his neck and lead him naked into the piazza before the people of Assisi shouting: "Behold the glutton who has grown fat on the meat of chickens which he ate without your knowing about it." Another brother was to get a bowl of ashes to sprinkle on Francis's head. While this second friar, "moved by pity and compassion," did not obey, Pietro complied. When they reached the square, Francis stationed himself on the stone reserved for criminals, the pillory where perjurers were made to stand.[3] Naked in the winter cold, he is said to have told the crowd: "You think I am a holy man, as do those who, on the basis of my example, leave the world and enter the Order and lead the life of the brothers. Well, I confess to God and to you that during my illness I ate meat and some stew."[4]

The extreme nature of Francis's behavior — having himself dragged naked through the streets like a criminal for having eaten a little meat while ill — led

2. Erich Auerbach, *Mimesis: The Representation of Reality in Western Literature* (Princeton, N.J.: Princeton University Press, 1953), 168, speaks of the story as bordering on farce. Arnoldo Fortini, *Francis of Assisi*, trans. and rev. Helen Moak (New York: Crossroad, 1981), 458–62, dates the incident in 1220–21, presumably because Pietro di Catanio is mentioned, both as a participant and apparently as Minister General. Pietro became Minister General in 1220 and died the following March 1221.

3. Fortini, *Francis of Assisi*, 461, n. j, makes the connection between the stone for criminals and the pillory for perjurers.

4. Thomas of Celano, *Vita prima*, 1.19.52, in *Analecta Franciscana sive chronica aliaque varia documenta ad historiam fratrum minorum* (Florence: Quaracchi, 1926–41), 10:40, hereafter 1 Cel., AF; *Scripta Leonis, Rufini et Angeli, Sociorum S. Francisci*, no. 39, ed. and trans. Rosalind B. Brooke (Oxford: Clarendon Press, 1970), 156, hereafter, *Scripta*; Bonaventura, *Legenda maior* 6.2, in AF 10:582–83, hereafter, *Leg. maior;* and it also occurs in *Speculum perfectionis* 61. Each has a somewhat different version, and I have followed the outlines of a reconstruction of the story in Fortini, *Francis of Assisi*, 458–62, who takes details about the "stone for criminals" from the *Leg. maior* and about Pietro Catanio from the *Scripta Leonis*. The early testimony of 1 Celano, the lack of miraculous events, and the kinds of detail in the various sources point to an authentic incident. Translations throughout have been taken either from the *Omnibus* or from the *Scripta*.

Bonaventure in the *Legenda maior* to caution against viewing his actions as exemplary:

> The onlookers were amazed at the extraordinary spectacle and . . . they were deeply moved, but they made no secret of the fact that they thought his humility was rather to be admired than imitated. His action certainly seems to have been intended rather as an omen reminiscent of the prophet Isaiah than as an example.[5]

By associating Francis's nakedness with that of Isaiah, who walked naked and barefoot as a sign and a portent,[6] Bonaventure endowed Francis's actions with a transcendent prophetic significance that insulated the ordinary world from the effects of his presence.

Bonaventure's interpretation of Francis's display of naked flesh as a sign of membership in the august company of saints and prophets accorded with hagiographic traditions,[7] but Francis's behavior cannot be isolated in this manner. Francis's choice of setting — the stone where criminals were made to stand in shame as a warning to the community — indicates that he intended his actions to be an example to others despite Bonaventure's denial of the exemplary meaning of his behavior. Both Thomas of Celano in his *Vita prima* of Francis and the compilers of the *Scripta Leonis* perceived the incident as having exemplary force. Celano says those watching Francis were "moved to a better way of life by so great an example," and in the *Scripta* the account of this event is immediately surrounded with texts that describe Francis's perception of himself as a model for others.[8]

But what does such extreme, even bizarre, behavior exemplify? If Bonaventure's reaction seems to miss the mark, how should an audience have reacted positively and appropriately to Francis? The search for answers leads back into Francis's own personal history and forward into the history of the construction of his order.

5. Bonaventure, *Leg. maior,* 6.2: "Igitur qui convenerant, tam ingenti viso spectaculo, admirati sunt, et quia ipsius austeritatem iam noverant, devoto corde compuncti, humilitatem huiusmodi magis admirabilem quam imitabilem proclamabant. Licet autem id magis videatur *portentum fuisse* instar prophetalis vaticinii quam exemplum." AF 10:583; *Omnibus,* 672.

6. The editors of the *Leg. maior* suggest Bonaventure had in mind Isaiah 20:3: "Servus meus Isaias, nudus et discalciatus, . . . signum et portentum erit," as the text to which he refers. See AF 10:583, n. 3. Donald Weinstein and Rudolph M. Bell, *Saints and Society: The Two Worlds of Western Christendom, 1000–1700* (Chicago: University of Chicago Press, 1982), 37, comment on the fine line in medieval society between acceptance and rejection of the extreme behavior of holy persons.

7. Brigitte Cazelles, *Le Corps de sainteté: d'après Jehan Bouche d'Or, Jehan Paulus et quelques vies des XIIe et XIIIe siècles* (Geneva: Librairie Droz S.A., 1982), 52–54, comments on the paradox that hagiographic depiction of the nudity of saints, particularly of female saints, emphasizes their inviolability and transcendence.

8. 1 Cel. 1.19.52: "Sicque *compuncti corde,* ad melioris vitae statum tanto provocabantur exemplo." AF 10:40; *Omnibus,* 273. In the *Scripta,* no. 38, p. 156, the sentence: "Propterea, sicut multotiens dicebat fratribus, quia oportebat ipsum esse formam et exemplum omnium fratrum, ideo non tantum medicinis, ed etiam cibis necessariis in infirmitatibus suis uti nolebat" immediately precedes the story. Also see *Scripta,* nos. 40–41, pp. 158–61.

Francis's public gesture occurred after he "nurtured" himself through an illness, which led him to feel that he was not living up to his obligation to practice self-denial and not living up to people's expectations about his asceticism. This tension between nurturing and asceticism is developed in the legendary account with an artfulness suggesting hagiographic elaboration: Pietro di Catanio's obedient complicity in Francis's self-abasement is contrasted with the other, unnamed friar's refusal out of pity and compassion to heap ashes on Francis's head. One should note that the friar who refused to do what Francis asked is not criticized for his behavior; his nurturant impulse has its place. Both compassion and ascetic self-abasement are positive values, and the reverberating clash between them can be heard in other contexts too — for example, in the Rule of 1221, the extant rule that most closely expresses Francis's personal views about his order. In Chapter 10, on the care of the sick, the friars are exhorted to care for those who are ill, while the ill, in turn, are exhorted to accept their illness as God's instruction and not to try to get medicine to relieve their physical distress.[9] While the story about Francis's having himself dragged through town emphasizes the importance of asceticism, it does not nullify the importance of nurturing behavior.

In his calculated bit of theater Francis put the conflict in his system of values on full display. Just as the Rule of 1221 was a public expression of Francis's personal beliefs, so was his daring instruction to Pietro. Francis did not just present himself before the world, expecting his exemplary nature to manifest itself to all. He actively injected himself into his social context, skillfully using various social mechanisms to stage-manage events for his purposes. In arranging his spectacle, he invoked the requirement of obedience to exact Pietro di Catanio's compliance with his wishes. He showed his knowledge of civic juridical theater in his choice of props — town square and pillory — that would represent his perceived hypocrisy as perjury. And in the act of subjecting himself voluntarily to punishment, he exploited the mechanism of shame. By shaming himself, he in turn shamed his audience who, as Celano reports, "weeping together with great sighs . . . were pierced to the heart."[10]

Francis created a bit of theater in which he had the lead role, but he was not just acting a part. He created a spectacle to benefit not just his audience but

9. *Regula prima*, chap. 10: "Si quis fratrum in infirmitatem ceciderit, ubicumque fuerit, alii fratres non dimittant eum, nisi constituatur unus de fratribus vel plures, si necesse fuerit, qui serviant ei, sicut vellent sibi serviri. . . . Si autem turbabitur vel irascetur sive contra Deum sive contra fratres vel forte postulaverit sollicite medicinas nimis desiderans liberare carnem cito morituram, quae est animae inimica, a malo sibi evenit et carnalis est, et non videtur esse de fratribus, quia plus diligit corpus quam animam." In *Opuscula Sancti Patris Francisci Assisiensis*, Bibliotheca Franciscana Ascetica Medii Aevi 1 (Quaracchi, 1949), 39, hereafter *Opuscula*. See *Omnibus*, 40–41. The *Regula bullata*, chap. 6: "Et, si quis eorum in infirmitatem ceciderit, alii fratres debent ei servire, sicut vellent sibi serviri" in *Opuscula*, 69, includes only this exhortation to care for the sick. See *Omnibus*, 62.

10. 1 Cel. 1.19.52: "Accurrebant proinde multi ad tam ingens spectaculum, et ingeminatis suspiriis collacrimantes. . . . Sicque *compuncti corde*" in AF 10:40. See *Omnibus*, 273; the shaming of the audience is made even clearer in the *Scripta*, no. 39, p. 158.

also himself: it was a penance for his "crime." This was penance with a difference, however, because it was he himself who chose and devised it. The priest of his order to whom he had apparently just made confession had little, if anything, to do with it. Indeed if that priest was Pietro di Catanio himself, as seems likely, we find him but a reluctant participant in Francis's penance.

Since Francis tailored his world to fit his own form, we cannot come to terms with him and understand what he was about without grappling with questions of psychology. In my efforts to devise questions that elicit a response from the source material, I have found the Freudian and Eriksonian schemas of psychohistory of less profit than the existential psychology of R. D. Laing. Laing's attempts to render the worlds of his patients intelligible in the context of family and community offer much that helps an historian deal with accounts of behavior that could easily be pigeonholed as inexplicable, bizarre, or mad. Laing's work provides the theoretical framework for what follows.[11]

The legends about Francis offer no stories about his childhood that would provide grist for a Freudian mill. One well-known account, however, tells the story of how his parents treated him when he entrusted himself as an oblate to the priest at St. Damian's. Francis, who had tried to give the priest some of the family money and hidden for a month from his father's irate attempts to get him back, finally faced the music by returning to town looking to the community like a madman. His father "seized him with many blows and dragged him home. Francis was then shut up in a dark cellar, and for . . . days his father used threats and blows to bend his son's will, to drag him back from the path . . . he had chosen."[12] When his father left on a business trip, though, his mother, disapproving of her husband's actions, let Francis go. Then, in the words of the *Legenda trium sociorum*, his father "added sin to sin by abusing his wife."[13]

Francis's father was legally within his rights to act as he did when Francis tried to give away money belonging to his family. The laws of Assisi granted

---

11. The early works of R. D. Laing have been most relevant, particularly *The Divided Self* (Baltimore: Penguin, 1971); *Self and Others,* rev. ed. (Baltimore: Penguin, 1972); and *Sanity, Madness and the Family* (with Aaron Esterson) (Baltimore: Penguin, 1972).

12. *Legenda trium sociorum,* 6.17, in Giuseppe Abate, "Nuovi studi sulla leggenda di San Francesco detta dei 'Tre compagni,'" *Miscellanea Francescana* 39 (1939): 390 – 91, hereafter MF. See *Omnibus,* 907; cf. 1 Cel. 1.5.12, AF 10:13. Even though the earliest manuscript of the *Legenda trium sociorum* dates from the fourteenth century, I am inclined to agree with those who believe it stems from 1246, the date ascribed to it by Arnold of Sarrant writing in the fourteenth century, and I have used the source accordingly. See *Omnibus,* 855 – 80 for a discussion of the so-called Franciscan question. Because of the uncertainty about whether this source depends on material gathered close to the time of Francis or on stories formulated a century later, wherever possible, I have used vignettes from the *Legenda* that also appear in the lives of Celano. Also, see Fortini, *Francis of Assisi,* p. 176, n. k, and p. 217, n. m, for a discussion of Francis's dedicating himself to the church as an oblate.

13. *Legenda trium sociorum,* 6.18: "peccata peccatis accumulans, intorquet convicia in uxorem," MF 39:391. See *Omnibus,* 908. Cf. 1 Cel. 1.6.13, AF 10:13.

fathers the right to confine a son to the family house in chains for "squandering the family patrimony."[14] But legally empowered or not, the father's choice to exercise his legal rights and to use blows and chains as means of persuasion says a great deal about the kind of man he was.

The authoritarian pattern of family relationships displayed in this story — father abusive to wife and son, mother siding with son against father — would create problems for many children,[15] and seems to have created for Francis a particularly difficult transition to adulthood. The crux of the difficulty, if one can judge from the sources, lay in Francis's inability to identify with his father sufficiently to make the transition from the childhood male roles of son and brother to the adult male roles of husband and father. For example, one of the two extant pieces of writing in Francis's own hand, a note to his close companion Brother Leo written around 1220, begins: "Brother Leo, send greetings and peace to your Brother Francis. As a mother to her child, I speak to you, my son."[16] Francis is defining here two relationships between himself and Leo — that of a brother to a brother and that of a mother to her son. The masculine role he allows himself, that of brother, arises in childhood and acquires no new obligations on the advent of adulthood. The adult role Francis assumes for himself, however, is a feminine one, that of a mother, not a father.

The value set upon the relationships of brothers and of mothers to sons is also evident in the Rule of 1221, where they are not just stressed but identified with each other: "The friars . . . are bound to love and care for one another as brothers, according to the means God gives them, just as a mother loves and cares for her son."[17] And the same imagery recurs in quite extended form in the guide entitled *Regula pro erimitoriis,* dictated c. 1217–22/24.[18] Francis decreed that hermitages should consist of three or four brothers, two of whom should act as "mothers" with the other one or two acting as the children. The

14. Fortini, *Francis of Assisi,* p. 221, n. o; p. 223, n. p; and pp. 224–25.

15. See Erik H. Erikson, *Childhood and Society,* 2d rev. ed. (New York: Norton, 1963), chap. 9: "The Legend of Hitler's Childhood," for a vivid discussion of the dynamics of the authoritarian family and the kind of effects it might have.

16. *Epistola ad fratrem Leonem,* "Ita dico tibi, fili mi, et sicut mater" in *Opuscula,* 116. In this letter Francis gives Leo advice and tells him to come to him if he should need to for the good of his soul. The exhortation gives an indication of how Francis conceived the relationship between "mother" and "son." See the discussion below about the maternal style of authority. And see *Omnibus,* 118.

17. *Regula prima,* chap. 9: "Et quilibet diligat et nutriat fratrem suum, sicut mater diligit et nutrit filium suum, in quibus Deus eis gratiam largietur." In *Opuscula,* 38. See *Omnibus,* 40. The *Regula bullata,* chap. 6, changes the wording to: "Et secure manifestet unus alteri necessitatem suam, quia, si mater nutrit et diligit filium suum carnalem, quanto diligentius debet quis diligere et nutrire fratrem suum spiritualem?" In *Opuscula,* 69. In that form, the passage makes less sense and quite changes the emphasis, indicating a certain uneasiness about this side of Francis among the other friars. Also see *Omnibus,* 61–62.

18. Kajetan Esser, "Die 'Regula pro eremitoriis data' des heiligen Franziskus von Assisi," *Franziskanische Studien* 44, no. 4 (1962): 406.

whole group was to live apart from outsiders, in obedience to a guardian minister, and the friars were to take turns assuming the roles of mothers and sons, as seemed best to them.[19] Paternal imagery is conspicuously lacking.

In fact the sources do not seem to contain any clear cases in which Francis assumes a paternal role. There are four ambiguous texts, all in Thomas of Celano's *Vitae*, that speak of father figures for the members of the order, and it is possible in each case that Francis identified himself in some way with them,[20] but Celano had a preference for the term "father" as a form of address for Francis and his preference may color the texts. The *Scripta Leonis* points out that in his letters Francis followed the injunction of Matthew 23:8–10, to call no one father, master, or teacher in respect for the Lord.[21] Matthew 23:9 is particularly apt: "Et patrem nolite vocare vobis super terram; unus est enim Pater vester, qui in caelis est." On this account Francis reserved the term "father" for God alone. The biblical injunction against using the term "father" for anyone except God might have been sufficient warrant for Francis to avoid the term, but he was not following any usual practice in confining the term to God in this way.[22]

19. *Regula pro eremitoris:* "1. Illi qui volunt religiose stare in eremis sint tres fratres vel quattuor ad plus. Duo ex ipsis sint matres et habeant duos filios vel unum ad minus. 2. Isti duo qui sunt matres, teneant vitam Marthae et duo filii teneant vitam Mariae, et habeant unum claustrum, in quo unusquisque habeat cellulam suam, in qua oret et dormiat. . . . 4. Et dicant primam hora qua convenit, et post tertiam absolvant silentium et possint loqui et ire ad matres suas, et quando placuerit, possint ab eis petere eleemosynam sicut parvuli pauperes propter amorem domini dei. . . . 6. Isti fratres qui sunt matres, studeant manere remote ab omni persona et per obedientiam sui ministri custodiant filios suos ab omni persona, ut nemo possit loqui cum eis. Et isti filii non loquantur cum aliqua persona nisi cum matribus suis et cum ministro et custode suo, quando placuerit eos visitare cum benedictione domini dei. 7. Filii vero quandoque officium matrum assumant sicat [sic] vicissitudinaliter eis pro tempore visum fuerit disponendum, quod omnia supradicta sollicite et studiose studeant observare." In Esser, "Die 'Regula pro eremitoriis,'"401.

20. 1 Cel. 2.4.98: "Cumque de die in diem infirmitas illa succresceret et ex incuria videretur quotidie augmentari, frater Helias tandem, quem loco matris elegerat sibi, et aliorum fratrum fecerat patrem, compulit eum ut medicinam non abhorreret, sed eam reciperet *in nomine Filii Dei.*" AF 10:75; 2 Cel. 2.39.69: "Fratribus autem quos urgeret infirmitas seu necessitas alia, mollem subtus ad carnem tunicam indulgebat, ita tamen quod foris in habitu asperitas et vilitas servaretur. Dicebat enim: 'Tantum adhuc laxabitur rigor, dominabitur tepor, quod filii pauperis patris etiam scarulaticos portare, colore solum mutato, minime verebuntur.' — Non *tibi,* pater, ex hoc *mentimur filii alieni, sibi* potius nostra *mentitur iniquitas.*" AF 10:173; 2 Cel. 2.139.184: "Respondit sanctus Franciscus, induens cuncta verba suspiriis: 'Tam multimodi exercitus ducem, tam ampli gregis pastorem nullum, fili, sufficientem intueor. Sed volo vobis unum depingere, ac manu iuxta proverbium facere, in quo reluceat qualis esse debeat huius familiae pater.'" AF 10:236; 2 Cel. 2.144.192: " 'Hinc', ait, 'relucet beatae huius familiae pulchritudo, cuius multiformis ornatus *patrifamilias* non modicum placet.'"AF 10:240.

21. *Scripta,* no. 65, p. 200; *Omnibus,* 1041.

22. Some of Francis's contemporaries show an unease with his use of maternal imagery. For example, Esser, "Die 'Regula pro eremitoriis,'" 408, n. 46, indicates that MS Breslau, Universitätsbibliothek cod. I.F. 271, f. 303vb, containing the *Regula pro eremitoriis,* systematically replaces the term *mater* with the term *pater* throughout the rule. Also see nn. 17 above and 24 and 26 below.

The conclusion that Francis himself preferred not to be called "father" gains further support from a report in Giordano's *Chronica*. At the Chapter of Mats, Giordano says that the minister general, brother Elias, "would bend down to listen to Francis, then straighten up and say, 'Brothers, thus says *the Brother*,' a term used for him by the friars."[23] In this case Francis appears with the appellation "brother," but the term "mother" also turns up. Celano includes a text in his *Vita secunda* in which Brother Pacificus uses the term "mother" to address Francis, saying: "Bless us, dearest Mother, and give me your hand to kiss."[24]

Evidence for Francis's identification with a maternal role appears as well in two dream visions attributed to him in the early biographical legends. One legend describes a dream in which Francis is a small black hen trying and failing to keep all of her chicks sheltered under her wings.[25] The other legend is in the form of a parable in which Francis identifies himself with a maiden living in a desert, married to a king, by whom the maiden has many children. Interpreting the latter vision, the legends have Francis designate the king as Christ and the children as the members of his order.[26]

In the end there emerges from Francis's own writings and from the legends that recount the details of his life a picture of Francis taking on himself a maternal or fraternal role, but not that of a father. Caroline Walker Bynum

---

23. Fortini, *Francis of Assisi*, p. 476, n. 121.

24. 2 Cel. 2.99.137: "Parati ad recessum vadunt ambo ad sanctum, *flexisque genibus*, dicit Pacificus sancto Francisco: 'Benedic nobis, *mater* carissima, et manum mihi ad osculandum praebe!'" AF 10:209; *Omnibus*, 473. The discomfort that the term *mater* as a mode of address for Francis produces in many commentators appears in a note the editors append to this passage, which says that since it is Brother Pacificus speaking here, the King of Verses, it is not surprising to see him use the term *mother*; see AF 10:209, n. 10.

25. *Legenda trium sociorum*, 16.63: "Quamdam nempe gallinam parvam et nigram, crura cum pedibus habentem pennata in modum columbae domesticae viderat, quae tot pullos habebat quod omnes sub alis suis no poterat congregare, sed ibant in gallinae circuitu exterius remanentes." MF 39:427. See *Omnibus*, 948–49. And cf. 2 Cel. 1.16.24, AF 10:145.

26. *Legenda trium sociorum*, 12.50–51, MF 39: 416–17. See *Omnibus*, 935–36. Cf. 2 Cel. 1.11.16–17, AF 10: 140–41. As Bonaventure tells the story in the *Legenda maior* 3.10, AF 10:571, Francis's identification with the mother is omitted. Thomas of Celano also shows a certain discomfort with the identification, saying "Mulier haec erat Franciscus multorum fecunditate natorum, non factorum mollitie." AF 10:141. In the *Legenda trium sociorum*, however, the compilers have Francis himself assert his identity with the maiden, clearly and without qualifications. The censorship that enters in here is an indication that Francis's identification with a maternal role was not always to his followers' liking. Celano, for one, persistently referred to him as "father."

The arrogation of feminine imagery in these cases is in no sense traditional. The dream of the mother hen evokes Matthew 23:37, in which Christ compares himself to a hen gathering her brood under her wings. This is one of the texts that Caroline Bynum found twelfth-century writers using to establish the image, which was so important in Cistercian circles, of Jesus as mother. See Caroline Walker Bynum, *Jesus as Mother: Studies in the Spirituality of the High Middle Ages*, (Berkeley and Los Angeles: University of California Press, 1982), 113–14, 120, 125–26. However, although Francis may here obliquely identify himself with a maternal Christ,

has shown that an extensive literature developed in the twelfth century incorporating maternal imagery into the definition of a good abbot or bishop. In the cases Bynum cites, however, the maternal imagery was added as a supplement to already existing paternal imagery in order to balance stereotypical paternal attributes of judgment and discipline with stereotypical maternal attributes of nurturing and mercy. Maternal attributes were thought to be necessary *along with* paternal attributes in order for someone to act as a wise ruler.[27] Francis, however, seems to have preferred not to identify himself with the paternal role at all. In his case the ambivalence toward authority that Bynum sees as the primary reason behind the twelfth-century feminization of authority[28] seems to have gone beyond the incorporation of maternal imagery into a paternal identity. He rejected paternal identity altogether.

This rejection left Francis in a dilemma. For a man, being a brother does not constitute a bridge from childhood to adulthood. Being a mother does constitute such a bridge but literally only for a woman, which Francis, of course, was not. We would, therefore, expect someone with his set of identifications to experience great difficulty making the transition to adulthood, and as Francis approached the age for marriage and family, he does indeed appear to have entered an acute crisis.[29]

To understand what Francis faced at this point, we may adopt a distinction proposed by Laing between those who are "ontologically secure" and those who are "ontologically insecure." The ontologically secure person "encounters all the hazards of life, social, ethical, spiritual, biological, from a centrally firm sense of his own and other people's reality and identity."[30] The ontologically insecure, by contrast, lacks a firm sense of social and physical place and resorts to a number of desperate maneuvers to create some kind of existence for himself or herself. As Laing puts it: "If the individual cannot take the realness, aliveness, autonomy and identity of himself and others for granted, then he has to become absorbed in contriving ways of trying to be real."[31]

---

it is not Christ who is the hen, but himself, and in the second vision, as if to belie the Cistercian imagery, Christ acts the role of father to Francis's mother. Again the imagery is atypical. It belongs tangentially to the literature that describes a mystical union with Christ in terms of the union of bride and bridegroom, an image characteristic of masculine piety in the period. See Bynum, *Jesus as Mother*, 110-69. However, while Francis does speak of himself here as the bride of Christ, it is for the purpose, not of mystical union, but of begetting children. The maternal, rather than wifely, role is what is emphasized. In fact, the legends do not indicate that Francis ever adopted the imagery of Jesus as Mother or the imagery that describes a mystical union with Christ in terms of the union of bride and bridegroom. Such imagery does occur in the *Fioretti* in descriptions of the pious visions of some of his later followers. See the visions of Brother John of Alverna, for instance, in *Little Flowers of St. Francis*, 49, *Omnibus*, 1414–20.

27. Bynum, *Jesus as Mother*, 113–25.   28. Bynum, *Jesus as Mother*, 154–59.
29. 1 Cel. 1.3.6, AF 10:9–10; *Omnibus*, 233–35; 2 Cel. 1.3.7–5.9, AF 10:134–36; *Omnibus*, 366–70; *Legenda trium sociorum*, 3.7–4.12, MF 39:381–86; *Omnibus*, 896–902.
30. Laing, *Divided Self*, 38.   31. Laing, *Divided Self*, 42–43.

The person whose identity is unclear adopts roles and parts of roles, clothing, and mannerisms from a variety of sources, from family and friends, and from oral and written traditions, in an effort to construct a self that will work, that will make sense to him or herself and also to others. Laing describes in detail one such ontologically insecure patient, David:

> The boy was a most fantastic-looking character — an adolescent Kierkegaard played by Danny Kaye. The hair was too long, the collar too large, the trousers too short, the shoes too big, and withall, his second-hand theatre cloak and cane! He was not simply eccentric: I could not escape the impression that this young man was *playing* at being eccentric. The whole effect was mannered and contrived. But why should anyone wish to contrive such an effect?[32]

Laing describes David's eccentricity as stemming from the difficulty he had in separating himself from what his mother had wanted him to be:

> *His* self was never directly revealed in and through his actions. It seemed to be the case that he had emerged from his infancy with his "*own self*" on the one hand, and "what his mother wanted him to be," his "personality," on the other; he had started from there and made it his aim and ideal to make the split between his own self (which only he knew) and what other people could see of him, as complete as possible. . . . His ideal was, *never to give himself away to others.* Consequently, he practiced the most tortuous equivocation towards others in the parts he played.[33]

As he grew older, however, following the death of his mother, David found it ever more difficult to prevent himself from becoming his mother, from being engulfed by the internalized persona he had acquired from her, and only his ever more bizarre eccentricity held this feminine self at bay.[34]

Descriptions of Francis's behavior during his adolescence show a number of parallels with Laing's depiction of the "ontologically insecure" David. The socially prescribed path for Francis required him to enter the family business and become a merchant like his father, and the legends indicate that he worked in the family shop and knew his father's trade.[35] He could not put on his father's mantle, however, without becoming like him, and that, from every indication, Francis was unable to do. He apparently tried for a while to avoid becoming the socially required extension of his father by adopting the values of the aristocracy. He gave the aristocratic virtues of hospitality and liberality precedence over the prudent saving appropriate to a member of the mercantile class. As the *Legenda trium sociorum* recounts:

> He was a spendthrift, and all that he earned went into eating and carousing with his friends. For this his parents often remonstrated with him, saying that in squandering such large sums on himself and others, his style of living made him appear not so much their son as the son of some great prince.[36]

32. Laing, *Divided Self*, 70.   33. Laing, *Divided Self*, 71.
34. Laing, *Divided Self*, 72–73.
35. 1 Cel. 1.4.8, AF 10:11; *Omnibus*, 236, and *Legenda trium sociorum*, 1.3, MF 39:378.
36. *Legenda trium sociorum*, 1.2: ". . . erat autem in expendendo largissimus adeo, ut omnia quae habere poterat et lucrari in comestionibus aliisque rebus consumeret; propter quod

But Francis's attempts to take on the life of a "prince" do not seem to have worked very well. His aristocratic identity rested uncomfortably on his shoulders. Friends and hangers-on took advantage of his generosity, and his liberality bordered on the extreme. In Celano's words: "he was a very kindly person, easy and affable, even making himself foolish because of it; for because of these qualities many ran after him, doers of evil and promoters of crime."[37] One revealing episode indicates Francis's own ambivalence toward the part he had chosen to play:

> In all things Francis was lavish, and he spent much more on his clothes than was warranted by his social position. He would use only the finest materials, but sometimes his vanity took an eccentric turn, and then he would insist on the richest cloth and the commonest being sewn together in the same garment.[38]

It is not clear whether Francis intended by this action to falsify the princely garb he had adopted, or whether he perceived this mixture of cloth as the dress of a jongleur or troubadour entertainer, another of the roles he sometimes took on,[39] but in either case he was showing himself a man of mixed mind, a figure of fun, a fool.

Francis's public stance, like that of Laing's patient David, seems unreal, like playacting. When portraying himself as a wealthy princeling, he exaggerated the role, clearly revealing that it was an identity beyond his reach at the same time that he seemed to assume it. The visionary, unrealistic character of Francis's desire to be an aristocrat becomes painfully clear in the accounts of his preparations to join the forces of Walter of Brienne fighting in Apulia for the papal interests, so that he might gain a knighthood on the field of

---

multoties arguebatur a parentibus dicentibus ei, quod tam magnas expensas in se et in aliis faceret, ut non eorum filius, sed cuiusdam magni principis videretur." MF 39:377; *Omnibus*, 891. Many of the biographers of Francis have structured their accounts of Francis's life around the theme of chivalry and knighthood, as though it provided the key to understand him. While the theme is apparent, particularly in stories about the early period of his life, I believe it is of secondary importance to family imagery and other kinds of imagery. The theme of chivalry is not particularly evident in Francis's own works. For biographies that emphasize Francis as a knight of God, see John Holland Smith, *Francis of Assisi* (New York: Charles Scribner's Sons, 1972), 12; Omer Englebert, *Saint Francis of Assisi: A Biography*, trans. Eve Marie Cooper, 2d ed. (Chicago: Franciscan Herald Press, 1965), 68–69; and Fortini, *Francis of Assisi*, 9.

37. 1 Cel. 1.1.2: ". . . homo tamen humanius agens, habilis et affabilis multum, licet *ad insipientiam* sibi. Quoniam multi ob hoc maxime post ipsum abibant, fautores malorum et criminum incentores." AF 10:7. The Quarrachi editors suggest that there is an echo of Ps. 21:3 in Celano's use of "ad insipientiam," although if there is an echo, it seems faint given the disparity of contexts. See *Omnibus*, 230.

38. *Legenda trium sociorum*, 1.2: "Ipse vero no solum in his erat largus, imo prodigus, sed etiam in indumentis multipliciter expendebat, cariores pannos faciens quam ipsum deceret habere. In curiositate etiam tantum erat vanus, quod aliquando in eodem indumento pannum valde carum panno vilissimo consui faciebat." MF 39:377; *Omnibus*, 891.

39. On the multicolored dress of some jongleurs, see, for example, Edmond Faral, *Les Jongleurs en France au moyen âge* (Paris: Librairie Honoré Champion, 1910), 64, n. 7. See *Scripta*, no. 24, pp. 130–33, and no. 43–44, pp. 162–71, for indications of Francis's interest in minstrelsy.

battle.[40] Contemporary descriptions of Francis speak of his short stature, his small hands and feet, and fine bone structure.[41] Even if an element of idealization exaggerates such descriptions, Francis was probably not built like someone who could wrest a knighthood for himself through feats of strength. If he had carried through with his plans, more than likely he would have ended up wounded, dead, or as he had in Assisi's war with Perugia, in prison. He started out on the journey to join the papal forces, but the sources tell us that he had a dream telling him to return home, a most fortunate dream under the circumstances.[42] Francis may have been immersed in a dream world, but he was not so immersed that he was unable to extricate himself from one dream by means of another, especially when the reality before him became too nightmarish and threatening.

The return to Assisi meant that Francis's attempt to achieve an adult male role, to separate himself from his mercantile father, had failed. At the age of twenty-three or twenty-four, he was plunged into great confusion. Behind the mask of princeling apparently lay hidden the desire to become a mother, and at this point that desire came to the fore. Francis retreated with a friend to remote and solitary spots, and the legends say that while praying in a cave he felt the devil bringing to his mind the image of one of the women of Assisi, a hunchback. The devil threatened to cast the deformity on Francis if he continued in the direction he was taking.[43] Not surprisingly, the fear of this image produced a great struggle in Francis. If at some level Francis wished to be like his mother, to go through pregnancy and give birth to sons of his own, then as a man he wished to be a distortion of himself. The vision in the cave confronted him with the full implications of his desire. If he persisted on the path he was taking, he would become like the hunchback, a twisted image of bizarre backward pregnancy.

As Francis continued to pray, he received an answer to the image that threatened him. A voice told him he should not retreat from his course but "hate and despise all that which hitherto your body has loved and desired to possess." The voice went on to say, "the things that formerly made you shudder will bring you great sweetness and content."[44] Thus he received divine assurance that he could disown all that he previously had loved — his

40. *Legenda trium sociorum*, 2.5, in MF 39:379; *Omnibus*, 893–94. Also see 1 Cel. 1.2.4, AF 10:8, and 2 Cel 1.2.6, AF 10:133; *Omnibus*, 232, 365. The identification of Walter of Brienne as the person for whom Francis wished to fight has been disputed. See Englebert, *Francis*, 425–26.

41. 1 Cel. 1.29.83, AF 10:62, for example.

42. *Legenda trium sociorum*, 2.6, MF 39:380; *Omnibus*, 894–95. Also see 2 Cel. 1.2.6, AF 10.133–34; *Omnibus*, 366.

43. *Legenda trium sociorum*, 4.12: "Nam quaedam mulier erat in civitate Assisii gibbosa deformiter, quam pluries viro Dei apparens daemon ad memoriam reducebat, comminando se, liberata muliere, praedictam gibbositatem eius iniecturum in ipsum, nisi a sancto proposito resilieret." MF 39:386. See *Omnibus*, 901–2. Also cf. 2 Cel. 1.5.9, AF 10:136; *Onmibus*, 369.

44. *Legenda trium sociorum*, 4.11: "'Francisce, omnia, quae carnaliter dilexisti et desiderasti habere, oportet contemnere ac odire, si meam vis agnoscere voluntatem; quod

family, his friends, his life of parties and fantasies — and accept the hunchback image of social deformity. It was not long afterward that Francis precipitated the break with his family by giving the family money to the priest of St. Damian's and resolved his own "ontological insecurity" in the famous scene in which he stripped himself before the bishop and returned everything he had, even his clothes, to his father, severing their relationship.

The legacy of this break endowed Francis with two roles for future use — that of mother, which he fulfilled in his creation of the Franciscan order, and that of a suffering son. Francis had engineered the separation from his family in a way that made it seem they had rejected him, not the other way around. When he tried to give the priest at St. Damian's money gained from selling cloth from the family shop, placing himself under the legal jurisdiction of the church as an oblate, he effectively nullified his father's authority over him. At the same time, through his act of illegal defiance, he incited his father to reject him[45] and made it seem as though the severing of ties came at his father's instigation. In order to effect his freedom, Francis embraced the role of suffering son. He removed himself from the control of Pietro Bernardone, his human father, and transferred his allegiance to a heavenly Father whose son also had suffered. Increasingly he identified with Christ's sufferings, until as a culmination he received the stigmata. The two identities of "mother" and "suffering son" weave in and out throughout the rest of Francis's life.

It is time now to return to the incident in which Francis had himself dragged to the public square after having eaten a little meat during his illness. The tension so evident in that moment between the requirements to nurture and to deny oneself is an expression of the tension between Francis's dual identities. Nurturing, which is at the heart of motherhood, demands that one take proper care of one's body, and the legends include a number of stories about how Francis forbade too great harshness in the ascetic practices of his followers.[46] In the *Vita secunda* Celano reports Francis as saying:

> Brother body should be provided for with discretion, so that a tempest of bad temper be not raised by it. So that it will not be wearied with watching and that it may persevere with reverence in prayer, take away from it every occasion for murmuring. For it might say: "I am weak with hunger, I cannot bear the burden of your exercise."[47]

---

postquam incoeperis facere, quae prius tibi dulcia et suavia videbantur erunt tibi importabilia et amara et e contra in iis, quae prius horrebas, hauries magnam dulcedinem et suavitatem immensam.'" MF 39:384; *Omnibus*, 900. Cf. 2 Cel. 1.5.9; *Omnibus*, 369. In Celano, the admonition to turn the world upside down comes after the vision of the woman; in the *Legend of the Three Companions*, just before.

45. See n. 12 above, and Fortini, *Francis of Assisi*, 217, n. m; and pp. 173–77.

46. 2 Cel. 2.160.210–11; *Omnibus*, 530–31, for instance, on the conflict and its relation to his own body.

47. 2 Cel. 2.92.129, AF 10:206; *Omnibus*, 468.

Through ascetic self-denial, however, Francis maintained himself in the role of suffering son. Immediately after recounting the story about "brother body," Celano comments that this was the only teaching in which Francis's deeds did not accord with his words.[48] The tension between these two values produced an inversion of the "brother body" story later in the *Vita secunda*, in which one of the friars found it necessary to rebuke Francis himself for not giving sufficient care to his body even though it had faithfully put up with all his exactions in the service of Christ.[49]

The two identities of mother and suffering son were not necessarily at odds. The medieval idea of conception, in which the woman served as a vessel for the child implanted within her, offered an image fusing the maternal and suffering roles. In his stigmatization, for instance, Francis not only imitated Jesus in the obvious way but could also become a version of Mary, taking Jesus into his own flesh. A concrete realization of this fused image occurs in art in the form of the *Vierge ouvrante*, a figure of the Virgin that opens to show Christ crucified or holding his cross.[50] Yet these two identities often did conflict, and in the story about Francis's exacting penance on himself in the town square, the contrast between the actions of Pietro di Catanio and those of the friar who refused to sprinkle ashes on Francis makes the tension plain.

The conflicts between the requirement to nurture and the requirement to engage in self-denial produced dilemmas that Francis and his followers had to resolve if they were to make decisions about ascetic practices and the care of the sick. The practical realities of governance brought frequent reminders of the difficulty. Exploring Cistercian concepts of authority, Caroline Bynum has shown how leaders of that order adopted complementary maternal and paternal imagery to express the full range of attributes necessary for the good ruler: the justice associated with a paternal style of authority required the mercy associated with its maternal counterpart; the strictures of command required the mitigation of nurturing.[51] No such easy balance was possible in the Franciscan case, however, since Francis had rejected paternal imagery for himself and in large measure for his order.[52]

---

48. 2 Cel. 2.92.129, AF 10:206; *Omnibus*, 468.

49. 2 Cel. 2.160.211, AF 10:251–52; *Omnibus*, 530–31.

50. See Marina Warner, *Alone of All Her Sex: The Myth and the Cult of the Virgin Mary* (New York: Alfred A. Knopf, 1976), plate 6, for an illustration of a Vierge-ouvrante from the Middle Rhine, c. 1300. Christ appears seated with his cross within a figure of the Virgin.

51. Bynum, *Jesus as Mother*, 154–59.

52. Engelbert, *Francis*, 215, discusses Francis's use of a maternal model in shaping the authority structure of the order. The *Regula prima*, chap. 5, enjoins any friar from wielding power or authority over the others, and describes the appropriate leadership role as one of being a servant to others; *Opuscula*, 31, and *Omnibus*, 36. Francis may have consigned his order to "father" figures when the feminine form of authority proved inadequate to the task. See n. 20 above for some texts that could be interpreted in this way.

What might authority of a stereotypical feminine kind look like? The *Legend of Perugia* contains a discussion about the nature of authority that seems to provide an answer. One of Francis's companions queried Francis about why he did not correct friars who departed from the way of life he had chosen for them. Francis replied:

> My duty, my mandate as superior of the brothers is of a spiritual order because I must repress vices and correct them. But if through my exhortations and my example I can neither suppress nor correct them, I do not wish to become an executioner who punishes and flogs, as the secular arm does.[53]

In this account Francis ruled out his own use of legalistic, corporeal forms of punishment, the sort his father had employed, and by implication ruled out the exaction of an involuntary obedience based on coercion and fear. He wished instead to exercise authority through example and preaching, mechanisms of authority that depended on voluntary obedience for their success. As opposed to the coercion and involuntary obedience characteristic of paternal authority, these constituted forms of authority compatible with a maternal identity.[54]

Voluntary obedience, the obedience undertaken in joining the Franciscan Order, functioned as the mechanism for negotiating conflicts between values. How this might work is evident in the story about Francis's having himself treated as a criminal for eating meat. Here Francis used obedience to override Pietro di Catanio's possible objections to dragging him through the streets of Assisi. But obedience could also function to override asceticism. When Francis was suffering from the progressive eye ailment that eventually robbed him of his sight, Brother Elias enjoined him under obedience to seek medical aid, something the requirements of asceticism and Francis's own rule of 1221 both prohibited.[55] In this case the requirement to nurture was made to take precedence over the requirement for self-denial. Yet the act of obedience, in itself a form of asceticism, also served to balance the act of nurturing that it required.

---

53. *Scripta*, no. 76, p. 220: "'Meum officium est spirituale, uidelicet prelatio super fratres, quia debeo dominari uitiis et ea emendare; unde si uitiis dominari et emendare non possum predicatione et exemplo, nolo carnifex fieri ad percutiendum et flagellandum sicut potestates huius seculi." See *Omnibus*, 1052. Cf. 2 Cel. 2.117.158, AF 10:222; *Omnibus*, 489–90, in which Francis's dilemma is similarly resolved through a message from God.

54. Kajetan Esser, *Repair My House*, ed. Luc Mély, trans. Michael D. Meilach, (Chicago: Franciscan Herald Press, 1963), 93–98, defends the view that Francis's attitudes toward obedience hardened in his later years. This may be the case, but the dialectical nature of Francis's position means that an emphasis on obedience in one text and on freedom in another may result from the need to keep a balance between the two values and from Francis's perception of the needs of his audience rather than from an evolution in Francis's thought. Esser's argument rests primarily on texts from the last few years of Francis's life, further supporting the alternative possibility of a dialectical, rather than evolutionary, process.

55. 1 Cel. 2.4.98, AF 10:75; *Omnibus*, 312–13. Cf. *Scripta*, no. 46, pp. 172–73.

Given Francis's maternal proclivities, however, the use of obedience to control others could become a problem if it were exercised in a coercive manner. Celano tells how Francis thought the command of obedience should be used only as a last resort, for "the hand must not be quickly laid to the sword."[56] Because obedience within the order functioned as a form of ascetic self-abnegation to which members of the order voluntarily subscribed, coercion was less apt to occur. The passages in Chapter 5 of the rule of 1221 and Chapter 10 of the *Regula bullata* of 1223, which exempted friars from the requirement of obedience if they were asked to do anything contrary to the Franciscan way of life or the demands of conscience,[57] underscore the point that obedience always had a voluntary dimension within the order. It functioned not so much as a weapon of authority as a carefully circumscribed mechanism for resolving conflict.

Hence even in the realm of command and obedience we find a "maternal" outlook on authority that relied on exemplarism and voluntary submission for its suasive power. The resulting system of governance succeeded in maintaining a balance between the perceived virtues of nurturant generosity and ascetic self-denial. Within the system he had constructed, Francis could exercise both his adopted roles — mother and suffering son — in turn and even simultaneously. In the drama in the piazza the maternal aspect of exemplarism fused with the suffering that characterized the exemplary action itself. There was no need for him to resort to the authoritarian character of a paterfamilias in order to sway his audience.

Yet authority by example has its dangers, and Bonaventure was eager to remove the account of Francis's morality play from the ranks of exemplary stories. He preferred to regard it instead as an awe-inspiring tale, sensing that trouble might arise if those exposed to the deeds of the saint responded by simply aping his deeds. Literalism of this gestural kind did have its appeal to medieval eyes. In fact Francis himself displayed it when he adopted as the model for his life the instruction that Jesus gave his disciples at the time he commissioned them to preach the kingdom. Francis tried, as Celano says in the *Vita prima*, to carry out the texts "to the letter."[58]

Such literalism was not always acclaimed, however. Celano relates a story in the *Vita secunda* about Brother John, "a very simple man," that indicates

---

56. 2 Cel. 2.113.153: "Per obedientiam itaque raro praecipiendum censuit, nec primo fulminandum iaculum, quod esse deberet extremum. 'Ad ensem,' inquit, 'non cito manus mitenda est.'" AF 10:219; *Omnibus*, 485. For a discussion of the tension between freedom and obedience, see Kajetan Esser, "Gehorsam und Freiheit," *Wissenschaft und Weisheit* 13 (1950): 142–50, and ibid., *Repair*, 99–113.

57. *Regula prima*, chap. 5: "Si quis autem ministrorum alicui fratrum aliquid contra vitam nostram praeceperit vel contra animam suam, frater non teneatur ei obedire, quia illa obedientia non est, in qua delictum vel peccatum committitur." *Opuscula*, 30; *Omnibus*, 35.

58. 1 Cel. 1.9.22: "Non enim fuerat Evangelii surdus auditor, sed laudabili memoriae quae audierat cuncta commendans, ad litteram diligenter implere curabat." AF 10:19; *Omnibus*, 247.

an awareness that this sort of copycat posture had its limits. After Francis recruited Brother John for his order, John followed Francis around, and copied whatever Francis did. If Francis spit, John spit; if Francis coughed, he coughed; if Francis sighed, he sighed; and so on. When Francis asked him why he acted that way, Brother John replied, "I have promised to do everything you do; it is dangerous for me to omit anything." As Celano tells it, Francis responded with ambivalence, rejoicing in John's simplicity and recommending his life for imitation, yet at the same time forbidding John to copy him that way anymore.[59]

Fearing just such literal-minded imitation, Bonaventure proposed that the flamboyant behavior Francis displayed in the piazza at Assisi be interpreted anagogically. Bonaventure suggested that Francis, by stripping himself, became like Isaiah, a prophet and sign of great future events.[60] In so doing, he removed himself from the world of ordinary human affairs. He ceased to be a model himself but was instead assimilated to another model, that of Isaiah. Thus Bonaventure shifted the force of the example from the arena in which Francis confronted his audience to the arena in which scripture confronted Francis.

In practice, exemplarism thrived neither at the level of naive literalism nor at the level of anagogical appropriation. Bonaventure suffered under the disability that during the Middle Ages there was no very effective way to talk analytically about the density of accomplishments in human interaction. Masters of the social game were able to produce mimetic descriptions of great sophistication, but there was only a limited vocabulary available to analyze human behavior. Bonaventure was apparently unable to convey to his audience the true complexity of Francis's acts because he had the choice of either representing them literally or resorting to the hermeneutics of biblical exegesis.[61]

Francis taught by example through dramatic subversions of the socially expected. Sometimes he accomplished his task by staging events. Celano relates in the *Vita secunda* how one Easter the friars prepared a festive table

---

59. 2 Cel. 2.143.190: "Eunte sancto Francisco iuxta villam quamdam prope Assisium, quidam Ioannes, vir simplicissimus. . . . Cum igitur in aliquo loco ad meditandum staret sanctus Franciscus, quoscumque faciebat gestus vel nutus, protinus in se repetebat et transformabat simplex Ioannes. Nam spuente spuebat, tussiente tussiebat, suspiria suspiriis iungens et fletus fletibus. . . . Advertit hoc sanctus, et quaerit aliquando, cur faciat talia. Respondet ille: 'Omnia,' inquit, 'promisi ego facere quae tu facis; periculosum mihi est aliquid praeterire.' *Congaudet* sanctus purae simplicitati, blande tamen prohibet, ne de caetero faciat. . . . Cuius vitam frequenter sanctus imitandam proponens, non fratrem Ioannem, sed sanctam Ioannem iucundissime nominabat." AF 10:239; *Omnibus*, 514–15.

60. See n. 6 above.

61. See Judson Byce Allen, *The Ethical Poetic of the Later Middle Ages* (Toronto: University of Toronto Press, 1982), for a discussion of the interconnections between biblical hermeneutics, ethical exemplarism, and literature. The analytical tools at Bonaventure's disposal would come from the fields of rhetoric, literary criticism, and ethics — fields intertwined in medieval thinking.

with linens and glassware. Seeing what his fellow friars had done, Francis pretended to be a beggar and came asking alms at the door. When he was given a dish, he sat alone, putting the dish in the ashes and saying: "Now I am sitting as a Friar Minor should sit."[62] When asked to dine with lords or high churchmen, he would collect alms and come to the table carrying as his portion the scraps he had gathered.[63] At other times he accomplished his task of subversion by treating creatures and events as indicative of spiritual matters, ignoring their everyday uses and associations. When one of the brothers spoke uncharitably about a poor man, Francis is said to have told him: "When you see a poor man, Brother, an image is placed before you of the Lord and his poor mother."[64] All creatures, he thought, were signs of their Creator and members of a single family under the same heavenly Father, hence brothers and sisters to Francis and his friars.[65] Francis made parables out of what he did, and those in his audience reacted most "correctly" when they read these acts as messages and acted upon the precepts they contained. To ape such actions in the manner of Brother John or to raise them up in awe in the manner of Bonaventure was to stray on either side of their intended effect. As should now be clear, however, Francis's messages could be disturbingly complex, involving finely balanced contradictions and alarming subversions of social convention. Hence neither Brother John's retreat to literalism nor Bonaventure's to anagogy is greatly surprising.

How then might one read the message contained in the account of what Francis did after nurturing himself when ill? At the center of the story lies the problem of hypocrisy. The ultimate message of Francis's actions — beyond the issues of nurturing, asceticism, and obedience — was: "seem to be good and be as you seem to be." He found himself in need of confessing to the crowd at Assisi that he had eaten meat, precisely because they revered him for his asceticism.[66]

---

62. 2 Cel. 2.31.61: "Factum est quodam *die Paschae*, ut fratres in eremo Graecii mensam accuratius solito albis et vitreis praepararent. Descendens autem pater de cella, venit ad mensam, conspicit alto sitam, vaneque ornatam; sed ridenti mensae nequaquam arridet. Furtim et pedentim retrahit gressum, capellum cuiusdam pauperis, qui tunc aderat, capiti suo imponit, et baculum manu gestans *egreditur foras*. Expectat *foris ad ostium*, donec incipiant fratres comedere. . . . 'Amore Domini Dei, *facite*,' inquit '*eleemosynam* isti peregrino pauperi et infirmo.' . . . Datur petenti scutella, et solo solus recumbens, discum ponit in cinere. 'Modo sedeo,' ait, 'ut frater Minor.'" AF 10:167 – 68; *Omnibus*, 414 – 15.

63. See 2 Cel. 2.42.72 and 2.43.73, AF 10:174 – 75; *Omnibus*, 424 – 25.

64. 2 Cel. 2.124.165, AF 10:225 – 26 demonstrates the general point, and see 2 Cel. 2.52.85: "Cui dixit sanctus: 'Cum pauperem vides, o frater, speculum tibi proponitur Domini et pauperis Matris eius.'" AF 10:181; *Omnibus*, 433.

65. The most famous example is Francis's "Canticle of Brother Sun," but numerous other examples occur in the legends. Celano notes in 2 Cel. 2.124.165: "Fraterno vocat nomine animalia cuncta." AF 10:226. The most startling instance of Francis's determination to include all creation in his family is found in the story in which he called the fire with which his doctors cauterized his temples to treat his eye ailment, his brother. See 2 Cel. 2.125.166, AF 10:227.

66. Bonaventure, *Leg. maior*, 6.2: "'Non est', inquit, 'conveniens, ut populus abstinentem me credat, et ego e contrario carnaliter reficiar in occulto.'" AF 10:582; *Omnibus*, 672.

The injunction "to seem to be good and to be as you seem" is not, however, an easy one to follow. It points tersely to two of the fundamental difficulties faced by those who try to lead an exemplary life. Such people confront, on the one hand, the interior problem of harmonizing their personal values with their exemplary role and its definition, and on the other, the exterior problem of engaging in an effective interactive process with an expectant audience. The admonition urges the necessity of resolving these two difficulties but offers no indication of how one might go about it. The stories about what Francis said and did offer a picture of how he went about resolving them.

In accounts of Francis' life, the saint first comes into view as a person caught in a struggle to create an external persona that would meet the expectations of family and community but not at the same time be repugnant to himself. His first attempt, seizing on the role of aristocrat and knight, failed to bring an end to his struggle. Only after his dramatic gesture before the bishop, in which he rejected not only knighthood but all status and social place in Assisi — every claim Assisi might have on him to be this sort of person or that — did he gain the freedom to develop the role of mother and its concomitant role of suffering son. Only then could he seem to be what he was and relegate false seemings to the past.

The possibility always existed, however, that he might lose the hard-won fruits of freedom. Insufficient diligence in the difficult task of maintaining a new, authentic persona against the pull of habit, public opinion, and uncooperative reality could always lead to the reemergence of falsity. At a number of points a critical discrepancy arose between Francis's perception of who he really was and the figure his community had come to perceive him to be. This signaled the return of a great sense of insecurity, threatening the loss of much, if not all, that he had gained. The name for false seeming was hypocrisy, and both scripture and tradition excoriated it.[67]

There are a number of vignettes about Francis's life, in addition to the story in which he confessed having eaten meat, that give evidence of a deep concern about hypocrisy.[68] Once when Francis fell ill during his last years, his guardian and companion obtained a fox skin to sew into his tunic as protection against the winter cold. Francis would permit the fox-skin liner only if a piece of the fur was also sewn on the outside of his tunic so that no one would be fooled by the garment's patched outer appearance into thinking Francis was being more ascetic than he was.[69] In another story the saint is

---

67. See Caroline Walker Bynum, *Docere Verbo et Exemplo: An Aspect of Twelfth-Century Spirituality*, Harvard Theological Studies 31 (Missoula, Mont.: Scholars Press, 1979), for a discussion of the tradition prior to Francis, especially pp. 14–18.

68. For example, see 2 Cel. 2.94.131, AF 10:207; *Omnibus*, 470; 2 Cel. 2.123.166, AF 10:227; *Omnibus*, 494; 2 Cel. 2.138.183, AF 10:235; *Omnibus*, 508.

69. 2 Cel. 2.93.130: "Acquiescente tandem guardiano, pecia supra peciam suitur, ne alius foris quam intus Franciscus esse monstretur." AF 10:207; *Omnibus*, 469. See 2 Cel. 2.39.69, cited above in n. 20, for a story in which Francis recommends maintaining the outer roughness

said to have kissed the feet of a peasant who admonished him: "Never be other than you are expected to be."[70] In this case, of course, he had created the peasant's expectation by his previous behavior, so that the social expectation was compatible with the person Francis really wanted to be.

In Chapter 7 of the Rule of 1221, in reference to Matthew 6:16, Francis urged the friars to let everyone see that they were happy in God and not to appear gloomy or depressed like hypocrites.[71] In applying the scriptural text, Francis and his fellows viewed the opposition between joy and gloom as marking the opposition between authenticity and falseness, safety and danger. Celano reports Francis as saying, "The devil rejoices most when he can snatch away spiritual joy from a servant of God. . . . Devils cannot harm the servant of Christ when they see he is filled with holy joy."[72] Francis took joy of this special kind, involving the acceptance of whatever God provided, as the sign of inner righteousness:

> If the servant of God, as may happen, is disturbed in any way, he should rise immediately to pray and he should remain in the presence of the heavenly Father until he restores unto him the joy of salvation. For if he remains stupefied in sadness, . . . it will generate an abiding rust in the heart.[73]

Francis used scripture to structure his life and interpret events around him. Thus joy and authenticity, sadness and hypocrisy, formed a complex of ideas and emotions connected with security and insecurity. Holy joy was the sign for Francis that he had well and truly made the transition from being the son of Pietro Bernadone to being the son of his Father in heaven.

The importance for Francis of maintaining harmony among inner regard, role definition, and audience expectation means that ultimately it is inadequate to describe his actions in terms of an analogy with the theater. Francis did employ many techniques associated with theater to engage his audience: he set scenes, used props, and adopted character roles. But the roles he

---

of garments even when softer inner garments are worn because of illness. The point of these two stories is the same, however, to avoid scandal and hypocrisy.

70. 2 Cel. 2.103.142: "'Stude,' ait rusticus, 'adeo bonus esse, ut ab omnibus diceris, quia multi *confidunt de te*. Quare te moneo, ut numquam de te sit aliter quam speratur.' *Vir autem Dei* Franciscus haec audiens, de asino se misit in terram, et coram rustico *provolutus, osculabatur pedes eius* humiliter, *gratias agens ei*, quod eum dignatus est monere." AF 10:212; *Omnibus*, 477.

71. *Regula prima*, chap. 7: "Et caveant sibi fratres, quod non se ostendant tristes extrinsecus et nubilosos hypocritas; sed ostendant se gaudentes in Domino et hilares et convenienter gratiosos." In *Opuscula*, 34.

72. 2 Cel. 2.88.125: "Dicebat enim: 'Tunc postissimum exsultat diabolus, cum *gaudium spiritus* servo Dei potest subripere. . . . Non possunt daemones offendere Christi famulum, ubi eum viderint sancta *iucunditate repletum*.'" AF 10:204; *Omnibus*, 465.

73. 2 Cel. 2.88.125: "Dicebat autem: '*Servus Dei* pro aliquo, ut assolet, conturbatus, illico surgere ad orationem debet, et tamdiu coram summo Patre persistere, donec *reddat ei sui salutaris laetitiam. Si* enim in moestitia *fecerit moram*, . . . nisi per lacrimas expurgetur, mansuram generabit in corde *rubiginem*.'" AF 10:204; *Omnibus*, 465–66.

adopted could not be playacted.[74] To be effective, he had not only to play but to be the beggar at the door on Easter, and when he went to the pillory in Assisi, he was not only playing the liar but dramatizing what he felt to be true about himself. Inner conviction had to shine through, or his attempts to shame his audience into reform would fail.

The conflict between the values of asceticism and nurturing contributed greatly to the difficulties Francis faced in trying to synchronize who he was with the role he had adopted. He found it difficult always to give each value its due. When one threatened to edge out the other, Francis would begin to sense he was something other than he wished to seem, and he would proceed to redress the balance.

The problem of hypocrisy was probably more acute given the kind of exemplary role Francis adopted than it was for canons and preachers of his era, who also tried to live out the idea of teaching by word and example.[75] The power of priestly office functioned in spite of the misdeeds of the priest, and the words of the preacher might have merit even if the preacher did not. But the effectiveness of Francis's morality plays depended on a unity of self, role, and audience perception. Without this convergence, his actions lacked authority. When he confronted an audience in his unfamiliar habit, modeled after the clothing of the Apostles, as a living example of the *vita apostolica,* and with his convictions intact, he had the power to discomfit. Like the vegetarian at the dinner party, his very presence induced his contemporaries to take stock of their own values. Just by being who he was, he called into question the way of life of those around him. But if this question mark placed next to their lives was to have an effect on their consciences, shaming them into changing their way of living, the question had to be hard to dismiss. The powerful inducement Francis presented to his contemporaries to lead lives of greater virtue ultimately depended less on how well he was able to be who others expected him to be than on how well he was able to be who he said he was.

74. See 2 Cel. 2.157.207, AF 10:249; *Omnibus,* 527–28, for another apt instance of Francis's stagecraft.

75. See Bynum, *Docere,* for a study comparing the attitudes of regular canons with the attitudes of monks on teaching by word and example as a way of fulfilling the *vita apostolica* during the twelfth century.

THREE

Prophet and Saint:
The Two Exemplars of Islam

William M. Brinner

The position of Muhammad within Islam remains a topic of misunderstanding in the West in spite of all that has been written on the subject by both Muslim and non-Muslim scholars. In part this misunderstanding is simply a function of the complexity of Islam. For all the majesty and apparent simplicity of its vision, the religion encompasses great variety, not only in its vast geographical range, which extends from the jungles of Indonesia to the deserts of Arabia and the glaciers of the Pamirs, but also in its ideational span, extending from the faith of urban intellectuals to the "rustic" Islam of the villager. Hence there is plenty of room for differing views about the nature and role of the Prophet, even though it was he who set out the limits of Islam and demarcated it from other monotheistic faiths.[1] A second cause of confusion lies in the difference between what Muslims, Jews, and Christians mean by "prophet." Unlike the prophets of the Hebrew Bible — Amos, Isaiah, and the like — whose words and messages are immortal but whose lives and daily deeds are of supreme unconcern to the believing Jew, every recorded word and action of Muhammad serves Muslims as a model for behavior.[2] Finally there is the matter of the relation between the one peerless Prophet, to whose example Muslims can turn for guidance in life, and the lesser "saints" who serve as foci for the piety of so many Muslim believers.

1. Annemarie Schimmel, *Mystical Dimensions of Islam* (Chapel Hill: University of North Carolina Press, 1975), 214.

2. See James E. Royster, "Muhammad as Teacher and Exemplar," *The Muslim World* 68, no. 4 (1978): 235–58, where he writes: "Not only did Muhammad act as teacher and exemplar, but his teaching and example constitute an exhaustive and, from the perspective of many Muslims, a perfect code of thought and conduct that shall remain in effect until the end of time" (p. 235). Schimmel, *Mystical*, 213. See also the review article by Maxime Rodinson, "A Critical Survey of Modern Studies on Muhammad," in *Studies in Islam*, trans. and ed. Merlin L. Swartz (New York: Oxford University Press, 1981), 23–85.

By directing attention to the saints and prophets of Islam, as I shall do in this essay, I may appear to be ignoring or denying the ultimate uniqueness of Muhammad, the Prophet or Messenger of God. Yet my aim is hardly to detract from his central and supreme position. Indeed it is the opposite. I intend to show just how central that position is; how it was challenged and shared for a time, at least in the popular view, with another, different group of figures; and how its uniqueness and supremacy are being reasserted in more recent days. In this last respect the present essay is to some extent an updating and expansion of the seminal chapters on the same subject by the great Islamicists Ignatz Goldziher and Gustave von Grunebaum, which were written at different points before the most recent upsurge of Islamic revival movements.[3]

In any examination of Islamic piety and devotion from the Middle Ages until modern times, one is struck by the coexistence of two polar figures— exemplars whose personalities, while strikingly different at the theoretical and creedal level, are closely aligned and indeed almost merged in popular perception. These figures are the Prophet Muhammad, on the one hand, and the saint, on the other. While the Prophet is unique in his position within Islam, the saint is realized in a dazzling array of figures from different areas of the Islamic world, bearing different names, venerated in different ways, and often incorporating a variety of local pre-Islamic and non-Islamic concepts and figures.[4] It has been noted that whereas the rank of prophethood is closed in Islam, the rank of sainthood is open to all who can accept the cost of following it. While there is no question about the exemplary status of the Prophet, as we shall see, only certain saints served as models for their followers. Thus Prophet rather than saint serves as exemplar to pious Muslims. Under contemporary circumstances the two figures may and do become symbols of what are at times violently rival ideologies within Islam.

In our examination of these two different exemplars we will begin with the older of the two in Islamic history and tradition, the Prophet or Messenger Muhammad.

Muhammad, the divinely sent Messenger of Islam, is seen by Muslims to be the paragon of all human virtues. This attitude stems directly from Qur'ānic phrases such as "Verily in the messenger of God you have a beautiful model [or, good example]"[5] or "Whoever obeys the messenger obeys

---

3. Ignatz Goldziher, "Veneration of Saints in Islam," in *Muslim Studies*, ed. S. M. Stern, vol. 2 (London: George Allen and Unwin, 1971) [originally *Muhammedanische Studien*, 1890], 255–341; G. E. von Grunebaum, "The Prophet and the Saints," in *Muhammadan Festivals* (New York: Henry Schuman, 1951), 67–85.

4. On this theme, see below, p. 44.

5. Qur'ān 33:21. Qur'ānic citations will be given in a slightly modified version of the translation by M. M. Pickthall, *The Meaning of the Glorious Koran* (London: George Allen and Unwin, 1957).

God."[6] Citing these verses, Annemarie Schimmel writes, "His *sunna* [way, or tradition] became normative wherever Muslims lived, a reason for the amazing uniformity of life style in all Muslim countries."[7] While this statement seems, as written, to be a simple assertion of fact, it contains a complex dilemma: how can a perfect individual, an incomparable paragon, serve as a practical example for his followers, the community of believers? Islamic civilization contains, however, another similar dilemma, this one involving the divine revelation, the Qur'ān itself. Its language, God's own speech, is inimitable, and yet has served for the past 1300 years as a model, albeit unattainable by definition, of perfect Arabic usage.[8] The paradox built into these two exemplars is that they both serve as models yet are at the same time unattainable by ordinary human beings. As other chapters of this volume will show, the concept of an unattainable ideal that one must nonetheless strive to emulate is not unique to Islam. However, it has its peculiarly Islamic form, which we can come to know by asking in what ways the Prophet serves as an exemplar for other Muslims. Does he succeed? Are there any mortals who, while clearly unable to attain to his perfection, approach it more closely than others? Who are they, and what are their characteristics?

As we begin this search, we may once again take note of the diversity of Islam and make the usual distinction between what may be called the "great tradition" and the "folk tradition" in Islam. The former, the literate tradition in the keeping of urban scholars, is passed on in books, theoretically accessible to all but in fact the province of a learned few. The latter is more emotive and ecstatic, accessible to the less-educated urban and rural masses, and passed on through holy lineages, religious brotherhoods, and saints.[9] The tension between these two traditions has varied in intensity and bitterness over the centuries but is in Islam today a serious, divisive issue.

Common to both of these traditions is the figure of the Messenger of Allah, the Prophet Muhammad, whom the Qur'ān describes, in the passage cited earlier, as a "good example" or "beautiful model." Yet the book also emphasizes the limited, mortal, human status of Muhammad, who is instructed to say: "I do not say to you that I possess the treasures of God, nor that I

---

6. Qur'ān 4:82.

7. Annemarie Schimmel, *As Through a Veil: Mystical Poetry in Islam* (New York: Columbia University Press, 1982), 172.

8. M. Khalafallah, "Arabiyya," in *The Encyclopedia of Islam* [New edition], vol. 1 (Leiden: E. J. Brill, 1960–), 567. He writes: "Thus the first and foremost Islamic literary work in the Arabic language became the most authentic model for literary usage. ... [It] had ... another aspect in which it influenced the course of the literary language, namely its miraculous unsurpassable excellence. The literary Arab celebrities admitted impotence before its challenge, and Muslims down the ages looked up to it as their literary guide and linguistic authority."

9. Ernest Gellner, *Muslim Society* (Cambridge, England: Cambridge University Press, 1981).

have knowledge of the unseen. And I do not say to you: Lo! I am an angel. I follow only what is inspired in me."[10] Further:

> For myself I have no power to benefit, nor power to hurt, save what God wills. Had I knowledge of the Unseen, I should have abundance of wealth, and adversity would not touch me. I am only a warner, and a bearer of good tidings to people who believe.[11]

Twice the Qur'ān has Muhammad repeat, "I am only a mortal like you,"[12] strengthened further by God's statement to him: "Lo! you will die, and lo! they will die! Then lo! on the Day of Resurrection before your Lord you will dispute."[13] And again: "Muhammad is but a Messenger, messengers have passed away before him. Will it be that when he dies, or is slain, you will turn back on your heels?"[14]

These forthright, unequivocal statements stress the mortality of Muhammad and the limits of his personal involvement in his divinely appointed mission as God's messenger. They are further reinforced by the explicit denial, recorded in God's own words, that the ability to work miracles necessarily attends the messenger's role:

> Verily We sent messengers before you, among them those of whom We have told you, and some of whom We have not told you; and it was not given to any messenger that he should bring a sign except by God's leave.[15]

This issue reflects a problem that Muhammad faced when called upon by doubters to bring forth a sign or miracle that would prove his mission: "They say: Why has no sign been sent down upon him from his Lord? Say: Lo! God is able to send down a sign. But most of them do not know."[16] Again: "Those who disbelieve say: If only some sign were sent down upon him from his Lord! You are only a warner, and a guide for every people."[17] But God reassures Muhammad by saying: "If you came to them with a miracle, those who disbelieve would exclaim: You are just tricksters."[18] And God gives the Qur'ān itself as Muhammad's sign and proof; ultimately this is the miracle that justifies him as a true messenger of God.[19]

In the body of oral tradition that was collected over the years into the canonical corpus of *hadīth*, this early, simple view of a very human messenger, taken from his everyday world by God to bring his message to his people and eventually to all humanity, still shines through later, embellished texts. As time passed, however, this matter-of-factness about Muhammad's daily life and dealings with his fellow human beings was gradually combined with an

---

10. Qur'ān 6:50. See also 11:31.
11. Ibid. 7:188.   12. Ibid. 18:111, 41:6.   13. Ibid. 39:30.   14. Ibid. 3:144.
15. Ibid. 40:78.   16. Ibid. 6:37.   17. Ibid. 13:7.   18. Ibid. 30:58.
19. Khalafallah writes: "The new Holy Book, by its excellence, proved to the Arabs as miraculous as the turning of a stick into a snake, or the healing of the sick was to former peoples" ("Arabiyya," 567).

ever-growing attitude of awe that turned Muhammad into a distant, almost superhuman figure.

An example of the first, matter-of-fact approach, emphasizing the Prophet's humanity, is the following passage from the *ḥadīth*:

> A'isha said: God's messenger used to patch his sandals, sew his garment and conduct himself at home as any one of you does in his house. He was a human being, searching his garment for lice, milking his sheep, and doing his own chores.[20]

Another passage, although from the same collection of *ḥadīth*, shows the beginnings of the process by means of which Muhammad was distanced from ordinary mortals. It contains the Prophet's reply to A'isha's observation:

> A'isha reported God's messenger as saying, "If I wished, A'isha, mountains of gold would accompany me. An angel whose waist was as high as the Ka'aba came to me and told me that my Lord sent me greeting and said that if I wished I could be a prophet and a servant, or if I wished I could be a prophet and king. I looked at Gabriel and he gave me a sign to humble myself.[21]

Central to this change of attitude — both as one element in the process and a symptom of it as well — are the stories connected with Muhammad's fabled night journey from Mecca to Jerusalem and his ascension to heaven from the latter city. Both these story cycles are ultimately linked to rather enigmatic verses in the Qur'ān through an involved technique of textual interpretation.

Three separate elements in the account of the night journey and ascension story are usually, though not always, combined into a single connected narrative: (1) the cleansing of Muhammad's heart in preparation for the vision of his Lord; (2) the journey by night from Mecca to Jerusalem; and (3) the ascension to heaven in the company of Gabriel and the meeting with God.[22] Each of these motifs has its basis in a single verse in the Qur'ān. The verse "Have We not caused your bosom to dilate?"[23] becomes the textual base for the first element. It appears in the later biography of the Messenger, the *Sīrah*, in which Muhammad says:

> [Gabriel] split all between here and here — i.e., from the hollow of his throat to his pubic hair — and drew out my heart. Then there was brought a golden basin filled with faith in which he washed my heart and my bowels and then they were returned [to their place].[24]

In like manner the night journey and the ascension to heaven have their Qur'ānic base in the following verse: "Glory be to Him Who took His

20. al-Marghinānī, *Mishkāt al-Maṣābīḥ*, trans. James Robson, bk. 26, chap. 20 (Lahore: Sh. Muhammad Ashraf, 1963), 1248.

21. Ibid., 1250.

22. This is based on various traditional accounts. Many commentators and scholars see the entire narrative as referring to a single event.

23. Qur'ān 94:1.

24. al-Baghawī, *Maṣābīḥ al-Sunna*, quoted in Arthur Jeffrey, ed., *Islam: Muhammad and His Religion* (New York: Liberal Arts Press, 1958), 35.

servant by night from the sacred place of worship to the more remote place of worship, whose precincts We have blessed, to show him some of our signs."[25] The assertion that this passage refers to the night journey and ascension is reinforced by a verse in the same chapter recounting the doubts of Muhammad's fellow citizens of Mecca and the divinely inspired response thereto:

> [We will not put faith in you until] you ascend up into heaven, and even then we will put no faith in your ascension till you bring down for us a book that we can read. Say: Glory be to my Lord! Am I but a man, a messenger?[26]

Finally, the following verse is taken to refer to Muhammad's vision of his Lord at the climax of the ascension:

> And verily he saw Him yet another time by the lote-tree of the utmost boundary, nigh unto which is the Garden of Abode. When that which shrouds did enshroud the lote-tree, the eye turned not aside nor yet was overbold. Verily he saw one of the greater revelations of his Lord.[27]

Here is a seemingly inimitable complex of events. Some of the earliest Muslim commentators make it less so, perhaps, by speaking of these happenings as dreams rather than physical transportations, and even A'isha, the Messenger's wife, is quoted in the *Sīrah* as saying that "the Messenger's body remained where it was but God removed his spirit by night."[28] Other commentators, in addition, speak of the "more remote place of worship" as referring to heaven, not Jerusalem, the name of which is not explicitly mentioned in the Qur'ān. Still, the lines of the story soon become set — and in a fashion that seems to place it totally outside the experience of ordinary mortals.

The surprising thing, however, is that for many Muslims, and especially for the mystics and pietists known as Sufis, it is precisely this journey account that comes to serve as the exemplar for all other spiritual journeys. As Geo Widengren has pointed out, the spiritual "ascension" of a Sufi like al-Bisṭāmī parallels the ascension of Muhammad and serves as a model for other Sufis in their search for divine union.[29] Widengren has broken down the essential stages in the varying versions of Muhammad's ascension into ten steps:

1. He ascends to heaven.
2. He drinks a cup of water or of milk.
3. He is chosen as the "friend of God."

---

25. Qur'ān 17:1.

26. Ibid., verse 93.   27. Ibid. 53:10–12.

28. Ibn Ishaq, *The Life of Muhammad: A Translation of Sirat Rasul Allah*, trans. A. Guillaume (Lahore: Oxford University Press, 1955), 183.

29. Geo Widengren, "Muhammad, the Apostle of God, and His Ascension," *Uppsala Universitets Årsskrift* 1 (1955): 92. Also cited by Royster, "Muhammad," 248.

4. The Qur'ān is revealed to him.
5. Esoteric knowledge is revealed to him.
6. He exhibits his wisdom.
7. He gives thanks.
8. He is sent to all the people of the earth.
9. He is promised all the earth for himself and his community.
10. He descends to earth and is sent forth.[30]

Each of these steps is understood to be replicated in any experience of ascent toward the divine. In this way, in at least one of the many Muslim traditions of piety and worship, the few enigmatic Qur'ānic phrases about a mysterious series of events in the life of the Messenger become transformed into a paradigm for the spiritual journey possible in the life of every believer.

The "elevation" of Muhammad from mortal Messenger to a semidivine figure at the center of a "cult of Muhammad" receives its greatest impetus in the folk practices and beliefs of Islam, whether they can be defined as mystical or not. This elevation is especially noticeable in Muslim religious devotions — not in the prescribed ṣalāt, the five daily prayers, but in the du'āt, the private petitions or devotions often composed by saints and founders of various Sufi orders for their followers. One can see the Prophet's elevation in the following litany, which ranges from the human to the superhuman aspects of Muhammad in a series of phrases evoking his many roles:

The man of the stalwart staff
The man who wore sandals
The man of argument
The man of sound reason . . .
The hero of the night ascent
The hero of the sword
The rider of Buraq . . .
He who traversed the seven spheres
The intercessor for all creatures . . .
The man at whose departure the palm trees wept and sighed
He whose influence the birds of the desert sought . . .
The apostle to whom was given the privilege of access
The spreading dawn
The brilliant star. . . .[31]

It is striking to see how in Sufi literature the heart yearns for union not only with its Lord but with the Prophet as well, as the following prayer indicates: "Unite me with him as Thou hast united the spirit and the soul, outwardly and inwardly, waking and sleeping. Make him the spirit of my being in all

30. Widengren, "Muhammad," 114.
31. Constance E. Padwick, *Muslim Devotions* (London: Society for the Propagation of Christian Knowledge, 1961), 146 – 47.

aspects, in this life as in the next."[32] Such prayers are not without their context. They rely on a series of arresting, even surprising traditions in which the Prophet is cherished and union with him is sought. An example is the following, found in the *ḥadīth* of 'Umar:

> Dearer art thou to me, O Apostle of God, than all things save the soul within my body. And the Prophet said, "Thou wilt not truly be a believer until I am dearer to thee than thine own soul."

> And 'Umar said: "By Him Who sent down the Book to thee, thou art indeed dearer to me than my own soul"; and the Prophet said, "Now, 'Umar, thy faith is complete."[33]

Looking at this whole spectrum, then, one can see how the self-doubting, at times rather frightened, and in all very human figure of Muhammad becomes transformed, especially in folk Islam and in certain Sufi circles, into an almost superhuman figure. As such, the Prophet comes to parallel the saints of Islam in healing and intercessionary powers. In fact, strange as it may seem, the cult of saints probably antedates the cult of Muhammad, though a Muhammad mysticism begins to appear as early as the eighth century C.E. As the cult of the Prophet developed, it took on features of the earlier cult of the saints.[34]

When we speak of saints in Islam, we face the difficulty — amounting at times almost to an impossibility — of translating terms across cultural boundaries. This quandary becomes even more extreme when we touch questions regarding religion. The very term *religion* has such strong Christian overtones that scholars have questioned its utility as a description of non-Christian traditions. The Arabic term *dīn*, for example, is simply not "religion" in the usual Western Christian sense, no matter how useful the latter may be as a shorthand translation.[35] Similarly, terms such as *prayer* (for *ṣalāt*) and *mysticism* (for *taṣawwuf*) have been subjected to serious question. Above all, the use of the term *orthodox* in relation to Islam has aroused strong objection. All this may serve as a warning that the Muslim "saint" is not to be equated with his Christian namesake.

The Arabic term usually translated as "saint" is *walī* (plural *awliyā'*), which means in a more literal sense a "friend" or "protégé," someone "near to God" or whom God has taken into a close relationship, as in these words of the Qur'ān, which are recited by Muslims when they visit the tombs of saints: "Lo! verily the friends of Allah are those on whom fear does not come and who do not grieve."[36] Furthermore, God himself is called *walī* in the Qur'ān, as in the verse: "God is the Friend of those who believe."[37]

32. Padwick, *Devotions*, 151.
33. Padwick, *Devotions*, 148. Compare Matt. 10:38, 39; Luke 14:26, 33.
34. Von Grunebaum, *Festivals*, 70.
35. See, for example, Wilfred C. Smith, *The Meaning and End of Religion* (San Francisco: Harper and Row, 1978) [originally 1962], especially chaps. 2 – 4.
36. Qur'ān 10:63.   37. Ibid. 2:257.

The special relationship between God and His *wali* differs greatly from what is usually implied in Christian concepts of sainthood. While possessing boundless aura and authority, the *wali*'s charisma is routinized, to use Weberian categories. Instead of operating on an individual, virtuoso basis like the Christian saint, the *wali* generally employs powers that are transmitted from father to son or alternatively from teacher to disciple and then from father to son.[38] As Schimmel points out, the role of the *wali* "is closely connected with the mystery of initiation and progress on the spiritual path, leading through a well-established hierarchy, the members of which surpass each other according to the degree of their love and gnosis."[39] These processes of initiatory or genealogical succession give rise to the phenomenon of "living saints" or "sacred lineages," which are still to be found, albeit in attenuated form, side by side with the veneration of the tombs of dead saints.

This striking difference between Christian and Islamic ideas of sainthood probably exists for several reasons, not the least of which is differing attitudes toward the social and moral values of sexuality. In Islam, unlike Christianity, there is no tradition — certainly no requirement — of celibacy among those who are the most logical candidates for sainthood. Hence, it is possible to see the rise of sacred lineages in certain Islamic societies. The sons of saints or the sons of a saint's disciples become a hereditary lineage of "saints" continuing, at times, for centuries. This hereditary transmission of saintliness helps justify the phenomenon rather than diminish it. In many instances, in fact, a saintly lineage is traced back to the Prophet himself. That these genealogies are usually invented — a fact often known and recognized — does not detract from their acceptance and social importance.[40]

The saints, found in popular religion in Sunni and Shi'i lands alike, are of different origins and types. While some are Sufis, often founders of orders or brotherhoods, others are tribal ancestors, heads of sacred lineages, or founders of dynasties. Often the saints are of humble origin, even, as we find frequently in late (that is, eighteenth- and nineteenth-century) chronicles and biographical dictionaries, "half-deranged persons, *madjdhūb,* whose peculiar or incoherent utterances are often regarded as inspired, or even the simple-minded, *bahlūl.*"[41] Modern scholars have traced some saints to origins as varied as ancient local cults and heroes, as well as to deities connected with woods, stones, and springs. Some are patrons of villages, towns, and even entire provinces; others watch over trades and guilds.

Although the concept of sainthood in the person of the *wali* does not seem to occur in the earliest stages of Islamic development, by the ninth (that is, third Islamic) century, we meet it in connection with the growing movement

---

38. See, for example, Gellner, *Muslim Society,* 131.
39. Schimmel, *Mystical,* 204.
40. Gellner, *Muslim Society,* 116.
41. B. Carra de Vaux, "Wali," in *Shorter Encyclopedia of Islam,* ed. H. A. R. Gibb and J. H. Kramer (Leiden: E. J. Brill, 1961), 629–30.

of *taṣawwuf* or Sufism. During this period, for example, we find a leading writer of the Hanafi school of law, Abū Ja'far al-Taḥāwī (d. 933), protesting against a growing predilection for saints as against prophets.[42] This theme of the opposition between saints and prophets — the one symbolizing the popular, nonscholarly, ecstatic, and sometimes quasi-heretical form of Islam, and the other symbolizing the essential purity of the Islamic message — begins to appear in the ideological struggle between the traditionalists and the Mu'tazilites. This latter group, who called themselves the "Party of God's Unity and Justice," used styles of argumentation borrowed from the Greeks in their vigorous defense of what they considered to be true, monotheistic Islam against aberrations such as dualism, anthropomorphism, and other features of what came to be popular religion. Their traditionalist opponents, on the other hand, calling themselves the "Party of Tradition and Community," considered themselves to be the true champions of pure monotheistic Islam, against those who refused to recognize God's omniscience and omnipotence. As a party more closely connected with popular religious expression, they were more accommodating to ideas like sainthood, which may have had their ultimate origin among new converts from other religions — most likely Christianity in a majority of cases. The Mu'tazilites, on the other hand, denied that there were men possessing special gifts, holding instead that every believer who obeys God is a *walī*.[43]

In the course of the bitter debate between the two parties, the traditionalists found it necessary to develop creedal statements and, later, catechisms to guarantee the propagation of correct ideas about subjects such as God, prophecy, revelation, predestination, and free will, as well as the priority of certain individual companions of the Prophet over others. One of the important creeds developed during that period (its exact date is not known), called *Fiqh Akbar II*, states in its sixteenth article: "The signs (*ayāt*) of the prophets and the miracles (*karāmāt*) of the saints are a reality."[44] Most later creeds and catechisms repeat this assertion in regard to both signs and miracles, but it is important to note that a definite distinction is made between the two. An examination of this distinction between signs (*ayāt*) and miracles (*karāmāt*) — though the English translation is hardly adequate in either case — may help us see the contrast between the special relationship between God and his prophets and the one that pertains between God and his saints.

We begin with the category of prophet, messenger, or apostle — a fundamental one in Islam. Belief in God and his Messenger Muhammad makes up the essential Confession of Faith (*shahāda*) that the Muslim is obliged to repeat daily in the call to prayer and in prayer itself. This belief receives no mention at all in the earliest forms of the creed, which seem to take these

42. A. J. Wensinck, *The Muslim Creed*, (London: Frank Cass, 1965), 225.

43. Carra de Vaux, "Wali," 629.

44. Wensinck, *Muslim Creed*, 193.

essential elements for granted, but in those forms dating from the tenth century onward we find all the elements of the formulation:

> I believe in Allah, His angels, His books, His apostles, the resurrection after death, the decree of Allah, both the good and evil of it, the computation of sins, the Balance, Paradise and Hell; and that all these are real.[45]

From the Qur'ān itself we are able to make some distinction between the two terms familiarly used to designate Muhammad: prophet (nabī), the somewhat earlier appellation, and apostle or messenger (rasūl). The exact difference between these two categories of special human beings cannot be explained with great clarity, but in general prophets were sent to "peoples of the book" — that is, recipients of divine revelations — while apostles or messengers were dispatched to other peoples as well. Each community or people (umma) received only one messenger who was, in addition, their leader. While every apostle or messenger is at the same time a prophet, not every prophet is an apostle. One catechism — and learned opinion in general — stated that there were about 120,000 prophets, among whom only 313 (or according to some, 315) could be counted as apostles. But all are free from sin after having been called to their vocation by God.[46]

According to Muslim commentators on the creeds, the signs (ayāt) are facts that deviate from God's customary way of ordering the universe ('āda, literally "custom," "what is usual"). These ayāt are granted to the prophets to prove their vocation and sincerity in such a way as to put their opponents to shame and thus silence them. Such things are also called mu'jizāt, a term often simply translated "miracles" but one that denotes acts of an overwhelming nature that serve as "proofs of the Faith." In Islamic scholasticism, God's activity in the customary course of events ('āda) consists of creating a series of universes with a certain regularity from one time-atom to the next. When God wishes to support his prophets or messengers visibly, he abandons the sequences he usually follows in recreating things: the dead are revived, mountains are thrown down, and so forth. This concept of what a miracle involves is based on the so-called atomistic philosophy of Islamic scholasticism.[47]

The karāmāt of the saints correspond to the mu'jizāt of the prophets insofar as they imply deviation from the ordinary course of events, but they are not meant to silence opponents. Rather, they are a sign of the grace of God toward the saint through whom they are manifested. Karāma, the miracle as a sign of God's favor rather than as a conclusive point of debate, is one of the two major distinguishing features of Islamic saints. The second is baraka, a word meaning literally "blessing," but connoting divine grace and the

45. Ibid., 188.
46. Ibid., 203–4.
47. Ibid., 224–26.

power of sanctity, or, as one scholar has put it, "virtue as inherent spiritual power."[48]

At times, however, one finds in Islamic writings about the Prophet tales of miracles that fit the category of *karāmāt* more closely than they do *mu'jizāt*. One of these is startlingly reminiscent of the miracles of Jesus:

> Jābir related that the people thirsted on the day of Hudeiba, and they came to the Prophet complaining of their thirst. There was a leather water-bucket before him with a little water in it. He put his hand into the bucket and made the water well forth from between his fingers as springs gush out. Jābir was asked, "How many were you?" He said, "Had we been a hundred thousand it would have sufficed us. We were fifteen hundred." Among his signs was the blessing of a little food till it sufficed a great multitude.[49]

As an example illustrating the veneration accorded saintly figures, we may choose one from among the multitude of saints — namely 'Abd al-Qādir al-Gīlānī, one of the "poles" discussed in a moment — to illustrate the type of veneration accorded to such figures. As Schimmel puts it,

> There is no end to his miracles. It was he who, according to the Balochi folk tradition, approached the Prophet during his heavenly journey when he drew close to the Divine Presence, and while Gabriel had to recede, 'Abdul Qādir offered the Prophet his neck to step on when descending from his heavenly mount Buraq. Gratefully the Prophet made 'Abdul Qādir's foot stand on the neck of every other saint.[50]

Not only is this saint thus awarded a special position among the saints, but he is shown able to stand where even the angel Gabriel had to recede.

It is thus clear that the major features shared by the Prophet and the saints, in popular religion at least, are the powers of performing miracles (though they are variously categorized) and of making intercession with God. To the Shi'a, the *imāms*, 'Ali and his descendants, are the saints and intercessors par excellence, while to Sunnis, with their myraid saints arranged in hierarchies, the chief intercessors after the Prophet are a small group of four saints (*aqṭāb* or "poles" about which the earth revolves) of the twelfth and thirteenth centuries who possess universally accepted intercessory powers. These are the aforementioned al-Gīlānī, as well as Aḥmad al-Rifā'ī, Aḥmad al-Badawī, and Ibrāhīm al-Dasūqī. While the Prophet's intercession can only be hoped for on the Day of Judgment, these four figures have the power to intercede in the affairs of this world. It is said, for example, that their *baraka* causes rain to fall and plants to sprout in the spring.[51]

---

48. J. Spencer Trimingham, *The Sufi Orders in Islam* (London: Oxford University Press, 1971), 301. See also Padwick, *Devotions*, xxv – xxvii.

49. Padwick, *Devotions*, 147.   50. Schimmel, *Veil*, 161.

51. There are many discussions of the hierarchies of saints. See, for example, Carra de Vaux, "Wali," 629; Schimmel, *Mystical*, 199-202; von Grunebaum, *Festivals*, 71. Regarding the intercession of the Prophet, Schimmel writes: "It is this trust in his help at the terrible Day of Judgment that has largely colored the popular veneration of Muhammad" (*Mystical*, 217).

The heavenly ordination of al-Gīlānī as universal intercessor has been depicted as follows by one writer:

> And the Truth Most High said to him in the language of mysterious ecstasy, "Verily today art thou firmly installed before us and trusted." And He caused him to sit with the spirits of the prophets on a seat between this world and the next, between the Creator and the created, between the visible and the spiritual, between the perceptible and the imperceptible. And He gave him four countenances, one to look towards earth, one to look towards the other world, one to look towards created beings, and one to look towards the Creator.[52]

Here the blurring of lines between saint and prophet is extreme and seems more to register the extraordinary force of the personality of al-Gīlānī than to indicate an overall doctrinal development in Islam.

If there is one place where the image of Muhammad seems to be almost totally merged into that of the saint, it is in some of the poetry of love and praise that is directed toward the Prophet. One can see this in the composition that has for the past six centuries at least been the most popular poem of praise of a nonmystical type — the *Burda* or Mantle poem written by the Egyptian poet al-Būṣīrī (1212–ca. 1295).[53] Translated into all of the major languages of the Islamic world, it is recited not so much for its poetic value, which is negligible, as for its supposed semimagical qualities. The poem was inspired by a dream in which the Prophet placed his mantle over the poet, who had been paralyzed by a stroke; upon awakening, the poet found himself cured. For many years the very paper on which the verses are written has been used as a curative charm or amulet, and the verses are recited at funerals to obtain the Prophet's intercession for the dead. No other Arabic poem has achieved such renown.

A few examples of the verses of this poem will show the attitude of veneration that it exudes. The supremacy of the Prophet is referred to as follows:[54]

45. For verily the superiority of the Messenger of God has no limit. . . .

46. If his miracles had equalled his worth, his [very] name, when called upon, would have restored to life moldering bones, crumbling to pieces.

Comparing Muhammad to other, earlier messengers of God, al-Būṣīrī writes:

51. And all the signs that the noble messengers wrought of yore, pertained to them only through his glory.

---

52. Padwick, *Devotions*, 240, quoting from Shaikh Ibn al-Qāsim ibn Bakr Ahmad, *Bahjatu l'asrār*. There is no question in Islamic theology about the superiority of Muhammad over all other prophets.

53. See *Encyclopedia* [new edition], 1:1314, s. v. Burda.

54. The translation used here (with modifications) is by W. A. Clouston, ed., *Arabian Poetry for English Readers* (Glasgow: Privately Printed, 1881), 323–41.

52. For he is, indeed, the sun of superiority, to which they are the stars. They show their lights to people in the dark [but the sun (that is, Muhammad) is seen by the day].

The Prophet's curative powers are also mentioned:

85. How many who were diseased has his hand cured by the touch? How many has he skillfully set free from the bond of insanity?

Then the wonders of his chief miracle, the Qur'ān itself, are delineated:

96. Its eloquence repels the pretensions of the disputer. . . .

97. Its miracles [that is, *ayāt,* also "verses"] have meanings like the ocean's waves at full tide, and are more beautiful and precious than its pearls. . . .

100. If you recite it out of fear of hellfire's heat, its recitation extinguishes the heat of hell's pit.

Finally, considerable space is devoted to the Prophet's night journey and ascension:

107. You travelled by night from one sacred site to [another] sacred site, as the full moon journeys in the deepest darkness;

108. And you continued to ascend until you reached the stage of Two Bow-shots, one neither reached nor attempted by another;

109. And all the prophets and messengers gave you precedence — the precedence of the served one over his servants;

110. And with them you traversed the seven strata [of the heavens] in a procession in which you were the standard bearer

111. Until you left no further limit for any to go beyond you in closeness [to God's throne], nor any ascending stair for anyone mounting.

112. You debased every degree by comparison, when you were invited to go up higher, like the sole distinguished guest,

113. That you might have an interview with one hidden in such a special manner from the eyes [of humanity] and [the communication of] a secret hidden in such a profound degree.

Given the strength of this amalgamation between the figures of prophet and saint, especially insofar as both have stood as exemplary models for ordinary Muslims, it is striking that in recent centuries a wedge has been driven between the two. From the eighteenth century onward, the person of the Prophet has become ever more prominent in Islamic thinking — there has been a great interest in his life and his sociopolitical role — at the same time as the saints and their cults have increasingly become objects of suspicion. Gellner has characterized this cleavage as a "contrast between reverence for the Law and for the sacred person, which emerges in Sunni Islam as the opposition between scholar and Sufi."[55] This description is insufficient,

---

55. Gellner, *Muslim Society,* 43.

however, to explain the force of currents that have been operating in the Muslim world, and that are symbolized, at least, by a perceived polarity between prophet and saint.

Both Sufism and the cult of saints associated with some of its forms were instrumental in spreading Islam after the close of its age of conquest. Incorporating local sacred places and figures, they naturalized Islam especially in areas such as India, Indonesia, and Africa. Of course, certain Muslim scholars throughout the ages have inveighed against the cult of saints. This opposition was expressed not only by the ninth-century al-Taḥāwī at the very beginning of the phenomenon but also by later medieval figures such as Ibn Taymiyya (d. 1328) and Ibn Qayyim al-Jawziyya (d. 1350). In most cases their reasoning was that saint worship negated the full monotheism of Islam and detracted from the status of the one true intercessor and protégé of God, the Prophet Muhammad. With the approach of the modern age and the penetration of modern, Western values into the world of Islam, a variety of external impulses gave added force to voices such as these. The modern-day attack on the cult of saints, with its reassertion of the primacy of the Prophet and its uncompromising insistence on his purely human character, can be traced to several movements. These movements have varied in strength and importance during the past century or so as they have responded to external pressures and influences, but all of them can ultimately be traced to indigenous Muslim movements that arose in the late eighteenth and early nineteenth centuries. However we label these movements — nationalist, liberal, reformist, modernist, fundamentalist, revivalist — they have shared a common lament. Each has looked with considerable dismay at the condition of Islam in the modern era. Each has descried the sad spiritual and moral state of the *umma,* the community of Islam, which seemed unable to compete with or stem the tide of the aggressive West. The latter, in turn, is often perceived not as a secular force but as the vanguard of Christendom.[56]

Almost without exception these modernist-reformist-revivalist movements have not only renewed their veneration of the Prophet but have launched attacks on the cults of the saints and on saintly lineages — all saints, both living and dead. Depending on the point of view of the writers involved, the cult of saints has been seen as non-Islamic and essentially alien to the spirit of the faith or as antimodern and antinationalist. Fundamentalist or radical religious reformers emphasize the first point; supporters of modernization, the second.

Westernizing modernists of the late nineteenth and early twentieth centuries, who saw no contradiction between rational Islam and modern science, urged the Muslim world to enter the modern era of science and technology

---

56. See especially Emmanuel Sivan, *Radical Islam: Medieval Theology and Modern Politics,* (New Haven, Conn.: Yale University Press, 1985), for a presentation of the view of the crisis of Islam by the radical revivalists: chap. 1, "The Mood: Doom and Gloom."

while retaining its own religious values. In doing so they pictured Muhammad as the fount of all modern science and progress, while denigrating the saints and all who venerate them as representatives of backwardness and superstition — an inadmissible perversion of authentic Islam. In some cases their attitude was strengthened by the antinomian, antiritualist tendencies present in certain Sufi orders and associated with some of the saints. More often, however, Sufis and saints were perceived as the enemy. As Gellner has pointed out, Islamic reformers in North Africa under the French tended to view the saintly lineages as antinationalist collaborators with the colonial power.[57] And in Turkey, Atatürk and his followers fought the powerful and widespread Sufi orders and their saints, driving them underground if not destroying them entirely.

Modernists, Westernizers, and nationalists are not the only groups who have fought against saint worship, however. The revivalist Wahhabis in Arabia and Shaykh Waliullah in India, both eighteenth-century phenomena, as well as other "revivalist" groups, have preached against pilgrimage to the tombs of saints.[58] The Wahhabis went so far as to destroy such tombs as they swept across Arabia, and they fought against other manifestations of the worship of saints as well.

For reformers of both types — modernist and revivalist — the Prophet Muhammad has been seen as embodying the pure, original nature of Islam, untainted by "foreign" influences. He has symbolized its originality and uniqueness as well as its "national" character. Especially among the radical revivalists this latter aspect — a stress on the uniqueness of the *umma* or community of Islam as against all the other religious groupings in the world — becomes supremely important. Whereas saints are "foreign" imports or medieval accretions, the Prophet represents authentic, pure Islam and is the sole worthy exemplar for his people during this period of Islamic crisis and renewal. Thus one has a rather peculiar situation. In attempting to cleanse Islam of its veneration of saints and to cast doubt on the worthiness of the aspiration of believers to align themselves with them, the radicals and reformers of modern Islam appear to be chopping away at much of the very piety that was responsible for securing such an exalted position for the Prophet over the course of Islamic history. Whether a healthy veneration of the Prophet can survive for long in such changed circumstances remains to be seen.

57. Gellner, *Muslim Society*, 32, 133, 148.

58. Waliullah's successor, Barelvi, created a new Sufi order aimed at placing Muhammad and the divine law above all saints. The struggle against saint worship was pictured as one against Hindu influences in Islam. See Aziz Ahmad, *Studies in Islamic Culture in the Indian Environment* (Oxford: Clarendon Press, 1964), 201–18.

FOUR

Morality Beyond Morality in the Lives of Three Hindu Saints

John Stratton Hawley

Westerners in search of Hindu ethics often proceed by a direct and unswerving path to *The Laws of Manu,* a classical textbook of codes compiled some two millennia ago, which depicts the proper relations that obtain in a society structured by caste.[1] What it describes is called *varṇāśrama dharma,* a set of proper obligations (*dharma*) that apply differentially depending on one's status in society (*varṇa*) and one's stage in life (*āśrama*).

While it is true that the spirit, if not the letter, of *The Laws of Manu* has set the tone for much Hindu thinking about ethics, Manu is hardly the final word. Indeed if one were to listen for moral lessons in village conversations or to seek them out in the bookstalls that fill the towns and cities of modern North India, chances are slim that one would come up with anything very close to the system bearing Manu's name. Instead of codes and formal prescriptions, one might find oneself attending to legends and tales — accounts of the god Rām, for example, who abandoned his throne in order to serve the dictates of *dharma,* or of his dutiful wife Sītā, who sacrificed every desire of her own to serve her husband. Or perhaps one might hear the story of king Hariścandra, who gave up his wealth, his kingdom, and his very wife and family to honor the demands of his Brahmin teacher. Or perhaps it would be Sāvitrī, the woman whose determination to save her husband's life was so great that she managed to hound Death himself into submission.

These stories show how the rules of *dharma* are embodied in people's lives — what it means in the most extreme circumstances to carry out obligations to one's father, teacher, husband, or society. But by emphasizing the extreme circumstances, they do something more. They teach character in

1. On *The Laws of Manu,* see P. V. Kane, *History of Dharmaśāstra,* 5 vols. (Poona: Bhandarkar Oriental Research Institute, 1930–1946), and Robert Lingat, *The Classical Law of India,* trans. J. Duncan M. Derrett (Berkeley and Los Angeles: University of California Press, 1973); in regard to its date, 92–96, 123–32 of the latter.

addition to precept; they praise personal resourcefulness and tenacity in a way that codes scarcely can.

Another genre of moral literature moves yet a step further from propositional *dharma*. It too advances from the realm of codes into narratives, but now the stories serve less to reinforce the conventional prescriptions enunciated by Manu and his ilk than to call them into question. Whether published as sober-looking religious tracts or as cheap paperbacks, even comic books, such tales record the life stories of the great *bhakti* saints, heroes of an important devotional strand in Indian religion that extends back at least as far as the sixth century A.D. *Bhakti* means, broadly, love — love of God — and poses the most serious questions to the canons of *dharma*.

Yet even here *dharma* is not left entirely behind. One could argue that the stories of these enthusiastic *bhakti* saints are not told merely to test *dharma* but to supplement it. Taken as a whole, they present a *dharma* of their own, an ethic based on certain qualities of character and communal identification that are not quite ignored but certainly obscured in the teaching of traditional *varṇāśrama dharma*. In effect they present to their readers a new version of *dharma*: a *bhakti dharma*, an ethics of character that focuses on love.

In what follows, I would like to investigate several aspects of this *bhakti dharma* as it emerges in the work that is the grandfather and prototype for most of the hagiographical collections one finds in North India today. This is the *Bhaktamāl*, the most important such anthology in Hindi, four centuries old but still widely available and widely read. I will focus on the portraits of three sixteenth- and seventeenth-century saints — Mīrā Bāī, Narasī Mehtā, and Pīpā Dās (together with his wife Sītā) — whose lives are depicted in the *Bhaktamāl* and its accompanying commentary, the *Bhaktarasabodhinī* of Priyā Dās (A.D. 1712). Each of these saints serves to highlight a particular virtue: fearlessness in the case of Mīrā, generosity in the case of Narasī, and community service in the case of Pīpā and Sītā. Though these virtues emerge with special clarity in their life stories, they are shared in various measure by other saints described in the *Bhaktamāl*, and they work together to set out three aspects of a single notion of saintliness. It is a saintliness that cannot be compounded on the basis of the "secular" or "ordinary" virtues one might deduce from the prescriptions and presuppositions of *varṇāśrama dharma*. Indeed the *Bhaktamāl* sometimes begins its devotional sketches by noting how these saints left that sort of *dharma* behind. Yet the saintliness depicted in the *Bhaktamāl* does not do away with all *dharma* either. Rather, it describes a more fundamental morality, which, if manifested with the naturalness that these saints evince, would lead to right living in the absence of all code and precept.

THE BHAKTAMĀL

The *Bhaktamāl* ("Garland of Devotees") is the best known "Lives of the Saints" in North India today.[2] Among Hindi works, it may also be the oldest, though precedents can be found in other Indian vernacular languages;[3] certainly it is more catholic than sectarian hagiographical collections such as the *Caurāsī Vaiṣṇavan kī Vārtā* ("Accounts of Eighty-four Vaiṣṇavas"), a product of the Vallabha Sampradāy. The *Bhaktamāl* seems to have been composed near the beginning of the seventeenth century by one Nābhājī. Little about him is definitely known, since his autobiographical comments are limited to indications of who his guru was. The commentator Priyā Dās, however, writing near the beginning of the eighteenth century, depicts Nābhājī as a devotee of Rām and associates him with the well known ashram at Galatā, near Jaipur in Rajasthan.[4] As for Priyā Dās, he identifies himself as a resident of Brindavan and devotee of the fifteenth-century Bengali ecstatic Caitanya. This makes him, presumably, a member of the Caitanya or Gauḍīya Sampradāy. Taking Nābhājī and Priyā Dās together, then, we already have a work of sectarian breadth; that breadth has had much to do with its wide readership over the centuries. Indeed the telegraphic Nābhājī is almost always read together with his commentator, and when I use the term *Bhaktamāl* in the present essay, I mean to denote that composite hagiography.[5]

2. I shall be referring to the following edition: Nābhājī, *Śrī Bhaktamāl* (Lucknow: Tejkumār Press, 1969). Critical work on the *Bhaktamāl* has recently been undertaken by Narendra Jhā in his *Bhaktamāl: Pāṭhānuśīlan evam Vivecan* (Patna: Anupam Prakāśan,1978). The texts he offers differ insubstantially from those given in the Tejkumār Press edition. In addition, one may consult two articles of Gilbert Pollet: "Eight Manuscripts of the Hindī *Bhaktamāla* in England," *Orientalia Lovaniensia Periodica* 1 (1970): 203–22, and The Mediaeval Vaiṣṇava Miracles as Recorded in the Hindi 'Bhakta Māla,' "*Le Muséon* 80 (1967): 475–87.

3. Lists of the Tamil Śaiva saints began to appear in the eighth century and were expanded into full-blown hagiographies in the eleventh and twelfth centuries. On the Vaiṣṇava side, Tamil hagiographies begin to appear in the thirteenth century with the *Ārāyirappaṭi Kuruparaparāprapāvam,* though the *Divya Sūri Carita* has sometimes been thought to be a century earlier. The *Śūnyasaṃpādane* of the Vīraśaiva community in Karnataka was produced in the fifteenth century. A century later the Maharashtrian saint Eknāth went on to compile a hagiographical collection in Marathi. On the Tamil materials, see Kamil Zvelebil, *Tamil Literature* (Wiesbaden: Otto Harrassowitz, 1974), 91, 170, 173–75; in addition, I have benefitted from a personal communication from Dennis Hudson (March 1983). On the Śūnyasaṃpādane, see R. Blake Michael, "Aṣṭāvaraṇa in the *Śūnyasaṃpādane*" (Ph.D. diss., Harvard University, 1979). On Eknāth, see L. R. Pangarkar, *Marāṭhī Vāṇmayācā Itihās* (Pune: Vidarbh Marāṭhavāḍā Book Company, 1972 [originally 1935]), 242. In regard to the hagiographical tradition that followed Nābhājī, see Kailāś Candra Śarmā, *Bhaktamāl aur Hindī Kavya mẽ unkī Paramparā* (Rohtak: Manthan Publications, 1983), 65–159.

4. *Bhaktamāl,* 41–46. In regard to the dating of Nābhājī's text, see Gilbert Pollet, "Early Evidence on Tulsīdās and His Epic," *Orientalia Lovaniensia Periodica* 5 (1974): 157–58 (sec. 3.2). Corroborating evidence adduced in sections 3.3ff., however, seems problematical, especially insofar as it relies on biographies of Tulsī Dās whose early date is doubtful. On this point, see Philip Lutgendorf, "The Quest for the Legendary Tulsīdās" (Paper delivered to the American Academy of Religion, Los Angeles, November 1985).

5. On Priyā Dās, see R. D. Gupta, "Priyā Dās, Author of the *Bhaktirasabodhinī,*" *Bulletin of the School of Oriental and African Studies* 32, no. 1 (1969): 57–70; also Philip Lutgendorf, "Kṛṣṇa Caitanya and His Companions as Presented in the *Bhaktamāla* of Nābhā Jī and the *Bhaktirasabodhinī* of Priyā Dāsa" (Master's essay, University of Chicago, 1981), 24–29.

The first section of the *Bhaktamāl* presents a galaxy of mythological figures who can be considered devotees (*bhaktas*) of Krishna or Rām, the principal manifestations (*avatārs*) of the god Vishnu in the human sphere. Other gods in the pantheon, such as Shiva, Brahmā, and Lakṣmī, are drawn into this worshipful array. Thus the *Bhaktamāl* begins at the beginning, as any good Hindu *purāṇa* should. Its bulk, however — the second section — concerns historical personages, denizens of this degenerate age (*kali yug*). Nābhājī starts with the four theologians whose names had by his time come to symbolize the four main teaching traditions (*sampradāys*) among Hindus who principally venerate Vishnu or one of his *avatārs*. His purpose, apparently, is to set the present world-age off on the right footing, but he dispenses quickly with these four venerable figures of the twelfth and following centuries and moves on toward saints who lived closer to his own times. When he relates some of their stories, he seems genuinely at home, and Priyā Dās elaborates at even greater length. Evidently they held great significance in Nābhājī's and Priyā Dās's day, and many of them continue to do so in the present as well. Among these are the portraits of Mīrā, Narasī, and Pīpā, which we will now consider one by one.

MĪRĀ BĀī: FEARLESSNESS

Among all the singer-saints of medieval North India none is better known today than Mīrā Bāī. Songs attributed to her are sung from one end of the subcontinent to the other; the bards of her native Rajasthan keep alive an ample cycle of songs about her; and not one but several feature films have taken her as their heroine. Her story is a gripping one, and the *Bhaktamāl's* version of it is the earliest to have come down to us.

Like all subsequent accounts, the *Bhaktamāl* presents Mīrā as a Rajput princess so absorbed in the love of Krishna from early childhood that she understood herself to be his bride and therefore regarded her earthly marriage as a matter of secondary importance at best. Depicted in this way, she vividly replicates the devotion of the cowherding women and girls (*gopīs*) who peopled the land of Braj, just south of Delhi, when Krishna dwelt there. They too had husbands. But even if they had dedicated themselves to the lifelong service of their mates — their "husband-gods" (*patidev*), as the Hindu expression tellingly puts it — they instantly abandoned the demands of conventional morality at the sound of Krishna's flute. They dropped their brooms, churning sticks, and cooking implements, and even slipped away from the conjugal bed itself, to rush out into the forest to dance the dance of love, Krishna's circular *rās* dance. Mīrā's urge was the same: to seek out the company of quite a different "family" from that to which *dharma* had assigned her — a family composed of those who sang the praises of her Lord. This put her constantly at loggerheads with that family's earthly rival.[6]

6. This is a fundamental tension in the life stories of many of India's best-known women saints, though it is not always worked out in the same terms that it is in Mīrā's case. Variations

To present Mīrā, the *Bhaktamāl* begins with the poem in which Nābhājī
sets forth the major themes that her life displays:

1   Mīrā unravelled the fetters of family;
        she sundered the chains of shame to sing
        of her mountain-lifting Lover and Lord.
2   Like a latter-day *gopī*, she showed the meaning
        of devotion in our devastated age.
3   She had no fear. Her impervious tongue
        intoned the triumphs of her artful Lord.
4   Villains thought it vile. They set out to kill her,
        but not even a hair on her head was harmed,
5   For the poison she took turned elixir in her throat.
        She cringed before none: she beat love's drum.
6   Mīrā unravelled the fetters of family;
        she sundered the chains of shame to sing
        of her mountain-lifting Lover and Lord.[7]

The very first line sets up an opposition between conventional modesty
(as defined by family bonds) and singing of Krishna, and the second line
confirms that Mīrā's life displays the tension that the *gopīs* experienced, but
on an earthly plane, or rather, as the Hindu concept has it, in the degenerate
world-age of which we are a part. Mention is then made of the fearless,
shameless quality of Mīrā's personality, which is presented as if it emerged
from her singing. The poem then cites the great example of Mīrā's fearlessness: the episode in which she gladly drank the poison her husband or in-
laws served up to her. As if in consequence of her fearlessness, she had no
reason to fear, for the poison turned to ambrosia in her throat. The poem
concludes in the same vein, making reference to her outspoken *bhakti* musicianship again (she is said to have beat the great annunciatory *nisān* drum)
and drawing attention again to its effect: it broke asunder the chains of
ordinary morality.

The rest of the account — the part added by Priyā Dās — fleshes out the
details. We are told that as a child in her father's house in the princely state
of Merta, in Rajasthan, Mīrā fell deeply in love with Giridhar — Krishna in his
role as lifter of Mount Govardhan, a heroic image of the Lord and very much
Mīrā's favorite. When she was betrothed to an unspecified *rāṇā* from another
state and followed him around the marriage fire, the mantras she said in her

on the theme are explored by A. K. Ramanujan, "On Women Saints," in J. S. Hawley and
Donna M. Wulff, eds., *The Divine Consort: Rādhā and the Goddesses of India* (Berkeley:
Berkeley Religious Studies Series, 1982), 316 – 24, and by Anne Feldhaus,"Bahiṇā Bāī: Wife and
Saint," *Journal of the American Academy of Religion* 50, no. 4 (1982): 591 – 604. Further
materials have been presented by R. Blake Michael in "The Housewife as Saint: Tales from the
Śūnyasampādane" (Paper delivered to the American Academy of Religion, New York, 1979).
    7. *Bhaktamāl*, 712 – 13.

heart were all directed to her other husband, the Mountain Lifter.[8] Instead of a dowry to take with her to her new home, she asked only for Him, the image of Krishna to which she had become so attached. And when she arrived at her in-laws' house, she refused to bow her head to her mother-in-law, as Hindu custom prescribes, or to the goddess who was the chosen deity of the household into which she had married. Her mother-in-law was humiliated; the *rāṇā* was put to shame (the text does not specify whether the term *rāṇā* refers to her father-in-law or her husband, but it was probably the former since the text calls him "the king");[9] and her behavior cast discredit on the honor of her own father's lineage as well. All family bonds were threatened by Mīrā's sense of having already offered herself totally to Krishna.

But that did not mean that Mīrā was left with no family at all. Though her earthly family would rather poison than nourish her, Mīrā retained another family in "the company of the saints" (*sādhu saṅg*) who are, as the text says, "attached to the will of Syām" — that is, Krishna (*jinhāi lāgī cāh syām kī*).[10] Her sisters-in-law tried to dissuade her from associating with such *sādhus* but to no avail; the *rāṇā*, on hearing of the state of things, dispatched a cup of poison. The poison was sent in the guise of a liquid offering (*caraṇāmṛt*) to the feet of Krishna, Mīrā's deity, since the king knew well that Mīrā was bound to consume whatever was left over from the table of her divine Lord. The irony is that, as she drank it, the poison became exactly the "immortal liquid from his feet" that the term *caraṇāmṛt* implies. It made her glow with an even greater health and happiness than before.

In the section that follows, the *Bhaktamāl* takes a closer look at the nature of Mīrā's chosen family — the *satsaṅg*.[11] First the *sādhus* who customarily

8. The term *rāṇā* refers to a male member of a royal or princely family and is in use in southwest Rajasthan. In the *Bhaktamāl*'s version of Mīrā's story, this *rāṇā* is later said to have been the ruler of Jodhpur (*Bhaktamāl, 722*).

9. *Bhaktamāl,* 718: *despatī*.

10. *Bhaktamāl,* 717. The term *sādhu* (or *sādhū*) has come to refer specifically to a religious mendicant in modern Hindi. I have translated it here, however, as "saints" because the term had a wider range of meaning in medieval Hindi, as the gloss offered by the text itself suggests.

11. *Satsaṅg* means "the gathering (*saṅg*) of the *sants*" (of which word *sat* is a shortened form). I translate the term here as "gathering of the good" or "company of saints," though the word "saint" bears no etymological relation to *sant*. The term *sant,* deriving ultimately from the Sanskrit participle of a verb that means both "to be good" and "to be real," comes into vernacular north Indian usage with several meanings. In fifteenth- and sixteenth-century usage, it generally connotes "the good," almost invariably with the specific sense of those who are worshiping and singing of God. A somewhat different connotation has come to be attached to the term in intervening centuries. *Sant* is taken to refer to one of a group of holy men whose lineage can be traced back to the Nāth Yogīs and who espouse what has come to be referred to familiarly as *sant mat,* "the point of view of the *sants*." This is the usage given the term by H. P. Dwivedi, Charlotte Vaudeville, W. H. McLeod, and others. Finally, in current Panjabi usage the term *sant* has come to refer to any holy man who lives apart from ordinary society. I shall use the term here in the first sense, the one that I believe is most directly in line with medieval usage. Further on this point, see J. S. Hawley, "The *Sant* in Sūr Dās," in *The Sants: Studies in a Devotional Tradition of India,* ed. Karine Schomer and W. H. McLeod (Berkeley: Berkeley Religious Studies Series; and Delhi: Motilal Banarsidass, 1987).

gathered around her eventually stopped coming, which saddened her but showed that not even those who pass their lives singing of God always possess the fearlessness that such a life requires and, if pursued in truth, generates naturally. Mīrā is left with only Krishna for her *satsaṅg*. But the departure of the *sādhūs* is providential, since at that time the *rāṇā* extends his murderous jealousy from Mīrā to any with whom she might speak. It has been rumored that she has liaisons with other men. Indeed someone overhears her cooing to a lover behind her door. The *rāṇā* is summoned, appears hastily with sword in hand, demands to be admitted to her chamber, and asks her to show him the man with whom she has been conversing so lovingly. Her response is that the one he seeks is standing directly in front of him — her image of Krishna — and that he is not one to shy away from an encounter. The *rāṇā*, flustered and angry, freezes "like a picture on the wall" and retreats.[12] Note that it is he, her "true" husband, who fearfully flees, not the one who appears to worldly eyes her paramour, her illegitimate consort. And the way in which the *rāṇā* goes deepens the sense of irony that the *Bhaktamāl* takes pleasure in conveying: he, though flesh and blood, turns stonelike, a mere image of reality, when faced with the image who is much more than an image, more than "real life" itself.

The next episode provides yet another instance of Mīrā's fearlessness, and again the battle is fought over the issue of marital fidelity and sexual propriety. This time Mīrā is truly faced with a vile and dissolute would-be lover, a man who comes to her in the guise of a *sādhū* and urges her to submit to his advances on the strength of the claim that Giridhar himself has commanded it. We learn nothing about sagacity or credulity from Mīrā's response; the lesson has to do, again, with absence of fear. She simply replies that she accepts Giridhar's orders in all humility, and with that she offers him food and has a bed made. But she goes him one better. She lays out the bower in the presence of the *satsaṅg*, urging on him that same fearlessness that is by now her trademark, and in that open, communal context she urges him to have good fun as well — another Krishnaite virtue. The result is that it is he, not she, who fears and feels shame. He blanches, loses any desire for corporeal contact, and begs her to help him attain the godly devotion that she displays.

Thus Mīrā's place in the *satsaṅg* is tested from without (by the *rāṇā*) and within (by the false *sādhū*), and in both cases it is her absence of shame in the

---

The term *bhakta*, meaning "loving devotee" and related to the Sanskrit root meaning "to participate, to share," is often distinguished from the term *sant* according to the second meaning of the latter term. The effect is to apply the term *bhakta* to those medieval poet-devotees who approved of the worship of God through image and drama (the *saguṇa*, "with qualities," approach) and *sant* to those who insist that such avenues are misleading (the *nirguṇa*, "without qualities," approach). In medieval usage, however, the two are much more synonymous than this distinction would suggest.

12. The phrase is *likhayau citra bhīt māno* (*Bhaktamāl*, 719).

presence of Krishna that makes her defenselessness a true defense. By breathing the expansive magnanimity of her Lord, she shames the shameless.

By the same token she charms the great. The Moghul emperor Akbar — a frequent figure in the hagiographies of the time — is drawn from afar to hear her sing. Accompanied by his chief musician Tānsen, he comes to Mīrā's presence disguised as a commoner, which teaches that neither rank nor religious affiliation (Akbar is a Muslim) are relevent to *satsaṅg,* and before long Tānsen is moved to song.

Not everyone is so impervious to issues of status and boundary as Akbar, however, even within the *bhakti* movement itself. In the next episode Mīrā travels to Brindavan, the great center of Krishna worship in Braj, and is refused an audience with the important Vaiṣṇava philosopher Jīv Gosvāmī. The reason is that Jīv has vowed never to have concourse with a woman. Mīrā sets him straight with a message in which she reminds him that in Brindavan there is really only one male, Krishna. All the rest are *gopīs* before him. The lesson, once again, is not only that *satsaṅg* is an open reality, devoid of the marks of hierarchy, but that fear and modesty have no place in it.

Mīrā's last journey takes her to Dvarka, the great focus of Krishna worship in the west of India, in order that her service to Giridhar might be deepened one final measure. When she has been gone for some time, the *rāṇā* finally misses her and recognizes that she is the very personification of love (*bhakti kau sarūp*).[13] The lesson, perhaps, is that even the world of profane morality cannot survive forever without the higher dimension that Mīrā represents.

The *rāṇā* sends a delegation of Brahmins to persuade her to return, but she refuses. Driven to extremes, they try to win her back with a hunger strike, which does indeed earn her sympathy, but Krishna himself prevents her departure. One day, as she worships, he draws her into his own image, and she is never seen again. The story ends, thus, on what from an ethical point of view is an ambiguous note. Mīrā may be willing to explore the possible coexistence of earthly propriety and heavenly devotion, but Krishna, the great hero of music and antistructure, cannot bear to see her try.

NARASĪ MEHTĀ: ABUNDANCE AND GENEROSITY

Mīrā is a paragon of fearlessness; the word echoes over and over in the *Bhaktamāl's* portrait of her. And she needs to be fearless if she is to sing God's songs, because the milieu in which she belongs, that of a traditional Rajasthani princess, has definite, almost inflexible expectations for women. But other lives face other barriers, and in the life of Narasī Mehtā, the great poet-saint of Gujarat, the barrier is not family but money. Hence the virtue to which his inveterate singing leads is not social but economic fearlessness.[14] It

---

13. *Bhaktamāl,* 722.

14. Indeed a term that might be translated "fearlessness" (*niśamk*) is used to describe him, as it is various others of the saints of the *Bhaktamāl* — for instance, Sūrdās Madanmohan (*Bhaktamāl,* 679, 748).

would be a great understatement to call him generous, though this virtue
follows naturally from a life of song and divine service in the lives of a number
of other saints. Narasī is generous even when he has nothing to give; he offers
freely to others even when he has nothing to eat himself. He acts as if the
Lord's economy is an endless abundance, and it always turns out that he is
right. Just as Mīrā's fearlessness in the face of marital propriety turns the
world's poison to divine nectar, so Narasī's sense of God's abundance spreads
wealth in a world where the belief that all things are scarce leads to niggardliness and suspicion.

As in the *Bhaktamāl*'s chapter on Mīrā, the kernel poem in the section on
Narasī—the one composed by Nābhājī—announces the main theme. It
draws attention to a conflict between traditional, high-ranking Smārta
Brahmins and devotional Bhāgavatas (that is *bhaktas*) of the time Narasī
represents (though he too was born a Smārta). The poem reports that Narasī
succeeded in turning the Brahmin's desert into a lake. His actions provide
ample irrigation for a view of life and religion that was parched and dry.[15]

As the story proper begins — the part related by Priyā Dās — we learn just
what it is that Narasī does: he wanders. Nothing explicit has yet been said
about his musicianship, but the reader, knowing why Narasī's life is being
reported at all, immediately understands that he wanders because he sings: he
is preoccupied with songs of God.

The reader also understands why when Narasī returns to the home of his
brother and his brother's wife, where he has stayed since he has been or-
phaned, his brother's wife rebukes him. She takes him for a wastrel and a
drain on the family finances. When he asks for a drink, she accepts his request
only grudgingly, taunting him with the remark that unless he is given water
to drink, his work can scarcely be expected to proceed. The words she
chooses have another resonance than the harsh one she intends, however,
since the reader has already been introduced in the prefatory poem to the
knowledge that Narasī's work is precisely one that depends on the availability of water: his songs irrigate the faithful.[16]

Nonetheless, it is to her harshness that Narasī responds. Deeply hurt, he
turns away. He is content to let himself die, and goes off to a temple of Shiva
to await the inevitable. But in this divine hospice earthly inevitabilities prove
pliable. After seven days of waiting, Narasī is still alive. Indeed he is granted
a vision of Shiva, who removes his thirst and hunger and agrees to supply him
with whatever boon he might wish. The boy replies that he does not know
how to ask for anything and merely suggests that Shiva give him whatever
would make the god himself happy. Shiva does so, making known a desire
that he cannot even acknowledge to his own consort — the desire to become

15. *Bhaktamāl*, 673–74.

16. The imagery of irrigation and soaking is also used with reference to the lives of Pīpā Dās
and his wife Sītā (*Bhaktamāl*, 496–500), and liquid imagery is applied to Jīv Gosvāmī, Sūrdās
Madanmohan, and Tulsī Dās (*Bhaktamāl*, 610, 749, 756).

a *gopī* before Krishna — and immediately Narasī is assumed into the circle of Krishna's *rās* dance. He never wants to leave, of course, but Krishna assures him that whenever Narasī remembers Krishna or meditates on his form, Krishna will be present. No wonder, then, that as Narasī returns to the world, marries, establishes his own household, and begins to sing of the Lord, many saints gather to sing those praises with him. And there more trouble begins, for Narasī's popularity arouses the jealousy of the Brahmins.

Note the logic of these events. Narasī is refused the most basic sustenance by his own family, the very unit that is bound by canons of earthly morality to give him succor. But in the presence of Shiva, not only is he given what he asks, he is given what he does not even know how to request. Boons are normally given in response to a prior action, but here there is not even a hint of a bargain. The wish Shiva grants to Narasī is purely an overflow of what he himself desires, and its content merely underscores this sense of plenty freely shared. In the *rās* dance Krishna multiplies himself many thousandfold so that he can become immediately available to the *gopīs* who join in the dance. The motif of abundance is expanded a step further when Krishna assures Narasī that he has access to the magic circle of the *rās* at the drop of a hat, even when he is "gone" from it. In consequence, when Narasī begins to recall that circle in song, he is naturally joined by throngs of others who come to share the wealth of love.

Two economies have been described in the story of Narasī: that of the Brahmins, which is based on scarcity and exhibits on that account a begrudging niggardliness and angry jealousy, and that of God's musical fellowship (or rather sisterhood) in which there is infinitely much to give. The more is given, the more there is still to be dispensed.

The incidents that the *Bhaktamāl* reports from the remainder of Narasī's life underscore this contrast. The jealous Brahmins set themselves to scheming. Living as they do in Junagarh, on the road to the holy temple of Krishna at Dvarka, they are often presented with requests from traveling pilgrims to hold their funds in safekeeping. Then the pilgrims can continue along the dangerous road to Dvarka without fear of robbers. Upon arrival they can reclaim an amount equivalent to what they deposited at Junagarh by proceeding with an IOU to a relative or associate of one of the Junagarh Brahmins. Of course a commission is required for the service.

Now the Junagarh Brahmins know full well that Narasī is no moneylender like themselves. The thought of using family ties with Brahmins in distant places to extract interest from travelers has never occurred to him. But the Brahmins believe that by portraying him as someone like themselves, they may have a great deal to gain. Hence they send several pilgrims to his doors claiming that Narasī is well known for his wealth. Their hope is at least to embarrass Narasī. If he accedes to these *sādhūs'* requests and writes them an IOU, he will have no way of reimbursing them and will have to suffer years in jail or worse in order to pay for his sins.

Sure enough, the pilgrims make their way to Narasī's ramshackle house, where he greets them cordially. He is a little surprised and suspects that someone is playing a practical joke on these folk, but he interprets their arrival nonetheless as a gesture from on high. His habit is simply to accept what is offered, as if the world were a reflex of God's abundance. He makes out an IOU, as the Brahmins had said he would, but it is of an unusual form. It reads, "Sāh Sāṅval is very generous. Take this to him, get the money from him, and go about your business without a second thought."[17]

When the travelers arrive in Dvarka, they search assiduously for a merchant by the name of Sāh Sāṅval but to no avail. The money merchants in town have never heard of such a person. When the desperate pilgrims had just about given up, however, that very merchant appears to them, saying that he has been looking high and low for them. He has their money and is eager, in fact, to grant them 25 percent interest in addition to the principal rather than extracting the customary reduction. As his letter of confirmation to Narasī, he writes that he has plenteous funds on hand and that Narasī is welcome on any occasion to write promissory notes in his name.

The mysterious financier, of course, is none other than Krishna, for Sāṅval is a variant on Syām, one of his titles: "the Dark One." It is no surprise, on reflection, that the Brahmin merchants of Dvarka, despite their physical proximity to Krishna's great temple and apparent call to his service, were ignorant of his true identity. He trades in a currency whose principles they do not understand. Its effortless abundance causes the Brahmins' joke on Narasī to backfire. As Joseph says to his brothers at the end of the biblical story, "You meant evil against me; but God meant it for good."[18]

Similar events follow. When Narasī's daughter is married and gives birth to a son, she notifies her father that custom requires he should present a substantial gift to her parents-in-law. Narasī sets off for her house in a broken-down cart. When his daughter sees his condition, she blanches with anger and shame and asks him why he came at all if he came empty-handed. He tells her not to worry and to have her mother-in-law make a list of things that will satisfy her on the occasion. The haughty mother-in-law complies, but in anger. She demands everything she can think of and brings her list to a conclusion by requesting two stones — a special insult intended to illuminate the actual extent of what Narasī has to give. Again, however, evil turns to

---

17. *Bhaktamāl*, 679–80.

18. Genesis 50:20 (Revised Standard Version). The *Bhaktamāl* tells a somewhat similar story about the disinterested stewardship of another's wealth on the part of Ravi Dās. In gratitude for the simple hospitality the saint has offered him, a visitor decides to entrust his *pāras* stone to Ravi Dās for safekeeping. The *pāras* is no ordinary stone. It is capable of transforming base metals into gold, but this is a matter of no concern to Ravi Dās since he already has the stone he needs — namely, the image he worships. Because of the *pāras* hidden away in the thatch of his hut, however, Ravi Dās's assets begin to multiply whether he wills it or not, but this is all due to the desire of Hari himself, who wants the money used to construct a splendid new temple where many can come to sing his praises under the guidance of the diffident saint (*Bhaktamāl*, 474–75).

good: as Narasī takes up his simple drone instrument and begins to sing, not only do all the desired items begin to crowd about him in the poor hut where he has been assigned to stay but the two stones in the assemblage turn to gold and silver. The mother-in-law is apparently satisfied, but a more important result is that Narasī's daughter is won away from her earthly values. She converts and accompanies her father back to Junagarh.

In the last episode that the *Bhaktamāl* reports, Narasī is so lost in song that he forgets to attend the marriage of his own son, despite the fact that it represents a great coup. His son has been paired with the daughter of the rich and respectable family with whom every Brahmin in town would like to achieve an alliance. Again Krishna intervenes — this time accompanied by his wife Rukmiṇī, as is appropriate for the nuptial occasion — and they lead the procession of the groom's family, spreading out before Narasī a display of incomparable pomp and plenty. The father of the bride, who had come to bemoan the betrothal when the local Brahmins informed him about Narasī's financial straits, reconsiders his qualms in an instant. The lesson is that even the richest, most proper Brahmin need not fear for his daughter's welfare in a family governed by the economic rules that seem to pertain to Narasī. Time and again it is made plain that to sing of the Lord and not fear for want is to be the recipient of more than one could ever have imagined asking. To worldly vision, Narasī has nothing; yet, as events make clear, he has everything — provided he is giving it away.[19]

PĪPĀ AND SĪTĀ: COMMUNITY SERVICE

A third image of sainthood and its virtues is presented in the *Bhaktamāl's* account of Pīpā Dās and his wife Sītā. Here too one finds the fearlessness of Mīrā and the unconscious, improbable generosity of Narasī, but these virtues are now bound up more closely than ever with a third: the service of *satsaṅg*, God's society, from within. Pīpā and Sītā epitomize a new view of householdership. Their marriage is presented as the very antithesis of most Indian marriages, which are cogs in the wheel of *dharma*, synapses in the vast and

19. The motif of "unconscious wealth" is an especially common one in the *Bhaktamāl*. Hari Dās squanders great amounts of a donor's precious perfume by pouring it on the banks of the River Jumna, but the odor miraculously reappears in the temple for which the donor had intended it (*Bhaktamāl*, 602). Rām Dās is unjustly accused of stealing a valuable image and is required to pay for it. He says he has no gold whatever, but the accusing "devotees" remind him of his wife's earrings, which, when weighed, are found to be worth so much that they cannot even be lifted off the ground (*Bhaktamāl*, 451–53). The aphorism introducing Dhanā calls him the one whose crops grew in the absence of any seed (*Bhaktamāl*, 521). And many acts of unwonted generosity are attributed to various saints — for instance, King Caturbhuj, Sūrdās Madanmohan, and Tulsī Dās (*Bhaktamāl*, 708, 748, 766). A surprisingly different set of attitudes to work, wealth, and generosity on the part of a community that shares in the *bhakti* tradition is revealed in R. Blake Michael, "Work as Worship in the Vīraśaiva Tradition," *Journal of the American Academy of Religion* 50, no. 4 (1982): 605–19.

complex network of caste society. Pīpā and Sītā belong instead to the fellowship of the saints, the realm of devotion and song.

As the story begins, Pīpā and Sītā are king and queen, sitting at the apex of
hierarchy. But Pīpā defects, urged on by the secret wishes and obvious
example of some visiting *sādhūs,* and looks for a new mode of worship: love
(*bhakti*). People think him crazy, but he runs off to Benares to be accepted as
a pupil by Rāmānand, whom the *Bhaktamāl* depicts as the great guru of the
sants and father of their spiritual family.[20] But Rāmānand does not ratify the
simple bifurcation between *dharma* and *bhakti* that Pīpā's flight from the
throne implies. In accepting Pīpā as one of his own, he commands him to go
back where he came from and begin serving the saints right there.

Later Pīpā bolts again, desperate to loosen the ties that bind him to his
twenty wives (this is householdership with a vengeance!), but the youngest
among them, Sītā, refuses to let him go. She is willing to wear a humble torn
blanket as clothing — she cares nothing for modesty and rank — if only she can
be allowed to stay at her husband's side. Pīpā then orders her to go naked, so
anxious is he to slip away from his domestic life, but again she consents, and
at this point Rāmānand intervenes and orders his pupil to take her along.
Earlier Rāmānand has said that it matters little whether one's station is that
of householder or renunciant, and now he positively prevents Pīpā from
lurching too greatly to one side. To do so would be merely to embrace a social
role that the old, unregenerate order sanctions in any case: that of the
outsider, the wanderer, the crazy enthusiast. What is wanted instead is a new
understanding of what one already is, and a genuinely new society in which
the roles of householder and renunciant are not polarized.[21]

In what follows we see Pīpā and Sītā form the nucleus of that society
precisely because they are both householders and renunciants, never one
without the other. They remain married, but their marriage is a life devoted
entirely to others. They are married in their mutual self-renunciation. Like

20. *Bhaktamāl,* 494. Along with the hagiographical sketches of Anant Dās, the *Bhaktamāl* is
the oldest extant text to assert that Kabīr, Ravi Dās, Pīpā, and Dhanā were all pupils of Rāmānand.
The story of Pīpā goes beyond serial affirmations of guru-to-pupil succession by having the family
of "guru-brothers" (an expression Hindi freely uses) actually travel together (*Bhaktamāl,* 495).
For an examination of subsequent lengthenings of the Rāmānandī lineage, see Richard Burghart,
"The Founding of the Ramanandi Sect," *Ethnohistory* 25, no. 2 (1978): 121–39.

21. This is substantially different from the scorn heaped on the role of renunciant in the
course of praising that of the householder in the Vallabhite community, a position that can be
traced all the way back to the writings of Vallabha himself. (See his "Sannyāsanirṇaya," in
Kṛṣṇaṣodaśagranthāḥ [Bombay: Nirnaya Sagara Press, n.d.].) Still, the *Bhaktamāl* shows a
definite bias in favor of householdership, if rightly understood. Immediately after Dhanā
becomes a desciple of Rāmānand, for example, it is specified that he remained a householder
(*Bhaktamāl,* 524). In presenting Hit Harivaṃś, who was known to have left his family behind
to go and live in Brindavan, Nābhājī makes quite a point of the fact that his sons were married
to the daughters of some of Brindavan's Brahmins even so, as if to compensate for Hit Harivaṃś's derilection of family responsibilities. His, then, is another life story that bridges the false
dichotomy between the life of renunciation and that of the householder (*Bhaktamāl,* 598–600).

Narasī, Pīpā finds unexpected treasure, but he shuns it as useless. Thieves, however, overhear his astonished discovery of a box filled with gold coins and seek it out for themselves, whereupon they find it filled with nothing but vipers. Enraged, they lay the box at Pīpā's door and there, at the touch of his hands, the contents turn to gold again. Pīpā spends the treasure immediately to feed the saints, offering to others what he has renounced himself.

Sītā too gives all. She learns "true love of the family"[22] — God's family — from the example of a woman who, when she and her penniless husband are visited by Sītā and Pīpā, removes her very skirt so that her husband can sell it to provide something for the saints to eat. As they sit down to the meal, the poor wife is absent and Pīpā protests, explaining that in defiance of established hierarchical patterns of Indian hospitality, Bhāgavatas — the satsaṅg — eat together. It is then that Sītā goes to the kitchen to fetch her and finds her naked. Thus Sītā learns a convincing lesson in humility, generosity, and fearlessness. Sītā immediately tears her own sari in two and offers half to the poor woman, pulling her out into the full community of the satsaṅg. Indeed, so moved is she by the need of this poor man and woman that she rushes to the bazaar and presents herself as a prostitute to the lustful eye of every passerby in the hopes of earning some money to feed her host and hostess. Miraculously, as in the case of Mīrā, her fearlessness changes the quality of her clients' vision, and soon she has a great heap of grain and cash before her, for which she has had to pay no corporal price.

On another occasion Pīpā and Sītā are visited by a group of saints — they are the hosts, not the guests, this time — and again nothing is in the house. Repeating her earlier foray, Sītā sets out to bargain her body for food, this time by going to a particularly lascivious merchant she knows. He is only too anxious to strike such a deal, and she agrees to go to his house after serving her guests. It is the rainy season, however, and by the time the meal is done the roads have been deluged to the point of impassibility. Pīpā, who has already been delighted by his wife's willingness to put the welfare of the saints before any claims that their own marriage would make on her, insists on carrying her across the mud-soaked fields. When they arrive, he hides himself so that the merchant can satisfy his desires undisturbed. Such a scene is the sort of extreme situation that the Buddhist jātaka tales sometimes describe in recommending the virtue of selfless giving (dāna). But in this case divine providence prevents the sacrifice from being completed; when the merchant discovers Sītā at the door in spite of the miserable weather, he asks incredulously how she got there. As she tells him, his disbelief is transformed into shame, his eyes gush tears, and Pīpā, seeing his change of heart, initiates him into the fellowship of saints.[23]

The marriage of Pīpā and Sītā is a marriage for others, a marriage whose only rules of conduct are those that relate it to the satsaṅg, and a marriage

---

22. *Bhaktamāl*, 502: *ghar kī . . . rati sācī*.
23. A similar pattern is followed in other episodes (*Bhaktamāl*, 512–13).

that presupposes in that context both the fearlessness of convention that Mīrā evinces and the economy of abundance that Narasī Mehtā's life illustrates. As such, it makes a statement about a new kind of *dharma* — a *bhakti dharma* — and offers a paradigm of virtuous living that seems consciously intended to supplant the old. Surely it is no accident that Pīpā's faithful wife is called Sītā, for the story of their life together amounts to a new version of the Hindu marriage that is usually understood as the classic statement of virtue and self-sacrifice: the epic marriage of Rām and Sītā. Rām and Sītā too are willingly disenfranchised royalty; they too rely on the instructions of the husband's guru; they too shed the raiments of royalty and wander the forests. It is no wonder that the story of Pīpā and Sītā is full of references to animals, especially wild animals, as is the epic of Rām.[24] Once fear and false notions of society are dispelled, the very beasts are brought within the purview of human concerns. Once the passions have been domesticated, put to the service of saintly community, there is no reason to project their devouring presence onto the animal realm.[25]

THE DHARMA OF BHAKTI

One message that emerges clearly from each of these three hagiographies is that the life of *bhakti* has threatening consequences for ordinary morality. But this *bhajan sevā*, "service through singing" as the nineteenth-century commentator Sītārāmśaraṇ Bhagavānprakāś Rūpakalā calls it in explaining the *Bhaktamāl*'s portrait of Ravi Dās, is not so amoral as it first appears.[26] Rather, these exemplary accounts show that *bhakti* has an ethical logic that demands more, rather than less, from those who come under its spell. And it creates an ethically significant community of its own, the *satsaṅg*. Whereas worldly *dharma* establishes its ethical community by means of social differentiation and complementary function, *bhakti* does so by reuniting socially

24. *Bhaktamāl*, 492, 506, 507, 511, 523.

25. As several notes above have already suggested, these three hagiographies — of Mīrā, Narasī, and Pīpā and Sītā — present only some of the most extended, obvious profiles of the new virtues to which a life of divine singing and service leads. The lives of other saints are often salted with the same motifs, and not only in the *Bhaktamāl*. Ravi Dās and his wife, for example, are presented as being no less eager to feed the saints than Pīpā and Sītā (*Bhaktamāl*, 473–74). Such *sādhusevā* or *sant-bhakti*, as it is called in the story of Pīpā and Sītā (*Bhaktamāl*, 503), is also evinced by Dhanā, Nand Dās, and many others (*Bhaktamāl*, 521, 696, 708, 748, 766). Sūr Dās, because he accepts the same notion of God's abundance as does Narasī Mehtā, is credited in Harirāy's commentary on the *Caurāsī Vaiṣṇavan kī Vārtā* with being able to divine the location of lost coins and cattle, much as Narasī can direct pilgrims to unknown funds in Dvarka (*Caurāsī Vaiṣṇavan kī Vārtā*, ed. Dvārkādās Parīkh [Mathura: Śrī Bajaraṅg Pustakālay, 1970], 401–2). An early biography of Nānak states that he, like Pīpā, had a mysterious rapport with animals — he is able to bring a dead elephant back to life — and much is made of the monkey Hanumān in the *Bhaktamāl*'s telling of the story of Tulsī Dās (W. H. McLeod, *Guru Nānak and the Sikh Religion* [Oxford: Clarendon Press, 1968], 15, 39; *Bhaktamāl*, 762–63, 769–70).

26. *Bhaktamāl*, 474.

disparate elements in a common cause: the praise of God. This seemingly external referent does not so much cancel recognizably *dharmic* virtues, as it liberates them from the social codes and contexts to which they are usually subordinated.

There is nothing new about any of the three virtues we have discussed. Each has its place in a traditional Hindu view of life. Within the four-caste system, fearlessness (*abhaya*) is a virtue one expects of a warrior and therefore considers to apply by extension to the entire *kṣatriya* caste. But it also has a place outside the caste system, in the lives of ascetics who have renounced the strictures imposed by *varṇāśrama dharma* and wander at will. As with warriors, their fearlessness often makes them feared by others.

Generosity (*dāna*), by contrast, is one of the great virtues — perhaps the greatest — to which a householder should aspire. It too bears particular association with the *kṣatriya* caste but through the roles of kingship and governance as distinct from battle and protection. The virtue of generosity has a particular relation to the Brahmin caste as well, but it is an inverse one. Brahmins fulfill the role not of donors but of recipients; royal largesse, and that of all householders, is owed first and foremost to them.

Community service (*sevā*), finally, is a virtue especially incumbent upon those placed low in the caste hierarchy. It is their *dharma* to serve their betters. Thus each of these virtues has at least one particular niche in the *varṇāśrama dharma* system.[27]

When translated into the *bhakti* mode, however, the virtues look radically different. No one is more the object of protection in Hindu society than a woman, who is required by the *Laws of Manu* to be shielded all her life.[28] Yet in the *Bhaktamāl* it is none other than a woman who most directly incarnates this virtue. As for generosity, we have seen that Brahmins are paradigmatically its object, not its agent. Yet it is a Brahmin whose story most vividly describes what true generosity is. Finally, we expect service to emanate naturally from the low, but no one in the *Bhaktamāl* more clearly exemplifies the virtue of community service than a couple who are born king and queen.

Clearly *bhakti* inverts what is normally understood to be *dharma,* and the *Bhaktamāl* is very much aware that this is so. In introducing both Ravi Dās and Kabīr, Nābhājī notes that these saints explicitly challenged the authenticity of *varṇāśrama dharma*. Ravi Dās, he says, "left its conceits behind" (*varṇāśram abhimān taji*) and Kabīr "neglected to observe it" (*rākhī nahī varṇāśram . . .*), for he maintained that *dharma* was no *dharma* if it stood in opposition to *bhakti* (*bhakti bimukh jo dharm so adharam*).[29] Similarly, Hit

27. I am indebted to John B. Carman for suggesting the principal contours of what I have said in the last three paragraphs (Harvard University, 16 December 1982).

28. *Manu Smṛti* 5.146–49, trans. Georg Bühler, *The Laws of Manu* (New York: Dover, 1969 [1886]), 195.

29. *Bhaktamāl*, 470, 479–80.

heroes and heroines of *bhakti* care very little for its prescriptions. Only unconsciously do they act on its behalf.

If one were to reconcile *bhakti* and *dharma* the other way around, beginning from the side of *dharma* rather than from that of *bhakti*, quite a different configuration would emerge. An amusing example of this approach can be observed in the modern comic-book version of the life of Mīrā Bāī, whose story must have been considered too flamboyant to be promulgated to the masses in the terms set forth by the *Bhaktamāl*. Doubtless this was particularly the case because of Mīrā's sex. In Hindu society men may be allowed some moral latitude, especially in their youths, but never women.

If one has read the *Bhaktamāl*, one may be somewhat taken aback to find that in her comic-book incarnation Mīrā is represented as a paragon of wifely devotion. Indeed she is depicted as having been a dutiful wife before all else. Such a masterly metamorphosis is made possible by transforming the unidentified *rāṇā* in the *Bhaktamāl's* version into two separate personages: Mīrā's husband — who dies while she is still relatively young — and her husband's brother, who succeeds him to the throne (but not, of course, to the conjugal bed). The first is a model of virtue who quickly repents any shortsightedness to which he may fall victim, so obedience to him poses no great problem. The second *rāṇā*, however, wields the poison cup and initiates all the other assaults on Mīrā. Thus, she presents no great affront to *dharma* when she leaves him, especially since he is only her guardian, not her husband. The intensity and musicality of Mīrā's devotion to Krishna are portrayed on almost every page, and the force of such devotion traditionally was seen as a challenge to her marriage. But, lest any ethical confusion be aroused, the comic book assures its readers in no uncertain terms that Mīrā was "an ideal Hindu wife."[39] She is said to have been careful to complete her obligations to house and husband before before she went off to serve Krishna. (In a booklet that might well reach the eyes of children, the matter of her abstinence from conjugal sex fortunately need not be broached.)

Dividing the *rāṇā* into two figures accomplishes a further objective from a *dharmic* point of view. It makes Mīrā a dutiful wife in just the years when active participation in family and household is required by Hinduism's classical four-stage conception of the life cycle (*caturāśramadharma*) and conveniently assigns to her later years the moment when she decided of her own volition to leave her in-laws' house. At least for men, those later years are a time when it is considered entirely appropriate to shake off the obligations of one's home and hearth. When Mīrā does so, then, she conforms in another aspect to what conventional *dharma* would dictate. The tensions between a life of ecstatic devotion and wifely service have been all but wiped away, and

---

39. Kamala Chandrakant, *Mirabai* (Bombay: India Book House, n.d.), 4. Lest readers forget, Mīrā is again called "the true Hindu wife" on p. 11. The Mīrā comic book did not, of course, invent this bifurcation between good and bad husbands. It can be traced back at least a century in popular mythology.

with them the need for a resolution from the side of *bhakti*'s own implicit *dharma* rather than in terms of what convention would dictate.[40]

One rarely finds in the *Bhaktamāl* a sense that the life of *bhakti* needs to be justified in the eyes of conventional *dharma,* but there is apparently an exception that proves the rule. On one occasion the *Bhaktamāl* registers a corrective to the extreme forms of behavior that *bhakti* can engender. The story concerns the culmination of Pīpā Dās's pilgrimage to Dvarka, presumably the height of his devotional life.

We are told that when he arrived on the beautiful shores of the Arabian Sea, the musical fervor of his circle of *bhaktas* became so intense that he wanted nothing more than to jump into the sea and drown — presumably because he would then have had the sight of Krishna as his last earthly vision and the sounds of Krishna ringing in his ears for all eternity. Priyā Dās tells us, however, that Krishna saw things differently. He called the group back and sent them home, explaining that reports of religious drownings would not do much for his reputation in the world at large.[41]

At first blush this seems a minor victory for conventional *dharma,* but a closer look reveals that things are not so simple as they seem. No real compromise with worldly values is made, for if Pīpā bows in the direction of conventional morality, it is only at the behest of the object of *bhakti* itself: Krishna. Furthermore, the modification in Pīpā's behavior is such as to reinforce the *bhakti* virtue of which he himself is a paradigm: he is reminded of a better way to serve his flock and, by extension, the rest of the world. Indeed the exemplary function of the *bhakti* community is just what Pīpā has threatened to dissolve. Or to put the matter another way, when Pīpā's *bhakti* is in danger of becoming a simple rejection of every earthly convention, including the affirmation of life itself, he must be corrected. This redirection of Pīpā's impulse merely restates what he had learned at the outset of his devotional life. When Rāmānand accepted Pīpā into the *bhakti* fold, his first command was that Pīpā draw back from the life of a renunciant and accept the importance of householdership. To love God is not to leave the world but to transform it.

In the view of the *Bhaktamāl,* then, the life of *bhakti* is hardly a life without morality. Though saintliness is not constructed by any piling up of "secular" virtues, it does not exclude them if they follow from a life of love and devotion. Even the codes of the *varṇāśrama dharma* can be accommodated on occasion — though often seemingly by accident. A much firmer place is set

---

40. That the *caturāśramadharma* conception of the life-cycle applies to women in at best a secondary way has frequently been noted. (For example, Katherine Young, "One Stage, Three Acts: The Life-Drama of a Traditional Hindu Woman," paper presented to the American Academy of Religion, New York, November, 1979; current work on the subject is being undertaken by Mary McGee, Harvard University.) Even so, particularly for unusual and famous women, the *caturāśrama* model has a certain relevance.

41. *Bhaktamāl,* 498.

aside for the virtues that from time to time support these codes and infuse them with a meaning that is truly personal and social — virtues such as fearlessness, generosity, and service. The reality of the community created by *bhakti* welds them into patterns of complementarity that give them quite different locations from the ones to which they are assigned in traditional Hindu views of society. As we have seen, these virtues interlock in the lives of saintly individuals. They also serve to reinforce one another in that the *bhaktas* who especially manifest one virtue or another are linked in a single chain by means of the *Bhaktamāl* itself, "A Garland of Devotees." Indeed, as John Carman has pointed out, the virtues these saints exhibit are aspects of the divine character itself.[42] According to the vision of God that is dominant in the tradition of Vaiṣṇava *bhakti,* God quells all fear, shows incalculable generosity, and serves his devotees at every turn. It is therefore no surprise that those who worship him should manifest these virtues, both individually and collectively, and that such qualities of life are genuinely fostered nowhere else but in the community of devotion.

42. John B. Carman, oral communication, 10 February 1983.

FIVE

The Confucian Sage: Exemplar of Personal Knowledge

Tu Wei-ming

The Confucian conviction that virtue can be learned and that the highest exemplification of virtue, sagehood, is attainable has been a source of inspiration for both the educated elite and the general populace in China. Indeed a defining characteristic of Chinese culture is the faith in the human capacity for creative self-transformation. The belief that a humble person can become the exemplar of humanity and thus assume a godlike stature in the pantheon of the virtuous is widely held among modern as well as traditional Chinese. To them, sagehood is an authentic manifestation of humanity. The paradigmatic sage, Confucius, is a case in point.

For centuries Confucius has been a model of humanity. He exemplifies an ideal that is accessible to all, yet curiously elusive because learning to be fully human is continually and intensely personal. That is, what Confucius himself actually attained can never be repeated. As we strive to become fully human, we have no blueprint to follow. We can neither imitate Confucius nor learn to realize ourselves through him. Since he is remembered as having lived a life shaped by the critical self-awareness that sagehood was ever just beyond his grasp, he inspires us and provides a standard for us in our search for ultimate personal knowledge.

The paradigmatic sage, then, is not only a teacher but a learner, and the learning that he exemplifies has a definite shape. In this essay I will attempt to convey a sense of how the historical Confucius, who emphatically denied that he ever attained sagehood,[1] emerged in Chinese history as the preeminent sage. My main purpose, however, is not to give a narrative account of how this is thought to have happened but to suggest a way of understanding the Confucian persuasion that a mere human who takes the cultivation of his

---

1. *Analects* 7:34. See D. C. Lau, trans., *Confucius: The Analects* (Harmondsworth: Penguin Books, 1979), 90.

or her personal knowledge with utmost seriousness can become the exemplar for the human community as a whole.

When Confucius identified himself as a lover of the ancients and a transmitter of tradition rather than an innovator,[2] he had in mind the age-old wisdom that human beings must learn to be fully human through their own efforts; for that reason the mastery of culture, over and above instinct, is an essential human activity. Animals have little choice in what they are destined to be, but humans, individually and collectively, enjoy an immense range of possibility to make something of themselves. A salient feature of humanity is its malleability, thus its perfectibility.[3]

It is painfully difficult for us to do what Confucius believed that as ordinary human beings we should do. His personal knowledge in this regard is instructive:

> There are four things in the Way of the profound person, none of which I have been able to do. To serve my father as I would expect my son to serve me: that I have not been able to do. To serve my ruler as I would expect my ministers to serve me: that I have not been able to do. To serve my elder brother as I would expect my younger brother to serve me: that I have not been able to do. To be the first to treat friends as I would expect them to treat me: that I have not been able to do.[4]

In the light of the "five cardinal relationships" in the Confucian tradition, we might also add for the present-day Confucian husband that "to serve my wife as I would expect her to serve me: that I have not been able to do." We may simply take these statements to mean that Confucius humbly admitted that he fell short of living up to his own ideal of a son, a minister, a younger brother, a friend, and, to complete the full Confucian list, a spouse. Yet the underlying reason for Confucius's self-criticism is more subtle. It relates to his perception of what personal knowledge really entails.

A deceptively simple statement in the *Analects* is pertinent here. Confucius once insisted that the right kind of learning—the sort handed down by the ancient sages—was not learning to please others but "learning for the sake of one's self."[5] This message is not an individualistic, romantic assertion about one's existential right to be unique. The rights-consciousness prevalent

2. *Analects* 7:1, trans. Lau, 86.

3. For a general discussion on this issue, see Donald J. Munro, *The Concept of Man in Early China* (Stanford, Calif.: Stanford University Press, 1969).

4. *Chung-yung (Doctrine of the Mean)*, chap. 13, sec. 4. See Wing-tsit Chan, trans. and comp., *A Source Book in Chinese Philosophy* (Princeton, N. J.: Princeton University Press, 1969), 101.

5. *Analects* 16:25. D. C. Lau translates this critical statement in the *Analects* as follows: "Men of antiquity studied to improve themselves; men today study to impress others." See Lau, 128. In Lau's translation, this statement is identified as 14:24. For a thought-provoking discussion of this aspect of Confucian education, see Wm. Theodore de Bary, *The Liberal Tradition in China* (Hong Kong: The Chinese University Press; and New York: Columbia University Press, 1983), 21–24.

in modern Western culture is alien to the Confucian tradition. By advocating learning for one's own sake, Confucius did not suppose that the human self is an isolated or isolable "individuality." Nor did he even consider that the self is an autonomous entity distinct from and often in conflict with society. Indeed no one in his world and time entertained such an idea. The "individualists" in ancient China were apolitical but not antisocial. Like Confucius, they understood the self as a connecting point for relationships, an inseparable part of a network of human interaction.

In the Confucian perspective the self can never be reduced to a single dimension, for it acts as the focus for a number of relationships; it can never be considered purely a function of one or more forms of human relatedness.[6] Paradoxically, our uniqueness as persons is made possible by the ever-changing landscape of our social interactions. We may not be fully aware of the complexity of the network in which we are socialized to function in daily life, but as long as we continue to broaden our knowledge of ourselves in the context of our social intercourse, we do not lose "the unwobbling pivot"[7] (*chung-yung*) that acts as our personal center. Learning for the sake of oneself is precisely intended to preserve and strengthen that center.

Confucius's conscientious effort to take things at hand — ordinary daily affairs — as the basis for his ethical teaching makes Confucian learning an intrinsically moral activity at whose core is the task of developing a refined knowledge of oneself. As the exemplar Confucius taught by means of who he was. And he learned in substantially the same way; hence the style of education with which his name is associated is at heart a realization of personal knowledge. I will explore the traditional division of this personal learning into its "elementary" and "great" components and then consider the way in which the sage manages both to teach and to exemplify the process.

Education in the classical Confucian sense is learning to be human. It involves an integrated sequence according to which "elementary learning" is followed by "great learning." "Elementary learning" primarily involves the ritualization of the body, and "great learning" entails the sort of self-cultivation that aims at the "embodiment" of all levels of human sensitivity.[8] Both forms of learning focus on developing an increasingly refined self-awareness.

Personal knowledge in this sense can well be understood as the strenuous learning process by which we become acquainted with our bodies and minds

6. See Tu Wei-ming, "Selfhood and Otherness: Father-Son Relationship in Confucian Thought," in his *Confucian Thought: Selfhood as Creative Transformation* (Albany: State University of New York Press, 1984), 113–130.

7. Ezra Pound, *Confucius: The Great Digest and the Unwobbling Pivot* (London: Peter Owen, 1952), 97. "The unwobbling pivot" is Pound's translation of the title of the Confucian classic, *Chung-yung*, which is commonly rendered as *The Doctrine of the Mean*.

8. See Tu Wei-ming, "Li as Process of Humanization," in his *Humanity and Self-Cultivation: Essays in Confucian Thought* (Berkeley: Asian Humanities Press, 1979), 17–34.

so that eventually we become true masters of the "house" we inhabit. Confucius's autobiographical observation on this matter is suggestive:

> There are presumably men who innovate without possessing knowledge, but this is not a fault I have. I use my ears widely and follow what is good in what I have heard; I use my eyes widely and retain what I have seen in my mind. This constitutes a lower level knowledge.[9]

By stressing empirical knowledge as the means by which he learned to be human, Confucius made it explicit that, unlike the legendary sages Yao and Shun, he was not "born with knowledge."[10] Rather, he struggled hard to acquire the knowledge that eventually made him free and wise: "I followed my heart's desire without overstepping the line."[11] This awe-inspiring spontaneity, far from being the result of a sudden enlightenment, was the crowning success of Confucius's lifelong attempt at "accumulating righteous acts" (chi-i).[12] The message is clear: no one can afford to bypass "elementary learning" if true humanity is to be realized.

ELEMENTARY LEARNING

Confucians have always been aware that the process of learning to be human begins in infancy. For the baby, personal knowledge may simply mean standing steadily for a few moments or walking a few steps without falling down. To learn the art of centering oneself in its more advanced aspects, however, requires repeated practice and often entails the same experience of trial and error that infants must endure. The question in the beginning of the Analects— "Is it not a pleasure, having learned something, to try it out at due intervals?"[13]—draws attention to this common experience. Humans, like animals, learn many of the basic skills of life this way. In fact, the ideogram representing the Chinese term hsi, which was just rendered as "try it out at due intervals," depicts a young bird learning to fly by flapping its wings. The pleasure that one enjoys in perfecting an internalized skill through repeated practice can be seen as much in the radiant smile of an infant who has just negotiated his or her first steps as in the joy of a virtuoso lute player who has mastered a difficult score. The happiness evident in both cases has to do with the sense that what has been learned is not merely something external, something apart from the learner, but a feature of the learner's expanded vocabulary of self-expression. What has been learned is an aspect of the learner's personhood.

The focus of "elementary learning," education for the very young, is to create a healthy environment in which infants can discover their sensitive and

9. *Analects* 7:28, trans. Lau, 89.   10. *Analects* 7:20.   11. *Analects* 2:4, trans. Lau, 63.
12. A technical concept used by Mencius to designate the gradual process of learning to be fully human. See *Mencius* 2A:2.
13. *Analects* 1:1, trans. Lau, 59.

responsive bodies. For the very young, every simple act is a significant accomplishment in self-expression and communication. Gentle persuasion and proper encouragement are integral parts of this collaborative enterprise between the infant and the adults around him or her. Such encouragement helps a new member of the human community develop the first inklings of personal knowledge. At the age of six or seven, after a child has learned to speak and seems to be well-adjusted in the loving environment of the immediate family, adults may offer some structured guidance, intended to foster a sense of communal participation. In traditional China the child was first asked to perform easy tasks such as answering short questions and sprinkling water on the floor for cleaning. A more elaborate program of education then followed: instructions in the "six arts" of ritual, music, archery, charioteering, calligraphy, and arithmetic. All this was traditionally assumed under the heading of "elementary learning."

I have noted elsewhere that the "six arts" can be understood as ways of cultivating the body.[14] This training is not merely physical: it includes mental and spiritual disciplines as well. Yet the focus on ritualizing bodily behavior remains. The training represents a concerted effort to transform the body into a fitting expression of the mental and spiritual resources within. The individual aims not only to establish a social identity but also to cultivate the proper disposition. The art of archery, for example, is intended at once to improve one's skill as an archer and to discipline one's mind so that it is constantly tranquil. Furthermore, archery requires self-examination: if we fail to hit the mark, we must first search for the fault within ourselves.[15] The archer tries to produce a finely tuned disposition that informs every gesture of the body. Thus one becomes thoroughly familiar with one's mental states while learning to do the kinds of things archers do. Yet for all this mental discipline, the bodily form remains the basis of the enterprise, and is acknowledged as such in traditional Confucian education. After all, the body so conceived is no purely physical entity; it is inseparable from the mind and spirit.

The ritualization of the body is, therefore, appropriately more in the nature of invitation than command. The young child, far from being the unsuspecting target of a series of rules imposed from without, is bidden to play ritual games that lead to adulthood by enticement rather than coercion. If the child is not yet ready to play, he or she should not be forced to join in, and since premature ritualization is detrimental to the moral growth of the child, voluntary participation in the initial stage is both necessary and desirable. In fact, it is best if initially the child enters the ritual situation with a spirit of playfulness. The solemnity of ritual acts is not compromised so long

14. Tu Wei-ming, "The Idea of the Human in Mencian Thought: An Approach to Chinese Aesthetics," in *Theories of the Arts in China,* ed. Susan Bush and Christian Murck (Princeton, N. J.: Princeton University Press, 1984), 57–73.

15. *Chung-yung,* chap. 14.

as the child plays at them conscientiously. For example, in the traditional Confucian family, the oldest grandson (often a young boy) was commonly seated in the most exalted place, the one symbolizing the deceased ancestors. He would thus receive bows and prostrations from his father, uncles, and even grandfather in the performance of the ancestral cult, and would gain some sense of what it is to be the recipient of filial piety. The whole affair constituted an artfully designed, institutionalized effort to bridge the generation gap.

Seemingly minute daily routines are particularly important for training the child to appreciate the intimate involvement of ritual action in the proper behavior of a maturing person. Tzu-hsia's critical comment on Tzu-yu's obvious misunderstanding of the teaching of their master, Confucius, makes this point:

> Tzu-yu said, "The disciples and younger followers of Tzu-hsia can certainly cope with sweeping and cleaning, with responding to calls and replying to questions put to them, and with coming forward and withdrawing, but these are only details. On what is basic they are ignorant. What is one to do with them?"
>
> When Tzu-hsia heard this, he said, "Oh! how mistaken Yen Yu [Tzu-yu's other name] is! In the way of the gentleman [profound person], what is to be taught first and what is to be put last as being less urgent? The former is as clearly distinguishable from the latter as grasses are from trees. It is futile to try to give such a false picture of the way of the gentleman. It is, perhaps, the sage alone who, having started something, will always see it through to the end."[16]

Tzu-hsia captures the Confucian spirit well when he reminds his fellow student that simple ritual acts, such as helping one's parents sweep the floor, responding to simple questions, and greeting elders properly, are essential to the process of learning to be human. Strictly speaking, the various aspects of elementary learning are not branches of self-cultivation but its roots. Tzu-hsia's conception of the teacher as one who "having started something, will always see it through to the end" — or, in an alternate translation, as one "who can unite in one the beginning and the consummation of *learning*"[17] — apparently refers to elementary learning in the first instance and to great learning in the second. But more may be involved. Confucius described himself as an untiring teacher and indefatigable student.[18] The Confucian sage may thus be characterized as someone who brings elementary learning to full fruition.

The significance of elementary learning goes beyond the harmonization of relationships within the family. To Confucius, it serves as the foundation of

---

16. *Analects* 19:12, trans. Lau, 154.
17. James Legge, trans., *Chinese Classics*, vol.1 (Oxford: Clarendon Press, 1883), 137.
18. *Analects* 7:34.

good government as well. Actually, living the good life in the confines of one's domestic arena is in itself a profoundly meaningful political statement:

> Someone said to Confucius, "Why do you not take part in government?"
>
> The Master said, "The *Book of History* says, 'Oh! Simply by being a good son and friendly to his brothers a man can exert an influence upon government.' In so doing a man is, in fact, taking part in government. How can there be any question of having actively to 'take part in government'?"[19]

Implicit in elementary learning, then, is the realization, through practice, of the cherished Confucian affirmation that the ultimate meaning in life can be fruitfully attained in ordinary human existence. Confucius as an exemplar never performed miracles to impress his followers; in fact, he chose not to speak of such topics as "prodigies, force, disorder and gods."[20] The real magic is elsewhere: in an unassuming approach to living. Confucius's magnetic power radiated from his deep personal sense of what he really was:

> The Governor of She asked Tzu-lu about Confucius. Tzu-lu did not answer. The Master said, "Why did you not simply say something to this effect: he is the sort of man who is so immersed in his study that he forgets his meals, who is so full of joy that he forgets his worries and who does not notice the onset of old age?"[21]

Understandably, Confucius taught more by deed than by word. The *Analects* in this sense are as much a record of what the Master did as an account of what he said. Confucian personal knowledge is a form of self-understanding acquired through practice.

GREAT LEARNING

Once the body has been properly ritualized to serve as an instrument of self-expression and communication, a person is well on the way to becoming a full participant in society. In the Confucian perspective a young person involved in the process of socialization is not passively trying to adapt himself or herself to the adult world without being aware of the rules of the game. Children do not socialize themselves, and they do not know the mechanism that shapes every dimension of their lives. But they do participate actively in their own socialization by responding creatively to their elders' invitations. For they know with increasing sophistication that they are vital to the well-being of the community and that the elders share with them a deep concern for their healthy growth. As they learn that they can better enjoy themselves by taking part in an interactive venture with other members of

19. *Analects* 2:21, trans. Lau, 66.
20. *Analects* 7:21, trans. Lau, 88.
21. *Analects* 7:19, trans. Lau, 88.

their community, they become aware that being in the company of their elders enables them to discover their own humanity or "co-humanity," in Peter Boodberg's preferred translation of the Confucian term *jen*.[22] As their comprehension grows and they begin to see that what they have been taught and encouraged to do is not merely a game but the sacred mission of personal growth, they may even take an active role in helping adults to realize themselves further. At this time a "great learning" begins, for it presupposes the emergence of a communal critical self-awareness in the mind of the young adult.

Confucius's recollection that "at fifteen I set my heart on learning"[23] has been widely cited by later Confucians as a clear sign that the Master was by then ready to embark on his own journey toward becoming a fully realized human being. The transformation from elementary learning to great learning occurs at the point when a young adult assumes responsibility for his or her own education, and in the Confucian tradition rituals marked that passage. Yet no qualitative break separates a child from a young adult who is mature enough to leave childish preoccupations behind. Confucian great learning builds on elementary learning and often harks back to the simple ritual acts that enable a child to earn a niche in society.

Through elementary learning we acquire the personal knowledge necessary for preserving our individual centers as we enter into an ever-enlarging network of human relationships. But it is not enough to do the right thing at the right moment so that we can earn the approval of our elders as we assume responsible roles in society. More than self-preservation is at stake: the more demanding task is to strengthen the center in such a way that it can respond creatively to continuous change and generate virtuous transformation itself. Thus the purpose of great learning, as specified by the seminal Confucian text called *The Great Learning* (originally a chapter in the *Book of Rites*), is threefold: (1) to enlighten the enlightening virtue, (2) to care for the people, and (3) to dwell in the highest good.[24] "To enlighten the enlightening virtue" (*ming ming-te*) refers to the cultivation of our personal knowledge, "to care for the people" (*ch'in-min*) refers to our responsibility of helping others to realize themselves, and "dwelling in the highest good" (*chih yu chih-shan*) refers to our desire to strive toward moral excellence.

We cannot rely on external factors, whether the support of our elders or the encouragement of society at large, to attain these lofty goals. We need to nourish our internal resources and develop a sense of personal direction. This path involves disciplined, daily practice. In Mencian terms we need to go through the strenuous effort of "accumulating righteousness"[25] so that our

22. Peter Boodberg, "The Semasiology of Some Primary Confucian Concepts," *Philosophy East and West* 2, no. 4 (1953): 317–32.

23. *Analects* 2:4, trans. Lau, 63.

24. *Great Learning*, chap. 1. Cf. Chan, *Source Book*, 86.

25. *Mencius* 2A:2.

vital force can be substantially enhanced. Tseng Tzu has set a well-known example in this regard:

> Every day I examine myself on three counts. In what I have undertaken on another's behalf, have I failed to do my best? In my dealings with my friends have I failed to be trustworthy in what I say? Have I passed on to others anything that I have not tried out myself?[26]

Although Tseng Tzu's method of self-examination has been applauded in the Confucian tradition, his regimen was never intended to suit everyone's situation. Instead each person is expected to take an active role in designing his or her course of self-improvement. One aspect of the process, however, was held to be of universal importance: the deepening and broadening of communal critical self-awareness. Confucians wholeheartedly subscribe to the dictum that the unreflective life is not worth living.

There is nothing solipsistic or egoistic about such an inquiry. Since the Confucian self is the center of a nexus of relationships, not an isolated monad, it inevitably encounters other selves in the course of pursuing its own growth. Confucian self-cultivation does not take the form of searching for one's own inner spirituality in a lonely quest. Rather, it enriches the self by enabling it to participate in a confluence of many life streams. The idea of an isolated individual who hopes to become the recipient of divine inspiration without any reference to the human community is quite alien to the Confucian perception of the self. Hence it is not accidental that Tseng Tzu's queries to himself all strike an interpersonal note. Each reinforces a social conception of personhood.

Nevertheless, Confucians advocate more than what we normally understand to be social ethics. The first goal of the great learning, "to enlighten the enlightening virtue," draws attention not to the social milieu that makes learning fruitful but to the moral equipment that makes it possible. The phrase "to enlighten the enlightening virtue," which Ezra Pound elaborately renders as "clarifying the way wherein the intelligence increases through the process of looking straight into one's own heart and acting on the result"[27] and Wing-tsit Chan translates more straightforwardly as "manifesting the clear character,"[28] presupposes that all human beings are endowed with the "enlightening virtue." As personal knowledge develops, it is understood to be a manifestation of this virtue, and as such does not come from without but is inherent in one's original nature. The personal knowledge that we attain by rigorous practice is but the exposition and elaboration of the "enlightening virtue" that defines who we truly are from the start.

It may seem that we have an inconsistency here: if we are all endowed with "enlightening virtue" to begin with, what do we need to learn to become

---

26. *Analects* 1:4, trans. Lau, 59.
27. Pound, *Confucius*, 27.   28. Chan, *Source Book*, 86.

moral persons? Confucians do not see this as a problem. They believe that the inborn "enlightening virtue" is a precondition for self-cultivation but not the full expression of authentic humanity. In other words, ontologically we are all sages because the "enlightening virtue" inherent in our human nature defines who we truly are, but existentially we must strive to learn what we ought to be by striving to fully realize our potential, that which is originally in us. Learning enables us to clarify and manifest this virtue, transforming it from a latent potentiality into an actualized, daily presence. Each person has the possibility of becoming sagelike, but it takes lifelong work to know experientially that this is indeed the case.

That we are always in a position of having to preserve, clarify, manifest, and realize who we are is not in conflict with the Confucian faith in the goodness of human nature. The creative tension between the ontological reality that we are intrinsically sages and the existential fact that we can never become sages defines the human condition in a most vivid way: we are not what we ought to be, as dictated by our moral sense of rightness, but we learn to become what we ought to be by taking as our point of departure what we are here and now. This is possible because we have innate spiritual resources to tap.

What Confucius exemplifies, accordingly, is both a realistic appraisal of human limitation and an awe-inspiring demonstration of human excellence. There is an intrinsic safeguard against deification in the historicity of Confucius's personality. Mencius's apt characterization of the Master as the "timely sage"[29] prevents us from extracting Confucius from the moment in which he learned and taught. To be sure, Confucius has been venerated as a god — a god of culture, to be specific — for more than two millennia in China. But in the folk tradition he is honored more as a moral force than as a mysterious power. The popular image of Confucius as a bearded wise old man who is the foremost teacher of how to live the life of a civilized person is not far off the mark. It suggests a man who has lived through the entire process of human growth, from the humble beginning of a student to the attainment of exemplary personal knowledge.

In the tradition having to do with "great learning," eight steps are elaborated as belonging to this process. The first five are concerned with the

29. *Mencius* 5B:1. In characterizing Confucius as the sage "whose actions were timely," Mencius further remarked: "Confucius was the one who gathered together all that was good. To do this is to open with bells and conclude with jade tubes. [This refers to music.] To open with bells is to begin in an orderly fashion; to conclude with jade tubes is to end in an orderly fashion. To begin in an orderly fashion is the concern of the wise while to end in an orderly fashion is the concern of a sage. Wisdom is like skill, shall I say, while sageness is like strength. It is like shooting from beyond a hundred paces. It is due to your strength that the arrow reaches the target, but it is not due to your strength that it hits the mark." It seems obvious that, to Mencius, what Confucius's timeliness symbolizes is the confluence of many temporal features that cannot be imitated as a static model. See D. C. Lau, trans., *Mencius* (Harmondsworth: Penguin Books, 1970), 150–51.

mobilization of our inner resources for enhancing personal knowledge, and the remainder refer to an outer dimension — concrete appropriations of our self-awareness in the service of society. The eight-part sequence is as follows: (1) investigation of things (*ko-wu*), (2) extension of knowledge (*chih-chih*), (3) authentication of the will (*ch'eng-i*), (4) rectification of the mind (*cheng-hsin*), (5) cultivation of the personal life (*hsiu-shen*), (6) regulation of family (*ch'i-chia*), (7) governance of the state (*chih-kuo*), and (8) peace-making throughout the world (*p'ing t'ien-hsia*).[30] The following observation in the *Great Learning* clearly shows that the whole structure pivots on the fifth step, cultivation of the personal life:

> From the Son of Heaven down to the common people, all must regard cultivation of the personal life as the root. There is never a case when the root is in disorder and yet the branches are in order.[31]

The centrality of self-cultivation, however, is predicated on the conception of the self as an open system, forever learning from the external world by extending its sensitivity to an ever-enlarging network of interconnections. The "investigation of things" in this sense should not be construed as disinterested study of external facts by an outside observer. Rather, it signifies a form of knowing in which the knower is not only informed but also transformed by the known. To "investigate things" is to inquire into either natural phenomena or human affairs for the sake of understanding both the world around us and ourselves.

When we inquire into natural phenomena and human affairs as inside participants as well as outside observers, we "embody" in our sensitivity those aspects of nature and the world that have touched our hearts and minds. But even the cultivation of "enlightening virtue" involves, as Mencius insisted, a mutual nourishment between the internal and external.[32] Surely, the investigation of things in nature and the world adds to our information about the external, but it is the purification of the internal — the authentication of the will and the rectification of the mind — that enables us to be transformed by what we have come to know. Of that, Confucius stands as the great exemplar.

EXEMPLARY TEACHING

In the "personalist" interpretation of the Confucian approach to education that I have advanced so far, I have stressed the centrality of acquiring personal knowledge as a motive force for moral growth. I have also emphasized that self-cultivation is not a private matter. Given the Confucian perception of the self as a focal point for multiple relationships, the quest for one's own

---

30. *Great Learning*, chap. 1. Cf. Chan, *Source Book*, 86–87.
31. Chan, *Source Book*, 87.
32. *Mencius* 2A:2.

personal knowledge must be understood as an act of service to the community as well:

> A humane person, wishing to establish his [or her] character, also establishes the characters of others and wishing to enlarge himself [or herself], also helps others to enlarge themselves. To be able to take the analogy near at hand [for understanding others] may be called the method of realizing humanity.[33]

By the same token the Confucian view of the self necessarily casts the task of self-cultivation in social terms. Learning is a collaborative enterprise and is all-encompassing. We learn not only from our tutors and other elders but from our friends, colleagues, students, children, and acquaintances, and from people on the street. The famous statement about teachers in the *Analects* is relevant here:

> The Master said, "Even when walking in the company of two others, I am bound to be able to learn from them. The good points of the one I copy; the bad points of the other I correct in myself."[34]

Since we learn from both positive and negative examples, every human being is potentially a teacher to us. But how does such teaching transpire? Since the Confucian tradition regards teaching, like learning, as an embodying act, the teaching will have to be undertaken by the whole person; all levels of the self — body, mind, soul, and spirit — will be involved. Personal exemplification is the most authentic and therefore the most effective pedagogy. The Way must be lived and lived well to be truly efficacious, and good teachers embody the form of life they advocate. Confucian thinkers have always known that, though logical rigor and rhetorical ingenuity may dazzle the mind, only teaching that has the force of personal example can touch the heart, purify the soul, and evoke the spirit. Every aspect of the ritualization of the body is the result of exemplary teaching. We learn to stand up, sit down, walk, and speak by emulating models around us. And self-cultivation at the higher levels requires the presence of examples in no less measure.

When it comes to the highest learning of all, the learning of virtue per se, the best teacher to model ourselves after is one who perceives of himself or herself not strictly as a teacher but also as a learner. This makes it possible for a pupil not only to bear the teacher's stamp, in a relationship of complementarity, but ultimately to establish a sympathetic resonance with the teacher's whole being — from within, as it were. Again Confucius himself serves as the best model in this regard. His seemingly modest estimate of what he was about has come to be a classic statement of the mentality all teachers should cultivate: "How dare I claim to be a sage or a man of humanity? It might be said of me, that I learn without flagging and teach without growing weary."[35]

33. *Analects* 6:30.
34. *Analects* 7:22, trans. Lau, 88.
35. *Analects* 7:34, trans. Lau, 90.

As expected, Confucius's disciples responded to the Master's sober humility not with relief at the sense that their own shortcomings could thereby be excused but with a heightened apprehension of how much they had to learn and how painfully difficult it was to do so. Yen Hui, Confucius's best student, may serve as an example:

> Yen Yuan [a.k.a. Yen Hui], heaving a sigh, said "The more I look up at it the higher it appears. The more I bore into it the harder it becomes. I see it before me. Suddenly it is behind me. The Master is good at leading one on step by step. He broadens me with culture and brings me back to essentials by means of the rites. I cannot give it up even if I wanted to, but, having done all I can, it [the way of Confucius] seems to rise sheer above me and I have no way of going after it, however much I may want to."[36]

Equally telling is the response of another student of Confucius. On hearing the Master's humble words that he did not dare to claim sagehood and that he defined himself as an unflagging learner and a tireless teacher, Kung-hsi Hua said, "This is precisely where we disciples are unable to learn from you."[37] Confucius compelled his students to draw the conclusion that learning could not ultimately be a matter of imitation. Acts of virtue might be imitated, but the spirit that made such acts truly virtuous required a personal commitment beyond imitation. It had to be directed not only without but within. Yet the inimitability of the Master could never be an excuse for laziness in the cultivation of virtue:

> Jan Ch'iu said, "It is not that I am not pleased with your way, but rather that my strength gives out." The Master said, "A man whose strength gives out collapses along the course. In your case you set the limits beforehand."[38]

Confucius certainly did not "set the limits beforehand," but he fully acknowledged his inability to attain sagehood. In this peculiar way he was a sage to his followers but not to himself, and for that reason he became the exemplar of sagehood itself. As a sage he was, said Mencius, "the first to possess what is common in our minds,"[39] for the sage is the one among us who has fully realized the same "enlightening virtue" that is inherent in the nature of each of us. Mencius further observed: "Our body and complexion are given to us by Heaven. Only a sage can give his body complete fulfillment."[40]

Yet by his own admission the paradigmatic sage, Confucius himself, fell short of this ideal. He perceived himself as a person who was as yet on the way to "giv[ing] his body complete fulfillment." Thus Confucius, the sage, serves as an exemplary teacher of humanity, not only because of the extraordinary

---

36. *Analects* 9:11, trans. Lau, 97.
37. *Analects* 7:34, trans. Lau, 90–91.
38. *Analects* 6:12, trans. Lau, 82–83.
39. *Mencius* 6A: 7.
40. *Mencius* 7A:38, trans. Lau, *Mencius*, 191.

accomplishments that establish a distance between him and the rest of us, but because of those aspects of his humanity that bring him near to us and make him accessible. The sage, like us, practices the ordinary virtues. When he eats, he observes the same basic etiquette that the rest of us do. Yet there is a difference. While we eat to gratify our need for food or to satisfy our culinary desires, the sage knows the "taste" of eating in a fuller sense: he is able to appreciate the moral and aesthetic force inherent in the simple rituals that regulate the taking of food in a human setting.[41] The sage lives more sensibly, more intensely, more self-consciously than the rest of us; he lives with more feeling. His "allotment" (*fen*) or "fate" (*ming*) is something that defines him. It makes him, like us, a circumscribed historical being. As such, it is impossible for us to imitate him. Yet the personal knowledge that he displays can very well serve as a source of inspiration for all. Each of us can strive to adopt it in relation to who we are, and thus come close to what sagehood would mean in our own circumstances.

The Confucian sage attains the highest moral excellence without losing sight of the humanity that unites him with all other members of society. True, his greatness lies in his effort to transform himself from an ordinary mortal into something awesome: a good, true, beautiful, great, sagely, even spiritual being.[42] But he is enabled to do this, not by abrogating the roles incumbent upon him as one person in the presence of others, but by fulfilling his obligations and responsibilities as a member of the human community. Similarly, he earns the respect of his fellow human beings as the "foremost teacher" because he never ceases to be a dedicated student. He devotes himself to elementary learning and great learning in order to practice the art of living and never tires of cultivating the virtue that ultimately makes human beings human.

41. See Tu Wei-ming, *Centrality and Commonality: An Essay on Chung-yung* (Honolulu: University Press of Hawaii, 1976), 30–34.

42. *Mencius* 7B:25. See Tu Wei-ming, "On the Mencian Perception of Moral Self-Development," in his *Humanity and Self-Cultivation*, 57–68.

SIX

Sainthood on the Periphery: The Case of Judaism

Robert L. Cohn

Ask an American Jew to identify the saints of Judaism and you will most likely be met with bewilderment. The term *saint* conjures up images of haloes, shrines, and relics quite foreign to modern Jewish sensibilities. For modern Western Jews sainthood is a category irredeemably Christian. Despite this popular view, however, modern Jewish scholars have occasionally used the term *saint* to refer to various rabbis. Thus Louis Finkelstein entitled his biography of the famous second-century sage *Akiba: Scholar, Saint, and Martyr*, while Louis Ginzberg, in his book *Students, Scholars, and Saints*, treated sages from ancient to modern times without clearly distinguishing among the three rubrics.[1] More recently, Jacob Neusner has identified the Babylonian rabbis as saints, using the term in the general sense of "holy man."[2] But it is not clear just what the term *saint* adds to our understanding of these figures nor how they relate to "saints" in other religions.

If we want to employ sainthood as a category in the comparative study of religion and to investigate its application to Judaism, we must begin with a good sense of what we are looking for. *Saint* must mean more than "holy person" in general but must also be liberated from its specifically Christian definition.[3] As I use the term in this study, a saint is a type of religious authority who is both a model for imitation and an object of veneration. A saint so perfectly enfleshes the ideals and values of a religion that he or she

I am grateful to Professors Manfred Vogel and Jon Levenson for their helpful suggestions on earlier drafts of this essay.

1. Louis Finkelstein, *Akiba: Scholar, Saint, and Martyr* (Philadelphia: Jewish Publication Society, 1962); Louis Ginzberg, *Students, Scholars, and Saints* (Philadelphia: Jewish Publication Society, 1928).

2. Jacob Neusner, *There We Sat Down* (Nashville and New York: Abingdon, 1972), 79–86.

3. For a contemporary treatment of the idea of saints in Christianity with implications for cross-traditional studies, see Lawrence Cunningham, *The Meaning of Saints* (San Francisco: Harper and Row, 1980), esp. 65–85.

becomes holy in a distinctive way. The life of the saint acts as a parable for others, a beacon leading to fullness of life. The sanctity of the saints inspires other people to follow them, usually by dwelling piously on their stories (hagiography) and cultically revering their memory (hagiolatry).[4]

This description characterizes entire classes of holy persons in Christianity, Islam, Hinduism, and Buddhism. In classical forms of these traditions individuals function as paradigms for piety and their holiness inspires cultic veneration. Saints are vital to Roman Catholicism and Eastern Orthodoxy, as are the *walī* to Sufism, the *ṛṣi* and *guru* to Hinduism, the *arahant* to Theravada and the *bodhisattva* to Mahāyāna Buddhism. These figures stand at the center of the piety of these traditions. But classical rabbinic Judaism, by contrast, never officially designated a set of human beings as worthy of special reverence or models of pious behavior. The literary genre of hagiography is nearly absent from biblical and classical Jewish literature and appears only sporadically among later mystical groups.[5] Most tellingly, the Jewish calendar lacks any celebration or memorial devoted to a holy person; there are no saints' days or seasons celebrated throughout the Jewish world. With rare exceptions, Jewish graves did not become shrines, and relics are unheard of. Those saintlike figures that Judaism has produced have emerged not from its classical rabbinic center but from its periphery, from forms of Judaism localized in time or place. Thus North African Jewry, heavily influenced by Muslim practice, and Eastern European Hasidism, repelled by rabbinic formalism, both developed traditions of saints.

To investigate the category of sainthood with respect to Judaism, then, is first and foremost to explain why no institution of sainthood formed within rabbinic Judaism. Only then can we explore those manifestations of sainthood that do exist and see them in their proper perspective. Accordingly, we shall first examine the ways in which the shape of Judaism mitigates against a tradition of saints. In so doing we shall see how this comparative category aids in highlighting the distinctiveness of Jewish piety. Next, guided by Jewish specimens of hagiography and hagiolatry, we survey those figures who may be construed as saintlike. Finally, we describe the ideal human types that Judaism commends for emulation, for it is these ideals, rather than flesh-and-blood human beings, on which most Jewish aspirations have focused.

The minor role that sainthood plays in Judaism can be explained by analyzing several features inherent in the structure of Jewish religion and society. First, of major relevance is the Jewish faith's subordination of the individual to the community. The central Jewish myth sees God bound in covenant to the people of Israel as a whole; one's individual identity is discovered through membership in that people. By following God's Torah,

---

4. Joachim Wach stresses the impress of the saint on society by the force of his personal example and his posthumous effect in forging a new social entity. *Sociology of Religion* (Chicago: University of Chicago Press, 1944), 357–60.

5. See Haim Zafrani, "Hagiography," in *Encyclopedia Judaica* [hereafter *EJ*], vol. 7 (Jerusalem: Keter, 1972) cols. 1116–21.

his commandments, the Jew works toward the redemption of the whole people, toward the creation of a just society. Salvation is not primarily an individual but a group achievement. The idea of the saint as paradigm, by contrast, presupposes an individualistic form of piety. The saint is a spiritual elder who has cultivated a unique path and can help followers cultivate theirs. Moreover, the saints' journey to holiness endows them with the ability to aid or intercede for followers as they pursue life in this world. But Jews lack the need for individual intercession, because redemption is understood to come only when society as a whole is ripe for it. One rabbinic dictum insists that the Messiah would come if all Israel would only keep a single Sabbath. No amount of saintly intercession can produce that result; it is a matter of human will and energy properly directed toward obeying the injunctions of Torah. The way of Torah is not too difficult, says Deuteronomy (30:11); the law is public and even the humblest Jew can follow it. Rabbinic Judaism has no barriers that need to be crossed with supernatural helpmates and no *gnosis* that must be supernaturally revealed. The very goal of regnant Jewish faith renders the saint superfluous.

Furthermore, the centrality of Torah leaves no room for the paradigm of sainthood in many traditions: the unique founder. An impersonal law, not a personal life, molds Jewish piety. Unlike Christianity, Islam, Buddhism, and others, Judaism recognizes no superlative person whose experience and insight map the spiritual journey for everyone else. Saints often reenact the founder's life in their own by seeking to follow his path. They act as symbols who translate the founder's experience into terms that are understandable in their own time and place. Lacking such a central person, Judaism offered no master paradigm to spiritual seekers. Although Moses ("our rabbi") was seen to be the recipient of a unique mission, his life was the object of no special attention. God had assigned him a distinct role, but even he remained subject to the Torah, which he mediated. It, not he, focused religious devotion.

Because Jewish religion is inextricably linked to Jewish nationhood, conversion, which is a hallmark of many religious biographies, tends to be exceptional rather than standard. Most Jews become Jews by birth, not transformation, so the experience of conversion is not central to the faith of Jews as it is, for instance, for many Christians. In other religions saints provide models for potential converts by dwelling on their own experiences of conversion or transformation. Often these come as profound visions, auditions, or awakenings that suddenly or gradually change their lives.[6] Such transformation experiences are important to hagiographers, for they demonstrate how the most worldly person can become the most spiritual. But in

---

6. Cunningham writes about Christian saints: "A saint is a person so grasped by a religious vision that it becomes central to his or her life *in a way that radically changes the person* and leads others to glimpse the value of that vision" (emphasis added). *Meaning of Saints*, 65. See also Jonathan Sumption, *Pilgrimage: An Image of Medieval Religion* (London: Faber and Faber, 1975), 18.

Judaism such tales of transformation generally failed to exercise the religious imagination. In fact, Jewish custom forbids the recall of the prior life of a convert; what counts is the life shared with fellow Jews. Thus the spiritual transformation, the stock in trade of hagiography, has had little appeal in Judaism.

The correlation between the Jewish emphasis on nationhood and the dearth of saint veneration emerges most clearly in the two matchless indices to Jewish piety, the calendar and the prayerbook (*Siddur*).[7] The main festivals of Judaism commemorate national events: the exodus, the giving of Torah, the wilderness wandering. Even minor holidays such as Purim and Hanukkah, though they involve the praise of individuals, celebrate national salvation.[8] In fact, the Passover *Haggadah,* which retells the liberation from Egypt, mentions Moses, the great liberator, only once — and that in a proof-text from Scripture. Similarly, the *Siddur* devotes no petitions to individuals and recalls no individual lives. Even in remembering the martyrs of Judaism, the liturgies for the Day of Atonement and the Ninth of Av view them as a group rather than as individual saints. In the *Mahzor,* the high holiday prayerbook, individual supplications to God for forgiveness of sin are found in the first-person plural: we have sinned. Even on these days of awe when the individual Jew seeks atonement, he or she does so as part of a group — and directly, without saintly mediation.

The absence of any veneration of humans from the religious calendar and liturgy derives from a second distinctive feature of Jewish piety: its unrelenting aniconism. The second commandment's prohibitions of image making and serving other gods were interpreted to preclude also the veneration of any human being or earthly object. The abyss between God and human beings is absolute in Judaism; neither divine incarnation nor human apotheosis can occur. Thus a class of perfectly sanctified human beings rubs against the grain of Jewish faith. Like mosques, synagogues lack icons and employ few symbols in decoration. To be sure, the ban on images has been relaxed in various eras: Hellenistic synagogues, for instance, displayed zodiacs and their symbols, and even had drawings of biblical figures. Nonetheless, neither humans nor representations of them formed any part of Jewish worship.

Related to the prohibition of molded images and their use in worship is the biblical ban on necromancy — contact with the dead, the veneration of whom

---

7. See Joseph H. Hertz, trans., *The Authorized Daily Prayer Book,* rev. ed. (New York: Bloch, 1959).

8. In the realm of popular custom, however, the deaths of certain "martyrs" such as R. Meir and Jeremiah the prophet were commemorated in past eras. Also the death of Moses on 7 Adar was marked by reading the story of his death in Deut. 34:5 once every three years, when that passage fell on that date in the ancient triennial cycle of Torah readings. Certain Jewish groups also commemorated the deaths of other figures such as R. Simeon b. Yohai (on this, see below). Eric Werner, "Traces of Jewish Hagiolatry," *Hebrew Union College Annual* 51 (1980): 51, 55–58.

would compromise the exclusive worship of God. So the biblical tradition insists that the dead are gone for good. Deuteronomy 34:6 emphasizes that even the grave of Moses is unknown, thus precluding any cult dedicated to the dead liberator. And the shade of the prophet Samuel, the only dead man contacted by the living in the Hebrew Bible, is outraged that Saul disturbs him. But sainthood, especially in the Christian tradition, often relies on the power of the dead. The posthumous miracles of Christian saints are an important criterion for their canonization: wonders frequently occur in the vicinity of their graves or their relics. The only good saint, it has been suggested, is a dead saint.[9] But the Jewish refusal to countenance contact with the dead or to recognize their powers nearly eliminates this entire dimension of sainthood. Although from at least Second Temple times Jews commonly visited the alleged tombs of biblical and rabbinic worthies, these revered dead were not the objects of official cults.[10]

The distance that Jews kept from the dead proceeds also from a deep-seated sense of the impurity of corpses. In biblical law a dead body represents the highest degree of impurity and conveys uncleanness to everything that touches it or is in the same tent with it (Lev. 11:24–25; Num. 19:14–16). Those who have come in contact with corpses, like those who have touched lepers or had an issue from their sexual organs, must undergo purification rituals. Talmudic law extends the category "father of impurity" beyond corpses to entire burial areas.[11] These purity rules made nearly impossible any cultic contact with the dead or their relics. Jewish practice thus stands in marked contrast to the Christian fascination with corpses, their dismembered pieces, and their blood, as well as with objects that had come in contact with the dead. Indeed the rise of the Christian cult of saints took place in the cemeteries, where the faithful gathered to pay homage to and solicit the merit of the martyrs.[12] Gradually the tomb became a shrine, and the power of the dead became the foundation of the piety of the living. Eventually relics brought the power of saints to distant places. Since these developments could not occur in Judaism, there existed no real cultic basis for sainthood.

A final barrier to the development of sainthood in Judaism is sociological. Jewish piety tended to be egalitarian: all were bound by the same law and worshipped in the same synagogues. Separate and supererogatory piety, such

9. This is the thrust of G. van der Leeuw's discussion of the posthumous powers of saints. *Religion in Essence and Manifestation: A Study in Phenomenology* (New York and Evanston, Ill.: Harper and Row, 1963), 236–39.

10. For a general discussion of Jewish holy graves, see James W. Parkes, Raphael Posner, and Saul Paul Colbi, "Holy Places," in *EJ*, vol. 8, cols. 921–22.

11. See "Purity and Impurity, Ritual," in *EJ*, vol. 13, cols. 1405-14; Johs. Pedersen, *Israel: Its Life and Culture I–II* (London: Oxford University Press; and Copenhagen: Branner Og Korch, 1926), 481–84.

12. See Peter Brown, *The Cult of the Saints* (Chicago: University of Chicago Press, 1981), 1–12; and Michael Perham, *The Communion of Saints* (London: Society for the Propagation of Christian Knowledge, 1980), 15–21.

as is represented in other religions by monasticism, played no role in rabbinic Judaism. Jews could not escape from the world to find God; they met him in their daily lives. They saw their task to be sanctifying the world as given, not leaving it to find a higher way. The rabbis' goal was to "rabbinize" Israel, not to cultivate a separate path. So by refusing to recognize a higher terrain of piety, Judaism eliminated the main breeding ground for saints. In part, this position was an expression of the conviction that Jewish society as a whole was already separate from the "world" — that is, from the dominant Christian or Muslim society in which it lived. As a "nation within the nations" distinguished from them by its Torah, Judaism treasured its separateness, its higher calling. Because Israel saw itself as a "kingdom of priests and a holy nation" (Exod. 19:6) with respect to Christendom and Islam, it did not typically nurture a pious elite class within itself.

Furthermore, without an official hierarchy, Judaism lacked an authoritative means to canonize saints, to declare that certain holy persons were deemed fit as exemplars. Without an institution to sponsor them, local holy persons' reputations could easily wither. Indeed in Christianity it was the bishops' willingness to patronize the tombs of the martyrs and to exploit them for their own needs that created the cult of the saints out of what might have been private shrines.[13] Moreover, unlike many holy persons in other religions who lived and functioned at a distance from society, rabbis lived under the constant gaze of their disciples and colleagues.[14] Thus claims to special holiness were likely to have as many detractors as defenders.

The absence of a vigorous tradition of sainthood in Judaism in no way reflects despair about the human potential for holiness. Rather the very structure of Jewish religion and society discouraged the recognition of holy persons as models and icons. The primacy of the community over the individual in covenant and cult, the abhorrence of icons and the uncleanness of corpses, and the egalitarian nature of Jewish society all worked against the production of saints. Nevertheless, despite these limiting factors, certain individuals and groups of individuals in the history of Judaism may be construed as saintlike, given the impression they made on popular Jewish piety. Holy men (but not women!) have occasionally achieved a status analogous to that of saints in other religions.[15] Having explained why sainthood is rather peripheral in Jewish piety, we next look historically at the manifestations of sainthood on that periphery.

13. Brown, *Cult of the Saints*, 23–49.

14. For a discussion of the organization of rabbinic disciple circles and assemblies in Babylonia, see David M. Goodblatt, *Rabbinic Instruction in Sasanian Babylonia* (Leiden: E. J. Brill, 1975), 267–85.

15. Aside from the biblical heroines and Beruriah, the pious wife of R. Meir, very few Jewish women attained positions of influence in society or were celebrated in Jewish literature. This fact is simply part and parcel of the masculine-centered focus of *halakha* and Jewish piety. See Paula E. Hyman, "The Other Half: Women in the Jewish Tradition," *Conservative Judaism* 26, no. 4 (1972): 14–21.

SAINTLIKE MANIFESTATIONS IN JEWISH HISTORY

Biblical personalities have always occupied a special place in the Jewish imagination. Although no single one of them could properly be regarded as a saint for ancient Israel, together they display a range of imitable and inimitable qualities typical of saints. Many project values that biblical authors considered exemplary. Thus Abraham is a model of faith, Jacob of cunning, Joseph of wisdom, Moses of humility, David of repentance, and Jeremiah of compassion. And among females the narratives praise Sarah the patient, Rebekkah the determined, Ruth the loyal, and Esther the wise. Others display supernatural powers associated with saints. Thus Elijah and Elisha multiply food, heal lepers, and raise the dead. Even the bones of the dead Elisha have the power to raise a corpse (2 Kings 13:21). At the same time none of these figures is idealized, much less seen as a perfected being. Indeed biblical authors go to great lengths to depict the weaknesses of their heroes: Abraham lies, Jacob cheats, Joseph boasts, Moses refuses, Jeremiah complains, David murders, Sarah laughs at God, and Elisha misuses his powers to slay some children who have offended him.

The biblical tales, moreover, cannot be regarded as hagiographical in any meaningful sense. Although biblical historiography is structured around the deeds of individual characters, the narratives focus not on praising the hero but on illustrating his or her role in the history of Israel. Biblical historiography presents a succession of characters whose lives become windows to the ramifications of biblical faith. Episodes depict the virtues and vices of the biblical worthies but never comprise a devotional vita.

Although on one level the biblical characters seem to be too much like us to be considered saints, on another level they are too different from us to warrant that title. Nearly all of them are "called," divinely designated for a certain vocation. Abraham must forsake his past, Moses must lead his people, David must reign as king, and Amos can but prophesy. Their experiences are not repeatable, since no discipline of prayer, meditation, or asceticism has made them what they are. One cannot train for their vocations. Rather, they have been struck dumb by a God who gives them power to act or speak on his behalf. The prophet is in no sense a model to imitate; one should do what he says but cannot do what he does. Biblical sources retroactively apply the title "prophet," in the sense of a unique spokesperson for and intercessor with God, to Abraham, Moses, and others, while rabbinic literature terms all of the biblical heroes prophets.[16] One rabbinic tradition counts forty-eight prophets and seven prophetesses (*b. Meg.* 14a). Since the rabbis believed that prophecy ceased at the end of the biblical era, the designation "prophet" marks for them a unique set of inimitable individuals confined to ancient times.

16. See Louis I. Rabinowitz, "Prophets and Prophecy," in *EJ*, vol. 13, cols. 1175–76.

In Hellenistic Jewish literature various genres elaborate hagiographically on the laconic tales given in the Bible.[17] Testament literature, for instance, attributes lengthy deathbed testaments to biblical personalities such as the sons of Jacob, who commend particular virtues and condemn certain vices. In the many apocalyptic writings, ancient worthies such as Enoch, Moses, and Ezra are credited with incredible visions that map events in the time of the Hellenistic authors. Philo's *Life of Moses* represents a third genre: sacred biography. Here Moses is represented as the ideal king, the true priest and prophet, and the perfect lawgiver. Significantly, all of these hagiographical types were preserved not by Jews but by Christians.

Another Hellenistic genre, more significant for ongoing Judaism than these, is the martyr story. During the Antiochan persecution, the first time that individual Jews were persecuted and killed for adhering to Torah's laws, the martyr who dies rather than violate Torah became a new kind of Jewish hero. In 2 Maccabees, for instance, the tortures and deaths of the aged Eleazar and of a woman and her seven sons at the hands of Antiochus Epiphanes are related with a Greek rhetorical flourish that celebrates their courage and exemplary behavior (6:18–7:42). Writers soon read qualities of the martyr back into the lives of prophets whose biblical stories, except in the case of Jeremiah, gave only scant attention to the matter of suffering for one's beliefs.[18] Thus the Ascension of Isaiah memorializes the martyrdom of the prophet at the hands of the evil king Manasseh. Later the midrashim of the tannaim and later rabbinic sources count nearly all biblical heroes as martyrs—from Abel and Abraham to Zechariah and Daniel. Though as prophets these figures are inimitable, as martyrs they are exemplary. In this way they reflect the basic tension found in saints in other world religions.

Within the history of Israel and biblical literature itself there is little indication that holy men became the objects of special devotion or cultic worship. True, miracle tales such as those that surface about Elijah and Elisha may indicate a circle of disciples who revered the master's powers, and the tomb of the patriarchs and matriarchs at Machpelah seems to have been a holy place. Yet the strong biblical animus against any cult of personality or homage to the dead meant that any real veneration would have had to operate underground, beneath the official level of biblical writers. But by the Hellenistic period, sources reveal a lively cultic interest in the graves of biblical figures. Matthew 23:29 accuses the scribes and Pharisees of building and adorning the tombs of the prophets, a charge borne out by recent investigations into the role of biblical tombs in popular piety. Joachim Jeremias documents traditions about the graves of Joseph, Hulda, Isaiah, Zechariah,

---

17. For a brief introduction to these writings, see Leonhard Rost, *Judaism Outside the Hebrew Canon: An Introduction to the Documents* (Nashville: Abingdon, 1976).

18. See H. A. Fischel, "Martyr and Prophet (A Study in Jewish Literature)," *Jewish Quarterly Review* 37, no. 3 (1947): 265–80.

Rachel, David, Jeremiah, the patriarchs, and others; they were the object of pilgrimages from near and far.[19] References in Hellenistic Jewish literature and rabbinic midrashim indicate that, on the popular level, the holy person was believed to be still present in his grave and capable of hearing the prayers of the faithful and answering them. This popular piety, however, was soon repudiated by the rabbis, and grave veneration became an exclusively Christian practice. One source declares, "One erects no grave monuments to the dead; their lives perpetuate their memory" (*j. Shek.* 47a). Despite this official rejection, however, pilgrimages to tombs of biblical prophets are widely attested throughout the Middle Ages and have continued among eastern Jews until the present.[20]

Classical rabbinic literature — Talmud and midrash — does not focus on personalities, as does biblical narrative. In fact the structure of these texts, which map debates about interpretation of law and scripture, leaves no room for biography.[21] Not a single hagiographic sketch can be found in all of rabbinic writing. To be sure, sayings of and anecdotes about rabbinic sages appear everywhere, but nowhere is there an interest in an individual personality for its own sake. The rabbis did not see each other or their rabbinic forebears as possessors of a unique holiness worthy of devotion on the part of others. Yet rabbinic tales do attribute special qualities and merit to certain sages. The gentle Hillel is contrasted with the harsh Shammai, for instance, and R. Simeon b. Yohai is known for his mystical predilections; many others are praised for their great learning and wisdom. The five disciples of R. Yohanan b. Zakkai each have their characteristic virtues. The greatest of them, Eliezer b. Hyrcanus, is said to be "a plastered cistern which loses not a drop" (*m. Abot* 2:8), and others are credited with far-reaching wonder-working powers. Several Palestinian rabbis, like R. Hanina b. Dosa, are given the title *ḥasid* (enthusiast) and somewhat ambivalently celebrated for their cures and rain-making powers.[22] Many tales, similarly, relate the ability of a number of Babylonian rabbis to bring fertility, exorcise demons, and heal the sick.[23] One text even claims that people used soil from the grave of Rav to

19. Joachim Jeremias, *Heiligengräber im Jesu Umwelt* (Göttingen: Vandenhoeck and Ruprecht, 1958), esp. 118–43.

20. See E. N. Adler, *Jewish Travelers* (London: G. Routledge and Sons, 1930), for example, 64–99.

21. At a seminar at Northwestern University, May 1983, Professor William Scott Green suggested the "list" as the genre within which rabbinic writings should be understood. See also his "What's in a Name? — The Problematic of Rabbinic Biography," *Approaches to Ancient Judaism: Theory and Practice*, ed. William Scott Green, vol. 1 (Missoula, Mont.: Scholars Press, 1978), 77–96.

22. See Geza Vermes, *Jesus the Jew* (New York: Macmillan, 1973), 58–78; William Scott Green, "Palestinian Holy Men: Charismatic Leadership and the Rabbinic Tradition," in *Aufstieg und Niedergang der Römischen Welt*, ed. H. Temporini and W. Hasse (Berlin: H. Temporini; and New York: de Gruyter, 1979), vol. 19, no. 2, pp. 619–47.

23. See Neusner, *There We Sat Down*, 79–86.

bring down a fever (*b. Sanh.* 47b). But such powers were the stock in trade of magicians throughout the world of Late Antiquity; the influence of such Jewish magicians was primarily local and short-lived, not analogous to the lasting charisma of Christian saints.

More important for the subject of sainthood is the continued attention given to martyrs. The rabbis embraced the stories of the Maccabean martyrs and retold their stories in Talmudic literature.[24] In addition the deaths of rabbinic sages were interpreted in such a way that these sages would swell the ranks of those who preferred death to violating the dictates of Torah. Under the persecution of Hadrian many, such as R. Akiba, met their deaths, and their last moments were memorialized in tales that boast of their great courage. R. Akiba, for example, is pictured reciting the *Shema* as the Roman executioner flays his flesh (*j. Ber.* 14b). During the geonic period (seventh to eleventh centuries), martyr stories of ten teachers who were slain by Hadrian on a single day, according to legend, became the subjects of a special midrash ("The Ten Martyrs") also adapted for liturgical use.[25]

Tradition maintained that the selfless actions of these rabbinic martyrs and their biblical forebears earned merit for the community as a whole. Their deaths atoned not only for the sins of their own generation but also for the sins of their ancestors and descendents. Thus the deaths of the "ten martyrs" eventually were understood to atone for the ancient sin of the sale of Joseph, which had gone unexpiated. This idea of martyrs' merit forms part of the more general rabbinic tenet of the "merit of the fathers," the righteous biblical patriarchs.[26] As early as the Pentateuch Moses invokes the names of Abraham, Isaac, and Jacob when he seeks to avert God's destruction of Israel (Exod. 32:13). For the rabbis this merit continues to sustain Israel just as the merit of Noah sustains the Gentiles. Although there was opposition to the belief that the merit of the righteous in general and the martyr in particular might be called upon by later generations, it became anchored nonetheless in the prayers of fast days and the New Year. On the Day of Atonement, for instance, God is asked to remember the binding of Isaac, a near martyr, when he judges Israel. But this doctrine of merit, reminiscent as it is of the intercession of saints, did not focus on individual persons so much as it did on the collectivity of the righteous and the martyrs. Together their merit could elicit God's mercy toward his sinful people.

24. Gerson D. Cohen, "The Story of Hannah and Her Seven Sons in Hebrew Literature," in *Mordecai M. Kaplan Jubilee Volume,* ed. Moshe Davis, vol. 2 (New York: Jewish Theological Seminary of America, 1953), 109–22 (Hebrew).

25. Haim H. Ben-Sasson, "Kiddush Ha-shem," in *EJ,* vol. 10, cols. 981–82; "The Ten Martyrs," in *Jewish Encyclopedia,* vol. 8 (New York and London: Funk and Wagnalls, 1905, 1916), 355.

26. See the discussion of Ephraim E. Urbach, *The Sages: Their Concepts and Beliefs* (Jerusalem: Magnes, 1975), 496–511.

Martyrs continued to be thought of as possessing saintlike virtue among the Ashkenazic Jews of medieval Europe as the Crusades created an immense new wave of slaughtered Jews. Outnumbered and nearly defenseless Jewish communities in the Rhineland attacked by fringe groups of Crusaders (first in 1096) resorted to mass suicide rather than die at the hands of the uncircumcised.[27] Jewish chronicles and poets present these frenzied acts of desperation as the victims' saintly self-sacrifice for the sake of the sanctification of the divine name (*qiddush ha-shem*).[28] Following the rabbinic dictum that one must choose martyrdom over the commission of an act of idolatry, sexual crime, or murder, the victims willingly choose death over baptism. Chroniclers term these martyrs "holy ones" (*qedoshim*), for their righteous deaths not only earn them a place in the world to come but also atone for the sins of later generations. In fact, the chronicler Solomon bar Simson envies that generation chosen for its merit to be a sacrifice and witness to God's great name.[29] Although these martyrs are regarded as saintly and their memories are preserved not only in chronicles but also in *piyyutim* (poems) and *Memorbuchen* (memorial books) read in Ashkenazic synagogues, their individual vitae, like those of the "ten martyrs," are not emphasized. The chroniclers' stories of their martyrdoms are so highly stylized, in fact, that their individuality tends to disappear.[30] The Spanish Jewish poet and theologian Judah Halevi, who lived during the Crusades in the North, argued that since Christians and Muslims extol their martyrs, the Jews, an entire people of martyrs, should glory in them all the more.[31] But the martyrs' individual identity and potential sainthood pale before their function as representatives of Israel as a whole.

In addition to revering the martyrs, the Ashkenazim admired the leaders of the Ḥasidei Ashkenaz (pious ones of Germany), a mystical pietistic movement that developed in the wake of the violence of the Crusades.[32] Samuel of the Kalonymus family of Speyer, his more famous son Judah (1140–1217), and Judah's disciple, Eleazar of Worms, led an ascetic and penitential group of men who sought to live a continual martyrdom by dying daily to the pleasures of this world. Although they cultivated powerlessness, the Hasidim, especially their leader Judah, were credited with magical pow-

27. Salo W. Baron, *A Social and Religious History of the Jews*, vol. 4 (New York: Columbia University Press; and Philadelphia: Jewish Publication Society, 1957), 89–106.

28. Baron, *History*, vol. 4, pp. 139–47. See the chronicles now translated in Shlomo Eidelberg, *The Jews and the Crusaders* (Madison: University of Wisconsin Press, 1977).

29. Baron, *History*, vol. 4, p. 144.

30. See, for instance, the Chronicle of Solomon bar Simson in Eidelberg, *Jews*, 34, 43–44, 55–58.

31. See Hartwig Hirschfeld, trans., *Judah Hallevi's Kitab al Khazari* (London: George Routledge and Sons; and New York: E. P. Dutton, 1905), 78.

32. For background, see Gershom Scholem, *Major Trends in Jewish Mysticism* (New York: Schocken, 1954), 80–87.

ers. Because he denied himself everything, the *hasid*, in the popular mind, commanded the elements. Legends about the powers of Judah the *hasid* form the richest hagiographical cycle in medieval Jewish literature. Judah was transformed from a model of piety for the few into a magician venerated by the many.[33] He thus functioned as a popular saintlike figure despite his esoteric mystical orientation.

The propensity to revere mystical leaders as saints is even more evident among the Sephardic Jews, both in Spain and in the lands into which they were dispersed after their expulsion in 1492. Among these Jews, who were less fundamentalist than their Ashkenazic coreligionists, *kabbalah* (mystical tradition) developed in many directions. The classical document of *kabbalah*, the Zohar, written in late thirteenth-century Spain by the mystic Moses de Leon, featured the ancient rabbinic mystic, R. Simeon b. Yohai, as the expounder of esoteric doctrine.[34] His role as the fountainhead of mysticism indicates his unique position in the imaginations of Spanish mystics as a kind of patron saint. Until 1492 the *Zohar* and other mystical works belonged to a small elite, but after the expulsion from Spain they moved more into the public domain. To the new exiles mysticism offered an explanation for their fate and a discipline for bringing exile to an end. Especially in sixteenth-century Safed in northern Israel, pietists gathered under the tutelage of charismatic mystics to repent for the sins of Israel and prepare for the coming of the redeemer.

Foremost among these mystics was Isaac Luria, called *Ha-Ari* (the divine Rabbi Isaac), who interpreted the historical exile of the Jews as but a symptom of God's exile from himself and imprisonment in the material world.[35] Through prayer and fulfillment of the commandments, he thought, the Jew aids in the process of *tikkun*, whereby God is "restored" to himself, and thereby hastens the messianic age. By attributing cosmic significance to the experience of exile and the discipline he fostered to overcome it, Luria attracted a most serious following who regarded him as a *tsaddiq* (saintly man). For his part he encouraged this reverence by demonstrating clairvoyant powers. He "discovered" the graves of ancient worthies and, with his disciples, communed with these honored dead. Like all *kabbalists* Luria believed in metempsychosis, the transmigration of souls, and, like many, he claimed to be able to read in people's foreheads the identities of the ancient souls within them. In fact, he declared that he and his disciples reincarnated R. Simeon b. Yohai and his disciples, the heroes of the *Zohar*. His lasting influence was ensured by the writing of *Toledot ha-Ari*, a collection of his sayings and habits; one of the disciples who wrote it, Hayyim Vital, also composed an autohagiography as his own claim to be Luria's successor.

33. Scholem, *Major Trends*, 98–99.
34. Again, for background, see Scholem, *Major Trends*, 156–59.
35. Scholem, *Major Trends*, 273–75, 284–86.

Mystical enthusiasm and the tradition of open messianic speculation among Sephardic Jews gave rise to a large number of messianic claimants and movements.[36] These false messiahs illustrate the fate likely to befall a would-be Jewish saint. In the heat of apocalyptic predictions any Jewish leader recognized as especially holy may well assume the unique position of messiah in his own mind or that of his followers. But the public acclamation of a saint necessarily became the public condemnation of a sinner when the messiahship proved false. Such was the fate of all Jewish messianic pretenders: for them sainthood was an all or nothing proposition. Among the many figures who shared this fate, one might mention Solomon Molcho (1500–1532), a Portuguese Marrano who reverted to Judaism, preached in Salonika about the coming redemption, gathered many followers, and became convinced that he was the messiah. He even attempted to fulfill a Talmudic messianic legend by sitting in Rome as a beggar for thirty days (*b. Sanh.* 98a). His movement spread to Poland, and "relics" such as his banner are still on display in a Prague museum.[37] When the messianic age failed to dawn, however, his "sainthood" was discredited. As might be expected, Isaac Luria too saw himself in a messianic light, but because he was more circumspect in his claims, his messianic failure did not tarnish his *kabbalistic* influence. He only alluded to his belief that he was "the messiah, son of Joseph" and that he would die in fulfillment of his mission.

The most famous of these messianic personalities, Shabbatai Zevi, illustrates most dramatically how precipitously saint can become sinner in Judaism.[38] At the urging of his disciple and prophet Nathan of Gaza, Shabbatai proclaimed himself messiah on 31 May 1665 and soon declared 18 June 1666 to be the date of redemption. His prophecies, combined with his forceful personality and bizarre antinomian behavior, won him a huge following in Palestine and Turkey, and his fame spread rapidly through the Middle East and Europe. Everywhere the glad tidings of redemption evoked mass enthusiasm. His apostasy to Islam after he was arrested by Turkish authorities, however, brought an abrupt end to the messianic hopes of the vast Jewish society that supported him. Some groups continued to believe, seeing his apostasy as another manifestation of the "holiness of sin" that he earlier espoused, and they also converted to Islam along with him. For the great majority, however, apostasy was anathema, and the sudden collapse of the Shabbatean movement greatly diminished the respectability of messianism among rabbinic authorities and the credibility of this perilous mode of Jewish sainthood from the nineteenth century onward.

36. Gerson D. Cohen, "Messianic Postures of Ashkenazim and Sephardim," in *Studies of the Leo Baeck Institute*, ed. Max Kreutzberger (New York: Ungar, 1967), 121–25, 133–42.

37. Joseph Schochetman, "Molcho, Solomon," in *EJ*, vol. 12, cols. 225–27.

38. The career of Shabbetai Zevi is dealt with broadly in Scholem, *Major Trends*, 289–99, and in great detail in his *Sabbatai Sevi: The Mystical Messiah*, Bollingen Series 93 (Princeton, N. J.: Princeton University Press, 1973).

The expulsion of the Jews from Spain brought the Sephardim to the lands of the third major grouping of Jews to be considered here, those who made their home in the Orient, North Africa and the Middle East. In these Muslim lands Jewish attitudes toward sainthood were heavily influenced by Muslim practice. The ancient graves of biblical and rabbinic holy men were located here: in Palestine, Egypt, Syria, and Babylonia. The common Muslim practice of making pilgrimages to the tombs of the saints undoubtedly encouraged Jewish pilgrims to honor their dead in a similar way. Throughout the Middle Ages the itineraries of famous pilgrims from Europe were determined by these sacred tombs. The settlement of Jews in Turkey after 1492 greatly increased the number of pilgrims to the holy land. At the tomb of Samuel the prophet at Ramah, for instance, a spot also venerated by Muslims, Jewish pilgrims held annual communions and celebrations.[39] In North Africa Muslim worship at the tombs of *marabouts* prompted similar veneration among Jews at famous rabbis' tombs. In fact several such sites were shared by Jews and Muslims who revered the same or a different saint there.[40] Approaching such a tomb on the occasion of some important event, devotees would undergo purification, remove their shoes, light candles, kiss the tomb, eat a meal, and petition the rabbi for some favor.[41] The most famous of Moroccan rabbis so honored, R. Amran b. Divan, offered God his life if his ill son would recover. After his death in 1782 his tomb became an object of veneration, and his intercession was requested especially by barren women. Similar practices can still be observed among Oriental Jews at sites such as Rachel's tomb near Bethlehem, where women pray to "Rachel our mother" for fertility.

Annual collective pilgrimages to tombs occurred on the anniversary of the saint's death. Sometimes these were festive celebrations called *hilula* ("wedding"). The grandest of these was the *hilula* for R. Simeon b. Yohai, the hero of the *Zohar*, at his grave in Meiron in Galilee.[42] This festival is still celebrated by Sephardic and Oriental Jews on Lag Be'Omer, the thirty-third day after Passover. While other Jews mark this day by a lifting of the restrictions in force between Passover and Shavuot, the *hilula* celebrants conduct a joyful vigil at the grave of R. Simeon, lighting torches and bonfires, dancing and singing, and performing special rites such as cutting children's hair.

The most recent and most vigorous examples of sainthood in Judaism emerge from the Hasidic movement that took shape in late eighteenth-century Poland and the Ukraine. Led by the charismatic preacher and amulet writer Israel ben Eleazar (1700–1760), called the Baal Shem Tov, the move-

39. "Pilgrimage," in *Jewish Encyclopedia*, vol. 10, cols. 35–38.

40. For a detailed list and description of these tombs, see L. Voinot, *Pèlerinages judeo-musulman au Maroc* (Paris: Larose, 1948).

41. See A. Chouraqui, *Between East and West: A History of the Jews of North Africa* (New York: Atheneum, 1973), 71–79.

42. See Eric Werner, "Traces of Jewish Hagiolatry," 56–57; "'Omer Lag be-," in *Jewish Encyclopedia*, vol. 9, pp. 399–400.

ment appealed to simple Jews repelled by the elitism of rabbinic learning, disheartened by the failure of Shabbatai Zevi, and devastated by the harsh conditions of Poland after the Chmielnicki massacres (1666).[43] To them the Baal Shem Tov offered a warm and fervent piety rich in song and dance. In Hasidism many of the arcane notions of *kabbalah* reappear but are transformed for popular consumption to produce a practical mysticism appealing to the most unlettered soul. In the Baal Shem Tov his followers found more than a magician, a master of the divine name (*baal shem*). In him they found a living Torah, a personality that embodied the spirit of Torah and made it accessible to them directly. He showed the way to a personal redemption toward which individuals could strive by sanctifying the world around them and thus lifting their own souls to God.

After the death of the Baal Shem Tov his disciples gathered his sayings and stories but did not worship him as a dead saint. Rather, the living disciples themselves became the leaders of groups of Hasidim. In place of the one leader, then, multiple centers of authority developed, each of them focused on the *tsaddiq* or *rebbe*. With one important exception, Nahman of Bratslav, these *tsaddiqim* did not claim exclusive authority but were content to lead their own disciples in the tradition of the Baal Shem Tov as they understood it. Each *tsaddiq* had a distinctive personality and orientation, and attracted a following only partially determined by geographical proximity. Disciples would travel great distances to "their *rebbe*," often bypassing other Hasidic communities on the way. There they would find the *tsaddiq* who reached their soul, prayed for them and with them, answered their questions, and cured their ills. The *tsaddiq*'s very life served as a model for his disciples. Said one disciple of his master: "I did not go to the Maggid of Meseritz to learn Torah from him but to watch him tie his boot laces." The *tsaddiq* characteristically did not teach Torah by giving learned commentaries on it but by telling evocative tales that appealed to the emotions.

But if the *tsaddiq* was an exemplar, a living Torah, he was also inimitable, a saint whose powers transcended those of normal men. Then and now — for Hasidic communities still flourish — the *tsaddiq* functions as an *axis mundi*, a channel through which divine grace flows to the community and the agent through which the community approaches God.[44] A disciple of the Maggid of Meseritz reported that whenever he and his companions reached the town limits of Meseritz all their desires were fulfilled. Because the *tsaddiq* practices *devekut* (clinging to God), he can raise his disciples' prayers with dispatch. One influential Hasidic doctrine asserts that to be truly effective the *tsaddiq* must descend from the realm of purity in which he dwells and

43. Scholem, *Major Trends*, 34–50.

44. See Arthur Green, "The Zaddiq as *Axis Mundi* in Later Judaism," *Journal of the American Academy of Religion* 45 (1977): 327–47. Green shows that *axis mundi* symbolism is richest in the case of the *tsaddiq* Nahman of Bratslav.

encounter the evil world of the masses in order to lift up his followers with him. Though he remains inwardly bound to God, he goes out to the people to feel their sorrow, needs, doubts, and hopes and then to lead them from their current rung on the spiritual ladder to the realization of their highest potential.[45]

The inimitability of the *tsaddiq* reached its most extreme form in the Hasidic sect centered on Nahman of Bratslav.[46] Nahman considered himself to be an absolutely unique *tsaddiq* who rendered his contemporaries obsolete. He claimed to be the *tsaddiq ha-dor,* the sole *tsaddiq* of his time, and the last in a series that included Moses, R. Simeon b. Yohai, Isaac Luria, and Baal Shem Tov. He held, moreover, that as the final link in the chain he heralded the messiah. While the writings of other Hasidic sects portray their *tsaddiqim* as guides, teachers, healers, protectors, and intercessors, only the writings about Nahman depict the *tsaddiq* as a redeemer who battles sin for his disciples' sake.[47] One even finds among the Bratslavers the hope that he will return from death as the Messiah ben David. This Hasidic sect honored Nahman's claim to uniqueness by never recognizing a successor. Whereas in all of the other Hasidic sects a descendant of the *tsaddiq* became the link between God and community, in Bratslav Nahman reigned even after his death.

In the contemporary world the *tsaddiqim* continue to function as living saints. To witness the *rebbe* addressing his followers or casting scraps of food to them from his plate is to be shocked into the recognition that some Jews in the contemporary world venerate saints. To observe the *hilula* for R. Simeon b. Yohai at Meiron similarly convinces one that, despite modernity and Judaism's characteristic antipathy to sainthood, ancient holy men continue to exercise influence over Jews today.

We have seen that although traces of sainthood in Judaism are meager, it is undeniable that saints have been popularly acclaimed, especially by mystical groups. Here the stress on personality over law and on emotion over rationality has produced figures both imitated and venerated. And despite Judaism's abhorrence of veneration of the dead, the graves of the ancient heroes and their later descendants have proved to be powerful magnets drawing the faithful to commune with their holy past. Yet the saints that we have identified do not constitute the main focus of piety even for those who revere them. Even the Lurianic kabbalists followed the standard Jewish calendar; even the Hasidim read the Torah and soon studied Talmud as well;

45. This is the doctrine of Yaakov Yosef of Polnoy, the earliest Hasidic writer and the main source for the teachings of the Baal Shem Tov. His idea of the "descent of the *tsaddiq*" is explained in Samuel R. Dresner, *The Zaddik* (New York: Schocken, 1960), 148–90.

46. Arthur Green, *Tormented Master: A Life of Rabbi Nahman of Bratslav* (University, Ala.: University of Alabama Press, 1979) esp. 135–220.

47. Green, *Tormented Master,* 183.

even North African Jews prayed out of a *Siddur.* To understand the human ideals that shape Jewish piety we must look beyond the disconnected instances of Jewish sainthood. We must realize that although the sources of Judaism have much to say about the ideal Jew, they rarely dwell on specific human beings as models of perfection. Instead they talk about the ideal man in the abstract, using episodes from the lives of particular individuals to illustrate this or that quality. In the Hebrew Scriptures humans are directed to be holy, not perfect (Lev. 19:2; cf. Matt. 5:48). Thus the tradition stresses paths by which everyone can attain sanctity, rather than the special attainments of individuals who live a life apart.

THREE SPIRITUAL IDEALS

Plato understood the human soul to consist of three faculties: the spirited, rational, and appetitive, or in other words, the will, mind, and heart. Recently Robert Neville has used these Platonic categories as the basis for three models of spiritual perfection: the soldier, exemplar of psychic integrity; the sage, paragon of enlightenment; and the saint, embodiment of perfect love.[48] He analyzes the stages on the way to the development of their three perfections — a good will, a profound understanding, and a pure heart. Interestingly, Judaism offers three human ideals that correspond closely to Neville's categories: the *tsaddiq* or just man, the *talmid ḥakham* or scholar, and the *ḥasid* or enthusiast.[49] Although these types are not always clearly distinguished from one another in Jewish sources, they may usefully be separated here for purposes of discussion.

Without a doubt the premier ideal of Jewish piety is the *talmid ḥakham,* literally, the "pupil of a sage." This ancient rabbinic term for scholar emphasizes the continued studentship of even the greatest sage, for he always remains subordinate to the Torah he studies. Because Torah and its ongoing explication, interpretation, and application disclose the will of God, the ability to learn and teach it is Judaism's most prized skill. In the *talmid ḥakham* the mind traverses the most direct road to God, a road that beckons all to follow. Since Torah proceeds from God, to study it is to think God's thoughts after him. And Torah is never complete: each generation must appropriate, refine, and extend it as the flux of history demands. Talmudic reasoning seeks to find the principles behind every ruling, thus aiming toward the understanding of the basic structure of the universe. This process, as Jacob Neusner has said, represents the "perfect intellectualization of life."[50]

48. Robert C. Neville, *Soldier, Sage, Saint* (New York: Fordham University Press, 1978).

49. My analysis largely follows that of Gershom Scholem, "Three Types of Jewish Piety," *Eranos-Jahrbuch* 38 (1969): 331–48.

50. See Neusner's suggestive analysis in *Invitation to the Talmud: A Teaching Book* (New York: Harper and Row, 1973), 223–46.

God too studies Torah, rabbinic legend asserts; thus by applying his mind to Torah, the *talmid ḥakham* imitates God.

Rabbinic sages often viewed the study of Torah as an end in itself: *talmud torah lishmah*.[51] It should be studied for its own sake, not for the earthly or heavenly awards attendant thereupon. R. Simeon b. Yohai went so far as to condemn farmers who did not study but worked in the field: "They forsake eternal life and busy themselves with temporal life." Interestingly the same comment is ascribed to another sage, Rava, on the occasion of his observing R. Hamnuna at prayer (*b. Shab.* 10a). By saying what he is supposed to have said, he accounted prayer less significant than study. Indeed study becomes in Judaism a ritual act, a formalized mode of behavior through which the participant contacts God through his written word. The centrality of the rabbinic intellectual ideal is highlighted also by the abuse the rabbis heap upon the uneducated man, the *'am ha-'arets*.[52] Not to avail oneself of the chance to study Torah and thereby to merit eternal life makes one a stupid boor, and to study Torah in the presence of such an uncouth person, one source avers, "is as though he raped his betrothed before him" (*b. Pes.* 49b). Though other spokesmen for the rabbinic tradition are more charitable, such calumny reveals the importance of the ideal of the *talmid ḥakham*.

The rabbinic sage, as his image was recorded in the Talmuds of Palestine (400 c.e.) and Babylon (500 c.e.), became the dominant model of religiosity for all Judaism in the centuries that followed. No Jew could hope to attain a position of authority without thorough training in the classics of Torah literature. Whether he was a physician like Maimonides or a statesman like Don Isaac Abravanel, every ambitious Jew had the model of the *talmid ḥakham* before him. Even radical mystics like Isaac Luria began their careers studying Torah and continued to do so. The ancient biblical heroes too were transformed through legend into rabbinic sages: Abraham studied the whole Torah before it was given to Moses, and David donned phylacteries and prayed like a rabbi. Moses the greatest prophet became *Moshe rabbenu*, "Moses our rabbi," the spiritual forebear of all later sages. For most Jews through history the great names — the "saints" — have been the names of great scholars like Hillel, Rashi, Rambam, and the Vilna Gaon. Often their biographies were nearly unknown. Instead they were remembered and revered because of their contributions to Torah, the repository of Jewish wisdom. In fact, even the names of many rabbinic authorities were displaced by the titles of their commentaries.

Judaism's moral ideal crystallized in the figure of the *tsaddiq*, the righteous person. In Talmudic literature the term carries a variety of meanings: a man free from sin, a man who obeys Torah, a man declared not guilty at a trial, a

---

51. On the importance of study, see Urbach, *Sages*, 603–20.
52. On the *'am ha-'arets*, see Urbach, *Sages*, 632–39.

man who gives charity (*tsedaqah*).[53] Some traditions hold that any person who does his best to obey the law is to be accounted a *tsaddiq*. He may fail time and time again, but if he keeps his duty always before him and does not give up, he is righteous. Even a wicked person who repents of his sins may become a *tsaddiq*. In Talmudic literature there are tales of individuals deemed *tsaddiqim* because of a single righteous act. For example, a certain Pentakaka (whose name means literally "five sins"), though the resident manager of a brothel, is called a *tsaddiq* for selling his own bed to ransom from prison the husband of a penniless woman who would otherwise have been forced into a life of prostitution in order to ransom him (*j. Ta'anit* 1, 4, 64b).

The righteous benefit not only themselves but the world at large. Their deeds bring blessings to the world, and they intercede with God on behalf of humans. Through the notion of merit the effect of righteous beings on others is held to persist even beyond their deaths.[54] As we have seen, the merit of the patriarchs was in some quarters believed to sustain Israel. The martyrs form a special class of *tsaddiqim*: spiritual soldiers par excellence. Their moral courage stands in the tradition as an example of what every Jew ought to do in similar circumstances.

The ethical ideal of the righteous person is highly elaborated in medieval and modern philosophical and ethical literature. Just as the preeminence of a written revelation fostered the ideal of the scholar, so too the focus on the prophetic and social dimension of the commandments encouraged the development of the exemplary *tsaddiq*. Maimonides (1135–1204), for instance, sees the righteous man as the one who chooses the middle way. Everyone, he says, is free to become as great a *tsaddiq* as Moses or as infamous a *rasha'* (wicked man) as Jeroboam, the apostate king of Israel (*Yad. Tesh.* 5:2). Medieval moralists wrote ethical tracts that were meant to instill righteousness through rabbinic examples. For instance, the *Mesillat Yesharim* ("The Path of the Upright") of Moses Hayyim Luzzatto (1707–46), written on the eve of the modern period, declares itself a guide to *hasidut* (piousness) but understands that condition largely in terms of moral training.[55] Luzzatto laments pietistic practices such as reciting psalms, fasting, and soaking in ice and snow, which had given *hasidut* a bad name. Instead he offers a step-by-step program through which the learned person can cultivate proper traits of character and achieve true piety and, finally, holiness. Sanctity, for Luzzatto, results from the proper motivation in observing Torah's dictates.

In the nineteenth century an educational movement called Musar (moral) aimed at inculcating ethical ideals .in Eastern European Jewish

53. On the righteous man, see Urbach, *Sages,* 483–95.

54. See Urbach, *Sages,* 496–511.

55. Moses Hayyim Luzzatto, *The Path of the Upright,* trans. and ed. Mordecai M. Kaplan (Philadelphia: Jewish Publication Society, 1966).

society,[56] but its influence was felt primarily in the Lithuanian *yeshivot* (academies). Founded by Israel Lipkin Salanter, the Musar movement sought to resist the disintegrating trends of Haskalah (enlightenment), Hasidism, and Reform by infusing the study of Talmud and the practice of a traditional Jewish life with a high and dignified moral tone. Using Luzzatto's works and other ethical writings, Musar teachers had their pupils chant passages with plaintive melodies in semidarkness in order to create the proper emotional atmosphere for the internalization of their ethical teachings. In addition, sermons and other group activities encouraged the achievement of ethical goals. These practices created solidarity among the pupils and between each pupil and Torah, and these *yeshivot* successfully produced rabbinic leaders of high character and scholarship.

Although, as Gershom Scholem argues, the *tsaddiq* is by and large an ideal to which all can aspire, a fullness of moral virtue that all can attain with effort, nonetheless a different and richly developed strain in Jewish mysticism sees the *tsaddiq* as a supernormal person.[57] According to this tradition the *tsaddiq* is an individual whose existence sustains the world (*b. Ber.* 17b). R. Yohanan said, "The world exists for the sake of a single *tsaddiq,* as it is written: 'The *tsaddiq* is the foundation of the world' (Prov. 10:25)" (*b. Yoma* 38b). The Talmudic rabbis speculate about the number of *tsaddiqim* necessary in any generation to outweigh the world's sin; their estimates vary from forty-five to thirty. R. Simeon b. Yohai, with characteristic audacity, includes himself in their number and claims that even if there is only one *tsaddiq,* that one is he (*Gen. Rab.* 35:2). This notion evolves, as we saw earlier, into the mystical idea of the *tsaddiq ha-dor,* the unique sustainer of the world in his own and even in many generations. A final twist on this theme is the Yiddish legend of the *lamed-vovniks,* the thirty-six "just men" who covertly sustain the world though they themselves may not be aware of their true identity.

This tradition of the exceptional, inimitable *tsaddiq* brings us close to the third ideal of Jewish piety, the *ḥasid,* a figure usually also regarded as a unique individual. The *ḥasid* is a devotee who seeks an individualistic path to God, one that goes beyond knowing God's Torah (like the *talmid ḥakham*) and doing his will (like the *tsaddiq*). Whereas the *tsaddiq* is restrained, doing only what is right, the *ḥasid* is radical, going beyond the call of duty. The *ḥasid* displays the extremes of *ḥesed:* love, mercy, unbounded generosity. He follows the way of fervent prayer, ascetic discipline, or mystic rapture. Until the eighteenth-century Hasidic movement, the title *ḥasid* was given only to lone individuals, not to a social group.[58] In lists of Ashkenazic martyrs, for instance, some names are followed by the designation *ḥasid* or *ḥasidah* (fem.) to convey the highest honor. But even as extremists, *ḥasidim* were understood

56. Haim H. Ben-Sasson, "Musar Movement," in *EJ,* vol. 12, cols. 534–37.

57. See Green, *Tormented Master,* 117–19; 132, n.71.

58. This point is stressed by Scholem, "Three Types of Jewish Piety," 343.

as part of their communities and were not organized into exclusive pietistic conventicles. Not everyone was encouraged to be a *hasid;* emotional enthusiasm was an ideal for the few.

In Mishna and Talmud the name *hasidim rishonim* (*hasidim* of old) denotes men distinguished by the austerity of their halakhic rulings and their lengthy prayers.[59] "The *hasidim rishonim* used to tarry an hour before they prayed, that they might direct their hearts toward God" (*Ber.* 5:1). These men were also known for their wonder working. Honi the Circle Drawer, for instance, is credited with controlling rainfall. One can understand why miracles would be attributed to such pietists; spiritual intensity in religion often overflows into salvific acts.

More clearly illustrating the extremist's vocation are the medieval German pietists (*Hasidei Ashkenaz*). Out of the *Sefer Hasidim,* a book of popular teachings and examples, comes a radical ideal.[60] Though preserving his family life, the *hasid* was to renounce ordinary pleasures and aim toward an emotional equilibrium that would permit him to bear shame and insult without flinching. It is said, in fact, that the more he is abused, the greater will be his reward in the world to come. The *hasid* revered Torah yet marched to a different drummer, the "heavenly law" (*din shamayim*). His altruism forced him beyond the law, to a stricter interpretation: he might concentrate on the performance of a single commandment or undertake a radical act of penance such as sitting in an icy pond for an hour daily. By erasing all trace of ego, the *hasid* thus sought to do God's will out of pure love, and when his heart burned with this love, he was deemed worthier than a scholar.

If the medieval *hasidic* ideal stressed emotional control, the modern *hasidim,* the followers of the Baal Shem Tov, applauded emotional extravagance as the way to love God. In place of ascetic deprivations, joyful singing and dancing and fervent prayer became central. Thus, as Scholem notes, the term *hasid* referred no longer to the single religious enthusiast but to the mass following of a "super-*Hasid*," the *tsaddiq*.[61] Yet, as Arthur Green argues, although *hasid* and *tsaddiq* might seem to have been transposed in meaning in modern Hasidism, in fact the figure of the supernormal and exceptional *tsaddiq* has clear precedents in Talmudic and mystical tradition. Moreover, the new application of the title *hasid* to the many still carries with it the connotations of emotionalism and individualism of the old *hasidic* ideal. These new *hasidim* too looked beyond Torah, or rather found Torah in the person of the *tsaddiq* with whom they felt a deep emotional attachment. Each *hasid* needed to find his own master, his own link to God. As a group the modern *hasidim,* like the earlier individuals given this title, sought a piety

59. See S. Safrai, "Teaching of Pietists in Mishnaic Literature," *Journal of Jewish Studies* 16, nos. 1–2 (1965): 15–33.

60. See Scholem, *Major Trends,* 91–99.

61. Scholem, "Three Types of Jewish Piety," 346.

more intense than that available to them through the normal rabbinic channels. They took refuge in the fervor of a popular mysticism. In this movement, then, the narrow ideal of the *ḥasid* is opened up and becomes a life-style for the many.

The three ideals that I have sketched as distinct entities are not separated so neatly in Jewish sources. The *tsaddiq* and the *ḥasid* overlap, and the scholar should be a righteous and generous man. The Jew is encouraged to work toward all of the ideals at once: to study, observe, and pray. Indeed the *Shema*, the pivotal demand of Jewish faith, enjoins these ideals upon every person: "You shall love the Lord your God with all your heart, with all your soul, and with all your might" (Deut. 6:5). If we interpret this verse in a midrashic fashion, we may identify "heart" (the biblical seat of intelligence) with mind, "soul" (life) with will, and "might" (strength, energy) with enthusiasm. Thus the Jew is to love God with the mind, like a *talmid ḥakham;* with volition, like a *tsaddiq;* and with the emotions, like a *ḥasid.*

The study of the category of sainthood as applied to Judaism has yielded, in one sense, rather meager results. Saints — holy persons understood as models for imitation and subjects for veneration — have been an exceptional rather than a normal feature of Jewish religion. Characteristically, Jewish piety has not focused on the lives of paradigmatic and perfected human beings. Jewish tradition reveres many sages for their learning and wisdom but knows little about their spiritual lives. And tradition credits numerous holy men with gnostic, wonder-working, and even salvific powers but rarely enshrines them in any cultic devotion. If it recognizes extraordinary figures like R. Simeon b. Yohai, it almost never holds them up as models for the pious. There is little intersection between the paradigmatic and the perfected in Judaism. Only biblical personalities are universally recognized as simultaneously inimitable, because they are chosen, and yet exemplary, though in no way perfect, in the virtues they display. On the other end of Jewish history, the *tsaddiqim* of modern Hasidism represent the best examples of a tradition of personalities whose spiritual power rests in the tension between inimitability and otherness.

But if the yield of Jewish saints has been small, the light that the category sheds on Jewish piety has been substantial. For in trying to account for the dearth of Jewish saints, we were forced to examine some basic features of Jewish religion and society that inhibit the development of sainthood. Moreover, we saw that Judaism does not revere exceptional human beings but rather sets forth ideals of learning, righteousness, and enthusiasm for which all — not only the few — can aim. On the whole it is these holy ideals, rather than holy persons, that have guided Jewish society on its road to redemption.

PART II

Saints of the Modern World

SEVEN

The Buddhist Arahant: Classical Paradigm and Modern Thai Manifestations

Stanley J. Tambiah

In Thailand today a certain number of "forest monks" have combined "ascetic" (*dhūtaṅga*) practices with meditational exercises (of the *samādhi* and/or *vipassanā* kinds), and have established forest hermitages, particularly in the border provinces of North and Northeast Thailand.[1] Many of them are popularly acclaimed as *arahants* — literally "worthy ones" but in general usage "perfected saints." The best known of these *arahant* meditation masters are credited with charismatic powers, are well known "national" personages, and are associated with a cult of amulets. Lay sponsors mint these amulets, which are then blessed by the monks and consequently credited by the laity with sacred powers.

Traditionally, in all the Theravāda Buddhist countries of South and Southeast Asia, particularly Sri Lanka, Burma, Thailand, Laos, and Cambodia, the order of monks (*saṅgha*) has been divided into two kinds: the forest dwellers (*āraññavāsin*) and the town or village dweller (*gāmavāsin*). The former are usually associated with the vocation of meditation (*vipassanādhura*) and practice (*pratipatti*), and the latter with the vocation of books (*ganthadhura*) and learning (*pariyatti*). These labels, however, did not in the past and do not in the present apply to two exclusive groupings of monks. Meditation was and is frequently practiced by sections of urban monks, and certain communities of forest monks have always been at home with book learning. Still, the two labels are entrenched and describe two stereotypes of monks: one contemplative, reclusive, and devoted to meditation and ascetic practices; the other living amidst the laity, engaged in

---

1. These forest monk saints are the subject of my recently published book, *Buddhist Saints of the Forest and the Cult of Amulets* (Cambridge, England: Cambridge University Press, 1984). This essay deals with a small part of what is described in that book.

doctrinal learning and teaching, practicing rites and ceremonies, and inhabiting architecturally substantial monasteries. Traditionally, the village-and-town-dwelling monks have been the core of the mainstream ecclesiastical establishment, while the forest monk orders have tended to be excluded from honors and privileges conferred by the establishment. Thus, for example, the forest monks of Thailand do not participate in the monastic examinations and do not receive scholarly titles; indeed, they remain outside the *saṅgha's* system of royal and administrative titles altogether. The forest monks are referred to as Lūang Phāū and Lūang Pū (respectively "father" or "grandfather") and as Acharn (teacher), not as Chaokhun or Phrakhrū, names that signify the holding of official titles.

Certain "orthodox" Buddhist circles believe the *arahants* are exclusively heroes of the past; they maintain that present times are incapable of producing *arahants*.[2] But in both Burma and Thailand today, the possibility of a modern living saint is not ruled out, and some monks have recently been acclaimed as such. In fact the *arahant* remains an untarnished ideal among all Thai and Burmese Buddhists, and when the news spreads that a great monk has attained to the *arahant* status, his followers are aroused to great excitement and an awed recitation of his marvelous virtues.[3] The more saintly the monk is, the more virtues he is believed to possess, and the more sacred powers he is held to radiate. Thus the *arahant* ideal still glows as the jewel in the lotus of the Buddhist religion.

In the past history of Southeast Asian kingdoms one can see evidences of periodic royal fascination with forest monks, who were valued for their capacity to mediate between competing factions within the ecclesiastical establishment at the capital, or to serve as missionary pioneers who might travel with the flag into newly colonized frontier regions and thereby play a "civilizing" role on behalf of newly founded empires and dynasties. In recent times certain forest-monk meditation masters have figured conspicuously in the national scene in Thailand. The king and queen, the crown

2. In Southeast Asian countries a galaxy of *arahants* have been recognized, many of them being the most famous of the Buddha's own disciples. Examples are: Sāriputta, the "right hand" disciple of the Buddha, famous for his wisdom as propounder of the *abhidhamma;* Moggallāna, the "left hand" disciple of the Buddha, famous for the supranormal powers (*iddhi*) that accrue to those who engage in deep meditation; Ānanda, the Buddha's favorite disciple and master of the *Suttas;* Upāli, the expert on the disciplinary code (*Vinaya*); Rāhula, the Buddha's son who was eager for spiritual release; Revata, the younger brother of Sāriputta, known as a specialist forest monk and kind of foil to Ānanda, who was popular among the laity; and Mahākassapa, the elder who presided over the First Council and was reclusive by preference. In Burma, traditionally, others as well have been canonized and woven into local myths, legends, and festivals, notably Upagutta, Gavampati, and Sīvali.

3. John P. Ferguson remarks in his essay "The Arahat Ideal in Modern Burmese Buddhism" (unpublished paper, presented at the Annual Meeting of the Association for Asian Studies, 1977) that in Burma — and this would be true of Thailand as well — "The arahat ideal . . . exists as the ultimate model for any living monk, and the more saintly the monk, the more likely he will be assigned miraculous powers by his supporters."

prince, the ruling generals and ministers, and the managers of the largest banking and business houses have all sought these *arahants* in their remote habitations and have bowed before them, hoping to be edified and strengthened by their visits to them.[4]

In this essay I will describe the life that has brought such attention to monks in contemporary Thailand, but in order to make that life understandable I must first travel back in time to highlight the classical paradigm of the *arahant*'s salvation path. This route to salvation is outlined in the *Visuddhimagga*, which lists the virtues and capacities that the adept acquires as a result of following the path.

THE CLASSICAL PARADIGM

The *Visuddhimagga* (Path of Purification) was written in the fifth century A.D. by Buddhaghosa.[5] The book, which contains a detailed manual for meditation masters, is usually regarded as a principal noncanonical authority of the Theravāda school. It brilliantly illustrates the tenet that knowledge and practice are intertwined, and that wisdom in the abstract cannot be measured except through disciplined conduct. The *Visuddhimagga* is even today the authoritative source for the practice of meditation by Thai monks; virtually all manuals in use directly or ultimately derive from it.

The text sets out the dynamic relations between three kinds of practice: *sīla* (virtue), *samādhi* (concentration), and *prajñā* (insight or understanding). For monks the practice of *sīla* consists of the conscientious observance of the 227 disciplinary rules as set out in the *Vinaya*. *Sīla* emphasizes restrained behavior toward one's fellow monks and toward the laity, and underscores "the closing of the sense doors" and "the restraint of the faculties" as a prerequisite for the undertaking of the meditational exercises.

The meditational exercises are discussed under the rubrics *samādhi* (concentration) and *prajñā* or *vipassanā* (insight). *Samādhi* is training in reaching an intensity and depth of focus vividly described as "one-pointedness" of mind. The practice of *samādhi* bears the fruits of serenity, tranquility, and states of bliss. The book enumerates forty meditation subjects — ranging from *kasiṇas*, breathing in and out, to the contemplation of decaying corpses. These subjects are correlated with two factors: the temperaments of the meditators and the desired level of meditative consciousness, there being eight levels in all.

4. Thus a few years ago the king and queen flew from Bangkok to the Northeast to attend the mortuary rites of a famous forest saint called Acharn Fan, and another meditation master made the reverse trip to the capital by plane at the invitation of the crown prince. He camped out under his umbrella on the grounds of the crown prince's palace, and the prince daily carried food to him and received moral instruction from him.

5. See Bhikkhu Ñāṇamoli, *The Path of Purification (Visuddhimagga)* (Colombo, Sri Lanka: Semage, 1956).

Vipassanā is the path that produces understanding and wisdom, which are typically gained through the contemplation of one's body, feelings, mind, and mental formations, and the progress therefrom to the realization of the four noble truths concerning the nature, origin, and dissolution of suffering. Finally one ascends to *nibbāna*, the "signless state" of liberation, salvation, and void.

Samādhi and *vipassanā* are asymmetrically related, and the two practices usually have to be coupled before an aspirant can attain truth and end suffering. But the practice of *samādhi* alone cannot lead to *nibbāna*, while *vipassanā*, though it is usually preceded by the *samādhi* path, can be entered upon separately and directly.

DHŪTAṄGA PRACTICES

Now I want to highlight two phenomena discussed in the *Visuddhimagga* — namely, the *dhūtaṅga* (ascetic practices) and *iddhi* (supranormal powers). In the course of time these two facets have become widely linked with the forest monk vocation and with the technology of meditation in the Buddhist traditions of Southeast Asia. Indeed the *dhūtaṅga* practices, considered optional for monks in general, have become the hallmark of the wandering forest monk. They are so spectacularly conspicuous in the eye of the lay beholder that they effectively serve as diacritical markers of the forest monk's vocation.

The thirteen *dhūtaṅga* practices help the adept "shake off defilement." For instance, the refuse-rag-wearer's practice implies that a monk should use rags and discarded cloth for his robes. The alms-eater's practice stipulates that he eat only food that has been received as alms. The house-to-house-seeker's practice expects the strict monk to beg from all homes irrespective of their status and wealth; this impartiality on his part earns for him the name "gapless wanderer." The bowl-food-eater's practice implies that the monk receive all kinds of food in the same bowl and eat the food all mixed up, so as not to savor individual tastes. The forest-dweller's practice entails that the monk should live in the forest, not in human settlements such as villages and towns. The charnel-ground-dweller's practice recommends the contemplation of decomposing corpses in cemeteries as a way of exorcising fears and coming to understand dispassionately the processes of growth, death, and decay that shape us all.

The *dhūtaṅga* practices thus project in sharp relief the differences between the monk's ascetic regime and the lay householder's mode of life. The rules that the ascetic observe no social distinctions between houses as "the gapless wanderer," that he live without a roof over his head as a forest dweller, or that he possess the bare minimum of clothes and not amass possessions tell us, not only that he is removed from lay society, but also that he can be counted on to maintain his neutrality, impartiality, and ultimately his universal compassion for all beings by avoiding all durable and compulsory reciprocities with the laity.

Moreover, the ascetic monk strives for controlled experiences that set him apart from the layman's life of indulging the senses. Virtue for the monk demands that the senses be controlled, that wishes be made few, and that social intercourse be strictly limited. But, on the other hand, the monk also erases and supersedes the layman's cognitive and affective maps by crossing the boundaries that regulate lay life — its social and territorial spaces, culinary distinctions, and categorizations of what is true and what is not. The ascetic eats very sparingly, mixes all foods in one bowl to fuse tastes, wears discarded clothes, and wanders about the forest. Thus at the same time that the ascetic closes the sense doors that are in a layman left open, he also breaks open the layman's social codes and dissolves man-made cultural categories by which a layman orders the world and reifies it into a durable reality. A necessary corollary of the ascetic monk's resolution not to reify things is that he become a mindful observer of the processual character of life — its growth, decay, and dissolution. And what fitter subject does the monk have for contemplation than the human body itself, and what better viewing ground than a site of cremation?

IDDHI (SUPRANORMAL POWERS)

According to the *Visuddhimagga* the *iddhi* or supranormal powers become available in the course of meditative practice. They are produced as a result of passing from grosser material states of consciousness to the higher, "form-less" states. They are thus fruits of concentration. The Pali term *iddhi-vidha* literally means "kinds of success"; *iddhis* are the results of employing effective means, efficacies resulting from effort. *Iddhis* should not, therefore, be too facilely associated with "miracles" as the term is understood in Christianity. Miracles are a function of God's sovereignty, providence, and omnipotence; in a miracle God suspends the normal physical laws that govern nature. Buddhist *iddhis*, by contrast, are special powers that become available to the adept who attains to higher meditative levels because he is able to transcend and therefore encompass the lower realms of materiality and causality.

In contemporary Buddhist Southeast Asia the supranormal powers that become available to the adept are a focus of great interest and elaboration not only for the practitioners themselves but also for the public at large. Such *iddhi* powers include the following:

1. "Having been one, he becomes many." The adept becomes able to assume multiple forms, to appear and to vanish, and to reveal what is hidden, as the Buddha himself was able to part the sky and show the Brahma heavens to his devotees.

2. By means of "the divine ear" the adept can hear both divine and human sounds — sounds far off in another world-sphere as well as sounds occurring nearby.

3. The adept is able to penetrate the minds of other beings and persons.
4. He can recollect his past lives, transpiring over incalculable aeons of time.
5. He is blessed with "the divine eye," the knowledge of the passing away and reappearance of things. This is the power that makes possible a cosmic vision, by means of which one can witness the cycles through which the cosmos is formed and dissolved.

These *iddhi* powers are especially the fruits of *samādhi* concentration, in which the adept progresses through eight levels of consciousness. The "take-off," so to speak, is achieved at the fourth level, when the adept's body becomes light and malleable, "light as a tuft of cotton." At this point he experiences bliss and resolves to undergo further transformations. The adept is able, in addition, to recollect the past: starting with the memory of proximate events, his memory traverses through numerous births, and an infinite regress of this kind ultimately and cumulatively amounts to a full recall of the formation and dissolution of the cosmos. The basic transformations are from material to formless states; proximate events to remote events; familiar human sounds to faraway, subtle divine sounds.

An important implication of this meditative path is that the mental map of consciousness internal to the human adept is made homologous with and parallel to the cosmography of the world system, such that in the end personal and cosmic events are amalgamated. As the meditative path proceeds upward to cosmic reality and then downward to ordinary everyday reality, there is a striking parallel to the Buddhist story of the creation and dissolution of the cosmos as told in the canonical *Aggañña Suttanta* and in the medieval Thai cosmological treatise, the *Traibhūmikathā* (which acknowledges the influence of the *Visuddhimagga*).[6]

Finally we come to an interesting and ambiguous matter that has had vital implications for the motivation of meditative adepts down the ages. On the one hand, doctrinal strictures warn a monk against the danger of being seduced into enjoying the supranormal powers of *iddhi*, since that would obstruct his further progress toward salvation. Furthermore, a monk's false claim that he possesses these superior powers of the *arahant* is listed as one of the four principal *pārājika* offenses as set out in the *Vinaya* codes. At the same time, however, the *Visuddhimagga* celebrates the Buddha and his disciples,

---

6. In the text of the *Visuddhimagga* itself, for example, the destruction of the world system by fire at a certain level of the Brahma heavens, and the subsequent materialization of the world therefrom, is the exact reverse of meditative ascent to the fourth *jhānic* level and the leap from there into the subtle, ethereal, mind-made transformation.

For an analysis of the *Aggañña Suttanta*, the canonical genesis story, see Stanley Tambiah, *World Conqueror and World Renouncer* (Cambridge, England: Cambridge University Press, 1976), chap. 2. The *Traibhūmikathā* has recently been translated into English by Frank and Mani Reynolds, *Three Worlds According to King Ruang, A Thai Buddhist Cosmology* (Berkeley and Los Angeles: University of California Press, 1982).

especially Mahā Moggallāna, as marvelous exponents of *iddhi* feats. The following account, for instance, is familiar to innumerable Thai Buddhists:

> The Buddha lifted his feet and placed them on the summits of Mount Sineru and Mount Yugandhara, took up residence during the rainy season retreat on the Red Marble Terrace, and delivered his illuminating discourse on the *Abhidhamma* to the "deities of the ten thousand spheres." Then he informed the god Sakka of his intention to return to the human world, and the gods built "three flights of stairs, one of gold, one of silver, and one of crystal," so that the Buddha could descend, flanked by the deities.[7]

As we shall see, the themes that we have sketched in the *Visuddhimagga*, especially those concerning the *dhūtaṅga* ascetic practices and the contemplative technology producing *iddhis*, have a direct bearing on contemporary traditions concerning forest monks in Thailand and, by extension, Burma.

THE EXEMPLARY SAINT, ACHARN MAN, AND HIS LINE OF DISCIPLES

In contemporary Thailand most of the prominent forest monk meditation masters claim a link with a famous ascetic monk called Acharn Man, who was born in 1870 and died in 1943. He is the subject of popular legends and popular biographies in a Buddhist hagiographical style that is commonly encountered in Burma and Thailand. The most famous of these biographies was composed by a disciple, Acharn Maha Boowa, who is himself the founder of a well-known meditation hermitage on the outskirts of the town of Udorn in Northeast Thailand.

The galaxy of disciples who trace their "lineage" to their Master, Acharn Man, and who have established a loose network of monasteries at the peripheries of the country include the following: Acharn Fan of Sakhon Nakhaun, who died recently and whose mortuary rites were attended by the king and queen; Luang Pu Waen of Chiangmai, who is today the most sought-after saintly monk for the sacralization of amulets; Acharn Chaa of Ubon, who many would claim heads the most famous of the current meditation-teaching monasteries; Acharn Maha Boowa of Udorn, the biographer of Acharn Man and himself a recognized meditation teacher; and Acharn Thet of Nongkhai, who enjoys a similar reputation.

THE BIOGRAPHY OF ACHARN MAN[8]

As one might expect, Acharn Maha Boowa's biography of the Master is much shaped by hagiographical conventions, both literary and artistic. At the same

7. This paraphrase is indebted to Ñāṇamoli, *The Path;* quotations are from p. 428 of that work.

8. See Acharn Maha Boowa, *The Venerable Phra Acharn Mun Bhuridatta Thera, Meditation Master,* trans. Siri Buddhasukh (Bangkok: Mahamakut Rajavidyalaya Press, 1976).

time, however, the work is biographical in a meaningful sense: it includes many particulars about the life and person of Acharn Man. A fascinating problem is posed by this kind of text. On the one hand, the biography has been written retrospectively by a devoted disciple and it incorporates into the saint's life some aspects of the career (itself "mythologized") of the founder of the religion, Gotama Buddha. On the other hand, the saint himself clearly intended to mold his life to follow the ideal career of the founder and reproduced in his own milieu features of acts associated with the Buddha. Moreover, both the saint's life and its depiction by his disciple are influenced by the lives of a host of Buddhist saints, which themselves embody the same dialectic. If a hagiographical masterpiece is the account of a masterly life written by a masterly disciple, then Acharn Maha Boowa's work is certainly a masterpiece. It creates a marvelous fusion between the timeless, stereotypical features of a Buddhist saint's life and the colorful, particular, contingent features that accompany a life really lived — in a particular country and a particular epoch.[9]

Acharn Man was a peripatetic monk who wandered in and out of the forests of Laos and North and Northeast Thailand. He operated on the periphery of the country, territorially and socially, circulating among the remote, poor, and dispersed villages of the frontier provinces. Though ideally, according to the *Visuddhimagga*, a student of meditation should have a friendly teacher and guide (*kalyāṇamitta*), Acharn Man lacked one. His achievement of salvation was instead the result of a personal quest involving much trial and error and suffering. Yet this solitary man attracted numerous disciples, whom he inspired to form a multitude of fraternal cells. Though he was typically a lonely wanderer in the earlier part of his quest, Man would on occasion emerge from secluded meditation into the world of peasants and villages. At times he even visited urban areas to preach sermons and teach meditation, as when he reactivated an old *wat*, Wat Chedi Luang, in the historic city of Chiangmai.

Man's biography portrays his achievement of sainthood as occurring in two phases. First, after an initial phase of wandering, Man went into a period of seclusion, contemplation, and trance in the famous cave of Sarika, where he attained to the first stage of the *arahant*'s progress, that of "stream-enterer."[10] He then left the cave and spent some years wandering, teaching, and meditating. The second phase began with another period of intense, secluded contemplation in a high mountain cave in the wilds of Chiangmai in

9. Another Buddhist masterpiece I would identify as a notable achievement is the biography of Milarepa. See W. Y. Evans-Wentz, ed., *Tibet's Great Yogi Milarepa, A Biography from the Tibetan Being the Jetsun-Kahbum or Biographical History of Jetsun Milarepa, According to the Late Lama Kazi Dawa-Samdup's English Rendering* (London: Oxford University Press, 1978).

10. There are four stages or stations in the *arahant*'s progress: namely, stream-enterer, once-returner (that is, one last birth in the world before attaining *nibbāna*), nonreturner, and final fulfillment as *arahant*.

northern Thailand. There Man made the leap from the state of "non-returner" into fully enlightened arahantship. Once that was achieved, Man descended from the mountain and began his last extended tour of teaching. He is portrayed as a great and stirring teacher, who combined oratorical skills with austere ascetic practices. Subjecting his disciples to these ascetic practices, he insisted that they follow a strict regime that included begging for food, eating only one meal a day, mixing all kinds of food in the same bowl, and observing long periods of isolated contemplation. He limited "socializing" between monks to assemblies held at meal times or gatherings convened to hear sermons and homilies.

Much of the peripatetic wandering of the Master was undertaken during the dry summer months, when he and his traveling circle of disciples would take up brief residence near an isolated peasant village, and then move on to another. (Since no Buddhist monk in the Theravāda tradition is allowed to grow and cook his own food, he must always, even when meditating in lonely places, be within walking distance of settled villages so as to receive donations of food from the laity.) During the rainy season (*vassa*) of about three months, however, the disciplinary code (*vinaya*) stipulates that a monk must take up a single continuous residence. Each year Acharn Man would choose a different village *wat* for his retreat, and he would use the time for intensively training a large circle of monks and novices in the art of meditation. They would come from various nearby monasteries and daily congregate in the *wat* where the master had established his base.

We should appreciate the significance of this pattern of disseminating teachings and gathering followers on the part of ascetic *dhūtaṅga* wandering monks, who allegedly walk "lonely as a rhinoceros" in the jungles. Though a wandering adept steeped in *dhūtaṅga* practices and the techniques of meditation, Acharn Man established over the years cells of disciples in dispersed places. When they matured, these same disciples in turn started their own hermitages and attracted their own young disciples. Thus over time there emerged a series of parent hermitages and daughter houses, which constituted a loose, sprawling network of hermitages constructed out of master-pupil relationships.

Such relationships cannot, however, exist in a vacuum. These ascetic wanderers are ever dependent for food, medicine, and robes on the laity, and for that reason they are always in contact with rural folk — even if this contact is limited to begging and sporadic preaching. These lay folk develop great respect for the virtuosi who travel in their midst and in fact believe in their virtues, their capacity to show loving-kindness and compassion (*mettā* and *karuna*), and their ability to exercise supranormal powers (*iddhi*). Such laypeople circulate stories about the monks, attest their achievements, and initiate at the grass roots level the impetus that in due course builds up a regional and even national reputation. Once a monk becomes known on that scale, established powers at the capital are apt to become interested in appropriating some of the holy man's charisma for their own purposes. How does a peripatetic, meditating forest monk become recognized as a charismatic person and saint in the society at large? Such recognition is achieved by a widening, interacting series of pathways connecting cells of ordained monk-disciples and an outer penumbra of ordinary laity.

Let us return to the biography of Acharn Man. Its second part contains a rich, colorful, and sometimes hair-raising description of the Master's meditation experiences and other exploits. These include dialogues with and sermons to Sakka (Indra), the king of the gods, who reigns atop Mount Meru surrounded by his retinue of deities and divine angels; encounters with demons, *nāga* kings, and wandering ghosts (*pretas*), resulting in their conversion to the Buddhist *dhamma;* and the seeing of prophetic visions and the exercise of supranormal powers. The latter imply the ability to recall past lives, to assess future events and their consequences, and to read the minds of other persons — a faculty the Master exercised to the discomfort of his disciples whenever they were assailed by errant thoughts and desires.

Another notable set of encounters documented in detail and with some relish are those in which the Master pacified wild animals — fierce tigers, threatening elephants, screaming monkeys, and poisonous snakes — through his exercise of his cosmic love (*mettā*). These stories also include references to the Master's ability to speak to the animals in a kind of silent or nonverbal metalanguage described in the text as "the language of the mind, which is superior to all the languages in the Three Worlds."[11] The meanings conveyed by these confrontations between a nonviolent forest saint and the fierce creatures of untamed nature are striking. The tiger, for instance, embodies wild ferocious power and represents to Thai Buddhists the intensity of animal desires and defilements. By pacifying it, the monk is understood not only to subdue but to incorporate its powers. In a sense the ascetic monk and tiger are similar in that both are forest creatures, situated outside society. But the ascetic transcends the animal state and incorporates and transmutes its lower passions and gross energies. Thus these exchanges between renouncer and animal portray relations of similarity, contrast, encompassment, and transformation.

The final part of the biography of Acharn Man consists of his *parinibbāna,* his passing away. The Master knows beforehand of his impending death, prepares for it, and dies surrounded by his monastic disciples and lay devotees. This account contains certain close resemblances to episodes in the Buddha's own life. The hagiographical tradition is thus conspicuous when the saint's passing away and the subsequent mortuary rites are portrayed. Acharn Man dies, as did the Buddha, at the age of eighty; he dies, too, lying on his right side in "the lion's posture." His cremation is reminiscent of the cremation rites staged for the Buddha and described in the *Mahāparinibbāna*

---

11. Acharn Maha Boowa, *The Venerable Phra Acharn Mun,* 191.

Sutta. During the cremation the miracle of the rain cloud occurs, as it did when the Buddha departed this life. "Just as the fire was lit," says the text, "a small cloud appeared in the summer sky, and suddenly the cremation area was cooled by a drizzle that lasted fifteen minutes,"[12] and then the moonlit sky was bright and clear as before. The following day the ashes and bones of Acharn Man were collected and distributed as relics to various persons, and the biography concludes by describing miraculous things that happened: grains of ashes turned into crystals and jewels because, as the text explains, the mind of an *arahant* is absolutely purified and therefore can effect the transformation of the physical body.

ACHARN MAN: THE CONTOURS OF THE BUDDHIST EXEMPLARY SAINT

As mentioned earlier, Acharn Man had several pupils, who have become famous meditation masters in their turn and have established their own hermitages, each with branches of its own. In addition, surrounding the Master were two circles of followers: the inner circle, made up of his ordained disciples, and the outer circle, a penumbra of rural lay supporters. These two circles acted dialectically and cumulatively to produce the recognition of the forest monk as saint and to spread his saintly reputation.

When analyzing the role of the forest monk *arahant,* we must see two modalities and emphases. On the one hand, the *arahant* is a meditation master and teacher who combines knowledge with practice and has a "professional," exemplary relationship with his monastic disciples. He resides with them, takes them on his begging rounds, teaches them both the *dhamma* and the technology of meditation, and leads them through the path of purification. In all, he provides for them a model of the salvation seeker in the classical mode — someone to imitate and cathect upon, someone whose example they can interiorize. He is a role model for his ordained professional disciples.

On the other hand, this same *arahant* saint has a second circle of relationships — with lay devotees — and his significance in that context is quite different. The laity see him primarily as a "field of merit" (*puññak khetta*) in which they can cultivate and make merit through donations of food and material gifts (*dāna*). Although many of them congregate around him to listen to his homilies and even at times to engage in brief collective meditation sittings conducted by him, their main orientation to him is as a religious virtuoso, who has trodden an arduous, specialized, highly venerated path that contrasts markedly with the cares, ambitions, worries, and sinfulness in which their ordinary lives are enmeshed. In this light they are likely to see the saint as a radiant person who can cast his blessings upon the laity and

12. Ibid., 227.

transmit part of his charisma to them, very much in the mode of *darśan*, the visual interaction so well known to students of Hinduism.

In the spectrum of activities, capacities, and reputations associated with the Master there are two poles: the "rationalist" and the "tantric." The "rationalist" pole is represented by the "pure virtuoso," who is dedicated to the practice of meditation, who contemplates the philosophical truth that all the world is characterized by flux and dependent origination, and who cultivates the wisdom of *nibbāna*. One might say, echoing Max Weber's words, that the rationalist path portrays the extraordinary metaphysical achievement of Buddhism, which unites a "virtuoso-like self-redemption by man's own effort" with a salvation universally accessible and ties "contemplation as the path to salvation" to "an inner-worldly vocational ethic."[13] In this aspect the virtuoso shies away from the attentions and demands of the laity, devalues the cult of images and amulets, and deemphasizes merit-making rites. He has no desire for his hermitage to become a place of social gathering for the laity.

The "tantric" pole exists within the same virtuoso but describes the cosmic love he develops for people at large: he wants to convey to them some part of his mystic experience and psychic conquest. To echo Max Weber again, the tantric path represents the cultivation of a cosmic brotherliness and shows one way to escape the man-made cage of estrangement and alienation from one's fellow human beings and dependence on the inexorable power of material goods. In this aspect the virtuoso, as a man who has achieved charismatic powers, wishes to give all beings a taste of calm bliss, a measure of relief from their physical and mental sufferings. This sympathy causes the man of illumination to yield under pressure from the laity and to transfer his virtues to them through ritual action.

Now the Master under discussion, Acharn Man, was no crude dispenser of charms or amulets; he was a purist, a rationalist, and a practitioner of meditation. Yet he also affirmed his mystical experiences and visions, which were attested by his disciples, and was also driven to be a preacher who not only instructed his monastic disciples but also occasionally addressed vast gatherings of laypeople. He was acclaimed as an *arahant* in his lifetime, and this reputation rested on both aspects: his ascetic life and orthodox practices, on the one hand, and tantric experiences and supranormal feats, on the other. Given this fact, one might have expected that what was a single spectrum of divergent tendencies in the Master might become polarized orientations in the disciples, some abjuring the world in forest retreats, others welcoming its attentions. And in fact in some measure this has happened. As a cult developed around Acharn Man's relics after his death, and amulets stamped with his image began to be widely distributed, a certain group of Man's famous

13. *From Max Weber: Essays in Sociology*, trans. and ed. H. H. Gerth and C. Wright Mills (London: Routledge and Kegan Paul, 1948), 358.

disciples became centrally implicated in the cult, while others stayed away. The "worldly" ones bless these amulets, which the laity then regard as objectifications of their virtues and supranormal powers—objects capable, therefore, of furthering their worldly interests.[14]

THE CULT OF AMULETS

Traditionally in Thailand many kinds of sacralized objects (*khrūeang rāng*) are invested with supranormal power and are therefore the foci of devout attention. Examples include Buddha images, large and small; amulets in the form of medallions and clay tablets bearing the imprints of the Buddha, deities, and famous monks; and flags and pieces of cloth bearing *yantra* designs. The amulets currently being sacralized by famous forest saints and meditation masters such as Luang Pu Waen usually take the form of metal medallions, with the monk's face or bust imprinted on one side and the insignia of the lay sponsor—be it royalty, famous generals, or prosperous banks—on the other side. These amulets, then, are the product of a combined effort. The saintly monk allows himself to be represented iconically and is willing to sacralize the amulets, and the lay sponsor contributes or collects the funds necessary for minting the medallions and for staging the rites of sacralization. In recognition of these efforts, lay sponsors earn the right to have their insignias imprinted on the back of the amulet.

The forest monk transfers power (*saksit*) to the amulets in two ways. He chants sacred words, including *paritta* chants, which are thought to confer protection or prosperity upon the audience. In the case of amulets associated with Luang Pu Waen a cord is attached to the pile of amulets and held by the chanting monk, who confers potency to the amulets. He sits in meditation, engages in concentration (*samādhi*), and transfers some of his psychic energy through the cord. Similar rites for the consecration, animation, and activation of Buddha images have been performed traditionally in Southeast Asia. One phase of these consecration rituals (*buddha abhiseka*) is the opening of the image's eyes. The rites also typically include the recitation of the Buddha's biography—his victories and his triumphs—so that, once consecrated, the image is thought to radiate the Buddha's virtues and powers. The amulets of living saints—famous monks—do the same thing, transferring charisma to persons and objects through ritualized techniques. We may refer to this phenomenon as the objectification of charisma. It is known that the religious virtuoso is imbued with loving-kindness (*mettā*) for all humanity, and that his cosmic love enables him to cast his blessings on all in the spirit of detached action. If his charisma can be embodied in objects, it can more efficiently influence a layperson's worldly pursuits. Of course, the blessing of amulets

---

14. This cult of amulets in contemporary Thailand in which some forest monk "saints" participate is described at length in Tambiah, *The Buddhist Saints*, 195–289.

and talismans by holy men is no Buddhist peculiarity. In many religions the saints' or martyrs' tattered possessions, broken bones, or ash are credited with miraculous powers. It is tempting, therefore, to take up this issue as posing a general problem in the sociology of religion.

COMPARATIVE POINTS

At this point I would like to draw attention to Ernst Troeltsch's characterization of the way in which the medieval Christian Church redistributed the supernumerary good works of its ascetics as a process of "vicarious oblation" and "circulation of grace." These terms aptly illuminate the way in which the Buddhist ascetic saint's virtues are radiated to his devotees. Writes Troeltsch:

> The idea of vicarious repentance and achievement is really a living category of religious thought; the vicarious offering of Christ both as a punishment and as a source of merit is only a special instance of a general conception. . . . Thus the duty of those who live "in the world" towards the whole is that of preserving and procreating the race — a task in which ascetics cannot share, while they for their part have the duty of showing forth the ideal in an intensified form, and of rendering service through intercession, penitence and the acquisition of merit. This is the reason for the enormous gifts and endowments to monasteries; men wanted to make certain of their own part in the oblation offered by monasticism.[15]

Whereas Troeltsch makes it quite clear that in the "organic" whole of Catholicism a variety of tendencies already present in the early Gospels — ascetic, secular, and theocratic — existed side by side in a cosmos of mutual recognition, asceticism never occupied a position of supremacy in the medieval Church. In the Buddhist cosmos of callings, however, ascetic, contemplative renunciation is the apical exemplary calling, and the basis of the Buddhist saint's claim to special recognition has to be fitted into a comparative typology of charisma, more ample than that provided by Weber, whose fundamental paradigm, despite his comparative work, remained a Christian one.[16]

Other traditions come closer to the Buddhist case in certain respects than the Christian does. Surprisingly, one can look to the history of Judaism for an apt comparison. I have in mind Gershom Scholem's discussion of the Hasidic *tsaddiqim* venerated from the mid-eighteenth century onward.[17] Here was a group of saints of an ascetic, mystical, and contemplative kind, who achieved the highest virtues of their religious tradition and were celebrated as the

---

15. Ernst Troeltsch, *The Social Teachings of the Christian Churches*, trans. Olive Wyon, vol. 1 (New York: Free Press, 1949), 239–40.

16. I have attempted this in Chapter 21 of *The Buddhist Saints.*

17. Gershom G. Scholem, *Major Trends in Jewish Mysticism* (New York: Schocken, 1941). See also the foregoing essay by Robert Cohn in this volume.

radiating centers for the lives of their lay congregations. As the Hasidic movement sought to reinterpret the world of *kabbalah* so that it would be accessible to the masses, it acclaimed a new type of leader, the illuminate, "the man whose heart had been touched and changed by God,"[18] who was the very opposite of the ideal type of learned rabbi, the *talmid ḥakham*. Whereas the latter, as student of the Torah, was expected to display a deep knowledge of the Holy Law, which he could interpret to the community as the eternal and immutable word of God, the *tsaddiq* showed forth an inner moral revival. An inspired preacher and man of the holy spirit, he presented the secrets of the divine realm in the guise of mystical psychology, demonstrating that:

> It is by descending into the depths of his own self that man wanders through all the dimensions of the world; in his own self he lifts the barriers which separate one sphere from the other; in his own self, finally, he transcends the limits of natural existence and at the end of his way, without, as it were, a single step beyond himself, he discovers that God is "all in all" and there is "nothing but Him."[19]

It is worthwhile quoting *in extenso* Scholem's comment on this Hasidic "mysticism of the personal life":

> The whole development centers round the personality of the Hasidic saint; this is something entirely new. *Personality* takes the place of *doctrine;* what is lost in rationality by this change is gained in efficacy. The opinions particular to the exalted individual are less important than his character, and mere learning, knowledge of the Torah, no longer occupies the most important place in the scale of religious ideas. A tale is told of a famous saint who said: "I did not go to the 'Maggid' of Meseritz to learn Torah from him but to watch him tie his boot-laces." . . . The new ideal of the religious leader, the Zaddik, differs from the traditional ideal of rabbinical Judaism, the *Talmid Hakham* or student of the Torah, mainly in that he himself "has become Torah."[20]

In the light of the foregoing examples drawn from a limited strand in Catholicism and from a particular version of Jewish Hasidism, I find it interesting to probe whether, despite the obvious differences between the Buddhist, Christian, and Jewish traditions, one may find some general traits that draw together saints of the ascetical, mystical, contemplative type irrespective of the religious traditions in which they appear. In particular I am thinking of a quality of personal life that separates the Thai forest monk meditation masters from the "establishment" monks devoted to the vocation of books and to administering the ecclesiastical organization. Though they are outside the "establishment" and marginal to the ecclesiastical and government centers, they are, by another mode of counting within the doctrinal

18. Scholem, *Major Trends*, 328–29.
19. Scholem, *Major Trends*, 336.
20. Scholem, *Major Trends*, 339.

traditions of Buddhism, the greatest achievers. Like the Hasidic *tsaddiqim* and the ascetic saints referred to by Troeltsch, these forest monk saints are typically "illuminates." Rather than creating doctrine, they bring doctrine to life, especially for their lay communities. They are capable of circulating their grace and radiating their charisma as quintessential achievers of the highest values of their faith. In the end the personal, interiorized, mystical illumination of the saints in all three traditions is seen as flooding the vast spaces of the world with their cosmic love. In this sense religion is embodied in and proceeds from them, just as they, as individuals, interiorize the whole of religion.

EIGHT

Saints and Virtue in African Islam:
An Historical Approach

Lamin Sanneh

In 1893, André Gide visited Africa, desirous of resolving certain epicurean conflicts of the flesh while also obtaining the serenity of spirit with which virtue is prone to visit her children. He testified:

> The demands of my flesh did not know how to dispense with the consent of my spirit. . . . I saw at last that this discordant dualism might resolve itself into harmony. At once it became clear to me that this harmony should be my supreme aim. When in October '93 I embarked for Africa, it was . . . towards this golden fleece that my drive precipitated itself.[1]

Gide's carnal conflicts would strain the resources of most religions, but if any tradition could have met his needs, perhaps it was indeed African Islam, whose saints are so adept at mollifying the flesh without at the same time foregoing the spirit's consolation. In Africa, Gide's instinctive wish to transcend the conflict between flesh and spirit could be greeted as sound, even if the peculiar fierceness and introspective individualism with which he addressed it would continue to set him apart. His colorful excursions into the fleshpots of Morocco were not at bottom incompatible with the rather earthy understanding of virtue that prevails in Islamic Africa.

The saint in African Islam is distinguished by a strong social orientation rather than by retreat into the comtemplative life. The cultivation of virtue is in fact the cultivation of society, of the company of persons. The goal of the saintly life can be said to be the regard and devotion of the community, not the accumulation of charismatic power in the individual, as I shall attempt to show in later parts of this essay. The saint thus comes to embody the spirit of society — its scarcity and plenitude, its torments and triumphs, its egalitarianism and privilege, its materialism and spirituality, its esteem for tradition

1. André Gide, *Si le grain ne meurt,* cited in Ernest Gellner, *Muslim Society* (London: Cambridge University Press, 1983), 151.

and disposition toward innovation, and in one example we shall consider, its tendency toward messianic agitation and its need for prudent accommodation. The saints of African Islam may combine extremes and even espouse extremism, but they do so without forsaking the world.

Saintly virtue rests on this paradox of apparent spiritual extremism tied to a wisdom about what the world demands. The saint is at home in the confines of everyday routine, showing forth virtue by being unburdened by the world. If a saint gives up the material comforts of home, it may be only to seek similar conditions in unfamiliar surroundings. Thus material life is not disdained; rather, it is elevated to a higher plane. The body is not despised; rather, its gratification now earns meritorious favor as the saint's attention to the needs of the body displays his virtue. The extreme of self-denial (*zuhd*) evokes its fulfillment in the extreme of social eminence (*jāh*) and worldly acclaim.

I shall begin this essay with a consideration of the scriptural sources concerning sainthood in Islam and move from there to a study of sequential expressions of saintliness that emerged in North and West Africa as Islam expanded across the continent. In doing so I will distinguish, as Muslims do, between "saintship" (*wilāya*) and "sainthood" (*walāya*). The former concerns the organization and expression of saintly power, while the latter relates to the personality of the saint and the dynamics of saintly power. "Saintship" may thus be bequeathed and perpetuated in an organized fashion, whereas "sainthood" has to be acquired by individuals. "Sainthood" is personal charisma, while "saintship" is institutional charisma; though one may distinguish between the two, they are usually found in patterns of interplay. I shall also draw special attention to the Islamic concept of *baraka* ("favor," "grace") and its transmutation into indigenous social categories. Needless to say, the confines of space will dictate that only a few select items can be chosen to indicate what is typical and distinctive about saintly virtue as it charts a course from the eleventh century to the twentieth in African Islam and from the northern rim of the continent down its western coast.

SCRIPTURAL FOUNDATIONS

The common Arabic word for saint is *walī*, strictly speaking a "friend" or "patron." It occurs numerous times in the Qur'ān with this meaning, often with God being the "friend" or "patron."[2] The Qur'ān's major stress is on God as the only *walī* worthy of trust and dependence (*tawakkul*),[3] but a special place also is reserved for those whom God regards as his friends (*awliyā*).[4] A further step is taken when a forensic meaning is applied to the

2. Qur'ān 2:258; 3:61; 6:51, 69; 17:111; 41:34; 42:7, 27; 45:18; 2:101, 114; 9:75, 117; 13:37; 18:25; 29:21; 32:3; 42:6, 30, 42; 4:77, 122, 173; 6:14; 18:16; 33:17, etc.
3. Ibid. 7:2; 11:22, 115; 13:17; 17:99; 18:48, 102; 25:19; 29:49; 39:4; 42:4, 7, 45; 45:9; 60:1.
4. Ibid. 3:27; 4:91, 138, 143; 5:56, 62, 84; 7:28; 9:23; 10: 63; 60:9.

term and human patrons are given a status in contract law such that they may act as deputies for their clients.[5]

Given this range, there is some Qur'ānic justification for the claim made by and about many of the saints of Islam that God may enter into a relationship of special intimacy with his creatures, so that they hold the status of "friendship" or "nearness in favor" to God. They are close to him: "near ones" (*al-muqarrabūn*), who will receive the superlative reward of Paradise.[6] This word is from the same root (*q.r.b.*) that is at the base of the standard term for a relative or kin (*qurbā*). Making up for the abolition of natural kinship in Islam,[7] the Qur'ān assures believers that God himself will provide for them a next-of-kin, and the word used is the same as that for nearness.[8] Perhaps the most striking image of God's closeness to human beings occurs in the trenchant verse:

> We indeed created man; and We know
> what his soul whispers within him,
> and We are nearer to him [*agrabu ilyahi*] than the
> jugular vein.[9]

In Sufi circles and similar religious contexts, "nearness to God" has come to stand for a life marked by prayer and supererogatory acts of devotion. Consequently, the "saint" is one who leads a life of religious devotion, keeping close to God in prayer, praise, and supplication, and to the people in various acts of mediation and intercession. The "saint" becomes manifest to people after receiving the inner assurance of divine "friendship," although often the public manifestation of sainthood precedes final confirmation of the inner call.

THE ROOTS OF SAINTSHIP IN NORTH AFRICAN ISLAM

Contrary to the standard depiction of many Christian saints, saintly virtue in African Islam was typically cultivated with a militant end in view rather than exclusively for the sake of solitary retreat. From the military redoubts of Northwest Africa men emerged carrying in their hearts disdain for the non-Muslim world and in their hands the sword to overcome it. Ascetic practice (*zuhd*) developed alongside the study of law (*fiqh*), and together they helped sharpen the instruments of armed struggle (*jihād*). The religious recluse would typically occupy his time with the study of juridical sources, seeking in

5. Ibid. 2:282.

6. Ibid. 61:11; 83:21, 28.

7. See, for example, Reuben Levy, *The Social Structure of Islam* (London: Cambridge University Press, 1957; repr. 1965), 55 – 56. Qur' ān 49:13. Bayḍāwī, *Anwār al-Tanzīl*, ed. H. O. Fleischer, vol. 2 (Leipzig: F. C. G. Vogel, 1848), 276.

8. Qur'ān 19:5.

9. Ibid. 50:15. The translation is that of A. J. Arberry, *The Koran Interpreted*, vol. 2 (New York: Macmillan, 1969), 234.

the process to strip local practice of historical and circumstantial accretions and refine it to a purer Islam. Religious leaders thus came naturally to look upon worldly means as a legitimate instrument for their end. One modern authority observes in this regard that whereas elsewhere in the Muslim world the ascetics (*zuhhād*), who abandoned all worldly contact, were pitted against the jurists (*fuqahā*), who were immersed in worldly affairs, in North Africa they made common cause, and many religious figures in fact combined the two functions.

> In Ifriqiya, *fuqahā* became *zuhhād* without ceasing the study of *fiqh*, or cutting off relations with the *fuqahā* who demonstrated no interest in asceticism. As *zuhhād*, however, they did not become detached from the world, and they remained in constant communication with the people. They were guardians of the common people's interests, and challenged the rulers to show regard for these considerations. They were admired by the people for their piety, devotion, and independence with respect to rulers. They were not marginal to the mainstream of Islam in Ifriqiya, but rather its core. They were the true leaders of the people.[10]

Through this synthesis of jurisprudence and asceticism the *jihād* tradition was fomented; holy personages carried it into the citadels of power. Thus in the numerous eruptions of reform and renewal the saintly ideal — that is, the exemplary force of the holy and learned figure — was the ideological trigger and the guide for action. The military application of the doctrine of struggle (*jihād*) had its religious counterpart in the purification and discipline of the flesh (*nafs*), a combination that allowed the ascetic (*zāhid*) to assume leadership of affairs. Ascetic spirituality thus combined the prestige of learning and the power of religion to lay claim to political power.

It was one such religious figure, 'Abd Allah ibn Yaṣīn (d. 1059), who in 1040 C.E. launched the religious revolution in North Africa that was to lead to the establishment of the Almoravid Empire. Ibn Yaṣīn was a commanding, ascetic figure, and the sources describe how he was rewarded with miracles as God's recognition of his saintly stature. Thus the seal of *baraka*, of efficacious virtue, came to be attached to his person, and after his death he became a source of blessings for people who came to his tomb seeking rescue from various pains and obstacles in ordinary life. The Arab chronicler, al-Bakrī, writing in 1068 C.E., recounts how a cult grew up around the tomb of Ibn Yaṣīn.

> On his tomb stands today a mausoleum, which is well frequented, and a hospice [*rābiṭa*] always full of people. . . . Even now a group of them [the Almoravids] would choose to lead them in prayer only a man who prayed behind 'Abd Allah,

---

10. Nehemiah Levtzion, "'Abd Allāh ibn Yaṣīn and the Almoravids," in *Studies in West African Islamic History*, ed. John Ralph Willis, vol. 1 (London: Frank Cass, 1979), 80.

even though a more meritorious and more pious person, who had never prayed under the guidance of 'Abd Allah, was among them.[11]

Al-Bakrī reserves undisguised scorn for Ibn Yaṣīn and his followers, scrutinizing the man's heritage with the unsparing eye of a rigorist. The saintly heritage (*wilāya*) in Islam as a synthesis of *zuhd* and *fiqh*, of renunciation and the code, is held by scholars of orthodoxy (*'ulamā*) to be in excess of accepted guidance, and al-Bakrī represents their position. Yet the saints (*awliyā*) have often been the real architects of the changes that the *'ulamā* idealized in doctrine, thus giving practical expression to the aims of the code. A similar irony characterizes the Almoravid conquest of Spain (Andalusia), where the ascetic ideals of desert life triumphed over the cultured tastes of urban living. The rewards of saintship — victory in God's campaigns — were eloquent vindication of the superiority of virtue, and it is a bold individual who would say which made which: the saints or the rewards.

The legatees of the Almoravids were less equal to the challenge of living in the world and against it at the same time than the Almoravids had been. These were the Almohads, whose initial leader, Ibn Tumart (d. 1130), claimed the title of Mahdi, meaning Messiah, in 1127. He sought to make a firm distinction between *fiqh* and *zuhd*, between religious Thomism and free-wheeling experimentalism — a Thomism that stressed the binding authority of received tradition and an experimentalism that shifted the locus of authority to the individual and his cultivated insights, leading him to claim direct access to truth. In that cleavage he asserted his own towering authority, burdened by few scruples and buoyed by the single idea of a triumphant monotheism. Even in this stern, uncompromising opponent of Ibn Yaṣīn, then, worldly reward was understood to be the natural companion of religious virtue.[12]

The Almoravid movement and its Almohad reaction, feeding on earlier forms of religious activity, together combined to discharge an enduring element of devotion to jurisprudential sources (*'uṣūl al-fiqh*) into the stream of religious life and practice, and from that source Sudani Muslims of sub-Saharan Africa imbibed copiously. By that channel *fiqh* and *zudh* arrived in sub-Saharan Africa. Both Marty and Trimingham are correct in saying that a full-blown cult of saints as practiced in North Africa — centered around the tombs of the holy — did not take root in Black Africa, but other kinds of saint veneration took its place. Classical Islam accommodated itself to and mixed itself with local practice, as represented in charms, amulets, talismans, and

11. Al-Bakri, *Kitāb al-Masālik wa'l-Mamālik* ("Book of Routes and Realms"), ed. M. G. de Slane (Algiers: A. Jourdan, 1913), 168. The most recent annotated edition is N. Levtzion and J. F. P. Hopkins, eds., *Corpus of Early Arabic Sources for West African History* (London: Cambridge University Press, 1981), 74.

12. For a brief but authoritative account of Ibn Tumart, see Duncan Black Macdonald, *The Development of Muslim Theology and Jurisprudence* (Beirut: Khayat Books, 1965).

the whole field of divinatory practice, particularly in oneirology.[13] Amulets and charms with their indigenous associations were interpreted as the tangible vessels of saintly *baraka*. This is not to deny that Islamic law had an inhibiting effect on local needs, for Maliki law, the predominant code in West Africa, emphasizes exoteric (*zāhirī*) authority against esoteric (*bāṭinī*) understanding. But it is fair to say that considerations of legal sobriety, while publicly acknowledged, did not prevent the religious leaders from an equally calculated prudence in yielding to the popular demand for the worldly uses of religion and for saints who could correspond to the popular image of holy men.

CENOBITIC OVERTURES IN WEST AFRICAN ISLAM

The Almohad Empire eventually collapsed, in Spain first (1235) and then in North Africa (1269), although Hafsid rule in Tunisia continued the Almohad line. The religio-political unity of North Africa virtually ceased after the Almohads; the only carryover was the tradition of saintship, which continued unabated. The Sufi orders, inspired by Qādirī devotional materials and by the juristic sources in *fiqh* and *tafsīr* (exegesis), grew in power and influence. The Qādirī order, founded after the twelfth-century scholar and mystic 'Abd al-Qādir al-Gīlānī, spread widely in many parts of the Muslim world, spawning a number of smaller orders that developed their own autonomous rules. One such order was the Shādhiliyāh, founded after Abu'l-Ḥasan al-Shādhilī (1196–1258), although it was his disciple, Ibn 'Aṭa'Allāh (c. 1250–c. 1310), who established and popularized the order in the Maghrib. It had its base in Fez, and in the eighteenth century it was taken from there to sub-Saharan Africa by a returning student.

Our knowledge of the Shādhiliyāh in West Africa has hitherto been extremely fragmentary. Bits and pieces of information, picked up from a disparate spread of sources, are strung together in many accounts without a central organizing idea. The French administrator and scholar, Paul Marty, who published a number of pioneering studies from 1913 onward, drew attention to the presence of the order in French Guinea in a work published in 1921, but he was quick to belittle its religious influence while somewhat inconsistently exaggerating its political threat. The picture he paints is of an order that was haphazardly strewn through hinterland villages, alternately preying on simple folk and exploited by unscrupulous religious agents. Marty's commitment to the position that the cult of saints, so pervasive in North African Islam, was entirely unknown in West African Islam, came to determine his rather superficial handling of the material. Confronted with

---

13. For a good description of this subject in Muslim Africa, see Humphrey J. Fisher, "Dreams and Conversion in Black Africa," in *Conversion to Islam*, ed. Nehemiah Levtzion (New York: Holmes and Meier, 1979), 217–35.

undeniable evidence of both the organizational and devotional strength of the Shādhiliyāh, Marty stumbled after a conspiratorial menace in order to avoid recognizing its genuine religious force. Scholars who have followed him have been equally misled. For example, J. Spencer Trimingham, well known for his pioneering works on African Islam and much else, picked up Marty's view and elaborated it. When he had to deal with the widespread importance of *baraka* among the Shādhiliyāh, Trimingham dismissed it as thinly disguised magic and thus different, in his view, from its North African counterpart.[14] All this led to a very hazy picture of saint veneration in sub-Saharan Islam and suggested that the Sufi orders played little enduring role there.

The truth is quite otherwise. Under Sufi stimulus saintly virtue has been cultivated in a wide variety of situations in West African Islam: in battle, the study, and politics, as well as in marshaling students and disciples and in providing remedies for illness to the general public. The French scholar Vincent Monteil portrays a typical instance as follows:

> A marabout (*walī*) — or perhaps even a mystic — comes to settle in some part of town; as an eremite, his *baraka* renders him fame. He becomes indispensable to the population: he has charge of rain, of harvests, of troops, and of sickness. He intervenes in disputes. He is protector of the weak and the oppressed. He instructs children in the rudiments of the faith. He takes himself a wife from among the leading families, and becomes a *shaykh* or *muqaddam* [religious leader]. The people then build him a *zāwiyah* [religious center].[15]

Such patterns characterized the spread of a number of Sufi orders — the Qādiriyāh, the Tijāniyāh, the Mourides, the Hamalliyāh, and the Shādhiliyāh. Let us take the last, a little-known order, as an example of how saintly virtue had its impact on Islam below the Sahara.[16]

The man responsible for introducing the Shādhiliyāh to West Africa was 'Alī al-Ṣūfī, described in the sources as "the apostle of Shādhilism" in his part of Africa. He received the *wird,* the office of initiation, from a Moroccan spiritual director (*murshid*) in Fez and subsequently brought it to the plateau area of Futa Jallon in Guinea in the eighteenth century. The litanies he bequeathed to his flock emphasized an attachment to Fez as his spiritual birthplace, and his disciples went on to give it a veneration second in importance only to Mecca and Medina. A disciple of 'Ali al-Ṣūfī, Modi Sellu (1760–1813), the political head (*alfa*) of the district of Labé in Futa Jallon, expanded Shādhilism in Labé.

14. J. Spencer Trimingham, *Islam in West Africa* (Oxford: Clarendon Press, 1959), 66, 89–90.

15. Vincent Monteil, *L'Islam noir* (Paris: Seuil, 1964), 137.

16. On the Shādhiliyāh, see my "Islam and French Colonialism in Futa Jallon, Guinea: Tcherno Aliou, the *walī* of Goumba," forthcoming in *The Journal of Asian and African Studies,* University of Haifa, Israel. I am grateful to colleagues who participated in a meeting at the Truman Institute of the Hebrew University in 1983 for comments, criticisms, and supplementary notes on that paper.

Tcherno 'Isma'ila, a student of 'Ali al-Ṣūfī, made the order a political success. ("Tcherno" is a Fula title meaning "scholar" or "learned teacher.") At first he concentrated on broadening and deepening the spiritual resources of the movement, creating a religious center he called Diawia (*zāwiya*). Its focal point was the *missidi,* the word for "mosque" in the Fula language. The *missidi* was then replicated in numerous adjacent communities, resulting in a network of ideologically related centers. Diawia, in Labé, became the prototype, and from there sympathizers ranged far and wide.

The central organizing principle of the Shādhiliyāh *missidi* was the *diaroré* prayer ritual. Tcherno 'Isma'ila developed it as a complex technical exercise directed to both social and religious renewal. Through the discipline of retreat and renunciation, the *'ulamā* gave themselves up to the intoxicating fervor of the *diaroré,* sharing this with a motley crowd of social outcasts, ex-slaves, and economic insolvents. Thus the *missidi* offered a spiritual haven of social relief just as the *diaroré* offered mystical elevation. Through these two, the initiate was adopted into a religious community and invested with a new status. Thus rehabilitated, he upheld the authority of the Shādhilī *'ulamā* in their contest with the older political and religious elite. This bolstered the authority of the masters of *diaroré* while conferring on the disciple a sense of chosenness.

The *diaroré* consisted of the loud incantation of a *dhikr* formula — a cycle of litany "remembering" God in gratitude and expressing his praise — that was recited for several hours without interruption to help induce a state of spiritual intoxication. The more advanced *'ulamā* spent whole nights in *diaroré* retreat, and initiated novices in that setting.

Under the impact of such prayer the *missidi* became a model community — not exactly the *communitas* of Victor Turner, but still an egalitarian fellowship of religious radicalism.[17] Those who entered the camp of prayer were henceforth set apart from the mass by participation in a redeemed fellowship, a fellowship of virtue. Slaves, dispossessed peasants, refugees, and other flotsam and jetsam of society were incorporated into the ranks of the spiritual elite, their worldly stigma dissolved in the atmosphere of divine acceptance. At the head of the *missidi* was the *walī* under whose authority the devotees bound and consecrated themselves to serve. The *missidi* became the community of virtue, with the *walī* as a sort of spiritual commissar who wafted over his motley amalgam of *refuseniks* the breath of felicity.

Diawia came under a cloud following the death of Tcherno 'Isma'ila, although Shādhilism continued to expand in other areas. With the accession of Tcherno Mamadou Sharif, the youngest son of Tcherno 'Isma'ila, how-

---

17. Victor Turner, *The Ritual Process: Structure and Anti-Structure* (Ithaca, N.Y.: Cornell University Press, 1972). For a searching critique of Turner, see Humphrey Fisher, "Liminality, Hijrah and the City," *Journal of Asian and African Studies* 20:1 (1986): 153–77.

ever, the center went through a revival. Shādhilism once again regained the initiative and the *diaroré* rites, for a while interrupted, were reintroduced on an organized basis. All the Labé country was now engulfed by the rites, and from there the flame of devotion spread to numerous important locations in the Fula country and beyond. One leader, Tcherno Jaw (d. 1865), chief of the district of Ndama in Labé, gave the rites a strong political basis by refashioning his subjects into the butt of military operations against adjacent non-Muslim populations. These military thrusts were often called *jihād*, but they scarcely conformed to the classical specifications, in that they were not precipitated by a situation bringing danger to the Muslim community, and were not preceded by formal overtures of peace. Even if this was not *jihād*, however, it was certainly a fusion of religious ardor with political ambition, and Tcherno Jaw, as its sponsor, achieved an elevated status through it and was accordingly ascribed the title "the *walī* of Ndama" — another worldly saint.

Tcherno Jaw's initiative was inherited by his second son, Tcherno Ibrahima, whose influence extended much beyond Futa Jallon. The French wooed him in an effort to exploit his influence, but in 1899 the two sides collided on a path of inevitable conflict of interest. Tcherno Ibrahima and all his principal aides were subsequently arrested and sentenced to a term of imprisonment and exile in Gabon. Fortunately, Tcherno Ibrahima was saved from the outrage of infidel punishment: in 1902, before his sentence could be carried out, he died of natural causes. French involvement, however, compounded the incendiary urge that Shādhilism had exploited so successfully in an earlier era, and the perception that Tcherno Ibrahima's death before execution was caused by divine intervention added further fuel to the flame. All six of his sons founded retreat centers, and each prospered.

The man whose career brought matters to a head was Tcherno Aliou (c. 1828–1912) — frail, lame, and partly blind, but so considerable a force in the area that he was given the title "*walī* of Goumba." His retreat center at Goumba, situated on the lower escarpment of the Futa Jallon plateau, became a formidable challenge to the French, who responded to his influence by according him the treasonable status of Mahdi— "Messiah." In March 1911, a platoon of riflemen was sent to arrest Tcherno Aliou on suspicion of anticolonial subversion. Forewarned by his principal disciples, the feeble *walī* escaped on horseback to neighboring Sierra Leone, and the arrest party was ambushed with some loss of life. After a fierce struggle lasting three and a half hours, the bedraggled French troops withdrew to safety.

A reprisal ensued, and Tcherno Aliou was extradited by the British authorities of Sierra Leone to stand trail in Guinea on a capital charge, but he, too, died in detention before a sentence on him could be passed. Following the earlier pattern, Tcherno Aliou's disciples interpreted the manner of his death as evidence of divine intervention, but while this may have lifted the spirit, it could not ultimately counterbalance French military power. The French soon controlled the area and captured the centers of Shādhilī influence. Shādhilism had reached a watershed in West Africa, and the saintly virtue that propelled it, for so long a force to be reckoned with in the rarefied political atmosphere of the plateau, henceforth had to seek the low ground of accommodation with French colonial authorities.

The factual basis for any Mahdist claims by Tcherno Aliou, as alleged by the French, appears very thin indeed. When he testified at his own trial, Tcherno Aliou denied he had made such a claim, and there is no evidence he appealed to, or was familiar with, standard Islamic sources on Mahdism. Yet the historical issue this matter raises is less easily resolved. When the French perceived Tcherno Aliou as a Mahdist threat, they were responding to the power of the extraordinary devotion and loyalty that the saintly man's disciples lavished on him. Given the ferment of the times, religious activism reverberated with earth-shaking consequences, becoming an expression of deep grievances and fears. Under such conditions, it is of little relevance whether or not the *walī* made Mahdist claims and thereby fanned popular sentiments. French intrusion into hinterland Guinea had raised millenarian fears, and people turned to the *walī* as the all-competent broker of popular piety.

The history of Shādhilism thus shows that the links between West African and North African Islam were real and enduring, and that the synthesis of law and devotion and of involvement and retreat had assumed as viable proportions in West Africa as in the North. In neither area did the *awliyā* avoid controversy. On the contrary, they often became the focus of social and political issues. Since they perceived no dichotomy between the word of God and the world of politics, they had no hesitation in taking command of events to avenge their cause. For them saintly virtue was conceived as having a solid, worldly face to it; they expected worldly success to follow from inner virtue. In their minds form and content, dogma and practice coalesced naturally.

The *walī* was a moral exemplar. The power he possessed was proof of the intrinsic worth of virtue and the merit associated with his literacy in Arabic, the sacred tongue. Although he bore the stamp of humanity and carried the marks of earthly limitation, the saint was guaranteed divine forgiveness and acceptance should he fall into sin. This endowed him with the capacity to promise similar assurance to his disciples, and thus to act as intermediary between God and human beings. In some Islamic traditions the saint provided this link not only by bestowing spiritual blessings (*baraka*) on his followers but by instructing them in matters of doctrine so that God Himself might become directly accessible to the aspirant. In African Islam, however, this pedagogical role remained unimportant; instead the saint assumed, or was made to assume, the all-important role of guide and savior.

It is instructive to set this understanding of the saint alongside indigenous African conceptions. Unlike his counterpart in the indigenous culture who specializes in spells, incantations, and other forms of divination, the *walī* is distinguished by an organized following and public support. The organizational dimension of saintly power is therefore integral to the Islamic tradition: sainthood — individual charisma — is buttressed by saintship, an historically and even literarily transmitted line of succession. In traditional divination, by contrast, less stress is laid on a public code of conduct that regulates the exercise of sacred power. In such circles magicians are answerable chiefly to the demands of their art, not to any outside body of authority. For example, if the evil eye is potent enough to accomplish its work, then it is irrelevant whether the person being harmed deserves his or her fate. Magicians are vindicated by the results of their art, not by any moral consequences. This tradition is quite different from the Islamic notion of *baraka,* which implies both personal virtue (the saint is "the blessed person") and efficacious power.

Although writers like Trimingham tend to lump magic and *baraka* together, local populations are more discriminating. They recognize that the *walī* is different from the diviner or magician, whom they call *sirruyanké* (from Arabic *sirr,* "secret or esoteric knowledge").[18] Some *sirruyankés* have indeed aligned their practice with Islam. One *sirruyanké* adopted the feasts of Ramadan and the *ḥajj* as times to dispense prophecies and prescriptions. But Islam is only a veneer. Such diviners claim to be able to assume the form of a monkey or other animal and to receive from Allah communications that cause them to make predictions about events not in the Muslim calendar but in the farming calendar: rain, harvests, fat kine succeeding lean and vice versa.[19] Such predictions lend themselves easily to exploitation and extortion, and many *awliyā* have been careful to guard their reputations against such religious adventurism.[20] Even so, we should not press the division too rigidly. In the large grey area between genuine moral power and popular thaumaturgy it would need a saint of exceptional agility to avoid straying off the straight and narrow.

As we move to one last consideration of sainthood in West Africa, we shall see that only a faint line separates the refined power of *baraka* and its coarse

18. The term *sirr* occurs also in Sufi literature, where it is defined as "mystery," the infusion of the will of the *walī* with that of the All-Powerful. It became the intimate thought of the *walī* or *shaykh* as that was under the divine influence. Some authorities go so far as to make it the germ of the soul. G. C. Anawati and Louis Gardet, *Mystique musulmane: aspects et tendances — expériences et techniques* (Paris: Librairie philosophique J. Vrin, 1961), 226. Such pantheistic tendencies are slight in African Islam.

19. Paul Marty, *L'Islam en Guinée* (Paris: E. Leroux, 1921), 477.

20. On the *walī* of Goumba, for example, see Marty, ibid. In this connection mention should be made of the Jakhanke religious clerics, who saw themselves as standing firmly in the tradition of ethical moderation, an attitude that had a profound impact on the populations of Futa Jallon and beyond. Jakhanke clerics intervened in secular affairs to settle disputes, using their religious reputation to good effect in quiet diplomacy. L. Sanneh, *The Jakhanke: The History of an Islamic Clerical People of Senegambia* (London: International African Institute, 1979), 103–4, 107, 116. A segment of the Jakhanke community spread to Kano in the fifteenth century during the reign of Muhammad Rimfa (1463–99), who was so impressed by the saintly qualities of the Jakhanke clerical leader, 'Abd ad-Rahman Jakhite, that he asked to be buried by the latter's graveside so that, in his own words, "I might inherit his *baraka.*" (Sanneh, *The Jakhanke,* 31).

analogues in popular religion. As history moves forward and saints and disciples interact, that line can become blurred to the point of nonexistence.

SAINTHOOD AND SAINT VENERATION:
THE MOURIDES OF SENEGAL

The founder of the Mouride (Ar. *murīd,* "disciple") brotherhood of Senegal was Shaykh Amadou Bamba (c. 1852–1927), a man deeply influenced by the interior devotion of the Tijānī order of Sufis, although his own roots lay in Qādirī soil.[21] Over the course of time, his Mouride brotherhood outpaced its counterparts in vigorously cultivating the unthinking obeisance of rank-and-file neophytes, called by the Mourides themselves *tālibés* (Ar. *ṭālib*). The Mouride leaders' claim over the bodies of their disciples came to be complete and total, so much so that after a point religious instruction, with its accompanying initiation into grades of spiritual enlightenment, was almost entirely missing in the otherwise close relationship between the postulant and his spiritual axis. Instead the *shaykh* mounted the disciples like cavalry, driving them into virgin fields of submission and physical labor on the peanut plantations of the brotherhood, a cash-crop enterprise conducted for the exclusive benefit of the *shaykhs.* At its extreme form this submission may in fact, if not in theory, substitute for submission to God.

The manifestation of this kind of authoritative power over crowds of illiterates brought the Mourides to the hostile attention of the French colonial power. Paul Marty, whose acute analysis of the Mourides remains a classic, describes the extraordinary appeal of Amadou Bamba. Describing what he saw in 1913, Marty wrote:

> The mere sight of Amadou Bamba at prayer or giving his blessing with a stream of saliva on the prostrate faithful plunges some into hysterical outbursts which everyone wants to share. They roll at the feet of the saint, they kiss his sandals and the hem of his robe, they hold out their hands to him. With compunction he lets fall a stream of saliva on the open palms, which close up, clasp together, and spasmodically rub the face and body. Then there are shudderings, fainting fits, epileptic convulsions, followed by contortions and extraordinary leaps, all this accompanied by a horrible yelling. Madness finally takes hold of everyone.[22]

The French took strong measures to curb Amadou Bamba's power. He and his followers were harassed. Having first installed themselves at the village of Mbake-Baol in the rural hinterland of Senegal, the *shaykh* and his followers moved to a new center he built at Touba, also in Senegal, in 1887.

---

21. Fernand Dumont, *La Pensée réligieuse d'Amadou Bamba* (Dakar and Abidjan: Nouvelles éditions Africaines, 1975), 71–72.

22. Paul Marty, *Les Mourides d'Amadou Bamba* (Paris, 1913), 52–53. Cited in Donal Cruise O'Brien, *The Mourides of Senegal* (Oxford: Clarendon Press, 1971), 53.

Since there was no abatement in the hostility of local *commandants*, Amadou Bamba and his disciples removed to St. Louis, then the capital of colonial Senegal, in 1891. But proximity to power merely served to inflame official sensibilities further, and the *shaykh* was apprehended by French troops. He was sentenced to imprisonment and exile in Gabon from 1895 to 1902 on charges of political subversion. His popularity with the crowds turned him inevitably into a political figure, and in the eyes of the French his association with the Tijāniyāh, which was regarded in colonial circles as inherently subversive, established his culpability as needing no further proof. Amadou Bamba returned to Senegal in November 1902, but he was arrested again the following year and condemned to a fresh term of exile, this time in Mauritania, from 1903 to 1907.

Each French action against Amadou Bamba appears to have raised him in the esteem of his followers, who proceeded to ascribe miraculous powers to him. Historians of religion have still to decide whether it was a garrulous *shaykh* who led an ignorant and willing crowd, or an irrepressible crowd that molded the *shaykh*. The real picture seems a mixed one: the stimulus of popular expectation undoubtedly intensified the impulse to sainthood in Amadou Bamba, but the dramatic nature of his exilic absence increased the loyalty of his devotees too, and a cult of saintly personality grew up to fill the vacuum created by his absence. When he returned in 1907, he was a greater saint than when he left.

The spontaneous and overwhelming nature of the response to Amadou Bamba as *séringe* (Wolof for "holy man," "saint") cannot be explained solely on the grounds of strong Islamic influence. Most of his followers were ignorant of even the most basic tenets of the faith. For them Amadou Bamba cut the figure of the familiar charismatic personality, which in the pre-Islamic era was designated *borom bayré*, a Wolof phrase meaning "possessor of success and fame." The Muslim saint, when he appeared, was assimilated to this traditional African paradigm as both *borom bayré* and *borom barké*, a man of both worldly and spiritual achievement.[23]

This double level of understanding appears to have operated in Amadou Bamba's relationship with his disciples. In his own mind he was a devout, humble Muslim, eager to behave and think in strict accordance with orthodox requirements. Indeed, when first approached by an overzealous disciple who saw in him the marks of greatness, Amadou Bamba treated him with undisguised disapproval, sending him packing with the advice that he put his mind to better and more useful pursuits.[24] Even later in his career he forbade his disciples to render him the obeisance that he deemed properly due to God.[25] In his rules for novices he stressed submission to God above all else,[26] and in his prolific writings, the theme of obedience to God is the

23. Dumont, *La Pensée*, 21–22.   24. O'Brien, *Mourides*, 143.
25. O'Brien, *Mourides*, 54.   26. Dumont, *La Pensée*, 85.

persistent and incomparable standard alongside which all else fades into insignificance. He spoke at length concerning his unworthiness and expressed distress at evidence of his weakness. Praying to God, he said,

> I desire your help in the midst of terror and vengeance. Today my heart is overburdened with sadness. My being is too weak to bear what I face. Forgive. My misfortune is plain, and my heart is anguished.[27]

These words were spoken shortly before his first exile, an exile that was to resonate with the rising chorus of popular adulation.

Whatever his inner feelings of inadequacy, Amadou Bamba had to respond to the undeniable strength of his support among the peasant populations, and he tried to form order out of the chaos around him by moving in the direction of undisputed authority. In one of his devotional manuals he listed four qualities as necessary in the disciple: (1) a sincere and unshakable love for the *shaykh,* (2) unquestioning obedience to the commands of the *shaykh,* (3) abandonment of all opposition, including inward resistance, to the *shaykh,* and (4) the giving up of any preference for the disciple's own private thoughts.[28] Elsewhere he wrote that he who does not have a *shaykh* for his training will come to grief, "for he who does not have a *shaykh* for his guide will have Satan for his *shaykh.*"[29] "Truth," he said, "consists in the love for one's *shaykh.*"[30] In another work Amadou Bamba says that the *walī* inherits the power of miracles from the Prophet to whom the *walī* is attached by a mystical chain of initiation.[31] "Saints," he wrote, "are the authentic signs of the Prophet's religion, and of his truth. . . . Saints are preserved from error and invested with honor."[32] This point of devotion to the Prophet is stressed in the numerous details on performing the *dhikr.* At its height the *dhikr* is nothing but the imitation of the Prophet, the Perfect Man (*insān al-kāmil*) or the true intercessor (*shaffi', mushaffa'*).[33]

Recognizing in his disciples material requiring the iron hand of discipline rather than the persuasive pen of the scholar, Amadou Bamba elevated physical labor to the status of a religious principle. "Work," he contended, "is a part of true religion. The human body, since its creation, exists only to accomplish the work ordered by God."[34]

It would be unfair to blame Séringe Bamba entirely for the coarse bearing of his followers, for he was following where they led. Amar Sambe, a local Senegalese scholar, testified to the compelling interior impetus that a *shaykh's* following could develop by recalling that in his youth wandering,

27. Dumont, *La Pensée,* 123.
28. Dumont, *La Pensée,* 88.
29. Dumont, *La Pensée,* 90.
30. Ibid.
31. Dumont, *La Pensée,* 95.
32. Dumont, *La Pensée,* 96.
33. Dumont, *La Pensée,* 112.
34. Dumont, *La Pensée,* 114.

drunken *awliyā* were a familiar sight; yet their followers remained undaunted. He writes:

> When I was a child in Koranic school at Kébémer [Senegal], a marabout passed frequently in front of the school, staggering, held upright by his *tālibés*. The *séringe* always had a foot in the vineyard of the Lord. Despite this fact, his followers liked to maintain that their *shaykh* had so much *baraka* that strong liquor transformed itself into milk when it reached his stomach.[35]

Amadou Bamba was not nearly that idiosyncratic, but the anecdote suggests the wide margin of credulity available to the local *walī* if he wished to avail himself of it.

The central importance of discipleship per se in Mouride practice is dramatized in the nature of its simple initiation ritual, which has supreme value for the Mouride *tālibé*. It is called in Wolof *njebbel* (Ar. *bay'ah, talqīn*), meaning "personal and physical surrender," and is the crux of Mouride life and philosophy. In the *njebbel* the neophyte declares to his master, "I surrender to you my body and soul. What you forbid, I refrain from, and what you command I obey."[36] That unadorned formula binds the disciple to the *shaykh* in a relationship that is, for all practical purposes, indissoluble, though in theory the disciple can repudiate the link in an extreme crisis.[37] The neophyte is told by the *shaykh* to make unquestioning obedience his watchword. *Del deglu ndiggel,* he says: "You must hear words as commands."[38]

An extreme branch of the Mouride movement, called the Bay Fall, take the step of personal submission to its logical conclusion. According to them the canonical obligations of Islam are superfluous. In an arresting metaphor they ask, "Why carry your bags on your head if you are riding in a train?" The train is headed for salvation, Amadou Bamba is the locomotive engine, the carriages are the Mouride *shaykhs,* the passengers are the *tālibés,*[39] and the baggage, by implication, is the religious code. It follows from this that the servitude of the Mouride *tālibé* furnishes the basis of Mouride power. On the Mouride farm, called *dāra,* the *shaykhs* tether their *tālibés* in accordance with their right to command ultimate obedience. In the terminology of the Bay Fall, the *tālibé* is called *tak dêr,* "the laborer," after the wide leather belts used to hold their ragged clothes together as they toil unquestioningly on the fields of their masters.[40]

The Mourides are by no means unique in exploiting their followers for the benefit of their religious superiors. On the contrary, in the most representative tradition of Islamic education the schoolmaster in African Islam

---

35. Amar Sambe, *Diplôme d'études supérieures,* Faculté des Lettres, Université de Paris, 1964, p. 185. Cited in O'Brien, *Mourides,* 89.

36. O'Brien, *Mourides,* 85.   37. O'Brien, *Mourides,* 88.

38. O'Brien, *Mourides,* 85.   39. O'Brien, *Mourides,* 152.

40. O'Brien, *Mourides,* 165.

looks upon his students as indentured servants. Even the expectation that the
student will receive religious instruction is qualified by the view that the
schoolmaster has undisputed authority over mind as well as body.[41] The
Mourides are merely pressing this tradition to its logical conclusion and
building the entire edifice of saintly power on it.

We need a broader perspective to understand the true peculiarity of
Mouride extremism. Its counterpart in the large spectrum of Sufi spirituality
is the call to physical renunciation, an arming of the soul with the weapons of
struggle and vigilance against the lures of the carnal body. This, essentially,
is *zuhd*, and it was powerfully preached in the Tijāniyāh brotherhood, with
which the Mourides share some resemblance. There the devoted were urged
to beat the carnal self

> with the whip of the Book, bind it with the halter of reproach and judgment, set
> limits upon it with conscientious rebuke and reprimand, and place the saddle of
> firm intention upon it with the girth of determination. Then mount it with the
> profession of the holy law [*shari'a*] and ride it into the fields of Truth [*al-Ḥaqq*,
> a Sufi term for God].[42]

Even for the seasoned adept the challenges of genuine spirituality demand
superhuman resources, and the Mouride instinct to have recourse to saintly
intercession is fed from this reality. Unaided human effort is too bedeviled by
uncertainties to guarantee success. Through the servile channel of farm labor
the Mouride masters have taken individual responsibility out of the hands of
ignorant crowds and offered instead the privilege of collective subservience.

The power of the *shaykh* in the Mouride tradition is in exact proportion
to the adulation of the disciples. As Mouride theology says, the *shaykhs*
occupy the ranks of honor (Ar. *maqām*) to which they are carried by their
followers. It seems, therefore, that the cultivation of saintly eminence is but
a shorthand for the cultivation of society. Today, despite a number of
premature jeremiads, the Mourides number well over a million, and at the
Grand *Magāl*, their annual pilgrimage to Touba, up to half the total
membership may attend. One could scarcely ask for a more impressive
demonstration of group and religious solidarity, and of what has been called
the "versatility" of charisma.[43]

In the case of Mourides we seem to have a stunning example of how
even sober-minded *shaykhs* may be made to follow the lead of their followers
as they reap the reward of popular obeisance. But one should recall that the
Mourides are hardly alone in fusing concepts such as *borom barké* (spiritual

41. Sanneh, *Jakhanke*, 147–84.
42. Tcherno Bokar Salifu Taal (c. 1883–1940), as quoted by Louis Brenner, *West African
Sufi: The Religious Heritage and Spiritual Search of Cerno Bokar Saalif Taal* (London: Christopher Hurst, 1984), 114.
43. For example, O'Brien, *Mourides*, 302. O'Brien later revised his own position in "A
Versatile Charisma: The Mouride Brotherhood 1967–1975," *Archives européennes de sociologie* 18 (1977): 84–106.

success) and *borom bayré* (worldly renown) to understand who their masters are. These *shaykhs* exemplify a broader consensus of what sainthood means in African Islam. Saints are robust individuals. They are not just eminent souls who impart their blessing (*baraka*) to a few devotees in the isolation of retreat centers; they are leaders in the larger world. The blessings they distribute are not thought to have any intrinsic bounds, hence a claim to be near to God — to be God's "friend" — tends to become plausible in proportion to its social recognition.

"Sainthood," then, seems to be a domestication of *baraka*; "saintship," the social organization of saints, rises to greet it as devotees embrace their masters. The Mouride case is merely the extreme point of the spectrum: there the complex interaction of sainthood and saintship fairly squeezes utility from wildness itself.

NINE

Alourdes: A Case Study of Moral Leadership in Haitian Vodou

Karen McCarthy Brown

I have known Alourdes[1] since 1978 and addressed her as "mother" (a traditional title of respect for one's Vodou teacher) for the last five years. This ample-bodied, powerful, moody, loving, difficult, generous woman has taught me much of what I know about Haitian Vodou. It has not all been a simple matter of gathering scholarly data, for there have been broader life lessons learned under her tutelage. Among them have been many that relate directly to what we scholars would call the moral life. Through Alourdes I have glimpsed a deeply-rooted traditional value system that accepts conflict, celebrates plurality, and seeks the good through whatever enhances life energy.

Alourdes immigrated to the United States in 1963. Her brief career in Haiti as a singer with Troupe Folklorique ended when she married a man considerably older than herself, a man who worked for the Haitian Bureau of Taxation. In spite of the fact that he was able to provide her with security and comforts in striking contrast to her previous life of poverty, Alourdes was not willing to tolerate her husband's jealousy and need to control her life. However, living on her own in Port-au-Prince, the largest urban center in the poorest country in the Western hemisphere, proved extremely difficult. Her mother, though a well-known Vodou priestess in the city, was unable to help financially. By the early 1960s, Alourdes, not yet thirty, had three small children and was desperate to find some way to support them and herself. Moving to New York seemed the only avenue of escape, though it necessitated the wrenching decision to leave her extended family behind. On the day of her departure, Alourdes's mother invited her to come to the family altar and pray for the protection of the Vodou spirits in her new life. Alourdes

---

1. I use only Alourdes's first name in this essay to protect her privacy. I hope no one will read this as a sign of disrespect, for I intend none.

replied: "I'm going to New York; I don't need no spirits there." Each time she tells this story, she quickly adds: "And I was wrong!"

Once settled in Brooklyn, Alourdes went to work, first as a cleaning woman for the Pratt Institute, then as a pressing machine operator for Cascade Laundry. Finally, she began to hire out as a domestic on a daily basis, working mostly for wealthy families on Manhattan's upper east side. In this early period of her life in New York, Alourdes worked with language skills limited to three words of English: mop, pail, and vacuum. During this difficult time she became ill. Obscure and never adequately diagnosed pains in her stomach took her to the hospital three times. The second time a portion of her small intestine was removed. The second and third times she was in such bad condition that a Catholic priest was summoned to administer last rites. A series of significant dreams on the part of Alourdes, members of her family, and friends indicated that the spirits were causing her illness. They wanted her to return to Haiti temporarily in order to be initiated into the Vodou priesthood. In 1966, Alourdes made that journey home. She has had no recurrence of her illness since.

Alourdes understands herself to have been called to the priesthood by the spirits. She believes it was the spirits who made her sick as a way of reminding her of religious and family obligations. (The two cannot be neatly distinguished since one serves the Vodou spirits not just for oneself, but also for one's "family," whether that term is defined narrowly to refer to the members of the household or broadly to include ancestors long dead, as well as the typical Haitian penumbra of fictive "aunts" and "uncles," "cousins," "sisters," and "brothers.") Alourdes also credits the spirits with her current "luck." Although she, like most Haitians in the greater New York area, lives well below the poverty level, she owns her own home. Although, like many Haitian women, she has all the responsibilities of the head of household, she is surrounded by healthy children and grandchildren. Furthermore, since her initiation, Alourdes has been able to support herself without demeaning labor. She now works full time as a "technician of the sacred."

In her cramped and chaotic rowhouse in the Fort Greene section of Brooklyn, Alourdes functions daily as a *manbo*, "Vodou priestess." Nurse's aides, taxi drivers, dishwashers, and a smattering of persons with more lucrative professions come to see her at six-thirty in the morning before their workdays begin, or at eleven or twelve at night after they end. Mostly, though not all, Haitians, they bring to her a wide range of problems: love, work, health, and family relations. She reads cards to diagnose the cause of the trouble, determining first that the problem is nothing that comes from God,[2]

---

2. Those who serve the spirits in Vodou believe in a single god, Bondye, creator of all that is. Following the story from the Bible of the casting out of Lucifer and his coterie, they believe that the spirits were created by Bondye and subsequently banished to earth. However, these spirits are in no way understood as demonic or evil.

for she has no control over illness or trouble sent by God—only afflictions sent by the spirits. Virtually all spirit-sent problems, regardless of kind, are diagnosed as owing to some disturbance in the network of relations among people, often including a person's relationship to family members now dead. Healing is accomplished by ritually adjusting these interpersonal relationships. Alourdes cures through herbal medicine, prayer, "good-luck baths," charms, and talismans. In serious cases she is directed to the proper cures by her dreams and by consulting the spirits in trance sessions. The more recalcitrant cases may take time and extraordinary effort. For example, severely depressed persons, whom she is especially adept at curing, may be brought into her home to live for a period of several months. In addition to this intimate, problem-oriented work, Alourdes also holds several large feasts for individual Vodou spirits each year.

In scheduling these events, Alourdes follows the Catholic liturgical calendar, which dominates in Vodou ritualizing. Catholicism is an overlay on top of the layers of different African religious traditions that came together on the slave plantations of eighteenth-century Haiti to form Vodou. The Vodou spirits have both Catholic saint names and Afro-Haitian names, the latter being traceable in most cases to Yoruba, Dahomean, or Kongo counterparts. So, for example, Dambala the Dahomean snake deity is feted sometime around 17 March, the feast day of St. Patrick, who is pictured in the popular Catholic chromolithograph with snakes clustered around his feet. Each year Alourdes holds elaborate "birthday parties" for Dambala (St. Patrick) in March, Azaka (St. Isidore) in May, Ezili Dantò (Our Lady of Mount Carmel) in July, Ogou (St. James the Elder) also in July, and Gèdè (St. Gerard) in November. In addition she holds others when there is special "work" to be done that cannot wait until her spirits' feast days or involves another spirit with whom she has a less regular connection. Considerable effort and money (hundreds of dollars contributed by Alourdes and the members of her Vodou "family") are expended for each of these events. From late evening until early morning, praying, singing, and dancing go on in front of a "table" laden with the carefully prepared food and drink each spirit favors. Alourdes functions as the mistress of ceremonies, orchestrating the ritualizing throughout.

Almost always at these events it is also Alourdes who serves as the *chwal*, "horse," who is ridden by the spirit. After the brief struggle and confusion that routinely marks the onset of trance, Alourdes's body posture and tone of voice become those characteristic of the spirit called. She is dressed in a costume appropriate to the spirit, and is treated as if she were the spirit. On these ritual occasions the worshippers approach the spirits with the problems of their lives. The faithful are comforted, chastised, and given advice and blessings. Divine-human interaction becomes powerfully immediate as people are hugged, held, and handled by the spirits they serve.

From this brief description of Alourdes's life and her role as a Vodou priestess, it should be apparent that she is a competent, resourceful, and self-assured woman with an established reputation as a sacerdote and healer. It should also be clear that she, and those around her, believe that she was called to those latter roles by the spirits themselves. Yet none of this is sufficient to explain the position she enjoys within the Haitian immigrant community in New York. Haitian women are often strong and independent. In urban Haiti they frequently provide the main, if not sole, financial and emotional support for any number of children. Furthermore, the Vodou priesthood is not an office that guarantees a following. Many of the initiated never become leaders; and all initiates perceive themselves as having been chosen by the spirits. Building the reputation and steady following that Alourdes has requires further qualifications.

People speak about Alourdes as "strong," meaning that she is powerful and effective. They also speak respectfully about her "knowledge." Still, it is unclear how she might be related to the rubric of "saint" or "moral exemplar." Many of the people who are her clients and participate in her large ceremonies would spontaneously speak of her as a "good" woman. By this they mean that she responds readily and sympathetically to those in trouble; does not charge more than is fair for her services; is responsible to family and friends; and will have nothing to do with any kind of spirit "work" primarily designed to harm another person. Yet while this "good-ness" is not irrelevant to her leadership role within the Haitian Vodou community in New York, it does not explain it, and certainly would not be sufficient to guarantee it. If we can speak of Alourdes as a moral exemplar — and I think in one sense we can — it will not be because she exemplifies the good in its popular Western incarnations as fairness, humility, and equanim-ity. I believe Alourdes to be an ultimately fair person, but she is not humble or self-sacrificing, at least not in the way we usually understand these terms. Alourdes believes she has a right to respect and she demands it from those around her. She is not even-tempered. She will not put up with people who are inconsiderate. Her anger can be sudden and fierce, and her humor cutting as often as it is delightful.

There are two possible ways to approach the role of saints or moral exemplars in Haitian Vodou. I propose to pursue both of them here, although each case will require a significant redefinition of terms. The first approach is to examine not Alourdes herself but the spirits — or "saints" as the Haitians also call them — as they incarnate themselves through her. This tack will require that we relinquish the notion that what is saintly is good. The Vodou spirits are not good, but they are not evil either. They are whole — full, rich, complex character types. For example, Ezili Dantò, whom we will encounter later, though identified with two manifestations of the Virgin Mary, Our Lady of Mount Carmel and the black Virgin, Mater Salvatoris, is understood within the Vodou system to be an independent woman who will take lovers but never marry them and a fiercely defensive mother who will kill to protect her children. The second approach involves concentrating on Alourdes's leadership role. People bring life conflicts, many of them easily recognizable as what we would call moral dilemmas, to the Vodou system. In her community Alourdes is in charge of the process by which Vodou addresses these moral dilemmas. This line of questioning will require that we relinquish the notion that a moral leader is there to be imitated in the specifics of action or being. Alourdes is a moral exemplar not so much because of what she does as because of *how* she does what she does. In a deep sense it is a question of style. Moral sensibility and aesthetic sensibility are very close in the Vodou universe of meaning.

I will begin with a discussion of the exemplary nature of the Vodou saints, or *lwa,* another term the Haitians frequently use. Then I will move to an analysis of Alourdes's leadership role as I have come to understand it. Each of these discussions will be built around material from my field journals. In all cases the material will be drawn from events and interactions observed during the annual "birthday parties" for the spirits, since the high level of ritualizing and the presence of a full community at these events make it easier to observe the moral negotiation going on in the sacred context than it otherwise would be. I believe that essentially the same processes are involved in the more intimate and workaday ritualizing that Alourdes carries on, but in those cases the important role of the community is more implicit than explicit. I will conclude with a discussion of the coincidence of the moral and the aesthetic within the world of Vodou.

THE EXEMPLARY NATURE OF THE VODOU SPIRITS

The following is a selection drawn from my field journals describing the appearance of the warrior spirit Ogou in the latter stages of a fete held to honor the ancient and venerable snake spirit Dambala. All the most important spirits are saluted regardless of whose "birthday party" it is. Furthermore, since Ogou is the major spirit Alourdes serves, his actual appearance in one of his various personae is expected at all of Alourdes's Vodou feasts.

March 14, 1981
Feast for Dambala

It is Sin Jak Majè [St. Jacques Majeur, St. James the Elder] who comes, not Ogou Badagri, Alourdes's more usual Ogou manifestation. Maggie [Alourdes's daughter] says to me later that she is sorry Badagri did not come. "Sin Jak is mean! He have a mean expression on his face all the time. He never laugh or play. Sin Jak is hard."

Sin Jak's coming is marked with bravado. The first thing he does is pour rum into both ears. Alourdes's dress is quickly soaked through to her skin. Not long afterward, someone brings out Sin Jak's sword. This one looks like a fencing foil. He grabs it, unsheathes the blade and then thrusts it repeatedly in the air as if attacking an invisible enemy. Then, he lowers the blade and menacingly jabs it toward those standing nearest to him. Wary, though probably not genuinely afraid, most people take a step or two backward. Finally, he points the blade at himself. Resting the tip on his right hip, he pushes it in just enough to make the blade bend slightly — a gesture full of arrogance that hints at self-wounding. Next, he orders rum and then Florida Water [an inexpensive cologne often used in Vodou rituals] to be poured on the linoleum floor and lighted. People plunge their cupped hands into the blue alcohol flames and carry them upward, bathing face and arms in warmth. Sin Jak then directs some of the people to jump over the flames or to walk over them with legs spread apart. These are blessings from Sin Jak designed to raise life force but, like all his blessings, they contain a hint of danger.

Then people begin to queue up to speak with Sin Jak and he deals with them one by one, giving advice and ritualized blessings. For the most part, his blessings now take the form of spewing cigar smoke or rum over their bodies or directly into their faces. People grimace and hold their eyes tightly closed, but they do not turn away. Every once in awhile, Sin Jak rears back, puffs on his big cigar, puffs out his chest, and surveys the crowd with a calculating eye. As Maggie says, "Sin Jak is mean!"

Sin Jak Majè is the first in rank among the many Vodou spirits who go by the name Ogou. (It is, by the way, equally appropriate to speak as if there were one Ogou and as if his different manifestations were separate spirits.) The Haitian Ogou has his roots in the Gu of the Dahomean peoples and the Ogun of the Yoruba. The African Ogun was originally a deity connected to ironsmithing, whose sphere of influence subsequently expanded to include all the occupations connected with metal, including hunting, warfare, and most of modern technology. His cult is currently the fastest growing segment of traditional religion in Nigeria, and perhaps in all of sub-Saharan Africa. In addition to providing ritually enforced protection for the mobile, the marginal, and the isolated — ancient itinerant smiths as well as modern roughnecks in the oil fields — the Nigerian Ogun cult has also articulated a trenchant philosophy of modern technology. Ogun teaches that the power unleashed by human invention, unless ritually balanced, will turn on its creators.[3]

Haiti has had little of the modern technological world to contend with. Thus the Haitian Ogou, although grounded in the same dynamic as his Yoruba counterpart, has developed in different ways. His primary task has been to make sense of things military and, in particular, of the long and

3. "Ogun . . . focuses on humans' attempts to regulate the known, but out-of-control forces of culture. Fundamental to the cult is the belief that the power unleashed by man gains a momentum of its own. This momentum is of such magnitude that it cannot be controlled by the laws and sanctions of the supernatural. Once this out-of-control power is sacralized, it can be tapped for societal use." Sandra T. Barnes, *Ogun: An Old God for a New Age*, ISHI Occasional Papers in Social Change, no. 3 (Philadelphia: Institute for the Study of Human Issues, 1980), 29.

complex military history of Haiti itself. All of the Haitian Ogou are soldiers —
or by extension politicians. Those possessed by Ogou are often dressed in red
military jackets (Ogou's favorite color) with brass buttons and epaulets.
These military personae are highly evocative and complex images for Haitians. They contain references to the soldier heroes of their past, men such as
Toussaint L'Ouverture and Jean-Jacques Dessalines. These are the men who
led the successful slave revolution against the French that, in 1804, created
the second independent republic, and the first black one, in the Western
hemisphere. Yet this history is not unmixed. For example, people still debate
the justice of Dessalines's assassination at the hand of his own people. He was
the first president of Haiti and the leader responsible for restoring economic
order after the chaos of the revolution. However, he accomplished this
restoration largely through a system of forced labor that was undergirded by
threats and corporal punishment. For many Haitians, freedom became indis-
tinguishable from the slavery they had just escaped. Soldiers and politicians
of more recent vintage in Haitian history — from the American marines who
occupied the island in 1915 to the Duvalier family of more recent years — have
had a similar mixture of profit and pain to offer to the Haitian people.

Ogou repeats these lessons from history and keeps them alive in a variety
of ways.[4] Consider, for example, the ritualized gestures with the sword that
we saw Sin Jak perform and that are frequently executed at the opening of the
possession-performances of the other Ogou as well. The first gesture mimics
attack on the enemy; the next threatens the immediate community; the final
gesture points toward self-destruction. This Sin Jak performance was more
arrogant than usual. The most common ending to these maneuvers with the
ritual sword finds Ogou with the point of his sword placed, not in his hip, but
squarely in his solar plexus. Ogou's "dance" with the sword is to body
language what proverbs are to spoken language: a condensation point for
complex truths. Power liberates, power corrupts, power destroys.

People who serve Ogou are led through a rich and detailed analysis of a
certain way of being in the world. Ogou plays multiple, often clashing and
contradictory, variations on the theme of power. His warrior spirit is extended into all instances of anger, willfulness, and self-assertion. The arena of
his action extends beyond the military to include politics and governmental
bureaucracy, indeed hierarchy of any kind. Thus, Ogou serves as a model for
a full range of constructive and destructive possibilities inherent in the use of

---

4. There are African roots for Ogou's mixed messages about power. For example, the Yoruba
Ogun is said to become drunk with blood in battle and kill his own comrades. Also the Yoruba
Sango, who is conflated with Ogou in Haiti, is said to have been a king who foolishly and
arrogantly misused his power. Inadvertently, he called down lightning on his own palace, killing
his wives and children. Despairing, he hanged himself. See John Pemberton III, "A Cluster of
Sacred Symbols: Orisa Worship Among the Igbomina Yoruba of Ila-Orangun," *History of
Religions* 17, no. 1 (1977): 1–28. For the material relevant to Ogun, see p. 17; for that relevant
to Sango, see p. 20.

power. It is not surprising, then, that in song he is vaunted as a courageous warrior and at the same time satirized as a child throwing a temper tantrum.[5] Ogou plays all the roles in the power drama. This is what enables the people who serve him to see themselves in the mirror he holds up, regardless of where they are at the moment in relation to power.

Haitians have a great deal of experience with oppression. They know about hunger, poverty, and unemployment. They are also experienced in dealing with political oppression and abuse in their workplaces. The cumulative wisdom gained through these experiences clings to Ogou. He equips his "army" for a "war" that is quite simply life itself. By sanctioning anger and self-assertion, he empowers and restores dignity to those who face the "enemy" daily, for example, in the humiliation of a trip to the welfare office. But at the same time, by touching on themes such as broken families, isolation and loneliness, alcoholism and indigency, Ogou reminds his worshippers that the very same anger and self-assertive energy can be destructive when it is not properly balanced or is aimed at the wrong target.[6] The Haitians call Ogou a "saint" not because he is good but because he is whole, complete.

Perhaps it is true that in most cases fullness of vision must inevitably be sacrificed in the quest for clarity of expression, but Haitian Vodou seems to have refused the choice. The whole of Vodou ritualizing can be seen as driving toward those points where some particular way of being in the world, with all its complexities and contradictions, condenses into a single elegant image that can be held easily in the mind or heart. Let me be more specific: in Vodou, the word *pwen*, "point," is applied to anything—words, objects, gestures—that captures the essence or pith of a thing. *Pwen* are magical. They are charms or talismans that a person can use to negotiate his or her way in the world. *Pwen* can be sung, danced, or recited. They can be hung around the neck or over the door, buried in the yard in front of the house, or taken into the body. In Haiti, Ogou's sword is stuck into the earth in front of the Vodou altar and that is his *pwen*, his point. In a sense all the singing and dancing for Ogou, all the elaborate tables prepared with the hot and spicy food he loves, and all the performances of those possessed by him converge on the "point"

---

5. One of the songs for Ogou communicates both these messages simultaneously. It goes this way: Ki ki li ki o-ewa/ Papa Ogou tou piti kon sa/ Papa Ogou enrajè!, "Cock a-doodle do/ Papa Ogou all children are like that/ Papa Ogou enraged!" Such cryptic, ambiguous imagery is typical of Vodou songs. This one purposely leaves doubt as to whether Ogou is being counseled to be tolerant of his "children," his followers, or being caricatured as one who is behaving like a child.

6. See Karen McCarthy Brown, "Systematic Remembering, Systematic Forgetting: Ogou in Haiti," unpublished manuscript.

One of the Haitian Vodou songs sung for Ogou pictures him as a lonely beggar, thus capturing in one succinct image a worst-case study of one whose Ogou energy went wrong. Though anger and self-assertion are needed to make one's way in the modern world, they are also qualities that separate one from others. The beggar is Haiti's most poignant image of the person isolated from the all-important support of the extended family.

of his sword. They are the ritual context enabling that elegantly simple image to hold in apparent equilibrium a multiplicity of conflicting truths.

I would like to suggest a parallel way of understanding the exemplary role of the spirits in general. They themselves may be seen as *pwen,* condensation points for the complex and contradictory stuff of life. The Vodou spirits are personalities, and personality is perhaps the ideal vehicle for carrying such dynamic content. Yet, because they focus on one specific relational mode, one way of being in the world, they are much more like personality types than actual human personalities. This relative abstraction is what gives them clarity and allows them to be instructive.

In order to examine the moral function of the spirits in relation to actual persons, I return to the selection from my field journals quoted earlier, picking up where the previous narrative left off. Ogou was conducting audiences with the individual petitioners.

> In the middle of one woman's lengthy recitation of her family problems, Sin Jak raises his head and catches sight of a young man hanging back on the edge of the crowd. He cuts the woman off in mid-sentence, and bellows, "Come here!" The young man starts backing toward the door pretending interest in the zipper on his new black leather jacket. "Come here!" Sin Jak roars again. Hands begin to push the man forward. He is a tall, dark-skinned man, maybe twenty-five, who wears a black shirt open almost to the navel. He has several keys around his neck on a short gold chain. This strikes me as odd since they are quite ordinary keys and surely cannot be used on such a short chain. "Get down on your knees!" Sin Jak orders, his voice lower but still hard like stone. This time there are none of the usual ritualized greetings, no soothing preliminaries in which the spirit inquires about the general well-being of the petitioner and of his or her family. Instead Sin Jak throws a rapid-fire series of statements at the young man without giving him any chance to respond.
>
> "Ou ale tro vit." ["You're going too fast."]
>
> "Ou fè tro bagay." ["You're doing too much."]
>
> "Ou kone tro." ["You know too much."]
>
> "Ou pa kompran tou sa ou kone." ["You don't understand everything you know."]
>
> "Ou va tombe." ["You are going to fall."]
>
> "Fo ou desen enba." ["You have to come down."]
>
> The young man tries to protest, "Papa . . . ," but those standing around seem to be in general agreement and reinforce Sin Jak's words with little ejaculations such as, "Thank you, Papa," and "Grace, grace." Sin Jak, who had been bending close to the young man's face during this tongue-lashing, pulls himself up to his full height, takes a puff on his cigar and sets both hands firmly on his hips. Then he turns his back and strides away.

What Sin Jak was doing in this situation was what the Haitians would call "sending the point" or "throwing the point." This use of the word *point* relates to its talismanic use in the Vodou context described earlier. Here also, it signifies the essence or pith of a complex situation. Sending, singing, or throwing the point is a means of communicating charged feelings and information that is appropriately indirect though never off target. It is considered essential to the smooth functioning of relationships in Vodou circles and in the wider Haitian community. To understand the deeper significance of this social convention and how Sin Jak was using it, we need to explore a bit further.

An example drawn from outside the Vodou context seems to provide the clearest beginning. A Haitian friend told me this story: he was courting a young woman in Port-au-Prince; her mother disapproved of their union because it offered no economic advancement for her daughter. Rather than confront the man directly, the girl's mother chose to "sing the point." Working at her cooking chores, while the young man visited with her daughter, the mother sang over and over a well-known song with the refrain "dè mèg pa fri," or "two lean (pieces of meat) cannot fry." My friend got the point and let the relationship lapse. Two aspects of this means of communication deserve attention. First, the mother did not tell my friend what to do or force him into a situation in which he lost face; and second, her chosen method of communication needed my friend's active participation in interpreting and applying the message. She gave him an image. He is the one who used the image to make sense out of that particular social situation and, on the basis of what he saw, to decide what to do about it.

When Sin Jak called the young man out of the crowd and ordered him to his knees in preparation for a tongue-lashing, the spirit was also sending the point. This young man was not a frequent visitor at Alourdes's ritual events. I had never seen him before that evening and I never did learn much about him. Sin Jak, aggressive and "mean," acted characteristically in delivering his message without any polite preliminaries, but even he spoke in an imagistic code that gave away little of the content of the man's problem. The spirit's manner may have felt like that of a dutch uncle, but he actually gave him very little specific advice. "You have to come down" is open to many possible interpretations. After his encounter with Sin Jak, this man was left in the same position as the man who loved a woman he could not afford: he was left with an image. How the image applied to the specifics of his life was for him to decide. However he interpreted the message, though, one essential ingredient in his interpretation was the fact that it was Ogou who sent him the point.

In the West — that is in the European versions of Judaism and Christianity — a certain kind of thinking about religion and morality has been dominant. We feel that if we apply ourselves thoughtfully to our sacred texts and traditions, we can extract from them general principles that we can then hold up against our lives as measures of the moral quality to be found therein. The Vodou system is different. The relevant moral message does not measure a person's life so much as it reflects it. The various Vodou spirits are mirrors that may be held up to the ordinary human life. One song used to greet all the spirits begins with these lines: "Anonse o zanj nan dlo / bak odsu miwa," or "Announce to the angels in the water / down below the mirror."[7] Gazing into these mirrors — or better, interacting with them — gives the worshipper back nothing that is not already there. However, since the spirits are not actual characters so much as they are character types, what is reflected back to the viewer is a certain aspect of his or her life situation exaggerated for clarity and condensed into images that are easily retained. The Vodou participant does not turn to religion to be told what to do, but rather to be shown how to see.

ALOURDES'S LEADERSHIP ROLE

As we have seen, the Vodou spirits become available to the members of Alourdes's community through her possession-performances. In order to do justice to the indigenous understandings of the Vodou community, however, we must distinguish between what the spirits do and what Alourdes does. Regardless of how Western intellectuals might understand it to operate, any moral leadership manifest in the possession-performances would be attributed by Haitians to the spirits, not to Alourdes. Her role as *chwal*, "horse" of the spirits, is ideally seen as a passive one.

The initial confusion that marks the onset of trance is said to arise from the struggle between the *gro bonanj*, "guardian angel," of the *chwal* and the Vodou spirit who seeks to displace it. Loss of the guardian angel amounts to loss of self, so the resistance is instinctive. Initiation into the priesthood begins a long process wherein Vodou technicians of the sacred learn how to manage this perilous ego-exchange. They learn how to summon the spirits; how to enter trance, and thus surrender control to the spirits more easily; and how to prevent trance when that is necessary. Alourdes, who is considered quite advanced as a *manbo*, "priestess," moves readily into trance states with a short and more or less *pro forma* period of struggle. It is also said that total amnesia follows these periods of time in trance. The *chwal* claims to remember nothing of what transpired when the spirit had control of his or her body. This claim is yet another way of reiterating the Haitian belief that the spirit and the person possessed by that spirit are two separate entities.[8]

7. The Vodou spirits are said to dwell in Gine, "Africa," a watery world below the earth. It is from Gine that they are summoned to participate in Vodou ceremonies.

8. This reading of the situation has been reinforced by my own observations. Several times, I have heard the spirits chastise or contradict their own *chwal*, the very person possessed by them, as they are speaking. However, it is also my observation that individual possessions vary in the degree to which they achieve the ideal form. Trance appears to be somewhat like sleep: there are varying depths of it and, at these different levels, more or less of the old self with its consciousness, agendas, experiences, and information persists. I have seen a spirit remember a pot left cooking on a lit stove by an unpossessed *chwal*, much as we might rise from a dream to let the cat out. On the whole, I have been convinced that the post-trance amnesia is genuine, but there have also been times when bits of memory seemed to leak out.

Yet with this apparent separation, as with so many things in Vodou, conflicting perspectives coexist. Several aspects of Vodou ritual and language would reinforce a reading of the spirits as more closely tied to the person whom they "ride." For example, Haitians might remark: "Have you seen Alourdes's Ogou? He is strong!" This tying of person to spirit goes even further in the belief that spirits can be inherited in a family. So when Alourdes dies and her daughter takes over, as she likely will, people may talk of "Alourdes's Ogou in Maggie's head." A similar point is made in the Vodou rituals that give persons access to, and to some extent control over, their protective spirits. These rituals pay equal attention to "feeding" the spirits within the person and establishing repositories for the same spirits outside the person. In other words, the spirits are simultaneously addressed by these rituals as "in here" and "out there."

In the possession-performances of the spirits that occur in Alourdes's rituals, these two perspectives on the divine-human relationship coexist. In part, it is this dual perspective that lies behind my use of the term *possession-performance*. I am drawing a parallel with the theatrical context in which the individual actor's interpretation of a well-known character is one of the key ingredients in artistic success. However, I do not wish to signal by the use of this term that Alourdes's possessions are in any sense playacting or pretense. Haitians themselves condemn the occasional manipulative priest or priestess who will *pran poz*, "posture" or "act" as if possessed. Rather, this theater language is intended to make a point with which all Haitians would probably agree: some of the vehicles of the spirits are better than others, just as some actors are better at capturing a character than others. Alourdes has a sizeable and faithful following in the New York Haitian community for many reasons, one of the leading reasons being that she is a good *chwal*. People feel they have encountered the spirits and have been addressed by them when "the spirits come in Alourdes's head."

To examine Alourdes's leadership role in her community, I will eventually need to return to my field journals. The selection I will quote, like the earlier one, focuses on possession-performance; however, I wish to use this one for a broader purpose than the first. This time I want to explore the nature of group interaction and the modes of leadership operating within the group. One can handily locate these general, social processes within Vodou by beginning with a possession-performance, and this is as it should be if we are right in understanding the spirits as condensation points for existential complexities.

The interaction of a group of persons around someone possessed by a particular Vodou spirit is difficult to describe in language dependent on the assumptions we make about the nature of leaders and followers in Western, European-based culture. Our understandings of what it means to be a strong individual especially hamper our ability to comprehend a ritual scene such as the one that will be described here. To guard against importing such assumptions into the discussion, I have chosen to work with the passage in relation to an interactional model indigenous to Haitian Vodou culture.

Vodou drumming is thoroughly African in character.[9] In fact, some researchers claim that rhythms can still be heard in Haiti that have fallen into disuse in the areas of West Africa where they originated. Because of this close relationship between Haitian and African drumming, we can put to use John Miller Chernoff's illuminating study of the structure of African drumming in our analysis without fearing that it imports aesthetic values foreign to the Haitian Vodou context.[10] Chernoff's *African Rhythm and African Sensibility* is especially helpful in this enterprise because he focuses his study on the relationship between musical structure and social structure. I will use his work to discuss the social character of African music and of Vodou, the relation of the ordinary individual (listener, participant) to the total event, and the role of the leader within the performance.

Chernoff argues that the context and the content of African music are identical. In other words, the content of the music is the community that performs it. To support this point, he quotes a Takai drummer from Ghana who was one of his instructors during a seven-year drumming apprenticeship. Chernoff asked, "What is music?" Ibrahim Abdulai replied, "Music is something which does not conceal things about us, and so it adds to us."[11] Such a claim may also be made for Vodou ritual, and, as we shall see, Vodou carries on its socially revelatory work using many of the same interactional dynamics that Chernoff finds in African drumming.

African drumming is polyrhythmic. In it at least two rhythms, and often more, are always going on. The various rhythms, each carried by a separate drum, interweave in complex ways. Evidence of this complexity is illustrated in the fact that the music of African drumming ensembles cannot be reduced to Western-style notation without assigning different meters, as well as different rhythms, to each of the drums in an ensemble. Polymetric drumming creates the impression of different rhythms clashing and conflicting with one another.

Furthermore, no one, not even the drummers, can listen to all the rhythms simultaneously all the time. So what is, technically speaking, a simple repetition of the same patterning of sound is actually experienced as dynamic and changing because the participant's focus shifts from one rhythmic line to another. The resulting dynamic and unresolved character of African drumming leaves ears trained to Western harmony thoroughly confused. Western listeners, at least those of us who are white, become confused by African

9. In New York, people often cannot afford the drummers who are present at every sizeable ceremony in urban Haiti. In these situations, however, hand-clapping and statement-response singing reproduce many of the key dynamics in the musical performance being described here.

10. John Miller Chernoff, *African Rhythm and African Sensibility: Aesthetics and Social Action in African Musical Idioms* (Chicago: University of Chicago Press, 1979).

11. Chernoff, *Rhythm*, 35.

drumming because we try to listen to it in the same passive mode that we listen to our own music. Actually the only way to understand African music is to participate in it. When Africans are asked if they understand a certain type of music, Chernoff reports that they will say yes if they know the dance that goes with it.[12]

In this context dancing is not simply an accompaniment to music but a crucial ingredient in the process of music making. Exactly where we listeners accustomed to Western harmonic structure would expect to hear the most emphasis in this music, we hear the least. What we would call the main beat is missing.[13] The "main beat" in African music is supplied by clapping hands and pounding feet. It may also be supplied in the mind of the listener.

> We can say that the musicians play "around" the beat, or that they play on the off-beat, but actually it is precisely the ability to identify the beat that enables someone to appreciate the music. We begin to "understand" African music by being able to maintain, in our minds or our bodies, an *additional* rhythm to the ones we hear. Hearing another rhythm to fit alongside the rhythms of an ensemble is . . . a way of being steady within a context of multiple rhythms.[14]

This capacity to identify and maintain the integrating beat is what Chernoff, following Waterman, calls "metronome sense."[15]

With this brief review of the structure of African drumming as background, I now turn to the promised selection from my field journals. In this passage Ogou, who has possessed Alourdes, is just leaving. A chair is brought for Alourdes as her body collapses, signaling his departure.

July 21, 1979
Feast for Ogou
and Ezili Dantò

Before Alourdes's body has time to fully occupy the seat offered to her, Gèdè arrives. He leaps from the chair with a mischievous laugh; and a murmur of recognition and pleasure goes through the room. Gèdè's tricksterism always lightens the atmosphere and tonight, after more than two hours of Ogou, it is a special relief. Gèdè [spirit of death and sexuality, protector of small children, social satirist] calls for his black bowler and the dark glasses with one lens missing. Then he frolics and gambols around the room pressing his body against the bodies of various women present in his hip-grinding imitation of lovemaking. He remains a long time, passing out drinks of his pepper-laced *tafya* [raw rum] and joking with everyone. Gèdè is merciless with one elegantly dressed young man. After directing him to sit on the floor in front of him, Gèdè asks him over and over if he has a big penis. He steals the hat of another man; and when

12. Chernoff, *Rhythm*, 23.
13. Chernoff, *Rhythm*, 47.
14. Chernoff, *Rhythm*, 48–49.
15. Ibid., cf. Richard Alan Waterman, "African Influence on the Music of the Americas," in *Acculturation in the Americas,* ed. Sol Tax, vol. 2 (Chicago: University of Chicago Press, 1952), 207–18.

I try to take a picture, demands money. I give him some change. Later he comes back and tells me that was not enough. I give a dollar and take pictures uninterrupted. Gèdè collects money more or less continuously, appoints one young man treasurer, and every so often goes back to him and demands that he drag the money out of his pockets and count it. Gèdè says he wants to be sure no one is stealing from him. Ten to fifteen dollars is collected and earmarked for Gèdè's own feast in November.

It is five o'clock in the morning; people are restless; they look at their watches. Gèdè keeps singing: "M'ale. M'ale." ["I'm going. I'm going."] but he doesn't. He collapses into a chair, shuts his eyes, and then jumps up again in two seconds, remembering one more thing he has to say. This goes on and on and on. Everyone is aware that Dantò has yet to be called. This feast is for her, after all! Following some discussion with the elders present at the ceremony, Alourdes's daughter decides to begin the songs for Dantò even though Gèdè hasn't left. We sing slumped in our chairs barely able to keep our eyes open. while Gèdè satirizes our efforts and even injects dirty words into Ezili Dantò's sacred songs.

Finally, Gèdè leaves and the singing picks up. In only a few minutes, Ezili Dantò arrives like an explosion and we are all suddenly awake. Alourdes's ample body crashes into that of a man standing nearby. The spirit seems to spread to him by contagion and he, in turn, goes crashing into the food-laden table. Dantò's eyes dart out of her head. She utters one sound over and over: "dè-dè-dè." The pitch and rhythm change but the sound remains the same. A gold-edged, blue veil is brought and draped over her head madonna-fashion so she looks like the chromolithograph of Mater Salvatoris. She goes up to one man standing at the edge of the crowd. "Dè-dè-dè-dè-dè," she says softly. "Yes," he replies, "I will do it for you." She drags another to the elaborate table prepared for her and points to it emphatically: "Dè-dè-dè. Dè-dè-dè. Dè-dè-dè." A woman across the room yells out to the man: "She wants a table. She wants you to give her a party." "Dè-dè-dè-dè-dè-dè," she says to me, soothing, up-beat. Her hand brushes my cheek and she passes on. She strokes the belly of a pregnant woman next: "Dè-dè-dè-dè-dè-dè-dè-dè," she almost whispers and then roughly grabs the hair of the same woman and jerks her head back and forth: "DÈ-DÈ-DÈ-DÈ-DÈ-DÈ." "Your head washed," someone suggests. "She wants you to get initiated," another puts in. "That's right!" says a third and heads nod all around.

It is one thing to stand apart from Gèdè and Ezili Dantò and watch them interact with others through the distanced eye of scholarly objectivity. It is quite another to be in the place of one who awaits the attention of the spirits full of life issues and with a history of interaction with other persons present in the room. As we saw in the earlier discussion, African drumming requires that a person supply the integrating beat that clarifies what would otherwise be a chaotic clash of rhythms. Similarly, the participant in a Vodou ritual must pour his or her own life content into the polymorphic interplay of images found there. Otherwise nothing will have meaning. Because people must bring their lives into conversation with this ritualizing to make sense of it, Vodou ritual, like the music Chernoff describes, becomes "an occasion for the demonstration of character."[16] How I handle the intrusiveness of my camera; whether I try to buy my way into the community or pay appropriately and with humor; how I receive and how I am perceived receiving the gentle acceptance of Ezili Dantò at a time (1979) when my presence in the community was a source of some contention: all these things become occasions not simply for me to demonstrate character but also for me to learn what it means to have character in that context.

The way in which one "demonstrates character" in African music-making is through relationships.[17] No rhythm, not even the inner one, makes any musical sense in isolation. Meaning in African music arises from the mutual responsiveness of different rhythmic lines. For example, the dancers respond to the drummers *and* the drummers respond to the dancers. Drummers may shift their rhythmic patterning to match a particularly gifted dancer and then intensify it even further to urge her on to yet more energetic self-expression. This insight into the necessary involvement of all persons present and their interdependency in the process of music-making provides the key to Chernoff's insight that the content of African music is the social context in which it occurs.

Vodou rituals, like African drumming, usually occur in thickly meshed social situations, situations where people know one another well, and this is one of the key ingredients in their functioning.[18] Thus Chernoff's description of African music is equally apt as a description of Vodou ritualizing: both can be described as "a cultural activity which reveals a group of people organizing and involving themselves with their own communal relationships — a participant observer's comment, so to speak, on the processes of living together."[19] The criterion used to judge the success of a musical performance is, therefore, not the virtuosity of the drummers or their creative innovations, but whether the entire social event goes well.[20] Similarly, Vodou ritualizing is considered successful if everything comes together in such a way that what is going on within and among the people gathered there is expressed and clarified. This clarification is something that cannot be accomplished by one

16. Chernoff, *Rhythm*, 151.

17. Speaking of the individual musician, Chernoff says: "His individuality, like the rhythms that he plays, can only be seen in relationship." Making a similar point, Chernoff notes that, "in a context of multiple rhythms, people distinguish themselves from each other while they remain dynamically related" (*Rhythm*, 125–26).

18. In rural Haiti, Vodou ritualizing is a family affair. It takes place on the family land, where trees, streams, and wells are said to be the repositories of the spirits they serve, spirits inherited within the family. In urban Haiti and in the immigrant communities outside of Haiti, people who gather around a particular Vodou priest or priestess establish fictive kinship ties. The priestess or priest is called "mama" or "papa" and members of the temple refer to one another as "brother" and "sister."

19. Chernoff, *Rhythm*, 36.

20. Chernoff, *Rhythm*, 65.

person alone, not even a person of Alourdes's stature. That is why in the early
dawn hours when guests leave Alourdes's home after an elaborate Vodou
feast she has staged, it is not only they who thank her. She also thanks them
profusely for their help in the drama.

In the specifics of Ezili Dantò's possession-performances, we see more
precise parallels between Vodou ritualizing and African drumming. It is said
that Ezili Dantò had her tongue cut out as punishment for participating in the
Haitian slave revolution. That is why she cannot speak except to make the
one sound over and over. Dantò's performance, like any single rhythm in an
African ensemble, is meaningless in itself. It is only as the spirit interacts with
the group that her "dè-dè-dè" becomes articulate. As we saw in the passage
just quoted, Ezili Dantò supplies the emotional tone and general context of
her communications through body language and by varying the pitch and
rhythm of the "dè-dè." Yet it is actually the community, individually and
collectively, that supplies the specific content. The more conflict is present in
the message, the more the community is galvanized into offering interpretations. Such seemed to be the case when Dantò first soothingly patted the
stomach of the pregnant woman and then roughly shook her by the hair. The
interpretation of this message came from several sources and, in fact, drew
the tacit approval of the whole group.

Ezili Dantò is the woman-who-bears-children. Through the complex
ritualizing for Dantò, the many possibilities inherent in the mother-child
relationship are played out — from the mutually nourishing possibilities to the
mutually destructive ones. This spectrum of possibilities is quickly reviewed
in the reaction of Dantò to the pregnant woman. She first gives soothing
approval to the life growing in her womb and then aggressively reminds the
woman of her responsibilities to the larger kin group, the shoring up of which
can be said to be the main function of the initiation Dantò urges. Thus Dantò,
like Ogou, is a condensation point for the wisdom gained through an intense
exploration of one particular way of being in the world.

Her presence in the thick social weave of a Vodou ritual calls out meaning
on many different levels and in many different directions. On the whole, no
special attitude is required in Vodou ceremonies. People do not stop their
ordinary social intercourse while serving the spirits. As a result, a myriad of
small interpersonal exchanges are going on in relation to the words and
images of Vodou during the entire course of a ritual. It would be impossible
to describe all the ways in which persons present at that ceremony chose to
bring their own life rhythms into dialogue with the "dè-dè-dè" rhythm of
the spirit; however, I will cite one example. During Dantò's possession-
performance that evening, I noted a small exchange on the other side of the
room. As Dantò approached the pregnant woman, a mother reached out and
touched the arm of her daughter, nodding her head at the same time in the
direction of Dantò. With a look of exaggerated disgust on her face, the
daughter, who had been married some time without bearing children, looked
toward her sister, whose face, in turn, mirrored and confirmed that exaspera-

tion. Both daughters apparently agreed that their mother was overly eager about becoming a grandmother. Dantò's cross-rhythms, in this case played out as soothing approval (rubbing her belly) and forceful discipline (grabbing her hair), echoed through the room, creating a variety of meanings as they combined with the "cross-rhythms" of different life contexts. Thus, the ambiguous nature of the spirits' communications deepens and enriches their moral potential. This works in Haitian Vodou because the moral point in serving the spirits, like the aesthetic point in drumming, is not to strive toward an ideal form exterior to the context but to ritualize (and so clarify) the social forces already present within it.[21]

Ritualizing is essentially about balancing. In the Vodou context the Creole word *balanse* means, among other things, "to dance." By keeping the metronome beat with his or her own body, each dancer finds "a way of being steady within a context of multiple rhythms."[22] The polymetric clash and conflict of rhythms in African music has cosmological, social, and personal counterparts in the Vodou system. Chernoff notes the parallel between "multiple rhythms in music and the religious conception of multiple forces in the world."[23] This point can be extended to the social and personal realms by noting the parallel between polyrhythms and the Vodou system for describing the conflicting forces within and among persons according to the different spirits associated with them.

In Vodou each person is said to have one spirit who is the *mèt tet,* "master of the head." To some extent there is a mirroring between the personality of this spirit and that of the individual. For example, a particularly aggressive bit of behavior can be explained by the casual comment "li sèvi Ogou," or "she serves Ogou." Because people have different *mèt tet,* somewhat different behavioral expectations attend them. This is further complicated by the fact that, in addition to the *mèt tet,* there are two, or three, or four other spirits who are also said to "love" each person. Individual human character is consolidated by balancing in the midst of the polyrhythms of the different spirits "in one's head" and "around one's head." The neophyte who enters Vodou is told: "You cannot pray to Ogou alone. He is too hot. Light a candle for Dambala too." A moral person, in their terms, is thus one who can *balanse,* "dance," in the midst of forces pulling in opposing directions without missing the beat. The moral person is one who has a strongly developed metronome sense — that is, a strongly developed sense of self. Yet, as was said, no rhythm, not even one's own, has any meaning outside of relationship. In African drumming a rhythm must be in dialogue with one or more others before it can even be heard.[24] Chernoff calls the polyrhythmic

21. Cf. Chernoff, *Rhythm,* 37.

22. Chernoff, *Rhythm,* 49.

23. Chernoff, *Rhythm,* 156; cf. also 157–58.

24. "To a more sensitive ear, the flexible and dynamic relationships of various rhythms actually help one distinguish one rhythm from another, and on a basic level, *one rhythm defines another*" (Chernoff, *Rhythm,* 52).

structure of African drumming "music-to-find-the-beat-by."[25] We might call Vodou "ritual-to-find-the-self-by." The moral wisdom of Vodou lies in its teaching that it is precisely in responsive and responsible relation to others that one has the clearest and most steady sense of self.[26] In European-based culture we tend to oppose individualism and identification with the group. The two coincide in Vodou, where developing a strong sense of self leads not to self-sufficiency but to stronger and more sustaining social bonds.

The aesthetic sense emerging from African drumming delights in the skillful interweaving of rhythms that clash and conflict. The moral sense emerging from Vodou is one that, if it does not always delight in the conflicting forces of life, at least accepts them as somehow deeply and inevitably true. Vodou spirits, such as Ogou whose anger can equally liberate or destroy, are characters defined by conflict and contradiction. Gèdè, patron of the dead and guardian of human sexuality, wears dark glasses with one lens missing because he is said to see simultaneously into the worlds of the living and the dead. One supposes that seeing these two contradictory realities is also the source of his humor. To laugh is to balance and, like all balancing within Vodou, it is achieved, not through resolving or denying conflict, but by finding a way of staying steady in the midst of it.

Alourdes as *manbo* for a sizeable community of Haitians in New York is like the lead drummer in an African ensemble. It is her job to orchestrate her ritualizing in such a way that it becomes the context for the kind of personal and group self-disclosure that has been discussed earlier. This is a complex role that requires a full repertoire of moral-aesthetic skills.

The relation between the lead drum and the supporting drums in an African ensemble is more complicated than, say, the relation between a soloist and a supporting orchestra in Western music. The complexity of this relationship springs from the high degree of interdependency among the different players in an African ensemble. The lead drummer is the one who introduces change into an ongoing repetitive patterning of polyrhythms. However, he — all drummers are male — must do so carefully since too sudden or too drastic a change can throw his supporting players and the dancers into confusion. This means that a lead drummer must be extremely sensitive to the group, its mood, and what is going on within it, as he approaches a change point in his drumming. Before any change is effected, a polyrhythmic pattern must be allowed to repeat itself long enough for its depth to be revealed and its contour clarified, and the changes eventually introduced must be subtle ones skillfully enough executed

25. Chernoff, *Rhythm*, 50.

26. Compare this passage from Chernoff: "If you wish to sit alone in a bar, and you politely refuse an African's invitation to join his table, you may be cautioned in a friendly way that someone who sits alone may have crazy and meaningless thoughts, staying too long inside his isolated imagination and misperceiving things: it is better to develop one's thoughts with the open-mindedness ensured by the presence of other people. Their potential to reciprocate or to differ helps provide balance" (*Rhythm*, 158).

to allow one state of dynamic tension between rhythms to shift into another without losing the momentum of the music.[27] Consequently, the good lead drummer is one who does not need to show off his improvisational skill but can afford to wait and hold back, for as Chernoff says, "crucial as the changes are to keep the music dynamic, African music is more dependent on repetition."[28]

As a "lead drummer" in Vodou ritualizing in Brooklyn, Alourdes is constantly balancing repetition and change, respect for tradition and innovation. And she is doing this on a variety of levels. How many songs must be sung to greet a spirit? How many times must the verses of each be repeated? How much food must be prepared for the spirits, and can she take shortcuts in preparing it, since traditional ingredients are hard to find in New York and time is so much scarcer there? The possession-performances raise related issues. They are in themselves extremely skillful balancing acts between the traditional forms that make them recognizable and the delicate improvisations that make them relevant. Since the Vodou priesthood is charismatic, not institutionalized, Alourdes's followers would leave if they consistently felt that her tables were not well prepared or that the spirits who came to her lacked "power."

The improvisations of a master drummer cut across and redefine the other rhythms in the ensemble. Paradoxically, when they are well executed, they call attention not to themselves but to other parts of the ensemble.

> A drum in an African ensemble derives its power and becomes meaningful not only as it cuts and focuses the other drums *but also as it is cut and called into focus by them*. Rhythmic dialogues are reciprocal, and in a way that might seem paradoxical to a Westerner, a good drummer restrains himself from emphasizing his rhythm *in order that he may be heard better*.[29]

Alourdes, like a good drummer in an African ensemble, is continually stepping aside in order to be seen better. Trance is a particularly dramatic way in which she sets herself aside. Alourdes absents herself and her life concerns for much of the time during her feasts for the spirits. She does this in order that the spirits, through her, can address the life issues of those who come to her "parties." Paradoxically this very absenting of self confirms her presence and reinforces her leadership role within the community.

In a variety of other ways, too, Alourdes serves in order to lead. For example, I spent the day of the feast for Dantò described earlier helping Alourdes. By the time I left, well after dawn of the next day, she and I had spent seventeen hours without a break in preparing the food and feasting the spirits. Yet, while I was slumped in a chair at 5 A.M., barely able to keep my eyes open, Alourdes's body was being led by Gèdè through rambunctious sexual gyrations. Gèdè had emerged directly out of a two-hour possession by

---

27. "The connection between repetition and depth is one of the dominant themes emerging from the study of African music" (Chernoff, *Rhythm,* 112).

28. Chernoff, *Rhythm,* 114.   29. Chernoff, *Rhythm,* 60.

Ogou; and Alourdes returned to herself for no more than five or ten minutes after Gèdè left before Ezili Dantò came. These heroic expenditures of energy in the self-effacing service of the spirits ensure Alourdes's reputation as an accomplished leader among the Haitian immigrants in New York.

Furthermore, in Gèdè's reluctant departure that dawn, we gain some insight into the crucial sense of ritual timing that Alourdes must exercise in myriad ways — in and out of trance. In this also she is like the lead drummer in an African ensemble, whose skill can be said, like hers, to reside in a consummate sense of relationships.[30] The goal of all Vodou ritualizing is the presence of the spirits among the worshippers. They will not arrive, Haitians say, unless the group is *byen chofe*, "well heated up." The group that has eyes open, voices raised, hands clapping, and lives engaged with the ritual action is one which is "well heated up." Alourdes's skill as a technician of the sacred lies in being able to play subtly and wisely on the currents of energy that move through and among the persons who gather in her home for ceremonies. Doing so, she uses a variety of techniques similar to those employed by the African drummer.

I will give only one example of the subtlety and specificity of the connections between her techniques of ritual timing and those of the traditional drummers of Africa. Chernoff says,

> An African musician is not so much moving along with a pulsation as he is pushing the beat to make it more dynamic. The forceful quality of this orientation has led some people to speak of African musicians as playing their instruments . . . with "percussive attack," staying "on top of" the beat and imparting a rhythmic momentum to even the sweetest melodies.[31]

Percussive attack, which can be helpfully compared to the process of ritual heating up, is technically accomplished by delivering an anticipated beat just before or just after the point when it is expected.[32] The resulting tension has two outcomes. It forces the participant-listener into a heightened sense of his or her own metronome beat and also raises the general excitement and energy of the context in which that beat must be maintained.[33] Gèdè's hesitating departures and repeated reappearances performed an alchemical change on the waning energy in the room. By the dramatic technique of false departures the participants were called back to awareness of themselves, which took the form of awareness of time and anxiety about tomorrow's schedule. The expected beat — Dantò's arrival — was postponed long enough so that, when it did come, there was an awakening and resurgence of energy in the room.[34]

30. Chernoff, *Rhythm*, 150.   31. Chernoff, *Rhythm*, 56.

32. Chernoff, *Rhythm*, 96. The discussion focuses around a lengthy quotation from Waterman's "African Influence," 213.

33. Ibid.

34. Speaking of the lead drummer, Chernoff says: "A true master must time his utterances to replenish the dancers' physical and aesthetic energy at the right psychological moment" (*Rhythm*, 66).

This energizing in turn guaranteed the success of Dantò's visit. The people in the room were fully present to engage with her. The skill of a Vodou priestess such as Alourdes is rooted in her ability to give dynamic form to life energy. Thus, it might be said that Alourdes is a leader in the New York Vodou community because she is extremely skillful at using power.[35] This power, however, is best described as life energy and it should be noted that Alourdes does not exercise it over people so much as she organizes it around and through them.

One has only to watch Alourdes at ceremonies such as those described here to realize that her authority rests at least in part on the fact that she has an aesthetic sense rooted, not in the mere tolerance of clash and conflict, but rather in the positive enjoyment of it. She enjoys, and is accomplished at, the organization of power, of life energy. This point can be added to those made earlier to give us a fuller image of the aesthetic style that is the key to her leadership. In addition to her pleasure in giving form to energy, her aesthetic skill derives from a consummate sense of relationships and how these may be clarified and subtly changed to achieve a state that is at once dynamic and balanced. Furthermore, what enables Alourdes to do this is her ability to stay steady in the midst of conflicting forces. Many times I have heard her say, "I got plenty confidence in myself!" And it is precisely this highly developed sense of herself, what we have been calling metronome sense, that enables Alourdes to set herself aside in service to the community.

To sum up: in the first part of this paper we focused on the Vodou saints or spirits as condensation points for complex and conflicting truths about different ways of being in the world. In the second part we examined Alourdes's leadership role in the ritual context, and here we saw her as exemplifying a way of staying steady or balanced in the midst of the polyrhythms within and among these various ways of being in the world. Two conclusions emerge from this. First, although we are justified in calling Alourdes a moral exemplar, it is not because the specifics of her life or being (in or out of trance) represent an ideal against which the rest of the community is measured. In her role as priestess Alourdes does not stand over and against her community so much as she embodies it. She exemplifies a general style rather than specific actions or attitudes, and this is in keeping with the deep pluralism — cosmological, social, and personal — of Vodou. As a technician of the sacred, she has certain highly developed ritualistic skills, yet even these are not unrelated to those needed by the ordinary person who must negotiate conflict in life. The key to both a good ritual and a good life is high life energy and a strong sense of self balanced with responsiveness to others. The second and more general point to emerge from this analysis concerns the close relationship between the aesthetic and the moral within Vodou. I turn to this topic by way of concluding the essay.

---

35. "Proper performance of African music requires the respect and enjoyment of the organization of power" (Chernoff, *Rhythm*, 167).

AESTHETICS AND MORALS IN THE VODOU COMMUNITY

If the comparison between music and the social, therefore moral, interaction of Vodou ritualizing is to seem anything more than mere analogy, we must have some idea of how deep the connection is between the Haitian aesthetic and social senses of "how things are" and "how things ought to be." Chernoff notes that African children are soothed in lullabies whose rhythms *cut across* those of the arms that rock them.[36] I have observed the same process with Haitian infants. This intimation of the depth at which this particular aesthetic sense shapes, comments on, and organizes life for the Haitian people led me to stress Alourdes's enjoyment of what she does as well as her skill at doing it. In a deep art form such as Vodou ritualizing, which amplifies the earliest preverbal sense of how the world is, pleasure and significance coincide because art and life coincide there too.

Vodou operates as a moral system, not because it takes up what is good in life and human behavior and accentuates that, but rather because it takes up all of life and intensifies and clarifies it. The inclusive quality of its commentary on life explains why its mood is more generally celebrative than reverential, for there is nothing set apart to "worship." Indeed one of the most startling characteristics of Vodou ritualizing for one like myself, reared in the solemn rites of the Episcopal church, where only certain very selective forms of behavior are acceptable during services, is the degree to which people genuinely enjoy themselves in Vodou ceremonies. They eat, they drink, they joke and laugh, they cry. In short, the full range of emotional life finds play within the world of Vodou. Even sexuality has a place. This is yet another formulation of a by now familiar point: the context and content of Vodou ritualizing are the community itself. Rituals clarify and comment on the vast and complex intermeshing of human relationships represented there.

To the extent that change occurs in human lives because of these ritual processes, it does so through the subtle readjustments in relationships that occur as the individual "dancer" develops the skill of staying balanced within the existential push and pull represented in the rituals. The point is not to make conflict go away but to make it work for, rather than against, life. Cross-rhythms must be organized in just the right way for the baby to be rocked to sleep.

This view of life as defined by conflict is a morally neutral one. From the Haitian perspective, there is no evidence that humans live in a fallen or imperfect state; there is no Golden Age in the past, no Utopia in the future.[37]

36. Chernoff, *Rhythm*, 94.
37. There is no concept of heaven in Haitian Vodou. The souls of the dead, after existing for some time in a sort of limbo state, are "called" back to interact with the living once more, but this time in the form of spirits. *Lemò*, "the dead," though not to be confused with the *lwa*, the major spirits of Vodou, play a similar role in relation to the living. When well served, they guarantee good fortune; when neglected, they bring suffering and hardship. Some say that the

The moral pull within Vodou comes from the realization that the poly-rhythms of life can wound and destroy when not properly balanced; but when balanced, the same polyrhythms become the source of life-enhancing energy. This moral-aesthetic stance accounts for the high tolerance, indeed enjoyment, of pluralism on the cosmological, social, and personal levels. Haitians appear to believe that it is precisely the conflicts within people and the differences among them that make life worthwhile. From this perspective it would seem that there is no essential evil assumed to reside within specific persons or within specific areas of the world.[38] The moral problem is not evil but imbalance, both within and among persons. In the context of this pluralistic and conflict-centered description of life, the moral leader is not one who sets her own life up as a model for imitation. It is rather that person who, as a subtle and skilled technician of the sacred, can orchestrate ritual contexts in which each person discovers how to dance in his or her own way through a process of dynamic balancing with others who dance in their own way.

---

dead take up permanent residence in a land where their daily life is much as it was when they were alive. There is no sense in which this kind of existence is seen as superior to ordinary existence. In fact, it is probably understood as less desirable than being alive.

38. Haitian Vodou is notorious in the world of popular film and literature for its devil figures. Much of this is quite simply misinformation. There are, however, various sorts of negative spiritlike presences — for example, *lugaru, zobop, zombi,* and *baka.* Careful analysis of the stories that surround these malevolent figures, who are at any rate more figures of folklore than religion, indicates that virtually all of their malevolence can be traced to interrelational problems. For example, the *baka* may be the spirit of a murdered person. The disembodied soul of a person known as *zombi* may have been "sent" to do another harm because of trouble between the sender and the recipient. The *lugaru* and the *zobop* are spirit manifestations of living persons who are jealous or power-hungry.

TEN

Sathya Sai Baba's Saintly Play

Lawrence A. Babb

When my wife's South Indian singing teacher described her mother as a "saint," I thought I knew what I was hearing. After all, I had heard mothers characterized as saints before. Mothers are saints (or so speakers of American English mean to imply) when they are self-sacrificing, long suffering, and charitable. They are saintly, in other words, when they are paragons of certain virtues. My misunderstanding could not have been more complete. By this I mean to suggest, not that this particular mother was unvirtuous, but that her virtues (of which to this day I know nothing) were not the point of the remark. What made this woman saintlike, it later emerged, was that she was a holy person with a following of devotees. She possessed an extraordinary spiritual power that was manifested in, among other things, an ability to materialize objects from nowhere. Whatever speakers of American English mean when they refer to mothers as saints, it is, I think, rarely this.

It would be easy to say that my initial misunderstanding was the result of a fortuitous juxtaposition of two misusages of the English term *saint*. A self-sacrificing nature is not in itself saintliness, and neither is the ability to attract a personal following of devotees or the power to produce objects from thin air. And yet, upon reflection, it is not clear that the misunderstanding was as egregious as it seemed at first to be. Was my wife's teacher merely misusing an English word? Possibly, but saints do attract followings, and we frequently associate saintliness with the possession of miraculous power. And

The research reported by this essay took place in Delhi between July 1978 and May 1979, and was supported by an Indo-American Fellowship. I thank colleagues at the Department of Sociology, Delhi University, for their most generous hospitality and help during my stay in Delhi. I also thank the many devotees of Sathya Sai Baba who aided me in my inquiries. I am especially grateful to John Hawley for his trenchant comments on an earlier draft of this paper. All errors of fact or interpretation are, of course, my own.

when American mothers are sometimes described as saintly, is this merely a manner of speaking (perhaps ironic) that capitalizes on peripheral connotations of the term? Maybe, but we do think of saints as persons whose character is in some way morally instructive. The semantic problems arise because these apparently distinct senses of saintliness represent separate surfaces of a phenomenon that we intuitively recognize as real but have great difficulty characterizing as a unity.

Who is a saint? The confusion of the saintly mothers teaches us at the very least that real saints are more than one thing at once. Leaving aside the vexed (and important) question of whether other languages have terms that exactly represent this idea, let me suggest that in the symbolic infrastructures of various religions there exists the image of a certain extraordinary spiritual "type," a sacred character that seems to be more than the sum of its parts. Remarkable moral presence is frequently attributed to individuals who embody this idea, but they are recognized as extraordinary not because of this quality alone. They are also commonly believed to possess miraculous powers, but again they are not revered simply on account of such powers. Such persons, rather, blend and fuse the moral and the powerful in a way that generates a unique glow of spiritual energy. These saintly figures are the focal points of spiritual force-fields, and their personalities not only exert a powerful attractive influence on followers but touch the inner lives of others in transforming ways.

Was the music teacher's mother (now deceased) truly an example of a saint with these characteristics? I cannot say. However, another contender for such sainthood from India, one who also performs apparent miraculous materializations, comes immediately to mind. This is a celebrated Hindu holy man known as Sathya Sai Baba. There is probably no such thing as an uncontroversial saint. If one were to go to India and ask whether there are any Hindu saints alive today, many people would undoubtedly nominate this figure for that high honor, but others would just as surely dismiss him as a somewhat larger-than-life parlor magician or worse. Such controversies notwithstanding, ample justification does exist for calling him a saint; and in the course of explaining why this is so, I hope to be able to illustrate how miraculous power and moral presence can go together to make saintliness — or at least one kind of saintliness — possible.

Sathya Sai Baba is in all likelihood the most famous of modern India's holy men. His followers call him *bhagavān* (God) and consider him to be a modern *avatār* (descent of God) who has come to earth to restore righteousness in a benighted era, to establish what he and his followers call a "Sai Age." The chief basis of his fame, however, is his performance of miracles. As a type he is certainly not unique, for throughout India there are many men and women like him but whose renown is purely local. That he has risen to the top is largely a result of the power and influence of his principal constituency. He is, preeminently, the holy man of modern India's urban middle and upper-

middle classes, those whom Agehananda Bharati calls (perhaps too tenden-
tiously) "urban alienates."[1] Though his followers come from quite diverse
regional backgrounds, they tend to be educated, cosmopolitan, and in some
ways sophisticated. Many, though by no means all, are very wealthy. Largely
because of this, the public visibility of his cult is unparalleled, and he is
undoubtedly among the most important of modern India's great religious
figures.

I never met Sathya Sai Baba, and for reasons that will become obvious I am
not sure that anyone meets him in any meaningful sense. In the course of field
research on urban Hinduism, however, I did have many months of close
contact with members of his following in Delhi. I participated in a variety of
cult-related activities, and had numerous interviews and informal conversations with devotees about him, themselves, and their perceptions of who he
is and what he means to them. What follows is based on these encounters and
an extensive reading of the cult's literature.

If saintliness fuses the moral and the powerful, this is a case in which the
moral side of the balance is the more problematical. As we shall see, Sathya
Sai Baba is not a moral exemplar in any simple sense, nor is he an ethical
teacher of distinction. But the character he displays to the world nonetheless
teaches moral lessons, although in what may strike readers as a surprising
way. The primary focus of my account is the question of how moral meanings
are, and are not, embodied in Sathya Sai Baba's persona. My guiding assumption is that it is not always easy to appreciate moral presence for what it is,
especially when looking across cultural divides. This being so, we must
always be prepared to encounter forms of genuine saintliness that may depart
strikingly and perhaps disconcertingly from prevailing stereotypes.

HIMSELF

The first thing that must be said about Sathya Sai Baba is that the man himself
is nearly impossible to find. This may seem a strange thing to say, but I cannot
think of another way to put it: we will probably never know quite who he is.
Submerged somewhere in the hubbub and symbolic paraphernalia of his cult
is a person that we, as outside observers, would call the "real man." But
whoever this real Sathya Sai Baba is, he is inaccessible, hidden away not only
from outsiders but from his followers too — indeed perhaps hidden from them
most of all. For the most part the details of personal biography and manner
of life that might enable us to form an impression of an individual personality
are buried beneath a vast alluvium of hagiographic overlay. I suspect we will
never see an objective, warts-and-all portrait of Sathya Sai Baba, for it is
highly unlikely that anyone close enough to him to write such an account

---

1. Agehananda Bharati, *Hindu Views and Ways and the Hindu-Muslim Interface: An
Anthropological Assessment* (Delhi: Munshiram Manoharlal, 1981), 58–59.

would ever do so. In fact, it is not even clear that anyone *is* that close to him. Around this person, whoever he is, is a nearly impenetrable veil.

There is, however, another Sathya Sai Baba who is indeed knowable. He is the public Sathya Sai Baba, the one who is worshipped by devotees. This figure is not a human personality in the usual sense but a sacred persona, an image that draws its substance from the symbolism of certain forms of Hindu devotionalism. And if Sathya Sai Baba, the man himself, is largely hidden, the earthly career of this sacred figure is highly visible, especially in the hagiographic writings of his secretary and longtime devotee, N. Kasturi.[2]

These materials constitute a biography of a sort, but it is one that interestingly inverts what Western novels and psychoanalytic case histories have taught us to expect of portrayals of emergent character. By this I mean that Sathya Sai Baba's divine persona is not treated in developmental terms, as a continually growing product of a lengthening past. Rather, his character is presented as essentially timeless and constant — a completed pattern that is revealed, in varying facets, by events taking place over time. Episodic disclosure, not ontogeny, is the essence of Sathya Sai Baba's career on earth.

Some strict facts do exist. He was born on 23 November 1926 to a family of the *rāju* caste[3] in the village of Puttaparthi in what is now the state of Andhra Pradesh. His given name was Satyanarayana. But in Kasturi's rendering, facts grade off into symbolism. We are told that neither his birth nor his childhood was a normal one, for there were many evidences that his nature was of an extraordinary kind. We learn, for example, that the strings of a *tambūrā* were plucked by an invisible force prior to his birth, and that a cobra mysteriously appeared beneath the newborn infant's bedding — the same snake that serves as a bed for the god Vishnu. Sathya Sai Baba's childhood was generally reminiscent of Krishna's, displaying an amalgam of portents, miracles, and pranks: on one occasion he prevented a teacher from rising from a chair by causing it to stick to his backside. He was loving, magical, intelligent, wise, and innately charitable; he grew up an instinctive vegetarian. Even in early childhood he evoked devotional sentiments in those around him.

The first pivotal disclosure occurred when he was thirteen years old. Then attending school in the town of Uravakonda, he suddenly fell into a prolonged seizure that at first was thought to be the result of a scorpion sting. Fainting spells were punctuated by bouts of laughing, crying, singing, and scripture recitation, and at last his alarmed parents brought him back to his native Puttaparthi. Neither doctors nor an exorcist seemed to be able to help. Then one morning he began materializing sweets and flowers for members of

2. See N. Kasturi, *Sathyam, Sivam, Sundaram*, pt. 1, American ed. (Whitefield: Shri Sathya Sai Education and Publication Foundation, 1977); *Sathyam, Sivam, Sundaram*, pt. 2, 3d ed. (New Delhi: Bhagavan Sri Sathya Sai Seva Samiti, 1975); and *Sathyam, Sivam, Sundaram*, pt. 3 (New Delhi: Bhagavan Sri Sathya Sai Seva Samiti, 1975).

3. For further information on the *rājus*, see Edgar Thurston and K. Rangachari, *Castes and Tribes of Southern India*, vol. 6 (Madras: Government Press, 1909), 247–56.

his family and neighbors. His father was called to the scene, and in an outburst of exasperation at being asked to wash his hands, face, and feet before approaching his son, he threatened the boy with a stick. It was at this point that young Satyanarayana made his first declaration of identity. "I am Sai Baba," he said, and he went on to say that he belonged to the spiritual school of the sage Āpastamba and the spiritual lineage of Bharadvāja.

The key element in this remarkable announcement was that he claimed to be a reincarnation of a famed holy man known as Sai Baba, who years before had lived at the town of Shirdi in Maharashtra.[4] This claim was to become the first main element in his sacred identity. Shortly after this disclosure young Satyanarayana, now Sai Baba, declared to his brother's wife (he was living in his brother's home at the time) that he was no longer "your Satya." This signaled the decisive break with earthly kin that marks the careers of most holy persons in the Hindu tradition.

The second pivotal disclosure occurred years later, by which time Sathya Sai Baba had gained the allegiance of a vast following in North India as well as his native South. In June 1963, while at his ashram, he fell into another seizure. For several days he seemed to drift in and out of a coma, and he was able to communicate only with gestures and a few garbled words. After some slight improvement, on the eighth day of his illness he appeared before a large crowd of devotees. While propped in his chair, he asked one of his assistants to announce to the crowd that the illness was in fact not his, but something he had taken on himself on behalf of a deserving devotee. Then, by sprinkling water on himself, he effected what appeared to be an instantaneous and complete cure. This recovery was followed by a discourse in which he made another remarkable announcement. He was, he said, both Shiva and Shakti (Shiva's consort) in a single body. Although he had taken the illness on himself to save a devotee, the illness was also the same as that once contracted by Shakti because she had caused the sage Bharadvāja to become ill. And just as Shiva had cured the sage by means of water, Shiva had cured Shakti by the same means in Sathya Sai Baba's body. He further announced that his present incarnation was the second of three. Shirdi Sai Baba was Shakti alone, and Sathya Sai Baba is Shiva and Shakti together. Still to come is an incarnation of Shiva alone, to be known as Prem Sai, who will be born in Karnataka State.

Apart from his birth and the early manifestations of his divine character, these two disclosures have been the axial events of Sathya Sai Baba's career thus far. In the accounts of his life there is, of course, much more material, but for the most part it is of a sort that is easily summarized: his tours, his addresses to various groups, his visits (with legitimizing overtones) to various Hindu sacred centers, his confrontations with other religious figures,[5] and,

4. An excellent account of Shirdi Sai Baba and other figures (including Sathya Sai Baba) in the Sai Baba tradition can be found in Charles S. J. White, "The Sai Baba Movement: Approaches to the Study of Indian Saints," *Journal of Asian Studies* 31, no. 4 (1972): 863–78.

5. Visits to pilgrimage centers and debates with other divines are conventional features of Hindu hagiography.

above all, his encounters with devotees and his many miracles. He himself has stated that his earthly career will have a total of four phases. The first sixteen years were a time of playful pranks, and the next thirteen years a period for displays of miraculous power. The third sixteen years were for teaching and further miracles, and the remainder of his life will be devoted to the teaching of spiritual discipline to small groups of devotees. He will die, he says, at the age of ninety-six in the body of a young man.

One notable aspect of Sathya Sai Baba's career is the relative independence of his sacred authority from conventional patterns of spiritual succession. The legitimizing connections with Āpastamba and Bharadvāja do, of course, link him with recognized traditions, as does the claim to be a reincarnation of Shirdi Sai Baba. But it is, finally, not through the more usual channels of birth, propinquity, or discipleship that his sacred status is linked with other figures, but through miraculous connections that leap over space and time. The plausibility of his sacred authority seems to be based far more on his followers' direct responses to him than on any supposed spiritual links with the past. As D. A. Swallow points out, a purely practical effect of the additional projection of a third incarnation as Prem Sai is the obviation of any need to deal with potentially awkward succession issues within the cult.[6] Perhaps the most important implication of the series of Sai-successions, however, is that they establish Sathya Sai Baba's status as quite extraordinary, transcending more normal principles of spiritual inheritance.[7]

Another striking feature of Sathya Sai Baba's life, as it emerges in these materials, is an almost complete elision of individual personhood. What looks at first like life-history turns out to be something quite different: a suppression of unique life-history, and a removal of the life in question *from* history.[8] At virtually every turn individuating details are subordinated to one timeless mythic paradigm or another. His birth was not a particular birth but *the* birth of a deity-infant, as evidenced by the resounding of the *tambūrā* and the cobra under the bedding. His childhood was not a particular childhood but *the* childhood of a juvenile god, for which the ruling paradigm in India is the early life of Krishna. With the first of the two great disclosures, the image of the magical child is superseded by another — that of the archetypal holy man, as represented by Sai Baba of Shirdi. In the second disclosure this identity, in turn, is encompassed within yet another, which is not only wider, but universal. Now he is revealed to be Shiva and Shakti, who together represent the Absolute.

6. D. A. Swallow, "Ashes and Powers: Myth, Rite and Miracle in an Indian God-Man's Cult," *Modern Asian Studies* 16 (1982): 136–37.

7. My thanks to John Hawley for suggesting this interpretation.

8. For a parallel example of the suppression of individual personality in Hindu sacred biography, see Edward C. Dimock, Jr., "Religious Biography in India; The 'Nectar of the Acts' of Chaitanya," in *The Biographical Process: Studies in the History and Psychology of Religion*, ed. F. E. Reynolds and D. Capps (The Hague: Mouton, 1976). For a wider theoretic context, see Mircea Eliade, *The Myth of the Eternal Return*, trans. W. R. Trask (Princeton, N. J.: Princeton University Press, 1974).

In his identity as Shiva and Shakti, Sathya Sai Baba's persona opens out into transcendental inclusiveness and ambiguity. He is beyond all limiting categories. All times and all space are one to him. His character also transcends gender, for he is male and female in one body. By his own interpretation, Sai means "divine mother" and Baba means "father." He is the divine mother and father of all beings, blended in a single sacred personality.

As in a geological deposit, however, nothing is lost, for residues of older identities continue to exist below the newer and higher strata. Thus the playful, Krishna-like child lives on, as we shall see, in an important aspect of his present-day demeanor. And the identity of Shirdi Sai Baba is retained in his name and numerous aspects of his cult. But all these images are understood to be modulations of the most inclusive identity — that of the sacred, atemporal all. This final, ultimate identity as a divine being beyond the limits of time, space, and gender is, as I hope to show, an indispensable element in Sathya Sai Baba's character in the imaginations of his devotees. As for the remaining details of his life, they are largely reiterations of very basic gestures. Here we see a Sathya Sai Baba who again and again, once as always, accepts the devotion of his followers and responds with love and the granting of boons.

HIS MORALITY

Sathya Sai Baba is not a moral exemplar, or at least not in the usual meaning of the term. It would be impossible for most people to take his style of life as a model for their own and still discharge their worldly responsibilities. To begin with, he is celibate, not a householder. In this respect, to live as he does would be a clear dereliction of duty for most people, at least before a certain age. Sathya Sai Baba himself is quite clear on this point. For him the spiritual life is consonant with the fulfillment of one's duties in the world. He holds the householder's (*gṛhastha*'s) life in high esteem, and, in conformity with the spirit of the traditional *caturāśrama dharma,* he encourages celibacy only after the age of fifty or so. But his own conduct is also inimitable for another, deeper reason: his behavior is insufficiently structured by *any* single model to serve as a guide for the behavior of ordinary people. This explanation means, not that his behavior is amoral, but that the morality it expresses is in certain critical ways beyond the limited capacities of human understanding. As a fundamental feature of his sacred character, this quality will be discussed in detail later.

Yet if Sathya Sai Baba is not a moral exemplar, he is nonetheless a moral teacher, commending certain kinds of conduct to his devotees. His standards are neither rigid nor innovative. He encourages a moderate and *sāttvik* (in essence, vegetarian) diet and the avoidance of alcohol and smoking; these are not radical strictures in a Hindu context. He puts great stress on the obligation of the fortunate to aid the poor through charity and social service. He is an advocate of honesty, gentleness, tolerance, and kindness toward others. That there is nothing novel in any of these values does not decrease their importance: there exists no society in which adherence to Sathya Sai Baba's standards of interpersonal conduct would not be civilizing.

There is one domain, however, in which Sathya Sai Baba's judgments do have a particularly sharp edge, and this is the matter of India's cultural invasion by the West. He has stated many times that he believes that Indians who imitate Western ways of life have betrayed themselves and their heritage. His despair at this verges on the nativistic. He is particularly concerned about the decline in knowledge of the Hindu tradition among those who consider themselves Hindus. This is, in fact, a highly relevant critique of his own cosmopolitan and rather bicultural (Hindu and modern Western) followers. Many of my devotee-informants had only the sketchiest idea of the Hindu tradition, and this itself was sometimes gained only as a result of participation in Sathya Sai Baba's cult.

Perhaps the most basic point to be made about Sathya Sai Baba's moral teachings, including the last mentioned, is that they do not challenge traditional images of a just society. He advocates India's reform, but his reformism is basically that of a dharmic conventionalist; what he most seeks to do in this sphere is to reestablish traditional righteousness. Thus, for example, he views strikes as deeply misguided, in that they contradict what he regards as the proper relationship between employers and employees: noncompetitive complementarity.[9] This ideal of socioeconomic relations is of a piece with the ideology of caste, and while he is not an apologist for the caste system as such, his views on hierarchy in general are profoundly conservative. It is true that caste distinctions are spiritually unimportant, but it is also true that there are innate differences within the human family. How, he once asked, can there be human equality when "man" inherits "a multiplicity of impulses, skills, qualities, tendencies, attitudes, and even diseases from his ancestors and from his own history [that is, karmic history]?"[10]

His views on women are similar. He is much concerned for the welfare of women, and he has invested his cult's resources heavily in women's education, but he certainly does not advocate changes in conventional women's roles. Women are innately weak, compassionate, and humble. They should strive to realize *stri-dharma* (the specifically feminine virtues) in their conduct, which means, among other things, that they should be retiring and supportive of men.

In sum, Sathya Sai Baba is a moral teacher who urges his followers to treat others with decency and charity, but he can hardly be said to be the sort of illuminated moral presence who infuses a moral order with new kinds of

9. See, for example, N. Kasturi, *Sathya Sai Speaks*, vol. 8 (Tustin, Calif.: Sri Sathya Sai Baba Book Center of America, 1975), 80.

10. N. Kasturi, *Sathya Sai Speaks*, vol. 3, 2d ed. (Tustin, Calif.: Sri Sathya Sai Baba Book Center of America, 1970), 29.

energy and meaning. He asks his devotees to do good in the world, but his deep conservatism on fundamentals ensures that the good that is done is unlikely to prove unsettling to a social order in which the groups and classes from which his devotees mainly come are distinctly favored. Whatever else his saintliness is, it is not the saintliness of moral challenge.

But to anyone familiar with Sathya Sai Baba's cult this entire discussion of his teachings is likely to seem slightly disconnected from reality, since matters of doctrine, theological or ethical, are a poor guide to what matters most about Sathya Sai Baba to his devotees. When an observer talks with devotees, he or she immediately enters the world of the concrete. They speak of their personal encounters with Baba: seeing him, hearing him, touching him (especially his feet), visiting his ashram, being personally interviewed by him, and so on. Most of all, they talk about his miracles. It is because of the miracles that most of his devotees are drawn to him in the first place, and the miracles play a crucial role in his ongoing relationships with devotees. Indeed the miraculous, not doctrine of any sort, is truly central to Sathya Sai Baba's cult.

What does this mean? Does it mean that Sathya Sai Baba is merely a purveyor of amoral magicality? I think not. It would be mistaken to think of his ethical teachings as nothing more than a legitimizing smokescreen for magical tricks. Despite the cult's focus on the miraculous, his devotees do take these teachings seriously and so, I am convinced, does he. Even more to the point, it would be mistaken to think of Sathya Sai Baba's miracles as occupying an entirely separate sphere from morality. Rather, the miracles themselves have moral meanings. These pertain, however, to features of Sathya Sai Baba's character that lie at a completely different level from all that we have seen thus far, and in order to understand them we will have to examine his miracles in greater detail.

HIS MAGIC

Sathya Sai Baba's apologists are sometimes a bit disingenuous in the way they deal with his miracles. They often declare that the miracles are superficial — that the real miracles are those taking place "within" his devotees. Such a statement may be true, but as far as I am able to tell, it is rather remote from the attitudes of most devotees who, when asked to describe what Baba means to them, almost invariably turn to the subject of miracles they have witnessed or of which they have heard. Sathya Sai Baba himself characterizes his miracles as "evidence" of his divinity,[11] and sometimes speaks of them as his "visiting cards," signs of his power by which he may be known for what he is. Moreover, Sathya Sai Baba's fame in Indian society is based mainly on his reputation as a miracle worker.

11. Kasturi, *Sathyam, Sivam, Sundaram*, pt. 3, 139.

His devotees believe, quite simply, that nothing is beyond his powers. He can cure any illness and even bring the dead to life. He can see within the human heart and can tell his devotees what is on their minds before they open their mouths. He can magically travel to distant locations. He can be in more than one place at the same time. He can perform surgical operations from afar. He can effect transformations of objects and substances (he once changed water into gasoline). His most characteristic style of performing miracles, however, is to materialize objects and substances from nothing. He produces sweets, books, pictures of himself, watches, jewelry, statuettes of deities, and much more. The most important thing he produces is sacred ash (*vibhūti*), of which he is said to materialize over one pound per day.[12] Produced by a wave of his hand, the ash is given to devotees, and is usually consumed or applied to their bodies. The ash is a symbolic link with Shirdi Sai Baba, who also dispensed ash, and most of all with Shiva. Ash is one of Shiva's most important symbols — an emblem of his ascetic concentration and the power it yields; thus each materialization of ash is a dramatic reiteration of Sathya Sai Baba's identity as Shiva-Shakti.[13]

Devotees believe and report that Sathya Sai Baba's miracles are occurring everywhere and all the time, regardless of whether or not he is physically present. They sometimes smell his sweet odor in their houses and frequently experience his visitations in dreams. Associated with his cult, moreover, are numerous miraculous households in which his magical powers are continuously manifested from a distance. In these favored homes drinks are mysteriously drunk from glasses, bites are invisibly taken from edibles, objects change position, writing appears in closed notebooks, and pictures of Sathya Sai Baba exude sacred ash and other substances. Some of these households have become, in effect, unofficial subcenters of the cult.

The meaning of these various miraculous phenomena can be understood in three separate, but connected, frames of reference. The miraculous plays a role in recruitment to the cult; it provides a medium for certain kinds of transactions between Baba and his devotees; and it constitutes a theater in which a particular vision of the world, and of the self's situation in the world, is enacted as a dimension of his character. Because I have already treated these matters in another essay,[14] I will merely touch upon the recruitment and transactional dimensions of the miracles here, concentrating on the question of what Sathya Sai Baba's miracles mean as a total display of his divine persona.

Sathya Sai Baba's miracles play a major role in recruiting followers to his fold. Most of my devotee-informants first became aware of him because of the fame of his miracles, and for many the inception of personal devotion to

12. Kasturi, *Sathyam, Sivam, Sundaram,* pt. 1, 140.

13. On this point, see Swallow, "Ashes and Powers."

14. Lawrence A. Babb, "Sathya Sai Baba's Magic," *Anthropological Quarterly* 56, no. 3 (1983): 116–24.

him was virtually coterminous with an acceptance of their validity. The devotees I interviewed commonly characterized themselves as having been modern skeptics prior to their conversions. For such converts there was often a specific encounter with Sathya Sai Baba's miraculous power that proved decisive, a personal experience of some phenomenon that they felt to be completely inexplicable without assuming his divine powers. Most devotees seemed to feel that the beginning of this conviction was a true watershed in their life-histories.

With regard to the transactional dimension of Sathya Sai Baba's miracles, the key point is that his displays of magic usually involve the materialization of particular things or substances that then pass to his devotees. When devotees speak of his materializations, they naturally stress the apparent magic of the performance, but the denouement of the tale is typically the giving of the ash, the ring, or whatever, to some person or persons. Thus one of the most important aspects of the things he produces is the way they connect him to particular worshippers. In this respect Sathya Sai Baba's miracles exemplify a very common pattern in Hindu devotional worship. Throughout the Hindu world worshippers receive *prasād* (food-leavings) and other items that have been in intimate contact with a deity or august personage. Such transactions express hierarchical intimacy and, for the recipients, represent what McKim Marriott has called "biomoral" gain; the receiver ingests, absorbs, or assimilates the transferable virtues of a superior donor, and is thereby benefitted.[15] Sathya Sai Baba's magical productions function in a precisely analogous way. They are a particularly valuable form of his *prasād;* produced by his power, in a sense they *are* his power in mobile material vehicles. As such they can transfer the efficacy of his power (as his grace or favor) to his devotees.

A deep and constant theme in this aspect of Sathya Sai Baba's magical displays is personal intimacy with his followers. He is constantly surrounded by crowds, and sustained close contact with him is impossible except for the most privileged of his devotees. But true devotees nevertheless perceive their relationship with him as close and personal, and his miracles play an important role in buttressing this conviction. His miraculous multilocality is an obvious case in point: its purpose is to place Baba near his devotees in times of great need. Similarly, when sacred ash flows forth from his pictures in the miraculous households, it means that Baba is personally present in these households, appearances to the contrary notwithstanding. And when he produces by magical means items that can be ingested, the personal connectedness is intimate indeed. But the items in question need not be ingested.

15. McKim Marriott, "Hindu Transactions: Diversity without Dualism," in *Transactions and Meaning: Directions in the Anthropology of Exchange and Symbolic Behavior*, ed. B. Kapferer (Philadelphia: ISHI Publishers, 1976).

When Sathya Sai Baba gave one of my informants a ring he had magically produced, he stated that between the ring and himself would always be a "golden thread" that would ensure that he would always be near the wearer. Sathya Sai Baba's miracles deploy sacred power but not at random. This power moves in channels that are perceived to establish and deepen personal relationships between him and his devotees. It is not so much power in general as it is the power of his personal presence in the particular lives of particular others.

HIS PLAY

Yet another dimension to Sathya Sai Baba's miracles, and to his acts in general, is their apparent capriciousness. This element is intimately related to his sacred persona, and, as I hope to show, acts as a bridge between his magical displays and his devotees' most general perceptions of their own religious situations.

On this point we must begin with one of the most obvious facts of all about Sathya Sai Baba as he is perceived by his devotees — namely, his unpredictability. He is genuinely tricksterlike in his changeability. Where will Baba be? When will he travel? Whom will he see in interviews? When will he perform miracles? For whom will he materialize gifts? Questions of this sort are a constant background theme in the discourse of devotees when they talk to each other about Sathya Sai Baba. He simply cannot be caught in the net of any kind of expectations. His moods are mercurial, and he is constantly changing pace and direction, zigging and zagging across the landscapes of India and his devotees' imaginations. He promises one thing; he does another. He is expected here; he appears there. He is, one might say, as unpredictable as destiny itself.

The word used by devotees to characterize this aspect of Sathya Sai Baba's behavior is *līlā,* meaning "play," "sport," or "theatrical performance." That is, Baba's unpredictable, surprising, and often generous but sometimes mischievous acts are his play-as-display. Here is the youthful Krishna, Sathya Sai Baba the child-deity, still preserved as a fundamental part of his sacred demeanor.

The image of Sathya Sai Baba as playful is extremely significant; it brings us close, not only to the center of his own sacred character, but also to certain basic features of Hindu divinity in general. In what is perhaps one of the saddest legacies of a Judeo-Christian past, most Europeans and Americans have great difficulty finding any point of intellectual or emotional contact with the image of a playful God, but in the Hindu world this idea is quite natural. In this tradition the world was created in an act of divine play. The sportiveness of Hindu deities displays a liminal face of divinity. Prankster

Krishna, John Hawley shows, is a boundary breaker, a confounder of convention whose love floods over the barriers of social propriety.[16] There is a curious fusion of beyondness and nearness in this aspect of divine character. As David Kinsley points out, in their playfulness the gods are "other" because their actions simply slip through the meshes of theological and ethical systems, but in "playing with" their devotees they can also, and paradoxically, be very near.[17] Playfulness, it must never be forgotten, is a close sibling of love. Real love, like play, is utterly spontaneous, free, uncalculating, and its own justification. Therefore, devotional love and joyous play are deeply resonant with each other. The playmate-devotee enters a love affair with God, "an ovation of bliss in which the devotee and Kṛṣṇa delight and entertain one another, charmed by each other's beauty and drawn irresistibly by each other's love."[18] It is precisely because play is so careless of conventional structures that it can be a vehicle for unmediated, spontaneous connectedness. In ethnography this association is nowhere more clearly seen than in the northern Indian festival of *holī*, an occasion on which human celebrants leave their ordinary roles to become Krishna's cowherd and milkmaid playmates, and in the process renew their relationships with each other as well. Their sports become a "feast of love" in which "insubordinate libido" inundates "all established hierarchies of age, sex, caste, wealth, and power."[19]

Sathya Sai Baba's magic, and his persona in general, are unintelligible unless seen against the background of these ideas. Obviously the sheer magicality of his miracles is important, but what is vital to understand is that the miracles are not "mere" magic. In a Hindu milieu the miraculous hardly carries the weight it does in the pervasively skeptical West. What is significant about Sathya Sai Baba's miracles is, not the demonstration of apparently supernormal power as such (though this is indispensable to the total display), but what his devotees understand this power to signify. His devotees usually refer to his miracles as his *līlās*, his "sports." This is consistent with their insistent separation of his powers from all other magical powers. His miracles are not the same as the *siddhis*, the supernatural accomplishments, of human adepts. Rather, they are spontaneous, godlike play, and thus direct expressions of the "otherness" of his divine identity. But as evidences of his favor, and as expressions of a joyousness shared with his playmate-devotees, they are also manifestations of love.

One must not imagine that Sathya Sai Baba encounters no skepticism in

16. John Stratton Hawley, *Krishna, The Butter Thief* (Princeton, N.J.: Princeton University Press, 1983), 270–87.

17. David R. Kinsley, *The Divine Player: A Study of Kṛṣṇa Līlā* (Delhi: Motilal Banarsidass, 1979).

18. Kinsley, *Divine Player*, 202.

19. McKim Marriott, "The Feast of Love," in *Krishna: Myths, Rites and Attitudes*, ed. M. Singer (Honolulu: East-West Center Press, 1966), 212; also see Kinsley, *Divine Player*, 183–90.

Indian society. Indeed doubters do exist, and the character of their doubt is itself instructive. In conversations about Sathya Sai Baba with nondevotees, I encountered basically two attitudes. One was the view that his miracles are nothing more than some form of sleight of hand. This common response was, in fact, held by many of my devotee-informants before their conversions to the cult. The other view is that the magic is "real" enough but not extraordinary. People espousing this position often hold that his miracles are manifestations of humanly cultivated *siddhis,* or even of sorcery. It is in contrast to the latter form of skepticism that the inner spirit of "belief" in Sathya Sai Baba emerges with the greatest clarity. Belief in him is not just the belief that he possesses extraordinary powers; it is the belief that his powers have extraordinary implications. *Siddhis* and sorcery alike may be uncanny, extraordinary, or awe-inspiring, but they are explicable in ways that are, given certain premises, perfectly rational. But believers hold that Sathya Sai Baba's most definitively characteristic acts, his miracle-sports, are quite different — deeply and divinely unfathomable.

Yet his acts are not meaningless, and with this we are brought to what I believe to be a central feature of his character as it exists as a symbolic construct, and to what might be considered the crowning paradox of his nature. What does his capriciousness mean? Does it mean that his acts occur with the randomness of chance? Not quite, for although his human devotees cannot predict the things he does, or fully understand *why* he does the things he does, his actions are still susceptible to certain kinds of retrospective interpretation. In fact, he frequently offers such interpretations himself. For example, one of my devotee-informants was the father of a profoundly retarded boy. Knowing that Sathya Sai Baba can cure any illness, my informant once asked him why he did not cure the boy. Baba replied that it is sometimes best that the karmic effects of past lives be worked off quickly; thus, his apparent inaction was actually based on a calculation — one that only he could make — of the boy's best interests. Devotees themselves often interpret his acts within the same paradigm. An informant recalled his disappointment when Sathya Sai Baba failed to materialize a locket for him after promising to do so. But then my informant added that the broken promise was actually a much-needed lesson in humility, for he had wanted the locket only to "show off." His boons as well as his failures to act are often interpreted in the same way. For example, those who are favored by being allowed into the innermost circles of his cult are said to be reaping the results of past virtue. In other words, in ways that are not always obvious, Baba's devotees get what they deserve.

One important implication is that Sathya Sai Baba's capriciousness is only apparent. His seemingly chaotic acts are but the outer, visible surfaces of a deeper character that is necessarily beyond the limited capacities of human awareness to understand fully. As transmigrating souls, we wander in a night of forgetfulness. Though we carry the effects of our pasts in the form of unconscious tendencies (*sanskāras*), we remember nothing of our origins or our pasts, and thus we do not really know ourselves. Sathya Sai Baba, however, is believed by his devotees to be unbound by time or space. In a common formula they say he knows everything "past, present, and future." Does he sometimes fail to reward the virtuous? And does he sometimes seem, as many of his critics say, to favor men and women already too favored by a corrupt socioeconomic order? Maybe, but what must be kept in mind is that the widest, transtemporal questions of justice are totally beyond the powers of mere human moral judgment. We know little enough of ourselves, to say nothing of the transmigratory pasts of others. Therefore, Sathya Sai Baba's acts must seem inexplicable to us. But because his acts always serve a higher good in ways that only he can know, they are necessarily meaningful at a higher level, and their meaning is, in a manner that entirely transcends limited human moral sense, morally informed.

His devotees live in what at first glance seems to be a very curious kind of world. For them everything is determined. No occurrence, no matter how slight, happens without Baba willing it. And yet from the human standpoint, all possibilities are open, because the transtemporal awareness within which the things that happen have their rationale is one in which human beings, so long as they are bound to transmigratory careers, can never participate. Such a state of determined indetermination is, of course, vital to the plausibility of the karmic theory of destiny. It is precisely because we never know the entire pattern of an individual's world career that no twist of fortune can be either truly surprising or perceived as unjust. All is fixed, but nothing (from the limited human standpoint) is settled. Thus, the playlike indetermination of human life.

Karmic logic, with its critical escape clause, is the main link between Sathya Sai Baba's persona and the widest matters of morality and cosmic justice. His acts are a kind of enactment in miniature of the apparent moral nonsense of human experience that covers a deeper and unexperienced moral sense. And yet, as always with Baba, things are never simple. In a way that is never explicated with clarity (so far as I am aware), Baba's grace and will are not only viewed by devotees as working in partnership with *karma* but are also believed to supersede it if he wishes, for to him nothing is impossible. Thus in the end Baba is simply "beyond" all categories, ethical or otherwise. But devotees still know that whatever happens somehow serves their highest good in the long run.

It is not logic but love that finally cements this system (if that is what it is) together. At the basis of all talk about Sathya Sai Baba's acts there is always one fundamental assumption: that in his love and compassion for his devotees he can and will do anything. Devotees get what they deserve— sometimes perhaps better than they deserve. But what is most important, and what all devotees know, is that behind the operation of moral cause and effect is a loving presence who is concerned with them. More than anything else, what devotees believe is that Baba cares. His love transcends moral cause and effect, and even when it works through *karma,* it places karmic destiny in a new frame of reference. Baba's love, we might say, invests the cold logic of moral cause and effect with an aura of human plausibility.

The key word is *trust.* What a devotee's belief in Sathya Sai Baba really amounts to is total trust, through love, in the apparently untrustworthy. Indeed, by one of those curious tricks of conceptual levitation so characteristic of religious thought, Baba's apparent playful untrustworthiness is — to his devotees — evidence of his divinity, and thus evidence of his transcendental trustworthiness. In yet another paradox the divine child thus becomes divine parent, a universal mother and father.

HIS PEACE

His devotees say that their relations with Sathya Sai Baba result in inner serenity and peace of mind. For some, no doubt, this is a matter of soteriological optimism, a feeling of what is taken to be self-realization in union with the Absolute (that is, with Baba). But even though Sathya Sai Baba often employs the language of final salvation in his discourses, for most devotees the inner reward of devotion to him is no doubt on a completely different plane. For them, I think, it is largely a matter of the growth of a new and enlarged sense of self as the beloved of the Lord, and, by a kind of spiritual reflex, an altered sense of the self's situation in the world.

One of the most enduring insights of social psychology is that a person's sense of self arises from social interaction with others. Charles Cooley and George Herbert Mead long ago showed us how feelings of selfhood depend on acts of imagination in which a person comes to see himself or herself from the perspectives of others. In the imaginations of his devotees Sathya Sai Baba is such an "other," though obviously a very special one with whom interaction is of an extraordinary kind. He is the Lord, as shown by his miracles. And because he is the Lord, a devotee knows that the self that is real to him (and thus to the devotee himself or herself through him) is very different from the partial, temporally limited self with which the devotee and all normal social others are acquainted. The real self is transtemporally complete, ultimately unaffected by the vicissitudes of worldly life, and the object of limitless love.

Indeed this sense of Sathya Sai Baba's abounding love seems to be the root source of the spiritual energy of his presence in the lives of his devotees. In the cult's atmosphere of intense devotional intimacy this feeling of being personally loved by Baba is maintained despite the large numbers and general anonymity of devotees. To an outside observer it looks very different. Here is a religious leader of great force of personality surrounded by crowds of constantly demanding and importuning devotees. He cannot possibly deal personally with them all, and his occasional flashes of annoyance are quite understandable under the circumstances. But to his devotees he is seamlessly loving, and this feeling seems to be unchallenged by his apparent indifference, or even his anger. If he seems to be indifferent, it is only to disabuse a devotee of pride, and his anger likewise always has a higher purpose. Even to be ignored or scolded is to be loved. In fact, a large part of what it means to be a devotee of Sathya Sai Baba is to feel loved by him in the face of whatever evidence to the contrary.

But devotees also feel watched over, and this brings us to the question of how Sathya Sai Baba's devotees are situated in the world. In this matter we are simply dealing with another dimension of Sathya Sai Baba's love — a dimension that makes of his love a frame of reference for understanding the meaning of experience in general. If a devotee's sense of Baba's love must pass the test of his apparent indifference and occasional anger, so too a devotee's sense of being watched over by him seems to be a matter of maintaining a paradoxical sense of security in the face of the utter hazardousness of life in this world. Sathya Sai Baba's devotees certainly consider themselves to be less exposed to life's hazards than ordinary human beings. After all, he can cure the incurable, and all the rest. But to this the crucial fact must be added that there are no guarantees whatsoever. His devotees do get sick, they experience business reverses, they die. Yet even if life retains its usual vicissitudes, to a true devotee it *looks* different in the perspective of a personal relationship with Baba. Misfortune is only seeming misfortune, for Sathya Sai Baba's love ensures that even the most painful batterings of fortune are for one's own good in the end. As outside observers we cannot really know to what degree devotees actually feel this way, but the vision of the world projected by Sathya Sai Baba's sacred persona suggests that *to be able* to maintain this outlook is, in part, what devotion to him is really about.

When talking with devotees, one sometimes has the sense that for them the world is a place of endless enchantment in which signs of Baba's love are everywhere. For example, one devotee reported her momentary terror while descending through dark clouds in an aircraft. But then, just as she thought of Sathya Sai Baba, the plane passed through a reassuring shaft of sunlight. Another devotee tried to show me how the jumbled lines on the palm of his hand were really the roman characters S and R (standing for Saī Rām, a common salutation among devotees), magically put there by Baba. These are minor anecdotes, but they are typical of a wide genre. The point is that many of Sathya Sai Baba's devotees seem to live in a world that is, to them, saturated with his love. Any problem surmounted or trouble vanquished is a sign of his grace. But — and this is critical — what troubles remain are also interpreted as aspects of his omniscient, loving watchfulness, for nothing in this world happens by chance, and his love can be taken for granted. Baba's chaotic playfulness is, of course, the chaos of human existence itself. To learn to trust Baba, therefore, is to learn to trust life.

As to why Sathya Sai Baba's followers are drawn to him in particular, it is hard to say. There are many other figures in India whose divine personae project a similar appeal. No doubt his stress on the consistency of the pursuit of spiritual goals with the fulfillment of worldly obligations is an attraction to many of his successful, active devotees, but Sathya Sai Baba is hardly unique in this respect. The nativistic elements in his teachings may also have a special resonance with the concerns of people who, for reasons of education and background, feel alienated from their own tradition. As D. A. Swallow points out, these are people from a social milieu in which older ordering principles are felt to be weakening, and for them Sathya Sai Baba's cult may represent a way of reestablishing a personal sense of the relevance of respected, but poorly understood, Hindu symbols.[20] The basic simplicity of his teachings probably plays a role too. His cult represents an authentically Hindu devotionalism that makes less than rigorous demands on religious sensibilities that in many devotees are not very complex. Another factor that may draw some devotees is the simple social chic that has in some circles come to be associated with the cult's activities.

Sathya Sai Baba's genius — or perhaps the genius of the wider tradition in which he operates — is that, in the midst of a tangle of varied and often conflicting motives, he has found a way to deploy highly traditional devotional symbols in a fashion that is deeply satisfying to men and women who are quite untraditional. If the emphasis on the miraculous seems incongruously archaic from this standpoint, the incongruity is more apparent than real. Sathya Sai Baba's miracles are associated with an anything-is-possible optimism that actually accords quite effortlessly with the psychic extroversion of the affluent and up-to-date. Westerners on the whole are too inclined to believe that the modern world has no place for figures like Baba. If it teaches us nothing else, his cult at least shows us that the Hindu tradition has the capacity to respond creatively to the religious needs of individuals whose outlooks on life are deeply affected by the culture of modernity.

What is at issue here, however, is not Sathya Sai Baba's modernity or lack of it, but what kind of religious figure he really is. I have tried to show that there is much more to him than first meets the eye. He is certainly no mere magician but a teacher and moralist (of a sort) as well. In these matters he does not approach the status of, let us say, a Gandhi: his ethical teachings are really more reiterative than innovative. Great moral imaginations transvalue ethical systems by invoking deeper principles and finding fresh meanings in moral traditions. As far as I am aware, this has not been Sathya Sai Baba's forte. But, on the other hand, his divine persona certainly does not lack contact with wider moral meanings. In fact, one of the most important features of his divine character is that for his devotees it invests the widest field of human experience with a kind of unified moral sense. His distinctiveness is not a matter of the specific content of his ethical teachings, although it would be a mistake to think of this content, however conventional it may

20. Swallow, "Ashes and Powers," 153–55.

seem, as trivial. The overarching moral message of his persona (leaving aside the question of other messages) seems to be a recipe less for how to lead a virtuous life than for how to lead a life in which virtue has meaning.

As playmate-parent, what Baba mainly teaches is trust — trust in him, which to a true devotee is trust in existence. He teaches something akin to what Erik Erikson calls "basic trust": "that original 'optimism,' that assumption that 'somebody is there,' without which we cannot live."[21] This primordial confidence arises initially from the individual's earliest interactions with a maternal figure, the first social "other," and this may be echoed in the maternal overtones of Sathya Sai Baba's bisexual identity. It is consolidated and supported by later phases of parental care, and it is often given collective expression in religious images of surrender. This trust is the foundation of personality, underlying an individual's sense of self and feelings of meaningful participation in social life. As such, it is also an indispensable precondition for the moral life. Trust is not in itself morality, but no sustained inner sense of moral consequence can possibly flourish in an individual who does not believe that he or she is *someone* with a place in a meaningful, just, and ultimately beneficent cosmos.

This awareness is vital to human life, especially in its collective dimensions, and there is no medium more supportive of basic trust than a sense of being loved. I do not suggest that without Baba his devotees would be devoid of such feelings, but one basis of his general appeal is that for many his total persona makes such feelings easier to sustain. In a way that is saintly — to revert to that word at last — Baba uses the spectacle of his *līlās*, and above all the presumption of his love, as ways of teaching his devotees *how* to believe that life, in spite of its frequent moral and physical chaos, is a domain in which meaning, including moral meaning, is possible. There is really nothing very subtle about this; the essential ingredient is his devotees' absolute confidence in his love, and this confidence is powerfully supported by their own feelings of love for him in return.

Admittedly, this construction owes at least as much to the Baba who exists in his devotees' imaginations as it does to anything Sathya Sai Baba actually does. One must never minimize the aura of mystery that surrounds him: the very essence of his character is that he is profoundly loving and lovable but at the same time finally inexplicable. He embodies the paradoxes of human existence; he himself has said again and again that human beings will never fathom him. But perhaps one of the most saintly of virtues is the ability to present to the world a religiously energized character that is symbolically rich enough to provoke, but finally ambiguous enough to allow, the spiritual imagination to seek basic insights on its own.

21. Erik H. Erikson, *Young Man Luther: A Study in Psychoanalysis and History* (New York: Norton, 1962), 118; see also *Childhood and Society*, 2d ed. (New York: Norton, 1963). I am indebted to Catherine Bateson for alerting me to the possibility of connections between Erikson's theories and these materials.

ELEVEN

Saint Gandhi

Mark Juergensmeyer

In a reminiscence entitled "Saint, Patriot and Statesman," Henry S. L. Polak writes that when he first visited Gandhi he felt that he was "in the presence of a moral giant, whose pellucid soul is a clear, still lake, in which one sees Truth clearly mirrored."[1] Writing in the same anthology, *Gandhiji as We Know Him*, published in 1945, the Indian poet Sarojini Naidu unleashes a burst of adjectives likening the Mahatma to the Buddha and the Christ. In her mind they are each

> richly endowed with the loftiest and loveliest qualities of the human mind and spirit: an exquisite courtesy of heart, a wisdom at once profound and luminous, an unconquerable courage, an incorruptible faith, a surpassing love of suffering and erring humanity.[2]

Was Gandhi worthy of all these superlatives? When confronted with such adulation, he responded with a delicate modesty. "It is too early . . . to clothe me in sainthood," he wrote. "I myself do not feel a saint in any shape or form."[3] Elsewhere he assured his admiring followers that he was "not perfect," and was "only a humble seeker."[4]

Some of Gandhi's less admiring observers have felt that such protests were warranted. They have argued that he was morally arrogant, that he yearned for attention from Westerners and pandered to their tastes, that he slighted his family, and was less than successful in maintaining his vows of chastity.[5] Others have remarked that it took a lot of money to keep Gandhi in poverty;

1. Henry S. L. Polak, "Saint, Patriot, and Statesman," in *Gandhiji as We Know Him*, ed. Chandrashankar Shukla (Bombay: Vora, 1945), 45.
2. Sarojini Naidu, "Foreword," in Shukla, ed., *Gandhiji*, vi.
3. *Young India*, 20 January 1927.
4. *Harijan*, 6 May 1933.
5. See, for example, Richard Grenier, "The Gandhi Nobody Knows," *Commentary* 75, no. 3 (March 1983): 59–72.

they have claimed that, despite his image as a friend of the poor, the Mahatma was really the savior of the rich and an advocate of capitalist development.[6] Still others argue that Gandhi was inconsistent — perhaps even hypocritical — in applying his ethical principles. According to some observers, Gandhi's conduct of *satyāgraha,* a technique of fighting that requires the renunciation of coercion, was little more than a mask for moral manipulation.[7]

Yet somehow the facts of Gandhi's life and his apparent inability to live up to the moral expectations of those who revered him seem not quite relevant to the matter of Gandhi's sainthood. Saintliness, like beauty, exists largely in the eye of the beholder, and the point of view is as interesting as the object of attention. The fact that Gandhi was extravagantly revered presents us with a phenomenon worth considering in its own right, regardless of whether or not we feel that the man deserved it. Such adulation shows that sainthood is far from dead, even in the present day and even, perhaps, when the "saints" themselves — Gandhi included — disavow it.

It takes a great deal to qualify as a modern saint. Citizens of this century do not easily attribute extraordinary power and moral perfection to their fellows. Yet Gandhi's saintly image has captivated the attentions of educated people from a variety of backgrounds, both religious and nonreligious, and seems to have gained in popularity over the years. My primary material for reconstructing the Gandhian hagiography has come from the vast literature produced by an international group of admirers in the 1930s and 1940s. I will try to recreate that image and then compare it with traditional Christian and Indian views of saintliness, with the more recent portrayals of Gandhi such as one finds in Richard Attenborough's film *Gandhi,* and with Gandhi's own depiction of himself in his *Autobiography* and other writings. In doing so, I will try to understand, not just what was involved in Gandhi's saintliness, but the urge to sanctify in general, and why it persists even in the modern day.

By using the term *saint* to describe the Gandhi of popular veneration, I mean to suggest that his image carries with it the two characteristics that have defined saintliness in the Christian tradition: the possession of extraordinary power and the ability to convey that power to others. At the root of the word *saint* is the Latin word *sanctus,* indicating the power of holiness that the first saints, the Christian martyrs, were thought to possess, and that they demon-

---

6. See, for instance, Howard Ryan, "Mahatma Gandhi: New Look at the Father of Nonviolence," *It's About Times* (November 1985); and his *Nonviolence and Class Bias: From Mahatma Gandhi to the Anti-Nuclear Movement* (New Delhi: South Asia Publications; and Cupertino, Calif.: Folklore Institute, 1983).

7. B. R. Ambedkar, for instance, thought that Gandhi used the Untouchables as pawns in a political strategy: see his *What Congress and Gandhi Have Done to the Untouchables* (Bombay: Thackur, 1945). Reinhold Niebuhr, in *Moral Man and Immoral Society* (New York: Charles Scribner's Sons, 1932, 224–46), argues that Gandhi was coercive, despite his protestations to the contrary. And in my *Fighting with Gandhi* (San Francisco: Harper and Row, 1984, 55, 144, 147, 151–55), I describe instances when Gandhi was inconsistent and inflexible in applying the principles implied in *satyāgraha.*

strated by their ability to give their lives to the faith. The saints' power could be witnessed and received by those who venerated them. One accessible residue of saintly potency was to be found in the bones and relics of saints who died. And not only in Christianity was this the case: relics of holy persons have been revered in such disparate settings as traditional China, Southeast Asian Buddhism, and North African Islam. In the Europe of Late Antiquity the very names of saints were thought to be purveyors of strength. Parents would give their children names of saints with the hope that the very appellation would provide the child with a saintly guardian spirit.[8]

To my knowledge, Gandhi's bones are nowhere venerated: They were incinerated and the ashes have long ago floated down the River Jumna into the Ganges. And the number of Mohandases among the population of male children has not risen appreciably in India or abroad. Yet the underlying characteristics of saintliness — the possession of a purifying power and its transmission to others either by emulation or by a more direct transfer of gifts — may be detected in the several images of the Mahatma that Gandhi's disciples have projected. A look at these images will tell us something about the modern search for power and the way in which people of our generation think power can be transmitted.

THE EMERGENCE OF A SAINT

The canonization of Gandhi by those who admired him occurred rather early in his public life, but it would be difficult to assign it a definite date. One milestone, certainly, was the moment when he was first called a *mahātmā*, a "great soul," but it is not clear exactly when that was. The title is often said to have been granted him by Tagore when Gandhi arrived in India in 1915. A letter from Tagore to Gandhi in February of that year would seem to provide the evidence substantiating that legendary event.[9] The curious thing about the reference, however, is that the letter in which it is found was written several months before Tagore actually met Gandhi. It was Tagore's welcoming letter, so it is probable that he had heard the Mahatma being given that name on an earlier occasion by someone else. Much of what Tagore knew about Gandhi came from a mutual friend: C. F. Andrews, the former Anglican missionary who for some time had been a disciple of Tagore's and had met Gandhi in South Africa early in 1914. Andrews quickly became as much a devotee of Gandhi's as of Tagore's, for both Andrews and his traveling companion, Willy Pearson, were struck with the sanctity of the man on their very first meeting. Pearson, in an article he wrote for *The New Republic* in 1921, recalled the moment that he met the one whom he came to know as

8. Peter Brown, *The Cult of the Saints* (Chicago: University of Chicago Press, 1981), 58 and passim.

9. See Geoffrey Ashe, *Gandhi* (New York: Stein and Day, 1968), 144.

"an Indian saint": "I remember my first glimpse of him. . . . He was dressed in simple homespun, had no hat on his head and was barefoot. He is not striking in appearance . . . but I was forcibly reminded of St. Francis of Assisi."[10]

The term *mahātmā* was by no means a specifically Gandhian coinage. Before Tagore took it up and applied it to Gandhi, the name had been used to characterize other saintly figures in India, and in Britain and America the term had been adopted by the Theosophists, who used it to describe mysterious masters of wisdom from the East. It is a matter of record that before 1914 members of the Theosophical movement in South Africa, including Hermann Kallenbach, who befriended and supported Gandhi, had used the word to address Gandhi himself.[11] Andrews and Pearson may well have reported this fact in letters they wrote to Tagore while living in Gandhi's ashram near Durban in the early months of 1914. Naturally enough, even as sheer politeness, Tagore may have repeated the name when writing to Gandhi a year later.

The term was to stick with Gandhi for the rest of his life, and it probably does not make a great deal of difference how it was originally applied, or by whom. Yet it is interesting that the first recognition of Gandhi as a saint, and even the epithet in terms of which he was canonized, may have come not from his compatriots but from Westerners. Perhaps this should occasion little amazement. The intellectual and spiritual circles of which Gandhi was a part in England and South Africa prior to his return to India at age forty-five were composed largely of Westerners. Although he did take part in the movement to protect the rights of the Indian community in South Africa (but was not the sole leader of it, as is often supposed), Gandhi was largely surrounded by Westerners in the two communities that he founded, the Phoenix Farm and the Tolstoy Farm. To some of these Westerners, including those with Theosophical leanings, Gandhi must have appeared a mysterious Indian sage, and to his Christian admirers he was apparently even more. To Charlie Andrews and Willy Pearson he was a saint, and from them the rumor spread to the wider world.[12]

Andrews's writings about Gandhi were circulated in England, and in 1918 the Oxford classicist, Sir Gilbert Murray, made brief references to a remarkable Indian named Gandhi in an article he published in the *Hibbert Journal* on the concept of the soul.[13] This article provided an American clergyman,

10. Willy Pearson, "Gandhi: An Indian Saint," *The New Republic*, 21 July 1921, reprinted in Charles Chatfield, ed., *The Americanization of Gandhi: Images of the Mahatma* (New York and London, Garland Publishing, 1976), 98.

11. Ashe, *Gandhi*, 144.

12. Ibid. Andrews, like Pearson, compared Gandhi with St. Francis.

13. John Haynes Holmes, *My Gandhi* (New York: Harper and Brothers, 1953), 21. In addition to reading about Gandhi, Murray had actually met him when Gandhi was in London in 1914.

John Haynes Holmes, with his first knowledge about Gandhi, and stirred Holmes to search out a pamphlet containing a selection of the Indian activist's writings. Reading Gandhi had an enormous impact on Holmes, as he recalled in a subsequent reflection:

> Instantly I seemed to be alive — my vision clear, my mind at peace, my heart reassured. Here was the perfect answer to all my problems. . . . Something clicked within me, like the turning of a lock. Before I knew it, the supreme moment of my life had come.[14]

At the time he discovered Gandhi, Holmes was the pastor of the Community Church of New York City and one of the leaders of the liberal Protestantism of his day. So when he announced that he would give a sermon in the Lyric Theater in New York on 10 April 1921 on the topic "Who is the Greatest Man in the World Today?" it aroused a fair amount of public curiosity.[15] Who would it be? Lenin? Sun Yat-sen? Lloyd George? Woodrow Wilson? The overflow crowd that attended the lecture heard Holmes indeed extol the merits of Lenin, but he soon passed on to other luminaries. Next among his candidates for greatness was the novelist Romain Rolland, but the name that crowned the list was one that most members of the audience had never heard: Mohandas Karamchand Gandhi. Holmes said that Lenin may have been his generation's Napoleon, and Rolland its Tolstoy, but, said Holmes, "when I think of Gandhi, I think of Jesus Christ. He lives his life; he speaks his word; he suffers, strives, and will some day nobly die, for his kingdom upon earth."[16]

Tarak Nath Das, a professor at Columbia, and other Indian nationalists living in the United States were eager to use this unexpected publicity for their own political purposes and saw to it that Holmes's sermon was quickly reprinted and circulated throughout the country. It received much attention in India as well.[17] Thus was launched a lifetime career for Holmes, who became dedicated to interpreting and advertising Gandhi for American audiences; he is sometimes credited with being "the discoverer of Gandhi."[18] Holmes's efforts to spread the gospel of Gandhi took him beyond his own publication, however. In 1924, he arranged for an entire issue of the influential pacifist journal *The World Tomorrow* to be devoted to Gandhi. It included articles by C. F. Andrews, E. Stanley Jones, and, of course, Holmes himself.[19] Although Holmes had no personal acquaintance with Gandhi

14. Holmes, *My Gandhi*, 26 – 27.

15. Carl Hermann Voss, "John Haynes Holmes: Discoverer of Gandhi," in *The Christian Century* 81, no. 19 (6 May 1964): 603 – 606, reprinted in Chatfield, ed., *Americanization*, 590.

16. John Haynes Holmes, "Who is the Greatest Man in the World Today?" — a pamphlet published in 1921 and reprinted in Chatfield, ed., *Americanization*, 620.

17. Voss, "John Haynes Holmes," in Chatfield, ed., *Americanization*, 591.

18. Ibid.

19. *The World Tomorrow*, December 1924. The issue is entitled "Gandhi!" and it is reprinted in its entirety in Chatfield, ed., *Americanization*, 638 – 76.

until 1931, when they met in London, he held a clear image of the Mahatma in his mind. Gandhi was an example of moral integrity that gave him "incalculable help and guidance" as he faced life's trials.[20]

Holmes, perhaps more than any other person outside India, was responsible for broadcasting the saintly image of Gandhi throughout the world, but there were also other admirers. The rather sizeable American circle included Richard Gregg, Kirby Page, and Clarence Marsh Case, all of whom kept a stream of articles and books flowing throughout the 1930s and 1940s. This Gandhian coterie had much in common with a similar English circle that included Henry Polak and, when he was not in India, C. F. Andrews. Both groups had as prominent members leading liberal Christians who had been outspoken pacifists during World War I and whose political sympathies were with rapid social reform — in some cases, with socialism. Gandhi appealed to liberal Christians such as these because he presented in the political arena what seemed to many of them a perfect combination of religion and social concern. As one Christian pacifist writer put it, Gandhi like Jesus demonstrated "the political power of love."[21]

Liberal Christianity, with its promise of creating the kingdom of God on earth through love and social service, had reached a high water mark in the later decades of the nineteenth century with the hopeful theology of Walter Rauschenbusch and the Christian socialism of such religious visionaries as Tolstoy — who had, incidentally, a powerful influence on Gandhi during his years as a student in London. But exponents of the religious path to social progress had trouble finding a hearing in the years that followed World War I, when much of the optimism of the previous decades vanished. Christian theologians such as Karl Barth and Reinhold Niebuhr began to discover instead the biblical exposition of the darker side of human existence — everything associated with the notion of original sin, and especially the self-serving and destructive character of human pride. The pessimistic view of human nature that lay at the heart of their so-called neo-orthodox theology increasingly put the pacifist liberal Protestants on the defensive, and made them keenly receptive to the example of someone whose piety and moral power seemed to work, and who was actually able to effect social change by evoking the brighter side of human nature.[22]

"What we have under Gandhi's leadership is a revolution," Holmes explained in his 1921 sermon, "but a revolution different from any other of which history has knowledge."[23] Here was a man who was "shaking the

20. Sermon by Holmes, "The Dilemma of the Moral Life," quoted in Voss, "John Haynes Holmes," in Chatfield, ed., *Americanization*, 593.

21. Richard Gregg, "The Meaning of Gandhi's Fast," in *The World Tomorrow*, 1932; reprinted in Chatfield, ed., *Americanization*, 276.

22. Although Reinhold Niebuhr considered Gandhi's approach to be "sentimental," he did acknowledge its effectiveness in the political arena. See Niebuhr, *Moral Man and Immoral Society*, 248.

23. Holmes, "Who is the Greatest?" in Chatfield, ed., *Americanization*, 616.

British Empire . . . to its foundations."[24] Whatever imperfections Gandhi's revolution and its leader may have had were blurred in the distant vision of their American admirers. To Holmes and his circle, Gandhi was a citadel of moral power.

The image of moral force that Gandhi projected was not one that appealed exclusively to religious people, since it fit well with a certain strand of pragmatic idealism that has always been attractive to the secular American mind. For example, in an article that appeared in *Asia* magazine in 1924, the columnist Drew Pearson found it possible to compare Gandhi with Henry Ford. Pointing out that both members of this unlikely pair were "practical idealists," Pearson concluded that Gandhi and Ford were essentially "on the same road."[25]

Many Christians, however, compared the Mahatma with a more exalted figure, for Gandhi provided something that the aniconic heritage of Puritan Protestantism could never supply: the image of a saint, or to some pious minds, a vision of Christ himself. The emotion that Holmes reported experiencing at his first reading of Gandhi, which he likened to the feeling that Keats had when he first read Homer,[26] was like a conversion experience. And for C. F. Andrews, to know Gandhi was tantamount to knowing Christ. As he observed Gandhi during the Mahatma's twenty-one day fast in 1924, Andrews described a "frail, wasted, tortured spirit" on the terrace by his side, a man who bore "the sins and sorrows of his people." For Andrews the comparison was obvious: "With a rush of emotion," he said, "I knew more deeply . . . the meaning of the Cross."[27]

For liberal Protestants like Holmes who would have been embarrassed by the superstitious trappings and cultural parochialism of Christianity's own complement of saints, Gandhi served as the consummate exemplar: "a perfect and universal man."[28] In a reminiscence entitled *My Gandhi,* Holmes described the Mahatma as "my saint and seer."[29] Gandhi's impact on Holmes — rationalist Unitarian though he was — was enough to make him sound like a pious Baptist speaking about his Lord. "I carried Gandhi in my heart," Holmes proclaimed.[30] And Holmes was not the only one inspired to such language. When Gandhi encountered difficulties with the British, the liberal Protestant press reported the events in words taken straight from the gospels. One headline in *The Christian Century* depicted the event as "Gandhi Before Pilate." "Gandhi Lifts the Cross," proclaimed another.[31]

24. Ibid.

25. Drew Pearson, "Are Gandhi and Ford on the Same Road?" in *Asia,* 1924; reprinted in Chatfield, ed., *Americanization,* 316.

26. Holmes, "Who is the Greatest?" in Chatfield, ed., *Americanization,* 620.

27. C. F. Andrews, quoted in E. Stanley Jones, "The Soul of Mahatma Gandhi," in *The World Tomorrow,* December 1924; reprinted in Chatfield, ed., *Americanization,* 652.

28. Holmes, "Who is the Greatest?" in Chatfield, ed., *Americanization,* 620.

29. Holmes, *My Gandhi,* 9.   30. Holmes, *My Gandhi,* 13.

31. *The Christian Century,* 16 April 1930, and 18 October 1933.

The fact that this second coming did not manifest itself in an overtly Christian form seemed to matter little. E. Stanley Jones dismissed the discrepancy this way: "Just because Gandhi is a Hindu it does not mean that he could not be Christian in the very springs of his character."[32]

Actually, the cultural distance between India and America was of great help in fitting Gandhi to his biblical role, and many American writers emphasized the disparity by beginning their descriptions of Gandhi with his clothes, or lack of them. The fact that he wore "simple homespun"[33] or appeared "unclad but for a loin cloth"[34] made him look a great deal like what many Americans expected in a Messiah. This image was enhanced by the dark (yet not Negroid) skin that made him, as the title of one book put it, "that strange little brown man."[35] And behind his wizened appearance was the awesome cultural backdrop of India, which seemed to Gandhi's American admirers as distant from the modern age as Jesus' Galilee. Richard Attenborough's recent film about Gandhi capitalizes on just such preconceptions, and his image of a white-robed Gandhi radiating calm in the center of a restless mob has more than a little to do with the Christs who moved through biblical epics in films produced in the decades preceding *Gandhi*.

What made Gandhi truly a Christ figure for Westerners from Andrews to Attenborough, however, was not just that he looked the part. He acted the part, too — or at least his actions were amenable to that interpretation. He was regarded as a man who exhibited saintly qualities, and it is a matter of some fascination to see just what qualities were singled out for praise. They indicate the sort of Messiah that Gandhi's modern observers would have welcomed.

THE CHARACTERISTICS OF A MODERN SAINT

The descriptions of Gandhi that flooded European and American books and journals in the 1930s and 1940s were often based on firsthand visits to Gandhi's ashram near Wardha, which was as much an international guest house for Gandhian pilgrims as it was the experimental community that it has usually been portrayed. In books such as *A Week With Gandhi*[36] and *My Host the Hindu*,[37] these visitors recorded the seemingly idyllic existence of the Mahatma in his meticulously constructed Indian village, carefully block-

32. E. Stanley Jones, "The Soul of Mahatma Gandhi," in *The World Tomorrow*, 1924; reprinted in Chatfield, ed., *Americanization*, 653.

33. Pearson, "Gandhi, an Indian Saint," in *The New Republic*, 21 July 1921; reprinted in Chatfield, *Americanization*, 99.

34. S. K. George, "Gandhi Before Pilate," in *The Christian Century* 47, no. 16 (16 April 1930): 488–90, reprinted in Chatfield, ed., *Americanization*, 325.

35. Frederick Fischer, *That Strange Little Brown Man Gandhi* (New York: Ray Long and Richard R. Smith, 1932).

36. Louis Fischer, *A Week with Gandhi* (London: George Allen and Unwin, 1943).

37. M. Lester, *My Host the Hindu* (London: Williams and Norgate, 1931).

ing out the fact that the number of foreign admirers in residence there often rivaled the number of Indians.[38]

The focus of these accounts, however, is not so much the life of the ashram as the life of Gandhi. Almost all of them refer to his social and political power — either obliquely, by describing him as a "leader" or "statesman,"[39] or more directly, by describing his ability to sway the masses. Long before he had met Gandhi, Holmes was impressed that "great throngs come to him,"[40] and Kirby Page, in answering affirmatively the question "Is Mahatma Gandhi the Greatest Man of the Age?" reported an American bishop as having observed that Gandhi "appeals to the hearts of the Indian people as no other man has done, probably since the days of Buddha."[41]

Invariably reports of Gandhi's popular and political strength were balanced with observations of what seemed to be a contradictory fact: his weak and ineffectual physical appearance. "The majestic personality of the man," Henry Polak explained, "overshadows his comparatively insignificant physique."[42] Kirby Page seemed almost to dwell on the Mahatma's physical imperfections, noting that "with wretched teeth, large ears, prominent nose and shaved head, he is physically one of the least impressive of men."[43] Robert Bernays, a British member of Parliament who regarded Gandhi as "the true Messiah,"[44] nevertheless observed that he did not have "the traditional appearance of a Messiah."[45] In fact, Bernays thought he was "ugly to the point of repulsion."[46]

How could someone so homely and unimpressive be so powerful? In 1933, an English physician, Dr. Josiah Oldfield, puzzled over the paradox and supplied an answer:

> What is it that has raised a man of comparatively obscure birth, of no family influence, of small financial means, of no great intellectual capacity and of delicate constitution to such a pinnacle as Gandhiji has reached? My answer is character, and again, character.[47]

Unfortunately, Oldfield was wrong on virtually every count. There was nothing obscure about the family line into which Gandhi was born — they

38. For life in Gandhi's ashram, see Fischer and Lester, above, and Ved Mehta, *Mahatma Gandhi and His Apostles* (London: Andre Deutsch, 1977).

39. See, for instance, Syud Hossain, *The Saint as Statesman* (Los Angeles: Sutton House, 1937); S. L. Polak, "Saint, Patriot and Statesman," in Shukla, ed., *Gandhiji,* 33–46; and Fischer, *Little Brown Man,* viii.

40. Holmes, "Who is the Greatest?" in Chatfield, ed., *Americanization,* 620.

41. Kirby Page, "Is Mahatma Gandhi the Greatest Man of the Age?" — a pamphlet published in New York, 1930, and reprinted in Chatfield, ed., *Americanization,* 682.

42. Polak, "Saint, Patriot and Statesman," in Shukla, ed., *Gandhiji,* 45.

43. Page, "Mahatma Gandhi," in Chatfield, ed., *Americanization,* 681.

44. Robert Bernays, in *Gandhi as Others See Him,* ed. Joseph John (Colombo, Sri Lanka: W. E. Bastion, 1933), 67.

45. Bernays, in John, ed., *Gandhi,* 60.

46. Ibid.   47. Josiah Oldfield in John, ed., *Gandhi,* 18.

were prime ministers in the princely state of Porbandar — nor did they lack any influence in the region. Gandhi's own salary as an attorney in South Africa came to some six thousand pounds a year by 1902, which amounted to a small fortune by the standards of the day;[48] he was bright enough to secure a law degree at London; and his health was sufficient to weather the most bizarre diets and abusive schedules over a seventy-seven-year life span. Character he may have had, but it was only in Oldfield's imagination that this moral strength contradicted the putative weaknesses of other aspects of Gandhi's existence. Oldfield and the others clearly wanted Gandhi to be weak in worldly terms, and so they skewed the facts a bit to make it possible. The question is, why?

One answer is obvious: Gandhi was portrayed as weak so that his moral power would appear all the grander by contrast. But Gandhi's weakness was also consonant with a specific strand in Christian messianic expectation. As Jesus' own sayings on the subject proclaim, "the last shall be first" and "the Son of Man will come at the time you least expect him."[49] It is in fact quite appropriate for a Messiah to lack "the traditional appearances of a Messiah,"[50] if one means by that a regal mien. Messiahs should surprise. So it is understandable that Oldfield wanted Gandhi to be born in something approximating a Palestinian stable and to live like a simple carpenter, even if history had ample evidence to the contrary. Of course, to many Western eyes any specific efforts to weaken and impoverish Gandhi would have been beside the point. For them, all of India is a stable, and the mere fact that Gandhi came from a land of poverty, wore that culture's skimpy clothing, and boasted a physique no sturdier than that of the average Gujarati was enough to strip him of "the traditional appearances of a Messiah."

The last becoming first, David defeating Goliath — such reversals of roles, in which worldly weakness is countermanded by supernatural strength, are the stuff of myth and legend, and occupy a central place in the saintly icon that has been superimposed on Gandhi. In many religious traditions the logical dilemma presented by such paradoxes — apparently weak persons doing powerful things — is often resolved in an almost miraculous way. What makes it possible for weak constitutions to produce strong deeds is the ability to tap into a power that exceeds the normal sources of supply. Just as Moses' shyness indicated that his leadership skills came from above, and Muhammad's illiteracy seemed as proof that the Qur'ān was written by a divine hand, so Gandhi's alleged weaknesses are to his admirers clear manifestations of the extraordinary character of the moral power that gave him the social and political strength he possessed.

To have access to such a special source of strength is to be freed from the need to rely on mundane powers, and freed from the temptation to misuse

48. Ashe, *Gandhi*, 78.
49. Matthew 19:30, 24:44.
50. Bernays, in John, ed., *Gandhi*, 60.

and overindulge such ordinary agents of potency as food, sex, money, material goods, status, dependent relationships, and the like. So one would expect a saint to be in some significant measure an ascetic, a renunciant — and that not so much by choice but as in consequence of a saintliness already attained. Gandhi's famous acts of self-abnegation were not requirements he had to fulfill before he could be perceived as a saint but expressions of a saintliness already affirmed. And for that reason the marks of his renunciant personality were often cited with an enthusiasm and repetition that exceeded what the realities of the situation would have warranted.

Take sex, for example. Celibacy is not such an awesome achievement, even in the West. Thousands of Roman Catholic priests and members of religious orders practice it to no great public acclaim. And Gandhi's celibacy seems on the face of it rather less heroic than theirs. He chose it somewhat late in life — at age thirty-seven — after he had fathered four children and after he had lived what Gandhi himself reports to have been an enjoyably sensuous existence.[51] Yet Gandhi's vow of celibacy is often reported in the most hushed of tones and offered as certain proof of his sanctity. C. F. Andrews proclaimed that Gandhi's "body and soul" were thereby "kept clean from all sensual passion,"[52] and Robert Bernays believed that his sexual abstinence "mortified the flesh."[53] Andrews offered Gandhi's absence of sexuality as evidence that his love was "pure,"[54] and Bernays found in it proof that Gandhi had "that abundant love for humanity of the true Messiah."[55] For a variety of reasons, then, Gandhi's victory over sexual desire was something inspiring awe.

Much the same sort of admiration was shown for Gandhi's attitude toward food. It is true that Gandhi was obsessed with diets, and that his normal eating habits were spartan, but to many Western observers even a typical Indian meal would seem evidence of gastronomical stringency. For instance, Robert Bernays believed that "Gandhi's sainthood was perfectly genuine" because, among other things, "the naked faquir" he admired refused to "dine out."[56] The fact that Gandhi ate regularly at a vegetarian restaurant in London seems to have escaped Bernays's notice, as did the knowledge that in Hindu India, where prohibitions against commensality are strong, the custom of dining out is practically nonexistent. The important point, for Bernays, was that a saint like Gandhi had no need of such frills and easy pleasures as might have occupied a British gentleman.

51. See, for instance, the first chapter in Gandhi's *Autobiography,* in which he tells how he was, as a youth, "devoted to the passions that flesh is heir to." *The Story of My Experiments with Truth* (Ahmedabad: Navajivan Press, 1927), 13.

52. C. F. Andrews, ed., *Mahatma Gandhi, His Own Story* (New York: Macmillan, 1930), 80.

53. Bernays, in John, ed., *Gandhi,* 62.

54. Andrews, *Mahatma Gandhi,* 8.

55. Bernays, in John, ed., *Gandhi,* 67.

56. Robert Bernays, *Naked Faquir* (New York: Henry Holt, 1932), xiv.

Money and material possessions were also the sorts of things a saint should not require, and Gandhi was praised for his simplicity and parsimony. Again, however, the facts of the matter make one wonder how much praise was justified. It is true that he abandoned gainful employment rather early in what promised to be a lucrative career, and that he relied on donations from well-wishers to supply his needs. He showed no interest in amassing wealth for the pure pleasure of it. He even disdained life insurance. But for all that, he never lacked sufficient funds for food, travel, shelter, secretarial staff, or postage. His telegraph bills alone must have cost a small fortune, judging by the number of cables and telegrams reproduced in Gandhi's *Collected Works*. And compared with the millions of hungry, penniless poor in India, Gandhi's much-touted poverty seems a comfortable life indeed. Nonetheless one often hears it cited as another indication of his sanctity: "He embraced poverty," Mr. Bernays reported, "as deliberately as did the Carpenter of Nazareth."[57]

According to Herryman Mauer, who wrote a book-length tribute to the man just after Gandhi's death in 1948, the external features of his life — that he "dressed poorly," "renounced material wealth," and was "not smart philosophically" — were all to be expected of a "Great Soul" who "knew the presence of Truth as sharply as if it were something he could touch and see and hear."[58] And Marc Edmund Jones, in a similar eulogy written in the same year, concluded that Gandhi's frailty and poverty were entirely appropriate to "the greatest figure since Jesus."[59]

A HINDU SAINT OR A CHRISTIAN SAINT?

There seems little doubt by now that Gandhi satisfied criteria for saintliness that were widely shared by Western Christians of his own day and that have continued to have their proponents in the years since. He was a prime example of divine power acting through a seemingly weak and faulty human vessel. But we should not assume that this Western point of view was universally shared, and that Gandhi's Indian admirers saw him in the same light. Gandhi was and is greatly admired in India: he is seen as a hero, a legend, a father of the country, even as something of a holy man. But in India Gandhi is not quite a saint.

This failure to elevate Gandhi in his homeland did not come about because Indians hesitate to find saints in their midst. On the contrary, they easily embrace saints of all shapes and sizes, accepting it as axiomatic that certain persons are endowed with a spiritual weightiness that ordinary people do not possess. Such godly people are not just confined to mythology. Almost every village in India contains the bones of saints, or, better yet, the saints themselves, sitting beneath banyan trees and dispensing blessings. Ardent devotees

57. Bernays, *Naked Faquir*, 63.
58. Herryman Mauer, *Great Soul: The Growth of Gandhi* (Garden City, N.Y.: Doubleday, 1948), 13.
59. Marc Edmund Jones, *Gandhi Lives* (Philadelphia: David McKay, 1948), 3.

of such holy men and women place pictures of these gurus on the family altar and offer them prayers and praise.

There are rumors that some people in India have treated Gandhi's picture this way, but I have not seen it myself, nor is there any evidence that the practice is widespread. A taxi-driver in Delhi told me that he had attended the movie version of Gandhi's life in order to receive his *darśan* — the power that is conveyed through seeing a holy image — but this is usually as pious as the veneration gets. It is not much different from the awe that was accorded Indira Gandhi by the masses that crowded to receive *darśan* from her. No shrines have been erected for either Gandhi — Indira or Mohandas — nor are rituals or offerings performed in front of their pictures, and in India that is the sort of thing one would expect for those who are regarded as saints.

The prominent Indian admirers of Gandhi — Indian counterparts to John Haynes Holmes, Robert Bernays, and C. F. Andrews — seldom mentioned Gandhi's supernatural powers, nor did they dwell on his physical infirmities or efforts at self-abnegation.[60] Rather, they laid emphasis on his moral qualities. One of Gandhi's first Indian supporters, the great Indian nationalist leader G. K. Gokhale, proclaimed to the Lahore session of the Indian Congress in 1909 that Gandhi was "a man among men" and that he was "without doubt made of the stuff of which heroes and martyrs are made."[61] Rajendra Prasad, in his reminiscence, *At the Feet of Mahatma Gandhi,* written after Gandhi's death, praised Gandhi as an exemplar: "not only helping us in our material well-being by showing us the way to political independence, social justice and economic prosperity, but also [helping us] to catch a glimpse of the moral and spiritual heights."[62] Even the most fawning tributes to Gandhi, such as those crafted by Sarojini Naidu, the Indian poet who likened Gandhi to Buddha and Christ, emphasized Gandhi's human virtues rather than his ascetic and saintly ones. It was his worldly wisdom, courage, love, and humor — "the loftiest and loveliest qualities of the human mind and spirit" — that most impressed her, not his other-worldly asceticism.[63]

To Hindus there was nothing strange about what Westerners regarded as Gandhi's acts of renunciation. What impressed the Indians was that someone like Gandhi, who appreciated and acted out the traditional Hindu roles and virtues, was also such a modern man — well educated and articulate in English, and at ease with politicians and journalists and Protestant pilgrims from the West. In the opening pages of his published correspondence with Gandhi, G. D. Birla, the wealthy industrialist, praised the Mahatma as a

60. Ved Mehta quotes one of Gandhi's disciples as saying that he was "the ugliest man in the world," but she immediately qualifies that judgment with descriptions of his beautiful smile and his "soft and gentle" eyes (p. 4). In the remainder of the description she praises his bodily strength, his concern with health, and his iron constitution (Mehta, *Gandhi and Apostles,* 4).

61. Gopal Krishnah Gokhale, "A Man Among Men," in Shukla, ed., *Gandhiji,* 15.

62. Rajendra Prasad, *At the Feet of Mahatma Gandhi* (Bombay: Hind Kitab, 1955), vi.

63. Sarojini Naidu, "Foreword," in Shukla, ed., *Gandhiji,* vi.

social reformer — not a saint but a "real man" who had a religious vision of a just and egalitarian society.[64] Birla credited Gandhi with bringing Hinduism into the twentieth century; and it is true that he did much to reconcile Hindu concepts with the egalitarian values shared by many in the urban, mercantile, and administrative class from which Gandhi himself came. So to his fellow modern Hindus, Gandhi was widely respected as offering a model for progressive Hinduism and helping to achieve "the modernity of tradition," as Lloyd and Susanne Rudolph have described it.[65]

Gandhi himself seemed to be content with this view of him and was willing to be seen as an example of someone who seriously attempted to live a righteous life in the modern world. In his remarkable *Autobiography,* written in 1925, which amounts to a sort of gospel of Gandhi according to Gandhi, he lays out his moral successes and errors in dispassionate terms, describing them as "experiments with Truth."[66] Most of these "experiments" concern what may appear to be trivial matters — how he dealt with the temptation of being offered a cigar by boyhood friends, or yielded to irresponsibility in the face of obligations to his parents — and are trials with which all of us can easily identify. The interesting thing, however, is that Gandhi saw them as more. He lifted the minutiae of everyday life — from eating to making love — into the realm of serious moral discourse, and made it appear that the moral life is not a general attitude but a constant daily struggle.

The *Autobiography* portrays Gandhi as being morally powerful, but that power was attained only with a great deal of effort and testing. According to Gandhi's own testimony, he achieved moral awareness only gradually, only by practiced attention. His was not an inborn, intuitive saintliness. It was, as he implied in the title of his book, a science, not a gift, and because it was learnable, it was available to all. For that reason, it was something not to be admired but practiced. Elsewhere I have argued that Gandhi's most enduring contribution to the annals of saintliness has very little to do with the image projected on him by his admirers. It is rather his devotion to moral experimentation and his technique of *satyāgraha,* both measures that can be adopted by anyone who wishes to bring a measure of saintliness into his or her own life.[67]

THE PECULIAR POWERS OF A SAINT

Yet for many Westerners neither Gandhi's view of himself nor the view of him held by his Indian admirers was enough. Gandhi as an exemplar of a socially

64. G. D. Birlan, *In the Shadow of the Mahatma: A Personal Memoir* (Bombay: Orient Longmans, 1953), xiv; see also 1–3.

65. Lloyd I. Rudolph and Susanne Hoeber Rudolph, *The Modernity of Tradition* (Chicago: University of Chicago Press, 1967).

66. This is the subtitle given to his autobiography.

67. See my article, "Shoring Up the Saint: Some Suggestions for Improving Satyagraha," in *Gandhi's Elusive Legacy,* ed. John Hick and Lamont Hempel (London: Macmillan, forthcoming); and my book, *Fighting with Gandhi.*

conscious, progressive Hinduism or as an advocate of a technique of moral experimentation fell far short of the messianic expectations they had in mind. Dr. Josiah Oldfield, writing in 1933, proclaimed that "there is no saint that has been placed in Christian hagiology since the time of the Apostles who could be invoked to mould men's actions today to the extent that Mahatma Gandhi can."[68] And the author of the introduction to the volume in which Oldfield's remarks appeared went so far as to suggest that "perhaps Gandhism may one day be a recognized religion."[69] Oldfield, as if in anticipation of the reaction such excesses of piety might earn, explained: "The idea of a man being worshipped in his lifetime seems almost ludicrous to the Western mind. But why not?"[70]

Yet we might well turn Oldfield's question around and ask: why? Why did the Oldfields and the Holmeses of the 1930s and 1940s need to worship a man like Gandhi?

Any answer we give to this question will be based on speculation more than on irrefutable evidence, but several answers immediately come to mind. One is that the image of Christ and the saints that Christian tradition has supplied is inadequate for the global, rational, modern point of view. The old portrayals are culture-bound, and since they seem more mythical than real, they lack credibility. Yet, as Robert Bellah has said, even modern persons need symbols of transcendence that "integrate the whole, known and unknown, conscious and unconscious."[71] Gandhi, the English-speaking, London-trained Hindu is intercultural in his appeal — "a universal saint," as Holmes put it[72] — and enjoys the credibility that comes from being a present-day political actor as well as a religious mentor, someone whose multifaceted social and spiritual interests appear to have "integrated the whole" as few other people are perceived to have done. For these reasons many Christians, especially those of a liberal theological bent who shy away from an otherworldly view of Christ, feel that Gandhi fills that role as adequately as Jesus did.

Like Jesus, Gandhi was a symbol of power. The characteristics of the Gandhian image that we earlier observed indicate what diverse kinds of potency he was thought to possess: on one hand, he laid claim to social and political power, and, on the other hand, he had the power to renounce worldly things. These powers may seem to be contradictory, but both features of the powers ascribed to him testify to his ability to command the elements around him rather than be subject to them. Gandhi the social organizer and Gandhi the ascetic have in common the ability to assert control over those forces — external and internal to the self — that buffet the best

68. Oldfield, in John, ed., *Gandhi,* 18.

69. E. V. Ratnam, "Foreword," in John, ed., *Gandhi,* n.p.

70. Oldfield, in John, ed., *Gandhi,* 17.

71. Robert Bellah, "Transcendence," in *The Religious Situation, 1969* (Boston: Beacon Press, 1969), 907.

72. Holmes, "Who is the Greatest?" in Chatfield, ed., *Americanization,* 620.

intentions of ordinary folk. In society at large and in many personal lives the fear of disorder is a deep and terrifying reality. So it is no surprise that some of Gandhi's contemporaries should want to put on a pedestal a man whom they perceived to have mastered the social and personal forces, someone who, as Andrews said, was propelled solely by "inner self-discipline and a desire for purification."[73]

The themes of mastery and self-control that inspired witnesses of Gandhi in his own time remain central features in the heroic image one finds in the enormously popular film of Gandhi's life that was produced by Richard Attenborough in 1982. The appeal of the movie — which must have been one of the most watched films in history, considering its combined Indian and Western audiences — came, not simply from a moving story, richly filmed, but from the image that it projected of an extraordinary human being. In short, the movie was an advertisement for a global saint, and it succeeded for a time in rekindling the flame of Gandhiolatry.

Attenborough's film was an authentic recreation of the hagiography of Andrews, Holmes, and Oldfield. Like them, Attenborough fastened onto Gandhi's Christ-like charisma and his masterful actions. On the social plane we see Gandhi commanding vast and potentially unruly crowds, and challenging the authority of the organizational might of the British Empire with all its bureaucratic panoply. On a personal level we see the ever-disciplined Mahatma abjuring sex, food, and possessions, and creating around himself a simple and orderly allocation of time and space. He spins, for example, to utilize the idle moments of the day.

This image of mastery has great appeal for anyone who feels debilitated by indiscipline and the absence of self-control, which is to say, just about everyone. Anyone who has felt lost and pushed around in a crowd, or powerless and dehumanized after an encounter with some massive, insensitive bureaucracy, is apt to applaud Gandhi's apparent powers of social control. Anyone who has felt demoralized and numbed by an easy access to pleasurable things, enslaved by passionate desires, or frustrated by the untidy indiscipline of daily life will be impressed by Gandhi's display of control over himself and the events with which he was surrounded.

The film *Gandhi* presents a picture of someone who lives a full, simple, integrated, intentional existence, a life quite unlike the messy, complicated ones that most of us lead. For that reason, its image of Gandhi has the potential to judge us and make us wonder why we cannot live up to the standard that he achieved with such apparent ease. Why, then, doesn't this image of Gandhi make us feel inadequate and guilty? The answer lies, I think, in Gandhi's alleged sanctity. Because he is portrayed as essentially different from us, endowed with a spiritual power to which ordinary mortals are not privy, we can laud his moral achievements without feeling the necessity to live

73. C. F. Andrews, *Mahatma Gandhi's Ideas* (New York: Macmillan, 1930), 17.

up to all of them ourselves. Gandhi's peculiarities, especially from a Western point of view, heighten this distance and make it even less likely that viewers of the Gandhian film — or readers of Andrews, Holmes, and Bernays's literary tributes — will feel challenged to emulate such a life or castigate themselves for falling short. They might be impressed by Gandhi's renunciation of sex, food, clothes, and other material things, but they will not expect such extreme virtues to serve as guides in the quandaries of ordinary life.

Reinhold Niebuhr observed some years ago that the virtues of Jesus are dazzling precisely because they are not emulable. They are extremes of selfless love that provide ordinary Christians with a noble but ultimately unobtainable goal.[74] Gandhi's saintliness is similar: though close enough to reality to be credible, it is ultimately unattainable. And in Gandhi's case there is an additional element. Although it does not come across in Attenborough's idealized portrait of a sober and lonely leader, there was in many people's perception a sort of sublime wackiness that set Gandhi apart from others of his station and from other human beings generally. This too played a role in protecting Gandhi's admirers from condemning themselves too much for not measuring up to the master's example. He was so obviously different, his admirers thought — even odd.

Regardless of what Gandhi's real virtues may have been, the saintly role that was and still is thrust upon him demands a more powerful, a purer, and perhaps even a more idiosyncratic person than we encounter in daily experience. The Gandhi of faith is necessarily different from and more luminous than the Gandhi of history. He has taken on "subtler and more lasting shapes," as Forster put it, in the saintly image that endures.[75]

74. See Reinhold Niebuhr, *The Nature and Destiny of Man,* vol. 1 (New York: Charles Scribner's Sons, 1941), for Niebuhr's view of the nature of Christ.

75. E. M. Forster, *A Passage to India* (New York: Harcourt, Brace and World, 1952), 256. I owe this comparison between the legacies of Gandhi and Mrs. Moore to Ved Mehta, *Gandhi and Apostles,* x.

CONCLUSION: AFTER SAINTHOOD?

John A. Coleman, S.J.

Can we really speak seriously about sainthood in our own time? By "seriously" I mean the culturally anchored "serious discourse" that Michel Foucault has shown to underpin and reinforce societal practices.[1] The answer is probably not. There are surprising exceptions to the rule: Mother Teresa, Dorothy Day, and Mahatma Gandhi. But compared to a familiar world peopled and evoked by saints — the sort of pleroma implied in the nave of a medieval cathedral or present in that invisible universe of patrons known to Late Antiquity — our modern pantheon of saints seems narrow, cramped, and one-dimensional. For us, the notion of the saint conjures up little more than heroism, a life of intensity touched with altruistic resolves, the sort of immortality implied in the shout, "Che Guevara Lives!" And we have only vague ideas about what we might be looking for if we ourselves began to aspire to sainthood — a sainthood appropriate to our own age.

Several of the essays in this volume originated in a comparative course on religious exemplars and leadership types that was offered by John Hawley and Mark Juergensmeyer at the Graduate Theological Union in Berkeley in the spring of 1982. The majority of students were Christian seminarians and doctoral students; I joined as an observer. It was striking how alert the students were to the charismatic power evinced by Karen Brown's Alourdes, Indian fakirs and gurus, Hasidic rabbis, and Sufi dancing saints. But when they were asked to reflect on contemporary Christian analogies to such gurus, healers, sages, and tellers of tales, their imaginations seemed to fail them. They trotted out tame, almost banal, portrayals of clinical workers, parish organizers, and administrative pastors.

---

1. Michel Foucault, *The Archeology of Knowledge*, trans. A. M. Sheridan Smith (New York: Harper and Row, 1972). Cf. Hubert Dreyfus and Paul Rabinow, *Michel Foucault: Beyond Structuralism and Hermeneutics* (Chicago: University of Chicago Press, 1982).

These students cannot be blamed for mirroring a certain cultural numbness when faced with examples of religious power manifest in individual persons from different cultures and times. Like all of us, they lack the language tools necessary to speak of saints. Alasdair MacIntyre claims in his provocative book *After Virtue* that we have lost the essential vocabulary of virtue,[2] and by titling this essay "After Sainthood," I am proposing that we have experienced a similar loss in regard to saints. Taken together, these two losses indicate a considerable cultural disarray, which will not be easy to repair.

It has become commonplace to comment on the absence of any vital ideal of sanctity in modern secular cultures. Half a century has passed since John Mecklin wrote a book called *The Passing of the Saint*,[3] and in our own decade Lawrence Cunningham is still asking,

> After all, how often does one hear sermons about the virtues of the saints or reflect on their place in the life of the church? How many theologians write about the saints? Why is a dearth of decent hagiography in the bookstores today? What does the word "saint" conjure up in the mind of the average Christian?[4]

Even Karl Rahner, the one important contemporary Catholic theologian to have addressed head-on some of these questions posed by Cunningham, felt constrained to note the passing of the saint from contemporary Catholic piety. "The present situation," he writes, "is such that at least in the 'Cisalpine' countries of Europe veneration of the saints has suffered an extraordinary decline even among Catholics."[5] And in a careful anthropological study of popular religion in rural Spain, William Christian demonstrates that this wearing out of the cult of the saint is by no means restricted to high theology or Cisalpine Catholicism.[6]

The visual arts are equally poor. With the exception of the work of Henri Matisse and Georges Rouault, the iconography of the saint has passed from modern art. As Donald Weinstein and Rudolf Bell comment in their recent social history of the saints, "It is undeniable that there has been an overall great decline in the role of cult and of saints as intermediaries between the faithful and their God."[7] And yet, as Lawrence Cunningham argues, it may

2. Alasdair MacIntyre, *After Virtue* (South Bend, Ind.: University of Notre Dame Press), 1981.

3. John Mecklin, *The Passing of the Saint: A Study of a Cultural Type* (Chicago: University of Chicago Press, 1941), 5.

4. Lawrence Cunningham, *The Meaning of the Saints* (New York: Harper and Row, 1980), 49.

5. Karl Rahner, *Theological Investigations*, vol. 8 (New York: Herder and Herder, 1971), 21.

6. William A. Christian, Jr., *Person and God in a Spanish Valley* (New York: Macmillan, 1972), 64–65, 88–93.

7. Donald Weinstein and Rudolph Bell, *Saints and Society* (Chicago: University of Chicago Press, 1982), 161.

be an apt time to look again at saints, to consider what we have lost with their passing. Cunningham asks, "How have we come to ignore the traditional saints precisely at a time when there is a major preoccupation with exploring the roots of spirituality and a renewed appreciation of the role of story in theology?"[8] In his *Systematic Theology,* Paul Tillich claimed that Protestant theology needed a thorough rethinking of the problem of sainthood; Cunningham argues that Catholic theology is no less in need; and as this volume attests, the resources available to a search for a new kind of sainthood are even more ecumenical than current attempts at intra-Christian dialogue would imply.

I want to address three related questions here. First, what is lost to a culture when people cease to think and talk about saints? Or, what sort of gap does this absence leave in people's conceptual maps of the world and in their lives? The second question follows closely behind: what is the relation between sainthood and ethics? Are saints ethical beings, and what, if so, does a comparative study of saints tell us about virtue? How do the heroic virtues of saints guide the lives of ordinary devotees? It will be my contention that, as a comparative category in the study of religion, sainthood is not primarily about ethics. Religion always deals with a tension between the mystical and the ethical, and with sainthood the mystical dimension is the controlling one. Mystical experience shapes the way we must think about ethics, not the other way around. Finally, I want to broach the question implied in my title: what kind of saint might be appropriate to modern, Western, secular societies? The first and last questions set the agenda for the opening and closing sections of the essay, and the second states the concerns that guide the intervening sections. It will be plain to the reader that I write as a Christian scholar concerned mainly with the Christian saints, but I will attempt to situate my remarks about Christian saints and Christian virtue in a comparative context.

THE PASSING OF THE SAINT

The story of the passing of the saint coincides with the story of what we call "modernity." Notoriously, this modernity represents an assault on tradition, an attempt to launch a tradition of the new. The Christian notion of sainthood assumes, by contrast, a tradition built upon vital links between past, present, and future. It requires a world in which the living and dead commingle in an intercourse of mutual challenge and sustenance. The dead live on because we pray for and to them and they, in turn, intercede for us. Peter Brown points in his essay to "the resilience of bonds of invisible friendship with invisible protectors and with the company of the righteous" that "gave to the 'Christ-carrying man' a sense of resources lodged deep within himself."[9]

8. Cunningham, *Saints,* 8.
9. Peter Brown, "The Saint as Exemplar in Late Antiquity," 12.

Sainthood implies community. In its original meaning the phrase *communio sanctorum* refers to an indispensable communal bond between the living and the dead. Its piety is *memoria sanctorum*, the recalling of the saintly deeds of the dead, the power of God that made such saintly lives possible, and the crowning of life in this world below by a perduring life with God. The conviction is that in their heavenly state the holy dead remain concerned that we walk a path similar to theirs in our fragile lives. This sense of a past that continues to live serves to enlarge and vitalize the present and to impregnate it with drama and possibility. Cunningham states it well: "The life of the saint should act as a parable: it should shock us into a heightened and new sense of God's presence (and judgment) in our own life."[10] As the Letter to the Hebrews (Heb. 11:1–4) indicates, the possibility of our becoming saints hinges on there being saints before us.

Few moderns can comprehend, let alone embrace, such a notion of vital community with the dead. It may well be, as Robert Bellah and his associates have recently argued in *Habits of the Heart,* that without tradition there can be no vital communities — what they refer to as "communities of memory" — and without living communities of memory there can be no anchored sense of self, no ground to give meaning to death, suffering, love and commitment, citizenship and justice.[11] Lawrence Babb, speaking of urban Indians who face a similar sense of deracination, addresses the same theme in his essay on Sathya Sai Baba:

> The overarching moral message of his persona . . . seems to be a recipe less for how to lead a virtuous life than for how to lead a life in which virtue has meaning. . . . [N]o sustained inner sense of moral consequence can possibly flourish in an individual who does not believe he or she is *someone* with a place in a meaningful, just, and ultimately beneficent cosmos.[12]

Saints — in the Christian context, holy ancestors — anchor a sense of tradition by facilitating communities of memory. For Bellah and his colleagues, these represent the only real communities that exist. In losing them, perhaps, we risk losing meaningful society as well.

The traditional Christian saint had his or her place in a world long since vanished — a cosmos of mediations, intercessions, and hierarchies. The Protestant Reformation, reacting to exaggerations of the mediatory role of saints that eclipsed the unique mediation of Christ, tended to reject the cult of saints altogether. After Luther, therefore, as William Bouwsma has said, "Man could no longer count on the mediation either of reason or of other men in closer contact with the divine than himself."[13] Hierarchy in the realm of the

10. Cunningham, *Saints,* 79.

11. Robert Bellah, Richard Marsden, William Sullivan, Ann Swindler, and Steven Tipton, *Habits of the Heart* (Berkeley and Los Angeles: University of California Press, 1985), 152–55.

12. Lawrence Babb, "Sathya Sai Baba's Saintly Play," 186.

13. Cited in Charles Jones, *Saint Nicholas of Myra, Bari and Manhattan* (Chicago: University of Chicago Press, 1978), 439.

spirit gave way to an equality of status, and all humans were seen as *simul justus et peccator* before God.

We have paid a price for this pursuit of *homo aequalis*. As Louis Dumont has forcefully contended, we moderns can no longer even conceptualize a notion of hierarchy that is not intrinsically unfair. We know only how to compare equals; hence, moderns cannot relate two persons or statuses without leveling their differences. Dumont claims that without a sense of a hierarchy of values we cannot recognize the other. As he sees it, our modern world is far less pluralistic and respectful of true otherness than its vaunted praise of individual difference would suggest. Without some notion of hierarchy to guarantee the possibility of otherness, there is no interconnected world, only a congeries of unrelated equals.[14] Hierarchy need not be oppressive if it allows for communication across the boundaries it assumes. The saints facilitated this, and their demise seems to have played a role in sentencing us to a one-dimensionality that expects no genuine otherness and therefore constricts our access to the religious. As both Luther and Pascal knew, God is hidden; and as Pascal argued, no religion can be true that does not give an account of this hiddenness while at the same time identifying points of access to God. Saints have traditionally served as God's mediators, signs of the divine presence even at the level of the trivial, local, and everyday. As Peter Brown observes in his essay here, the holy man in Late Antiquity was made accessible: " 'Indeed,' said the monks to the Patriarch Athanasius, 'when we look at you, it is as if we look upon Christ.' "[15] Stanley Tambiah highlights a similar theme in Buddhism when he speaks of objectifications of charisma, vicarious oblation, and a circulation of grace. Saints invite us to conceptualize our lives in terms other than mastery, usefulness, autonomy, and control. As free instruments of a higher grace and vehicles of transcendent power, they provide a vision of life that stresses receptivity and interaction.

With the passing of saints, this sense of concrete providence — God's concern for the local and the little — tends to be eclipsed. Charles Hallisey reports that in Sri Lanka devotees invoke the Buddhist saints primarily for help in puzzles, muddles, and daily conflicts, much as Catholics once prayed to St. Anthony for help in finding some lost, often small, item.[16] Christians traditionally expected their saints to assist with everyday sufferings and concerns (finding a husband, a job, a cure for headaches) too trivial to catch the attention of the more transcendent God, yet of vital concern to the devotees.[17] A heaven of human scale, like the daily world, would naturally

14. Cf. Louis Dumont, *Homo Hierarchicus*, rev. ed. (Chicago: University of Chicago Press, 1980), 239–45; and *From Mandeville to Marx* (Chicago: University of Chicago Press, 1978), 23–31.

15. Brown, "Saint as Exemplar," 10.

16. Hallisey, personal communication, University of Chicago, 5 December 1984. Bernard McGinn and David Burrell were also helpful in deepening my knowledge of the literature on sainthood.

17. See Paul Molinari, "The Intercession of the Saints," in *The New Catholic Encyclopedia*, vol. 12 (New York: McGraw-Hill, 1967), 972–73.

know a division of labor in which patrons could serve as mediators for those they sheltered, "putting in a good word with the boss."

William James in his classic Gifford Lectures, *The Varieties of Religious Experience*, recognized something of what we have lost as a culture with the passing of the saints, but by defining sainthood in generic terms, he attempted to show that saintliness need not be absent even in a world that regards itself as beyond saints. James called saintliness "the collective name for the ripe fruits of religion in a character" and outlined four psychological consequences of a belief in saints:

1. "A feeling of being in a wider life than that of this world's selfish little interests";

2. "A sense of the friendly continuity of the ideal power with our own life, and a willing self-surrender to its control";

3. "An immense elation and freedom, as the outlines of the confining selfhood melt down"; and

4. "A shifting of the emotional center towards loving and harmonious affections, towards 'yes, yes' and away from 'no,' where the claims of the non-ego are concerned."[18]

In making this list, James showed how the cult of the saints crystallized a wider cultural ideal of altruistic generosity.

Toward the end of his life James's younger colleague at Harvard, the sociologist Pitirim Sorokin, made further attempts to link sainthood and altruism.[19] One feels the impoverishment of modern language, however, as Sorokin, in his book *Altruistic Love*, tries to find words that will express some difference between the saints and the more banal American "good neighbor" with whom he compares them. The latter he characterizes by culling through a sample of *Reader's Digest* readers' responses to inquiries about altruistic behavior, but he finds little way to indicate why the former were categorically more exalted. For Sorokin, saints are "masters and creators of love energy," "living incarnation[s] of the highest goodness, love and spirituality of a given society."[20]

In devising ways to "test saintliness by common sense" and its usefulness to society, as James put it, [21] both these social scientists implicitly wrestled with alternatives to the utilitarian individualism that Robert Bellah and his colleagues find so dominant in contemporary American culture. Both James and Sorokin attempted to articulate the social use of saints. If their studies fail

18. William James, *The Varieties of Religious Experience* (New York: Longmans, Green, 1923), 272–73.

19. Pitirim Sorokin, *Altruistic Love* (Boston: Beacon Press, 1950) and *The Ways and Power of Love* (Boston: Beacon Press, 1954).

20. Sorokin, *Altruistic Love*, 197.

21. James, *Varieties*, 331.

to inspire confidence in a contemporary retrieval of saints as social types, however, the failure underscores how difficult it is for modern Western society to speak a language other than that of utilitarianism and expressive individualism. Since saints inhabit — indeed, partly constitute — a more solidaristic community of memory, they resist being described as models of individual behavior.

Instead saints are mediators of the transcendently holy, and as such they mirror the ambiguity inherent in the religious realm. They are both like us and — so hard for individualists to conceive — above us. As such, their ethical status also carries an ambiguity that is hard for modern society to accept: always to be admired, they are not always to be imitated. Their lives and their deeds, as John Hawley points out in his essay on *bhakti* saints, often have "threatening consequences for ordinary morality."[22] Among Christian saints, too, as Henri Daniel-Rops has written, "the witness of sanctity has something disconcerting and, even, very often something scandalous about it."[23] St. Francis of Assisi could strip off his clothes in front of the bishop and make one of his monks eat the droppings of an ass in punishment for having kept a morsel of food for himself. And St. Benedict Labre tried to teach his eighteenth-century contemporaries that in spite of all their satins and flounces they would be eaten up by worms: he left his body unwashed and let lice live in his hair.

No one today raises children to become this kind of saint, and perhaps parents never did. Yet somewhere, if we are to make sense of the practices of saints, there must be schools for saints, institutions where they are not only expected but needed. Where can one find such schools — equivalents of St. Anthony's desert or the medieval monastery — in the institutions of the modern West?

As mirrors of the inherent ambiguity of the religious, saints frequently offer not merely a challenge to normal mores but a *coincidentia oppositorum,* a strange wholeness and integrity that fuses the transcendent dimension with what Leonardo Boff in his biography of St. Francis of Assisi refers to as "trans-decendence" — that is, an assimilation to the poor, exploited, leprous, impure as a reminder that "weeds have a place in every garden."[24] Hester Gelber's psychological study of St. Francis in this volume points to another, more this-worldly, example of Francis as a *coincidentia oppositorum:* she stresses his simultaneous quest to nurture and engage in ascetic self-denial, to be a mother and a suffering son. Holiness always has to do with "wholeness," but it often shatters our ordinary notions of what makes a human life whole. It is not just, as Hawley argues, that saints follow "an

22. John Hawley, "Morality Beyond Morality in Three Hindu Saints," 66.

23. Henri Daniel-Rops, "Holiness in History and Holiness Today," in *Holiness in Action,* ed. Roland Cluny (New York: Hawthorn Books, 1963), 14.

24. Leonardo Boff, *Saint Francis: A Model of Human Liberation* (New York: Crossroad Books, 1984), 37.

ethical logic that demands more, rather than less."[25] At base they do not really follow an ethical logic at all. Ultimately, holy wholeness depends on allowing oneself to be transformed by the encompassing logic of a life lived in and through God.

Despite William James's best efforts, saints do not quite pass any utilitarian test. Holiness is never really justified by its results. Witness Thérèse of Lisieux shut up in a convent at age eighteen, never again to emerge except at death, or Charles de Foucault going to live entirely alone among the Tauregs of the Hoggar in the desert of North Africa without the hope of baptizing even one of them. A famous remark of Voltaire about Vincent de Paul — "Monsieur Vincent is the saint for me because he is the saint of human misery" — led Henri Bremond to question whether ethics played the dominant role in saints' lives: "Vincent did not become a saint because he was charitable but he was charitable because he was a saint."[26] Ethics flows from holiness, not the other way round.

Phyllis McGinley claims in her *Saint Watching* that "the saints differ from us in their exuberance, the excess of our human talents. Moderation is not their secret. It is in the wildness of their dreams, the desperate vitality of their ambitions that they stand apart from ordinary men of good will."[27] Such wildness is rarely generated in a search for virtue, heroic deeds, or ethical goodness. It is more frequently an aspect of a thrust toward union with God, and virtue — in a sense we have yet to explore — flashes forth from that union.

It is precisely in their liminality — the difference we observe between their ethical way and our own worldly prudence — that saints intrigue us and attract us to a deeper, undifferentiated sense of communal belonging: *communitas*. I choose these categories of Victor Turner — liminality and *communitas* — to underscore the fact that saints belong primarily to a religious, rather than a simply ethical, set of categories. Turner argues that liminal figures who both belong and do not quite belong to ordinarily structured social reality sharply contest the boundaries (and narrow limits and injustices) of social structure by evoking a large, more inclusive, undifferentiated sense of community. This latter, an essential part of any healthy society, is called by Turner "anti-structure." It places a question mark beside the boundaries, rules, and ethical codes that define social structure.[28]

If saints are liminal figures in Turner's sense, we should expect them to stretch our ordinary notions of structured prudence and virtue. Several authors, picking up on this insight, claim that limit-figures and limit-language always point beyond the threshold they occupy to a larger, transcendent

25. Hawley, "Morality beyond Morality," 66.
26. Cited in Daniel-Rops, "Holiness in History," 15.
27. Phyllis McGinley, *Saint Watching* (New York: Viking, 1969), 19.
28. Cf. Victor Turner, *The Ritual Process: Structure and Anti-Structure* (Chicago: Aldine, 1969), 94–130.

whole. They represent the primary locus for the human experience of the religious.[29] As Durkheim argued, community itself is of fundamental religious importance.[30] By seeing saints as playing an indispensable social role within our world, yet going beyond it, we keep alive the ideal of a more inclusive community that stands in judgment on our ordinary, familiarly structured social roles. When the modern world eclipses the liminal role of saints, then, the stakes are high. To lose them is to experience, in Max Weber's famous term, a severe "disenchantment" in both the religious and the communal realms.

To summarize, then, modern Western culture seems to have lost the following strengths in allowing the saint to pass away as an important social ideal: (1) a vivid concept of tradition built around the communion of the living and the dead in "communities of memory"; (2) a notion of hierarchy and mediation that makes it possible to appreciate the other as other; (3) a mediated access to a hidden God; (4) a sense of God's concrete providence; (5) a rich resource for altruistic behavior; and (6) an important avenue toward appreciating the ambiguity of the religious realm as a *coincidentia oppositorum* — at once terrifying and fascinating.

SAINTS ACROSS AND WITHIN TRADITIONS

One way to recover something of the meaning of the saint as a social type is to engage in cross-cultural and historical studies that plunge us into the rich variety of forms of sainthood. It raises a hope such as the one expressed by Stanley Tambiah, that we may discover universal traits that accompany sainthood wherever it is found. Yet we must heed William Brinner's warning about "the difficulty — amounting at times almost to an impossibility — of translating terms across cultural boundaries."[31] I believe it is possible to carve out an intermediary position. A search for overlapping "family resemblances" may help to guide the task of translating the stories of saints from one tradition or era to another without doing violence to their inherent differences.

The notion of "family resemblances" was Wittgenstein's. He thought that any definition of a set or group typically included diverse traits that cover, in an overlapping way, the various cases that fall under a definition. Often no one of the cases includes all of the postulated traits. For Wittgenstein, definitions represent ideal types possessing traits that tie together the various subfamily groups among the case examples in a cumulative way, as a rope pulls together its several threads. The traits represented in a "family

29. On liminality as an essentially religious category, see David Tracy, *The Analogical Imagination* (New York: Crossroads, 1981), 160–72; and Mary Douglas, *Purity and Danger* (London: Routledge and Kegan Paul, 1969), 120–36.

30. Emile Durkheim, *The Elementary Forms of Religious Life* (New York: Free Press, 1952).

31. William Brinner, "Prophet and Saint," 43.

resemblance" group are comparative rubrics, often similarities rather than widely shared properties; only rarely are they fixed essences.

Family resemblances among saints might be said to include the following functions: (1) exemplary model, (2) extraordinary teacher, (3) wonder worker or source of benevolent power, (4) intercessor, and (5) possessor of a special and revelatory relation to the holy.[32] Other elements associated with saints are less widely shared. Let us review these five in an illustrative way, as they appear in the several traditions studied in this volume.

Exemplary Model

The Chinese ideal of the sage, as described by Tu Wei-ming, represents the clearest case of the exemplary ethical model. But the sagely ideal of self-cultivation presupposes a belief in the perfectibility of human nature by human means that is quite foreign to the Christian conviction that salvation must come by grace. Indeed the Chinese sage consciously chooses not to resort to the extraordinary and transmundane. This position contrasts sharply with the centrality of the miraculous among canonized Christian saints, Buddhist *arahants,* Sufi *walīs,* and the ancient Greek thaumaturgical heroes. What is exemplary in one tradition is not necessarily so in another.

Yet the ethical element is often important: Muslim portrayals of the Prophet Muhammad often amount to a catalogue of virtues, and traditional Catholic teaching has affirmed that heroic virtue is a necessary if not sufficient condition for the recognition of sanctity. In the Confucian case these are inner-worldly ethical norms. Taoism, however, with its exaltation of passionless unity with the absolute, already represents a different construction of saintly virtue, which is less governed by right ethical conduct. And in Shinto, to take a third example from East Asia, the mythical saints do not live "according to the standards of ethical perfection or exceptionally meritorious performance" at all.[33] They show their liminal power in areas other than the ethical. Thus we have cases of saints who are not ethical exemplars (Shinto), cases where ethical heroism is only part of the profile of a saint (Christianity), and cases in which virtue serves as the primary element in defining sainthood (Confucianism).

Teacher

In Hinduism and Confucianism the sage-saint is typically thought of as a teacher, someone endowed with exceptional, even esoteric, knowledge and with the ability to communicate it, again sometimes by extraordinary means such as the reading of hearts. Teaching, along with martyrdom, is one of the major aspects of the rabbinic saints described by Robert Cohn, and esoteric

32. These categories are derived from those used to describe saints in "Saints," in *Encyclopedia Britannica,* vol. 16 (Chicago: University of Chicago Press, 1971), 163–68.
    33. Ibid., 164.

teaching is an essential trait for the Sufi saints we meet in William Brinner's essay. As Brinner notes, when teaching is a major factor in sainthood, we often find a strong notion of living saints and sacred lineages — Sufi saints and their disciples, rabbis and their students, Hindu gurus and their close devotees. While Christian saints such as Saints Thomas Aquinas, Augustine, and Jerome were teachers, exceptional teaching ability was by no means understood as prerequisite for sainthood. On the contrary, any claims to esoteric knowledge often constituted an obstacle in the Catholic canonization process. Orthodox Christianity knows something of the esoteric teacher — witness the Russian *starets* monk — but Catholic canonization procedures tend to rely more on public witness: heroic virtue widely acknowledged and miracles that could be attested after death. Although Catholicism knows instances of living lineages of saints (Monica and Augustine, Ignatius Loyola and Francis Xavier, Benedict and his first great disciples), this trait looms less large than in Sufi Islam or Taoism. Catholicism generally downplays saintly lineages in its effort to stress sanctity as an individual phenomenon, a manifestation of God's intimacy in a given life. It relegates the teacher-saint to one subcategory, "doctors of the church," rather than making it a generally expected trait.

Wonder Worker

For practical purposes we can conflate the saintly traits of "wonder worker" and "source of benevolent power." I distinguish them because, as Karen Brown's study of Alourdes shows, the latter need not include the idea of miracles as such. Miracles, however, as a sign of the presence of the holy, are important manifestations of saintliness in many religious traditions. This is certainly true in Christianity. Donald Weinstein and Rudolph Bell argue in their historical study of Catholic saints spanning six centuries that "what interested the faithful was the holy life and, above everything else in that life, evidence of supernatural power."[34] Miracles, not ethics, drew devotees to saintly shrines, and the Catholic canonization process, a highly rationalized mode of perceiving sanctity that goes far beyond "popular religion," demands miracles, at least of those who are not martyrs. Without miracles, it was argued, one could not be sure that a saint's ethical heroism truly derived from God.

In *Miracles and the Medieval Mind* Benedicta Ward studies pilgrimages and miracles in twelfth- and thirteenth-century English shrine centers. She focuses especially on the relation of miracles to sanctity, and tries not to dissociate miracles from virtue. In the medieval English mind, she says, it was felt that "miracles should be edifying to the faithful and linked to the virtues of the person proposed" as a model of sanctity.[35] Yet not all of these medieval

34. Weinstein and Bell, *Saints and Society*, 142.

35. Benedicta Ward, *Miracles and the Medieval Mind* (Philadelphia: University of Pennsylvania Press, 1982), 185.

miracles were morally exemplary. St. Cuthbert's shrine, for instance, was famous for its "judgment miracles," which inflicted severe retribution on sinners. Some of these harsh miracles gave little evidence of the Christian virtue of forgiveness, though they may have called wayward members of a close-knit community back to right behavior, much as Alourdes's actions do in a Vodou seance. Much less closely associated with ethics were the so-called *joca sanctorum:* nonedifying, sometimes parapsychological wonders that were playful yet erratic — the sort of behavior we expect of poltergeists. And in some cases miracles after death actually seemed to compensate for virtue lacking in life, as with Thomas Becket. Through the miracles manifest at his shrine in Canterbury Becket did seem to show a heroic forgiveness of his enemies that was quite absent while he lived.[36]

The correlation between virtue and miracles is far from total. Though miracles may demonstrate virtue, they also fulfill two additional functions in devotion to saints. In popular religion they serve as tokens of power, *mana,* a source of benevolence for the everyday needs of ordinary devotees; and in more official accounts they prove that the saint's revelatory power truly derives from the holy. In either instance they alert us to the danger of interpreting saintliness as sheerly a manifestation of virtue, at least for families of saints in which unusual displays of benevolent power play a key role.

Intercessor

Intercessory power is a central element in classical Christian, Chinese, Sufi, and Buddhist notions of sainthood, though there is room for variation as to whether a living or dead saint best exhibits this power. In Christianity, for example, most saints display their intercessory capabilities only after death, while in rabbinic Judaism, as Robert Cohn points out, those who might be considered "saints" intercede while living. And Jains resist the idea that the Tirthankaras — "stream-forders" who go before ordinary mortals — have the ability to intercede and be more than simply moral exemplars.

Possessor of a Special Relation to the Holy

The four elements we have been looking at so far link up with a fifth, the saint's connection with the holy. In fact, only a special relation to the holy operates as a constant in the preceding set of traits. As such, it is the most important of the features defining "family resemblances" among saints of different traditions. Of course, the quality of sanctity varies and manifests itself in diverse ways. In some traditions the aura of charismatic holiness tends to be something impersonal, a power like *mana* that works through persons without necessarily transforming their lives into personal holiness.

36. Cf. Dom David Knowles, "Archbishop Thomas Becket, the Saint," *Canterbury Cathedral Chronicles* 65 (1970): 18; also Ward, *Miracles,* 97.

Perhaps the *vodouisante* Alourdes fits this description. In other cases intercession involves individual prayer and dialogue with a saint who has attained a definite and relatively unchanging personality. But the major point is that in saints' lives, normal virtue and the realm of what is usually called ethics are subordinated to a more charismatic dimension. Saints, as liminal figures, function to break down and transform ordinary notions of virtue.

SAINTS AND VIRTUES

One way to understand how this happens is provided by classical Thomist theory. According to Aquinas, one virtue — love, or charity — is so fundamental that it stands apart from the others and serves as their ultimate form, transfiguring them. Likewise, the life of a saint serves as an image of how ordinary reality ought to be reoriented to achieve its ultimate purpose. Although Thomas draws upon the Aristotelian account of the virtues, he stresses that they are intelligible not in themselves but in the end, the *telos,* that they serve.[37] That end, the goal of the moral life, is a friendship with God that mirrors the "friendship" existing within God himself: the Trinity. Friendship comes to life, Thomas claims, when friends agree on what constitutes the good, and it attains its ultimate virtue when friends strive to be like the thing they commonly love. We acquire authentic selves, then, in the measure that we acquire likeness to God.

In Thomas's scheme any virtue derives its meaning and form from its end or goal. Thus, if we develop a love other than the love of God, we end up with a happiness other than God. If we cultivate another kind of friendship or desire another kind of good than the good that God desires, we become strangers to him. We become what we love. While we need the natural virtues, those Aristotle described, to become God's friend and experience the life of virtue that flows from friendship with God, such a friendship transforms ordinary virtue. The fact that we are trying to become God's friend inculcates a different, specifically religious, sense of the virtues — something beyond what Aristotle analyzed in the *Nichomachean Ethics.* By seeking to do the good as God does the good, we experience the gift of love for God, which, according to Thomas, transvalues the natural virtues.[38]

In the Aristotelian view virtue consists of skillful habits derived from practices aimed at achieving personal and social goods of intrinsic value. Virtue is a form of mastery: it comprises skills required for living the good life. Aquinas alters this scheme. He insists that the primary power of virtues formed under the aegis of love consists in receptivity rather than mastery. They take on force by being open to the divine love through which we are

---

37. For St. Thomas's treatment of the virtues, see *Summa Theologiae,* 1–2 qq. 55–67, in *Summa Theologiae* (Rome: Marietti, 1950), 239–98.
38. *Summa Theologiae,* 1–2, q. 65, art. 3.

healed and transformed. Virtues are more gifts than achievements. We do not already know, from ordinary ethical codes, what constitutes virtue, hence holy people cannot simply be those who display known virtues in a superior way. Instead we recognize holiness in those whose lives transfigure our experience of virtue to reveal virtue's source — its deepest meaning and true face.

Paul Waddell has written tellingly on this point:

> A virtue's perfection, its achievement of excellence or goodness, depends on the love which formed it. That is why the virtues are displayed differently in really holy people, in the friends of God we call saints. Virtues are stretched to their perfection in the saints because God's love has so perfectly transfigured them that it becomes the form and principle of all they do. . . . In this respect, the saints, the very ones who seem so unlike us, are the ones in whom the virtues are normatively displayed, the people against whom our own goodness must be measured.[39]

In this Thomistic understanding of virtue the love infused into holy people through their friendship with God becomes the form that gives shape to virtue. Virtues are not the only things that are so infused. Thomas also speaks of infused "gifts" of the Holy Spirit. These are virtue's highest excellence; they render deeds and those who perform them good, as God is good.[40] Such gifts are, as Waddell says, "God acting not outside us but from within."[41]

Several of the essays in this volume stress a special conjunction between morality and extraordinary power — what Thomas would call the gifts of the Spirit — in the lives of saints. This idea suggests that we may be able to generalize Aquinas's point beyond its Christian setting. Lawrence Babb, for instance, contends that saints "blend and fuse the moral and the powerful in a way that generates a unique glow of spiritual energy."[42] Stanley Tambiah argues that the laity "are likely to see the saint as a radiant person who can cast his blessing upon the laity and transmit part of his charisma to them, very much in the mode of *darśan*."[43] William Brinner and Lamin Sanneh draw attention to the fact that the Arabic word corresponding most closely to *saint* means "a friend or protégé of God."[44] Aquinas's depiction of saints as friends of God seems closely related indeed, and in the Islamic case, as in the Christian, other virtues follow from this powerful intimacy.

---

39. Paul Waddell, "An Interpretation of Aquinas' Treatise on the Passions, the Virtues, and the Gifts from the Perspective of Charity as Friendship with God" (Ph.D. diss., University of Notre Dame, 1985), 162.

40. On the gifts, see Thomas, *Summa Theologiae*, 1–2, q. 68.

41. Waddell, "An Interpretation," 183.

42. Babb, "Sathya Sai Baba," 169.

43. Stanley Tambiah, "The Buddhist *Arahant:* Classical Paradigm and Modern Thai Manifestations," 121–22.

44. Brinner, "Prophet and Saint," 43; cf. Sanneh, "Saints and Virtue in African Islam: An Historical Approach," 128–29.

Virtues typically appear as a set and usually can be ordered in a hierarchy. In classical theories of virtue some master virtue — prudence, justice, or Stoic equanimity — was perceived as giving design to the series of which it was a part.[45] So if the controlling virtue is altered from justice, say, to equanimity, each of the subsidiary virtues also changes. The master virtue colors the others.

Cultural differences in understanding virtues often lie less in the presence or absence of a given value across traditions than in the hierarchical principle that governs the set that they constitute.[46] When Thomas insisted that prudence was to be understood not as a virtue in the service of the political common good — Aristotle's notion — but as a virtue in the service of a universal love patterned on God's agapeic love for us, he altered the meaning of "prudence" fundamentally. Similarly, the fathers of the Church recognized the importance of such hierarchy of virtues when they referred to pagan virtues as splendid vices. Now if we think of communion with the holy, the source of charismatic power, as the master virtue in saints' lives, we may be close to accounting for the paradox that emerges so persistently in the essays collected in this volume. On the one hand, the saints are expected to be somehow moral and to serve as models for ordinary devotees. Yet their morality transcends ordinary ethical codes. If the master virtue that appears in the saint, however, differs from the priorities that give shape to ethics, we can understand how it is possible for saints to display ordinary virtues in such unusual ways. This sort of pattern would explain what John Hawley hints at in discussing the Hindu *bhakti* saints: "Though saintliness is not constructed by any piling up of 'secular' virtues, it does not exclude them if they follow from a life of love and devotion."[47]

Even Alourdes seems to fit this model. She represents an unexpected juncture of the aesthetic and the moral that mediates an encompassing whole such as Durkheim described in characterizing religion as an expression of social forces. Alourdes's access to such a whole provides her with the power to mediate conflicts and balance differences, thus tranforming human relationships. In Vodou a responsive and responsible relation to the encompassing whole is the form taken by appropriate, transvalued virtue. Similarly, Tu Wei-ming's Chinese sage serves as a summing up of the whole, a unique "connecting point for relationships, an inseparable part of a network

---

45. For a broader treatment of virtue, see Stanley Hauerwas, *The Community of Character* (South Bend, Ind.: University of Notre Dame Press, 1983), and Hauerwas, *Truthfulness and Tragedy* (South Bend, Ind.: University of Notre Dame Press, 1977), chap. 2.

46. On the notion of differences in hierarchy as keys to explaining cultural differences, see F. R. Kluckhohn and Fred L. Strodbeck, *Variations in Value Orientations* (Evanston, Ill.: Row, Paterson, 1961) and Clyde Kluckhohn, "Toward a Comparison of Value Emphases in Different Cultures," in *The State of the Social Sciences,* ed. Leonard White (Chicago: University of Chicago Press, 1956), 116–32.

47. Hawley, "Morality beyond Morality," 71.

of human interaction." As an exemplar of *coincidentia oppositorum*, the Chinese teacher "can unite in one the beginning and the consummation of learning."[48] The key to understanding the virtue of the Chinese sage also lies in perceiving his special relation to a master virtue — in this case *ming te*, "brilliant virtue." It serves as a symbol of encompassing wholeness.

But how does such heroic virtue relate to the ordinary virtues of these saints' devotees? Even within one tradition many of the saints display quite different patterns of virtue. Hence even in Catholic Christianity, which emphasizes the prototypical paradigm of martyrdom, it seems impossible to find a single list of virtues exemplified by all the canonized saints — something one might detect in lesser form among ordinary mortals. What do the very ascetical St. Rose of Lima, the moderate and playful St. Philip Neri ("God's Jester"), and the learned St. Albert the Great have in common? Each was virtuous, but the precise virtues they displayed were quite dissimilar.

This lack of convergence on a single list of virtues should come as no surprise if we recall that one way of seeing saintly virtues is to view them as essentially correctives for human deficiencies and temptations.[49] Not every virtue presents the same difficulty for each person or epoch. Different character types and different ages stand in need of different correctives. Even so, if one takes the canonized Catholic saints as a group, one may perhaps find a full panoply of virtues. As Benedict XIV insisted when he laid down the rules of canonization, we should expect in our saints a range of natural virtues such as courage, justice, and sympathy; these provide at least some links between the saints' lives and the lives of ordinary Christians. But what Catholic Christianity calls the "heroic virtues" are not the same as the natural or ordinary ones, and though some measure of both is regarded as a necessary first test of sanctity, neither is a sufficient condition for the recognition of sainthood. Virtues have to be sealed by miracles.

The Church has, indeed, canonized several saints who lived relatively undramatic lives — St. John Berchmans, for instance — to show ordinary Christians the possibility of holiness even in everyday lives. The notion of the "hidden" saint, which is found in several religious traditions, seems to serve a similar function, linking the saintly ideal to the lives of ordinary believers and demonstrating that sainthood does not have to be flashy in order to be real. But this is not the dominant note in the exemplitude of the saints. Rather, they draw us to the center of the universe, the holy *coincidentia oppositorum* that alone gives adequate grounds to integrity and makes possible a total "fit" between the disparate virtues needed in a particular life. In respect to specific virtues the saints tend to remain inimitable; their attraction, instead, is their power to lure us beyond virtue to virtue's source. As Robert Cohn says in regard to the Hasidic *tsaddiq*, "the *tsaddiq* functions as an *axis mundi*, a

48. Tu Wei-ming, "The Confucian Sage," 75, 78.

49. See Philippa Foot, *Virtues and Vices and Other Essays in Moral Philosophy* (Berkeley and Los Angeles: University of California Press, 1978), 8 – 11.

channel through which divine grace flows to the community and the agent through which the community approaches God."[50] Similarly, Lawrence Babb refers to Hindu saints as "focal points of spiritual force-fields,"[51] and Stanley Tambiah claims about the Buddhist *arahants* that "in the end, the personal, interiorized, mystical illumination of the saints ... is seen as flooding the vast spaces of the world with their cosmic love. In this sense religion is embodied in and proceeds from them, just as they, as individuals, interiorize the whole of religion."[52]

The saints are friends of God who show how God acts in human lives, and thereby they also call the rest of us to a deeper friendship with God. Though far from being ordinary persons, they are also not representatives of a sort of vicarious religion, something ordinary people cannot attain. Rather, saints are revelatory tokens, signs of a benevolent power larger than what is usually experienced in life and therefore, as William James said, "the best things that history has to show."[53] James held that saints' lives functioned vis-à-vis ordinary lives in much the same way that utopian dreams criticize the mediocrity of ordinary schemes of justice.[54] Saints represent a critical nega-tivity, challenging the mediocre to a higher life. Just as societal justice tends to disintegrate into a defense of the *status quo* unless utopias are imagined to depict what is politically possible, so a society without saints tends to allow virtue to sink to the level of utilitarian value. Saints allow society to see life as a battle for the highest stakes, an art demanding creative, altruistic love. As James says,

> They are the impregnators of the world, vivifiers and animators of potentialities of goodness which but for them would lie forever dormant. It is not possible to be quite as mean as we naturally are, when they have passed before us. One fire kindles another; and without that over-trust in human worth which they show, the rest of us would be in spiritual stagnancy. . . . If things are ever to move upward, someone must be ready to take the first step, and assume the risk of it.[55]

Several of the essays in this volume strike a similar theme as they note, with Tu Wei-ming, the importance of maintaining a permanent social tension between the real and the ideal. William Brinner speaks of "an unattainable ideal" that Muslims must "nonetheless strive to emulate."[56] Other essays, such as those of Robert Cohn and John Hawley, stress the importance of hagiography in creating a pattern that, once it is known and assimilated into a culture, makes it possible for individuals to compare their own life-journeys with the paradigms set by the saints. The question for further study, however, is just how these biographies actually function as models. Do they tend to

50. Cohn, "Saints at the Periphery," 101.
51. Babb, "Sathya Sai Baba," 169.
52. Tambiah, "The Buddhist *Arahant*," 126.
53. James, *Varieties*, 259.
54. James, *Varieties*, 367.
55. James, *Varieties*, 358.
56. Brinner, "Prophet and Saint," 38.

exemplify a particular set of virtues, or rather do they tend to point toward a deeper relation to virtue's source and meaning? And in either case we are left with the question with which we began: can there be saints — can there be hagiography — in an age of secularity?

SAINTS AFTER SAINTHOOD:
NEW SAINTS FOR OUR TIMES

What would a saint look like "after sainthood"? In a society characterized by "the eclipse of the sacred" it may be difficult, if not impossible, to tell.[57] As Patrick Sherry remarks, "It is unclear whether a man who acknowledges the sanctity of some religious believers and yet refuses to admit God's existence is making a mistake and, if so, of what kind."[58] It is perhaps symptomatic that in the section of this volume entitled "saints of the modern world," there are no examples of saints native to modern, Western, industrialized societies. Gandhi, Sathya Sai Baba, even Alourdes may be saints for modern Westerners, but there is something distinctly unmodern and un-Western about them all.

I find the silence of Christian theologians about the contemporary meaning of saints quite puzzling. One would have expected, as Rahner has proposed, that this ought to have been a burning question for a Church that proclaims its visible holiness through appeal to an unbroken lineage of saints and grounds the catholicity of that holiness through its ability to bring forth in every epoch saints who show us how to be holy in particular places, times, and circumstances. The absence in today's churches of serious discourse about the meaning of sainthood for our time is rather shocking. The churches apparently mirror, rather than shape, the age. What our age can do to the notion of a saint is vividly displayed in a comic book version of the life of Assisi distributed by the Marvel Comics Group: *Francis, Brother of the Universe: His Complete Life.* Here the wolf of Gubbio growls "aarh" and Francis receives his stigmata with an "ugghh," but nowhere is there any hint of that famed and lovely Franciscan personage, "Sister Death." Francis has been sanitized. He is a one-dimensional saint, hardly a *coincidentia oppositorum;* he may be a hero, but not really a holy man.

An earlier generation, the one that lived just before World War II, seemed to feel the need for a new type of saint more keenly than we. In that era the French Catholic poet, Charles Peguy, exclaimed, "Saints of all kinds have been needed in the past and today we need yet another kind."[59] Simone Weil, the Jewish mystic who stayed outside of Catholicism because it was not

57. The phrase is that of S. S. Acquaviva, *The Decline of the Sacred in Industrial Society* (New York: Harper and Row, 1979), 200.

58. Patrick Sherry, *Religion, Truth and Language Games* (New York: Barnes and Noble, 1971), 111.

59. Cited in Daniel-Rops, "Holiness in History," 17.

catholic enough, pointed to a modern form of sainthood whose hallmark would be a stance of waiting with determination for God to reappear. Anticipating contemporary Latin American notions of sainthood, she looked for God and for sainthood among the marginal and poor of modern, industrial society, and she echoed Peguy in announcing, "The world today needs saints, new saints, saints of genius."[60]

Since saints no longer answer to a cultural expectation, their cultural work must of necessity be countercultural. Their lives must embody something at the limits, something paradoxical. They must live with joy a life that would not make any sense or give any joy if God did not exist. Nineteenth-century apologetics used to rely on miracles to prove the existence of God.[61] Today's saints, if any exist, constitute a kind of moral miracle whose lives show religious possibility to a world grown unaccustomed to the expectation of holiness. The very cultural "uselessness" of saints would serve as a judgment on the one-sided technical and utilitarian ethos of the wider society. More than ever, their virtues need to point beyond ordinary morality to virtue's source and ground because, as Alasdair MacIntyre contends, we moderns have lost a coherent sense of grounding purpose and unity in the universe and life.

The cultural work of saints for our times would point to the hiddenness of God in modern secular society and give an account of its meaning and purpose. Christians in today's North Atlantic nations, like the Hasidic Jews Robert Cohn describes, find themselves in a diaspora situation, and the saints who can sustain them are like the unknown *tsaddiqs* who served as invisible pillars of the world in Hasidic society.

Some of our modern writers — Graham Greene, George Bernanos, Flannery O'Connor, and Ignazio Silone — have provided us with hints of what such hidden saints, revealing the hidden God, might look like. These saints of modern fiction are discovered in situations quite unsupportive of their aspiration for holiness. Often they are unusually worldly, flawed sinner-saints like Greene's whisky priest in *The Power and the Glory,* who nonetheless display uncommon grace and lead exemplary lives in situations that can scarcely support them.

Changes in styles of hagiography often serve as the best clue to detecting the unique characteristics of the saint of a given epoch. For modern hagiography and perhaps uncanonizable saints we must turn either to such fictional characters or to uncanonized saints such as Dorothy Day, Thomas Merton, Dag Hammarskjold, Simone Weil, Dietrich Bonhoeffer, or Etty Hillesum.[62] Their biographies proliferate and become best sellers — the only

60. Cited in Daniel-Rops, "Holiness in History," 19.
61. Cf. Francis Fiorenza, *Foundational Theology* (New York: Crossroads, 1984), 6.
62. On the latter, see Etty Hillesum, *An Interrupted Life: The Diaries* (New York: Pantheon, 1984).

sacred biography that exists in our time. Such lives witness to the possibility of holiness in situations where it seems impossible: the pacifist Dorothy Day working with bums in the Bowery of New York City; Simone Weil in her slavish factory work; Hammarskjold, the mystic amidst worldly diplomacy; Hillesum's *joie de vivre* in the midst of a hellish concentration camp. In the desert places of modern life, where one does not expect God, just there the saint emerges.[63]

It is worth noting, indeed, that certain of the sayings and practices associated with desert monks have come back into vogue: the Jesus prayer and hesychastic breathing, with its centering prayer. We may lack decent hagiography for our own times, but the spiritual writings of the classical saints are enjoying a remarkable revival that may portend an attempt by a creative minority to retrieve the classic concept of the Christian saint.[64] The churches have their work cut out for them. Formal canonization procedures no longer give us the saints we need. Yet such saints may nevertheless exist in our midst — saints such as Iris Murdoch describes in her novel, *The Philosopher's Pupil.*

Her character, William Eastcote, is a man recognized as a saint by both his fellow Quakers and the unbelieving townsfolk by whom he is surrounded. During a Quaker meeting, just before he dies, Eastcote makes the following plea:

> My dear friends, we live in an age of marvels. Men among us can send machines far out into space. Our homes are full of devices which would amaze our forebears. At the same time our beloved planet is ravaged by suffering and threatened by dooms. Experts and wise men give us vast counsels suited to vast ills. I want only to say something about simple good things which are as it were close to us, within our reach, part still of our world. Let us love the close things, the close clear good things, and hope that in their light other goods may be added. Let us prize innocence. The child is innocent, the man is not. Let us prolong and cherish the innocence of childhood, as we find it in the child and as we rediscover it later within ourselves. Repentance, renewal of life, such as is the task and possibility of every man, is the recovery of innocence. Let us see it thus, a return to a certain simplicity, something which is not hard to understand, not a remote good but very near. . . . Above all, do not despair, either for the planet or in the deep inwardness of heart. Recognize one's own evil, mend what can be mended, and for what cannot be undone, place it in love and faith in the clear light and the healing goodness of God.[65]

Murdoch goes on to show that Eastcote was what he preached. Such homely saints surely exist both inside and outside of the churches, but for

63. Cf. Cunningham, *Saints,* chap. 5: "Saintliness and the Desert."

64. Indication of this is provided by the best-selling volumes in the Paulist Press series, "Classics in World Spirituality."

65. Iris Murdoch, *The Philosopher's Pupil* (London: Chatto and Windus, 1983), 204–5.

them to become a public ideal, we must again elevate talk about saints to the status of "serious discourse" in our culture.

Alasdair MacIntyre was correct, it seems to me, in his assessment of our situation. We are waiting for some new St. Benedict to build again — perhaps far from the centers of high technology and culture — a movement and a world with some resemblance to the one we seem so irretrievably to have lost with the passing of the saint as a cultural type. As the essays in this volume indicate, in losing our saints we have lost something not only unspeakably lovely but truly essential to human culture and imagination.

BIBLIOGRAPHY

Abate, Giuseppe. "Nuovi studi sulla leggenda di San Francesco detta del 'Tre compagni.'" *Miscellanea Francescana* 39 (1939).

Abbott, Walter M., S. J., gen. ed. *The Documents of Vatican II.* New York: Herder and Herder/Association Press, 1966.

Acquaviva, S. S. *The Decline of the Sacred in Industrial Society.* New York: Harper and Row, 1979.

Adler, E. N. *Jewish Travelers.* London: G. Routledge and Sons, 1930.

Ahmad, Aziz. *Studies in Islamic Culture in the Indian Environment.* Oxford: Clarendon Press, 1964.

al-Bakri. *Kitāb al-Masālik wa'l-Mamālik.* Edited by M. G. de Slane. Algiers: A. Jourdan, 1913.

Allen, Judson Byce. *The Ethical Poetic of the Later Middle Ages.* Toronto: University of Toronto Press, 1982.

al-Marghinānī. *Mishkāt al-Masābīh.* Translated by James Robson. Lahore: Sh. Muhammad Ashraf, 1963.

Ambedkar, B. R. *What Congress and Gandhi Have Done to the Untouchables.* Bombay: Thackur, 1945.

Anawati, G. C., and Louis Gardet. *Mystique musulmane: aspects et tendances — expériences et techniques.* Paris: Librairie philosophique J. Vrin, 1961.

Andrews, C. F., ed. *Mahatma Gandhi, His Own Story.* New York: Macmillan, 1930.

———. *Mahatma Gandhi's Ideas.* New York: Macmillan, 1930.

Arberry, A. J. *The Koran Interpreted.* New York: Macmillan, 1969.

Ashe, Geoffrey. *Gandhi.* New York: Stein and Day, 1968.

Athanasius. *De passione et cruce Domini.* In *Patrologiae Graecae Cursus Completus,* edited by J.-P. Migne, vol. 28, cols. 186–250. Paris: J.-P. Migne, 1857.

Athanasius. *Quaestiones ad Antiochum ducem.* In *Patrologiae Graecae Cursus Completus,* edited by J.-P. Migne, vol. 28, cols. 554–706. Paris: J.-P. Migne, 1857.

Athanasius. *Vita Antonii.* In *Patrologiae Graecae Cursus Completus,* edited by J.-P. Migne, vol. 26, cols. 835–975. Paris: J.-P. Migne, 1857.

Athanassakis, A. A., trans. *Vita Pachomii Graeca Prima* (The life of Pachomius). Missoula, Mont.: Scholars Press, 1975.

Babb, Lawrence A. "Sathya Sai Baba's Magic." *Anthropological Quarterly* 56, no. 3 (July 1983): 116–24.

Barnes, Sandra T. *Ogun: An Old God for a New Age*. ISHI Occasional Papers in Social Change, no. 3. Philadelphia: Institute for the Study of Human Issues, 1980.

Barnes, T. D. *Constantine and Eusebius*. Cambridge, Mass: Harvard University Press, 1981.

Baron, Salo W. *A Social and Religious History of the Jews*. Vol. 4. New York and London: Columbia University Press; and Philadelphia: Jewish Publication Society, 1957.

Bates, W. Jackson. *Samuel Johnson*. New York: Harcourt Brace, 1975.

Bayḍāwī, *Anwār al-Tanzīl*. Vol. 2. Edited by H. O. Fleischer. Leipzig: F. C. G. Vogel, 1848.

Bellah, Robert. "Transcendence." In *The Religious Situation, 1969*. Boston: Beacon Press, 1969.

——, Richard Marsden, William Sullivan, Ann Swindler, and Steven Tipton. *Habits of the Heart*. Berkeley and Los Angeles: University of California Press, 1985.

Bernays, Robert. *Naked Faquir*. New York: Henry Holt, 1932.

Bharati, Agehananda. *Hindu Views and Ways and the Hindu-Muslim Interface: An Anthropological Assessment*. Delhi: Munshiram Manoharlal, 1981.

Birla, G. D. *In the Shadow of the Mahatma: A Personal Memoir*. Bombay: Orient Longmans, 1953.

Boff, Leonardo. *Saint Francis: A Model of Human Liberation*. New York: Crossroad Books, 1984.

Bonhoeffer, Dietrich. *The Cost of Discipleship*. New York: Macmillan, 1963.

Boowa, Acharn Maha. *The Venerable Phra Acharn Mun Bhuridatta Thera, Meditation Master*. Translated by Siri Buddhasukh. Bangkok: Mahamakut Rajavidyalaya Press, 1976.

Bosworth, C. E. *The Medieval Islamic Underworld*. Leiden: E. J. Brill, 1976.

Brennder, Louis. *West African Sufi: The Religious Heritage and Spiritual Search of Cerno Bokar Saalif Taal*. London: Christopher Hurst, 1984.

Brooke, Rosalind, ed. and trans. *Scripta Leonis, Rufini et Angeli, Sociorum S. Francisci*. Oxford: Clarendon Press, 1970.

Brown, Karen McCarthy. "Systematic Remembering, Systematic Forgetting: Ogou in Haiti." Unpublished manuscript.

Brown, Peter. *The Cult of the Saints*. Chicago: University of Chicago Press, 1981.

——. *The Making of Late Antiquity*. Cambridge, Mass.: Harvard University Press, 1978.

——. *Society and the Holy*. Berkeley and Los Angeles: University of California Press, 1984.

Burghart, Richard. "The Founding of the Ramanandi Sect." *Ethnohistory* 25, no. 2 (1978): 121–39.

Bynum, Caroline Walker. *Docere Verbo et Exemplo: An Aspect of Twelfth-Century Spirituality*. Harvard Theological Studies 31. Missoula, Mont.: Scholars Press, 1979.

——. *Jesus as Mother: Studies in the Spirituality of the High Middle Ages*. Berkeley and Los Angeles: University of California Press, 1982.

——. "Women Mystics and Eucharistic Devotion in the Thirteenth Century." *Women's Studies* 11 (1984): 179–214.

Carra de Vaux, B. "Wali." In *Shorter Encyclopedia of Islam,* edited by H. A. R. Gibb and J. H. Kramer, 629 – 31. Leiden: E. J. Brill, 1961.

Cavallin, S., ed. *Vitae Honorati et Hilarii, Episcoporum Arelatensium.* Lund: C. W. K. Gleerup, 1952.

Cavinet, Maria-Teresa, and Pierre Cavinet. "La mosaique d'Adam dans l'église syrienne de Huārte." *Cahiers archéologiques* 24 (1975): 49 – 60.

Cazelles, Brigitte. *Le Corps de sainteté: d'après Jehan Bouche d'Or, Jehan Paulus et quelques vies des XIIe et XIIIe siècles.* Geneva: Librairie Droz S.A., 1982.

Chadwick, H. E. "Pachomius and the Idea of Sanctity." In *The Byzantine Saint,* University of Birmingham Fourteenth Symposium of Byzantine Studies, edited by S. Hackel. London: Fellowship of St. Alban and St. Sergius, 1981.

Chan, Wing-tsit. *A Source Book in Chinese Philosophy.* Princeton, N.J.: Princeton University Press, 1969.

Chandrakant, Kamala. *Mirabai.* Bombay: India Book House, n.d.

Chatfield, Charles, ed. *The Americanization of Gandhi: Images of the Mahatma.* New York and London: Garland Publishing, 1976.

Chernoff, John Miller. *African Rhythm and African Sensibility: Aesthetics and Social Action in African Musical Idioms.* Chicago: University of Chicago Press, 1979.

Chouraqui, A. *Between East and West: A History of the Jews of North Africa.* New York: Atheneum, 1973.

Christian, William A., Jr. *Person and God in a Spanish Valley.* New York: Macmillan, 1972.

Clouston, W. A., ed. *Arabian Poetry for English Readers.* Glasgow: Privately Printed, 1881.

Cobb, John B., Jr., and Gregory Baum. "Review of *The Analogical Imagination: Christian Theology and the Culture of Pluralism.*" *Religious Studies Review* 7, no. 4 (October 1981): 281 – 90.

Cohen, Gerson D. "Messianic Postures of Ashkenazim and Sephardim." In *Studies of the Leo Baeck Institute,* translated by Max Krentzberger. New York: Ungar, 1967.

––––––. "The Story of Hannah and Her Seven Sons in Hebrew Literature." In *Mordecai M. Kaplan Jubilee Volume,* edited by Moshe Davis, vol. 2. New York: Jewish Theological Seminary of America, 1953.

Cunningham, Lawrence. *The Meaning of Saints.* New York: Harper and Row, 1980.

Daniel-Rops, Henri. "Holiness in History and Holiness Today." In *Holiness in Action,* edited by Roland Cluny. New York: Hawthorn Books, 1963.

David, Ben J., and T. N. Clarke, eds. *Culture and its Creators.* Chicago: University of Chicago Press, 1977.

de Bary, Wm. Theodore. "Chu Hsi and Liberal Education." In *Liberal Tradition in China.* Hong Kong: The Chinese University Press; and New York: Columbia University Press, 1983.

Dimock, Edward C., Jr. "Religious Biography in India: The 'Nectar of the Acts' of Caitanya." In *The Biographical Process: Studies in the History and Psychology of Religion,* edited by F. E. Reynolds and D. Capps. The Hague: Mouton, 1976.

Douglas, Mary. *Purity and Danger.* London: Routledge and Kegan Paul, 1969.

Dresner, Samuel R. *The Zaddik.* New York: Schocken, 1960.

Dreyfus, Hubert, and Paul Rabinow. *Michel Foucault: Beyond Structuralism and Hermeneutics.* Chicago: University of Chicago Press, 1982.

Dumont, Fernand. *La Pensée réligieuse d'Amadou Bamba.* Dakar and Abidjan: Nouvelles éditions Africaines, 1975.

Dumont, Louis. *From Mandeville to Marx.* Chicago: University of Chicago Press, 1978.

———. *Homo Hierarchicus.* Chicago: University of Chicago Press, 1970.

Durkheim, Emile. *The Elementary Forms of Religious Life.* New York: Free Press, 1952.

Eidelberg, Shlomo, trans. *The Jews and the Crusaders.* Madison: University of Wisconsin Press, 1977.

Eliade, Mircea. *The Myth of the Eternal Return.* Translated by W. R. Trask. Princeton, N.J.: Princeton University Press, 1974.

Encyclopedia Judaica. Jerusalem: Kater, 1972.

Englebert, Omer. *Saint Francis of Assisi: A Biography.* 2d ed. Translated by Eve Marie Cooper. Chicago: Franciscan Herald Press, 1965.

Erikson, Erik H. *Childhood and Society.* 2d ed. New York: Norton, 1963.

———. *Young Man Luther: A Study in Psychoanalysis and History.* New York: Norton, 1962.

Esser, Kajetan. "Gehorsam und Freiheit." *Wissenschaft und Weisheit* 13 (1950): 142–50.

———. "Die 'Regula pro eremitoriis data' des heiligen Franziskus von Assisi." *Franziskanische Studien* 44, no. 4 (1962): 383–417.

———. *Repair My House.* Edited by Luc Mely, and translated by Michael D. Meilach. Chicago: Franciscan Herald Press, 1963.

Evans-Wentz, W. Y., ed. *Tibet's Great Yogi Milarepa, A Biography from the Tibetan Being the Jetsun-Kahbum or Biographical History of Jetsun Milarepa, According to the Late Lama Kazi Dawa-Samdup's English Rendering.* London: Oxford University Press, 1978.

Eyice, Semavi, and Jacques Noret. "S. Lucien, disciple de S. Lucien d'Antioche, à propos d'une inscription de Kirsehir (Turquie)." *Analecta Bollandiana* 91 (1973): 363–78.

Faral, Edmond. *Les Jongleurs en France au moyen âge.* Paris: Librairie Honoré Champion, 1910.

Feldhaus, Anne. "Bahiṇā Bāī: Wife and Saint." *Journal of the American Academy of Religion* 50, no. 4 (1982): 591–604.

Ferguson, John P. "The Arahat Ideal in Modern Burmese Buddhism." Paper presented at the Annual Meeting of the Association for Asian Studies, New York, March 1977.

Festugière, A. J., ed. *Vita Theodori Syceotae.* Brussels: Société des Bollandistes, 1970.

Fiorenza, Francis. *Foundational Theology.* New York: Crossroad, 1984.

Fischel, H. A. "Martyr and Prophet (A Study in Jewish Literature)." *Jewish Quarterly Review* 37, no. 3 (January 1947): 265–80.

Fischer, Frederick. *That Strange Little Brown Man Gandhi.* New York: Ray Long and Richard R. Smith, 1932.

Fisher, Humphrey J. "Dreams and Conversion in Black Africa." In *Conversion to Islam,* edited by Nehemiah Levtzion. New York: Holmes and Meier, 1979.

———. "Liminality, Hijrah and the City." *Asian and African Studies* 20, no. 1 (1986): 153–77.

Fisher, Louis. *A Week with Gandhi.* London: George Allen and Unwin, 1943.

Foot, Philippa. *Virtues and Vices and Other Essays in Moral Philosophy.* Berkeley and Los Angeles: University of California Press, 1978.

Fortini, Arnaldo. *Francis of Assisi.* Translated by Helen Moak. New York: Crossroad, 1981.

Foucault, Michel. *The Archeology of Knowledge.* Translated by A. M. Sheridan Smith. New York: Harper and Row, 1972.

Francis of Assisi. *Opuscula Sancti Patris Francisci Assisiensis.* Bibliotheca Franciscana Ascetica Medii Aevi 1. Florence: Quaracchi, 1949.

Gandhi, Mohandas K. *Collected Writings of Mahatma Gandhi.* 86 vols. New Delhi: Publications Division, Ministry of Information and Broadcasting, 1958–82.

———. *The Story of My Experiments with Truth.* Ahmedabad: Navajivan Press, 1927.

Gellner, Ernest. *Muslim Society.* Cambridge, England: Cambridge University Press, 1981.

Goldberg, A. "Der Heilige und die Heiligen: Vorüberlegungen zur Theologie des heiligen Menschen im rabbinischen Judentum." In *Aspekte frühchristlicher Heiligenverehrung,* Oikonomia 6. Erlangen: Copy Center 2000, 1977.

Goodblatt, David M. *Rabbinic Instruction in Sasanian Babylonia.* London: E. J. Brill, 1975.

Green, Arthur. *Tormented Master: A Life of Rabbi Nahman of Bratslav.* University, Ala.: University of Alabama Press, 1979.

———. "The *Zaddiq* as *Axis Mundi* in Later Judaism." *Journal of the American Academy of Religion* 45 (1977): 327–47.

Green, William Scott. "Palestinian Holy Men: Charismatic Leadership and Rabbinic Tradition." In *Aufstieg und Niedergang der Römischen Welt,* edited by H. Temporini and W. Hasse, vol. 19, fasc. 2. Berlin: H. Temporini; and New York: de Gruyter, 1979.

———. "What's in a Name? — The Problematic of Rabbinic Biography." In *Approaches to Ancient Judaism: Theory and Practice,* edited by William Scott Green, vol. 1, pp. 77–96. Missoula, Mont.: Scholars Press, 1978.

Gregg, R., and D. Groh. *Early Arianism: A View of Salvation.* Philadelphia: Fortress Press, 1981.

Gregory of Nyssa. *De hominis opificio.* In *Patrologiae Graecae Cursus Completus,* edited by J.-P. Migne, vol. 44, cols. 123–256. Paris: J.-P. Migne, 1858.

———. *De perfectione christiana.* In *Patrologiae Graecae Cursus Completus,* edited by J.-P. Migne, vol. 46, cols. 251–86. Paris: J.-P. Migne, 1858.

Grenier, Richard. "The Gandhi Nobody Knows." *Commentary* 75, no. 3 (March 1983): 59–72.

Guillaumont, A. "Une inscription copte sur la 'Prière de Jésus.'" *Orientalia Christiana Periodica* 34 (1968): 310–25.

Gupta, R. D. "Priyā Dās, Author of the *Bhaktirasabodhinī.*" *Bulletin of the School of Oriental and African Studies* 32, no. 1 (1969): 57–70.

Hauerwas, Stanley, *The Community of Character.* South Bend, Ind.: University of Notre Dame Press, 1983.

———. *Truthfulness and Tragedy.* South Bend, Ind.: University of Notre Dame Press, 1977.

Hawley, John Stratton. *Krishna, The Butter Thief.* Princeton, N.J.: Princeton University Press, 1983.

———. "The *Sant* in Sūr Dās." In *The Sants: Studies in a Devotional Tradition of India,* edited by Karine Schomer and W. H. McLeod. Berkeley: Berkeley Religious Studies Series; and Delhi: Motilal Banarsidass, 1987.

Herz, Joseph H., trans., *The Authorized Daily Prayer Book.* Rev. ed. New York: Bloch, 1959.

Hillesum, Etty. *An Interrupted Life: The Diaries.* New York: Pantheon, 1984.

Hirschfeld, Hartwig, trans. *Judah Hallevi's Kitab al Khazari.* London: George Routledge and Sons; and New York: E. P. Dutton, 1905.

Holmes, John Haynes. *My Gandhi.* New York: Harper and Brothers, 1953.

Hossain, Syud. *The Saint as Statesman.* Los Angeles: Sutton House, 1937.

Hyman, Paula E. "The Other Half: Women in the Jewish Tradition." *Conservative Judaism* 26, no. 4 (1972): 14–21.

Ishaq, Ibn. *The Life of Muhammad: A Translation of Sirat Rasul Allah.* Translated by A. Guillaume. Lahore: Oxford University Press, 1955.

James, William. *The Varieties of Religious Experience.* New York: Longmans, Green, 1923.

Jeffrey, Arthur, ed. *Islam: Muhammad and His Religion.* New York: Liberal Arts Press, 1958.

Jeremias, Joachim. *Heiligengräber im Jesu Umwelt.* Göttingen: Vandenhoeck and Ruprecht, 1958.

The Jewish Encyclopedia. Vol. 8. New York and London: Funk and Wagnalls, 1905, 1916.

Jha, Narendra. *Bhaktamāl: Pāṭhānuśīlan evam Vivecan.* Patna: Anupam Prakāśan, 1978.

John, Joseph, ed. *Gandhi as Others See Him.* Colombo, Sri Lanka: W. E. Bastion, 1933.

Jones, Charles. *Saint Nicholas of Myra, Bari and Manhattan.* Chicago: University of Chicago Press, 1978.

Jones, Marc Edmund. *Gandhi Lives.* Philadelphia: David McKay, 1948.

Juergensmeyer, Mark. *Fighting with Gandhi.* San Francisco: Harper and Row, 1984.

———. "Shoring Up the Saint: Some Suggestions for Improving Satyagraha." In *Gandhi's Elusive Legacy,* edited by John Hick and Lamont Hempel. London: Macmillan, forthcoming.

Kane, P. V. *History of Dharmaśāstra.* 5 vols. Poona: Bhandarkar Oriental Research Institute, 1930–46.

Kasturi, N. *Sathya Sai Speaks.* Vol. 8. Tustin, Calif.: Sri Sathya Sai Baba Book Center of America, 1975.

———. *Sathyam, Sivam, Sundaram.* Pt. 1, American ed. Whitefield: Shri Sathya Sai Education and Publication Foundation, 1977. *Sathyam, Sivam, Sundaram.* Pt. 2, 3d ed. New Delhi: Bhagavan Sri Sathya Sai Seva Samiti, 1975. *Sathyam, Sivam, Sundaram.* Pt. 3. New Delhi: Bhagavan Sri Sathya Sai Seva Samiti, 1975.

Khalafallah, M. "Arabiyya." In *The Encyclopedia of Islam,* vol. 1, p. 567. Leiden: E. J. Brill, 1960.

Kinsley, David R. *The Divine Player: A Study of Kṛṣṇa Līlā.* Delhi: Motilal Banarsidass, 1979.

Kluckhohn, Clyde. "Toward a Comparison of Value Emphases in Different Cultures." In *The State of the Social Sciences,* edited by Leonard White. Chicago: University of Chicago Press, 1956.

Kluckhohn, F. R., and Fred L. Strodbeck. *Variations in Value Orientations.* Evanston, Ill.: Row, Paterson, 1961.

Ladner, G. *The Idea of Reform.* New York: Harper Torchbooks, 1967.

Laing, R. D. *The Divided Self.* Baltimore: Penguin, 1971.

———. *Self and Others.* Rev. ed. Baltimore: Penguin, 1972.

———, and Aaron Easterson. *Sanity, Madness and the Family.* Baltimore: Penguin, 1972.

Legge, James, trans. *The Chinese Classics.* Vol. 1. Oxford: Clarendon Press, 1883.

Lester, M. *My Host the Hindu.* London: Williams and Norgate, 1931.

Levtzion, N., and J. F. P. Hopkins, eds. *Corpus of Early Arabic Sources for West African History.* London: Cambridge University Press, 1981.

Levy, Reuben. *The Social Structure of Islam.* London: Cambridge University Press, 1957.

Lingat, Robert. *The Classical Law of India.* Translated by J. Duncan M. Derrett. Berkeley and Los Angeles: University of California Press, 1973.

Lucian. "The Ignorant Book-Collector." In Loeb Classical Library, translated by A. M. Harmon, vol. 3, pp. 173–211. Cambridge, Mass.: Harvard University Press, 1969.

Lutgendorf, Philip. "Kṛṣṇa Caitanya and His Companions as Presented in the *Bhaktamāla* of Nābhā Jī and the *Bhaktirasabodhinī* of Priyā Dāsa." Master's essay, University of Chicago, 1981.

———. "The Quest for the Legendary Tulsīdās." Paper presented to the American Academy of Religion, Los Angeles, November, 1985.

Luzzatto, Moses Hayyim. *The Path of the Upright.* Translated and edited by Mordecai M. Kaplan. Philadelphia: Jewish Publication Society, 1966.

Macdonald, Duncan Black. *The Development of Muslim Theology and Jurisprudence.* Beirut: Khayat Books, 1965.

MacIntyre, Alasdair. *After Virtue.* South Bend, Ind.: University of Notre Dame Press, 1981.

Manu. *The Laws of Manu.* Translated by Georg Bühler. New York: Dover, 1969.

Marriott, McKim. "The Feast of Love." In *Krishna: Myths, Rites and Attitudes,* edited by M. Singer. Honolulu: East-West Center Press, 1966.

———. "Hindu Transactions: Diversity without Dualism." In *Transactions and Meaning: Directions in the Anthropology of Exchange and Symbolic Behavior,* edited by B. Kapferer. Philadelphia: ISHI Publishers, 1976.

Marrou, H. I. *A History of Education in the Ancient World.* Translated by G. Lamb. New York: Sheed and Ward, 1956.

Marty, Paul. *L'Islam en Guinée.* Paris: E. Leroux, 1921.

Mauer, Herryman. *Great Soul: The Growth of Gandhi.* Garden City, N.Y.: Doubleday, 1948.

McGinley, Phyllis. *Saint Watching.* New York: Viking, 1969.

McLeod, W. H. *Gurū Nānak and the Sikh Religion.* Oxford: Clarendon Press, 1968.

Mecklin, John. *The Passing of the Saint: A Study of a Cultural Type.* Chicago: University of Chicago Press, 1941.

Mehta, Ved. *Mahatma Gandhi and His Apostles*. London: Andre Deutsch, 1977.

Michael, R. Blake. "Aṣṭāvaraṇa in the *Śūnyasaṃpādane*." Ph.D. diss., Harvard University, 1979.

———. "The Housewife as Saint: Tales from the *Śūnyasaṃpādane*." Paper presented to the American Academy of Religion, New York, 1979.

———. "Work as Worship in the Vīraśaiva Tradition," *Journal of the American Academy of Religion* 50, no. 4 (1982): 605–19.

Molinari, Paul. "The Intercession of the Saints." In *The New Catholic Encyclopedia*, vol. 12, pp. 971–74. New York: McGraw-Hill, 1967.

Monteil, Vincent. *L'Islam noir*. Paris: Seuil, 1964.

Murdoch, Iris. *The Philosopher's Pupil*. London: Chatto and Windus, 1983.

Nābhājī. *Śrī Bhaktamāl*. Lucknow, India: Tejkumār Press, 1969.

Ñāṇamoli, Bhikkhu. *The Path of Purification (Visuddhimagga)*. Colombo, Sri Lanka: Semage, 1956.

Neusner, Jacob. *Invitation to the Talmud: A Teaching Book*. New York: Harper and Row, 1973.

Neville, Robert C. *Soldier, Sage, Saint*. New York: Fordham University Press, 1978.

Niebuhr, Reinhold. *Moral Man and Immoral Society*. New York: Charles Scribner's Sons, 1932.

———. *The Nature and Destiny of Man*. Vol. 1. New York: Charles Scribner's Sons, 1941.

O'Brien, Donal Cruise. *The Mourides of Senegal*. Oxford: Clarendon Press, 1971.

———. "A Versatile Charisma: The Mouride Brotherhood 1967–1975." *Archives européennes de sociologie* 18 (1977): 84–106.

Padwick, Constance E. *Muslim Devotions*. London: Society for the Propagation of Christian Knowledge, 1961.

Pangarkar, L. R. *Marāṭhī Vāṇmayācā Itihās*. Pune, India: Vidarbh Marāṭhavāḍā Book Company, 1972.

Parikh, Dvarkadas, ed. *Caurāsī Vaiṣṇavan kī Vārtā*. Mathura: Śrī Bajaraṅg Pustakālay, 1970.

Paulinus. *Wandering Scholars*. Translated by H. Waddell. London: Constable, 1927.

Pedersen, Johannes. *Israel: Its Life and Culture I–II*. London: Oxford University Press; and Copenhagen: Branner Og Korch, 1926.

Pemberton, John, III. "A Cluster of Sacred Symbols: Oriṣa Worship Among the Igbomina Yoruba of Ila-Orangun." *History of Religions* 17, no. 1 (1977): 1–28.

Perham, Michael. *The Communion of Saints*. London: Society for the Propagation of Christian Knowledge, 1980.

Pickthall, M. M. *The Meaning of the Glorious Koran*. London: George Allen and Unwin, 1957.

Polak, Henry S. L. "Saint, Patriot, and Statesman." In *Gandhiji as We Know Him*, edited by Chandrashankar Shukla. Bombay: Vora, 1945.

Pollet, Gilbert. "Early Evidence on Tulsīdās and His Epic." *Orientalia Lovaniensia Periodica* 5 (1974): 151–62.

———. "Eight Manuscripts of the Hindī *Bhaktamāla* in England." *Orientalia Lovaniensia Periodica* 1 (1970): 203–22.

———. "The Mediaeval Vaiṣṇava Miracles as Recorded in the Hindi 'Bhakta Māla.'" *Le Muséon* 80 (1967): 475–87.

Pound, Ezra. *Confucius: The Great Digest and the Unwobbling Pivot.* London: Peter Owen, 1952.

Prasad, Rajendra. *At the Feet of Mahatma Gandhi.* Bombay: Hind Kitab, 1955.

Rahner, Karl. *Theological Investigations.* Vol. 8. New York: Herder and Herder, 1971.

Ramanujan, A. K. "On Women Saints." In *The Divine Consort: Rādhā and the Goddesses of India,* edited by J. S. Hawley and Donna M. Wulff, 316–24. Berkeley: Berkeley Religious Studies Series, 1982.

Reynolds, Frank E., and Donald Capps, eds. *The Biographical Process: Studies in the History and Psychology of Religion.* The Hague: Mouton, 1976.

Reynolds, Frank, and Mani Reynolds, trans. *Three Worlds According to King Ruang, A Thai Buddhist Cosmology.* Berkeley and Los Angeles: University of California Press, 1982.

Rost, Leonhard. *Judaism Outside the Hebrew Canon: An Introduction to the Documents.* Nashville: Abingdon, 1976.

Rousseau, Philip. *Ascetics, Authority and the Church.* Oxford: Oxford University Press, 1978.

Rudolph, Lloyd I., and Susanne Hoeber Rudolph. *The Modernity of Tradition.* Chicago: University of Chicago Press, 1967.

Ryan, Howard. "Mahatma Gandhi: New Look at the Father of Nonviolence." *It's About Times* (November 1985): 6–8.

———. *Nonviolence and Class Bias: From Mahatma Gandhi to the Anti-Nuclear Movement.* New Delhi: South Asia Publications; and Cupertino, Calif.: Folklore Institute, 1983.

Safrai, S. "Teaching of Pietists in Mishnaic Literature." *Journal of Jewish Studies* 16, nos. 1–2 (1965): 15–33.

Sanneh, Lamin. "Islam and French Colonialism in Futa Jallon, Guinea: Tcherno Aliou, the *wali* of Goumba." *Journal of Asian and African Studies.* Forthcoming.

———. *The Jakhanke: The History of an Islamic Clerical People of Senegambia.* London: International African Institute, 1979.

Śarmā, Kailāś Candra. *Bhaktamāl aur Hindī Kāvya mē unkī Paramparā.* Rohtak: Manthan Publications, 1983.

Schimmel, Annemarie. *As Through a Veil: Mystical Poetry in Islam.* New York: Columbia University Press, 1982.

———. *Mystical Dimensions of Islam.* Chapel Hill: University of North Carolina Press, 1973.

Scholem, Gershom. *Major Trends in Jewish Mysticism.* New York: Schocken, 1961.

———. *Sabbatai Sevi: The Mystical Messiah.* Bollingen Series 93. Princeton, N.J.: Princeton University Press, 1973.

———. "Three Types of Jewish Piety." *Eranos-Jahrbuch* 38 (1969): 331–48.

Sherry, Patrick. *Religion, Truth and Language Games.* New York: Barnes and Noble, 1971.

Shils, Edward. *Center and Periphery: Essays in Macrosociology.* Chicago: University of Chicago Press, 1975.

Sivan, Emmanuel. *Radical Islam: Medieval Theology and Modern Politics.* New Haven, Conn.: Yale University Press, 1985.

Smith, John Holland. *Francis of Assisi.* New York: Charles Scribner's Sons, 1972.

Smith, Wilfred C. *The Meaning and End of Religion*. San Francisco: Harper and Row, 1978.

Sorokin, Pitirim. *Altruistic Love*. Boston: Beacon Press, 1950.

———. *The Ways and Power of Love*. Boston: Beacon Press, 1954.

Sozomen. *Historia Ecclesiastica*. 3 vols. Edited by Robert Hussey. Oxford: Typographeum Academicum, 1860.

Sumption, Jonathan. *Pilgrimage: An Image of Medieval Religion*. London: Faber and Faber, 1975.

Swallow, D. A. "Ashes and Powers: Myth, Rite and Miracle in an Indian God-Man's Cult." *Modern Asian Studies* 16 (1982): 123–58.

Tambiah, Stanley. *Buddhist Saints of the Forest and the Cult of Amulets*. Cambridge, England: Cambridge University Press, 1984.

———. *World Conqueror and World Renouncer*. Cambridge, England: Cambridge University Press, 1976.

Theodore. "Catechesis." In *Pachomian Koinonia*, vol. 3. Translated by A. Veilleux. Kalamazoo, Mich.: Cistercian Publications, 1982.

Thomas Aquinas. *Summa Theologiae*. Rome: Marietti, 1950.

Thomas of Celano. *Analecta Franciscana sive chronica aliaque varia documenta ad historiam fratrum minorum*. Florence: Quaracchi, 1926–41.

Thurston, Edgar, and K. Rangachari. *Castes and Tribes of Southern India*. Vol. 6. Madras: Government Press, 1909.

Tracy, David. *The Analogical Imagination*. New York: Crossroads, 1981.

Trimingham, J. Spencer. *Islam in West Africa*. Oxford: Clarendon Press, 1959.

———. *The Sufi Orders in Islam*. London: Oxford University Press, 1971.

Troeltsch, Ernst. *The Social Teachings of the Christian Churches*. Vol. 1. Translated by Olive Wyon. New York: Free Press, 1949.

Turner, Victor. *The Ritual Process: Structure and Anti-Structure*. Chicago: Aldine, 1969.

Tu Wei-ming. "The Idea of the Human in Mencian Thought: An Approach to Chinese Aesthetics." In *Theories of the Arts in China,* edited by Susan Bush and Christian Murck. Princeton, N.J.: Princeton University Press, 1984.

———. "Selfhood and Otherness: Father-Son Relationship in Confucian Thought." In *Culture and Self,* edited by Anthony Marsella, George De Vos, and Francis Hsu. London: Tavistock Press. Forthcoming.

Urbach, Ephraim E. *The Sages: Their Concepts and Beliefs*. Jerusalem: Magnes, 1975.

Vallabha. "Sannyāsanirṇaya." In *Kṛṣṇaśodaśagranthāḥ*. Bombay: Nirnaya Sagara Press, n.d.

van den Ven, P., ed. *Vita Symeonis Junioris*. Brussels: Société des Bollandistes, 1962.

van der Leeuw, G. *Religion in Essence and Manifestation: A Study in Phenomenology*. Translated by J. E. Turner. New York and Evanston, Ill.: Harper and Row, 1963.

Vermes, Geza. *Jesus the Jew*. New York: Macmillan, 1973.

Vie et miracles de S. Thècle. Edited by G. Dagron. Brussels: Société des Bollandistes, 1978.

Voinot, L. *Pèlerinages judeo-musulman au Maroc*. Paris: Larose, 1948.

Von Grunebaum, Gustave E. *Muhammadan Festivals*. Leiden: E. J. Brill, 1958.

Wach, Joachim. *Sociology of Religion*. Chicago and London: University of Chicago Press, 1944.

Waddell, Paul. "An Interpretation of Aquinas' Treatise on the Passions, the Virtues, and the Gifts from the Perspective of Charity as Friendship with God." Ph.D. diss., University of Notre Dame, 1985.

Walsh, P. G. *Ancient Christian Writers.* New York: Newman Press, 1967.

Ward, Benedicta. *Miracles and the Medieval Mind.* Philadelphia: University of Pennsylvania Press, 1982.

————, trans. *The Sayings of the Desert Fathers.* Kalamazoo, Mich.: Cistercian Publications, 1975.

Warner, Marina. *Alone of All Her Sex: The Myth and Cult of the Virgin Mary.* New York: Alfred A. Knopf, 1976.

Waterman, Richard Alan. "African Influence on the Music of the Americas." In *Acculturation in the Americas,* edited by Sol Tax, vol. 2. Chicago: University of Chicago Press, 1952.

Weber, Max. *From Max Weber: Essays in Sociology.* Translated and edited by H. H. Gerth and C. Wright Mills. London: Routledge and Kegan Paul, 1948.

Weinstein, Donald, and Rudolph M. Bell. *Saints and Society: The Two Worlds of Western Christendom, 1000–1700.* Chicago: University of Chicago Press, 1982.

Wensinck, A. J. *The Muslim Creed.* London: Frank Cass, 1965.

Werner, Eric. "Traces of Jewish Hagiolatry." *Hebrew Union College Annual* 51 (1980): 39–60.

White, Charles S. J. "The Sai Baba Movement: Approaches to the Study of Indian Saints." *Journal of Asian Studies* 31, no. 4 (August 1972): 863–78.

Widengren, Geo. "Muhammad, the Apostle of God, and His Ascension." *Uppsala Universitets Arsskrift* 1 (1955): 1–258.

Williams, Michael A., ed. *Charisma and Sacred Biography.* Chico, Calif.: Scholars Press, 1982.

Willis, John Ralph, ed. *Studies in West African Islamic History.* London: Frank Cass, 1979.

Wilson, Stephen, ed. *Saints and Their Cults: Studies in Religious Sociology, Folklore and History.* Cambridge, England: Cambridge University Press, 1983.

Young, Katherine. "One Stage, Three Acts: The Life-Drama of a Traditional Hindu Woman." Paper presented to the American Academy of Religion, New York, November 1979.

Zvelebil, Kamil. *Tamil Literature.* Wiesbaden: Otto Harrassowitz, 1974.

LIST OF CONTRIBUTORS

LAWRENCE A. BABB is Professor of Anthropology at Amherst College. He is the author of *The Divine Hierarchy: Popular Hinduism in Central India* (Columbia University Press, 1975), *Redemptive Encounters: Three Modern Styles in the Hindu Tradition* (University of California Press, forthcoming), and various articles dealing with diverse aspects of the Hindu tradition. Currently he is engaged in research on Jainism.

WILLIAM M. BRINNER, Professor of Near Eastern Studies at the University of California, Berkeley, has interests in Islamic history and religion and in the history and culture of Jews in the Islamic world. His recent publications include two translations: from Judeo-Arabic, *An Elegant Composition Concerning Relief after Adversity* (Yale University Press, 1978), and from Arabic, *Prophets and Patriarchs,* vol. 2 of al-Tabari's *History* (SUNY Press, 1986).

KAREN MCCARTHY BROWN is Associate Professor of the Sociology of Religion in the Graduate and Theological Schools of Drew University. Since 1973 she has done research and writing on various aspects of Haitian Vodou. A book, *Mama Lola: A Vodou Priestess in Brooklyn,* is forthcoming.

PETER BROWN, a Fellow of the British Academy and the American Association of the Arts and Sciences, is Professor of History at Princeton University. His publications include *Augustine of Hippo* (University of California Press, 1967), *Religion and Society in the Age of Saint Augustine* (Faber, 1972), *The World of Late Antiquity* (Harcourt, Brace, 1972), *The Making of Late Antiquity* (Harvard University Press, 1978), *The Cult of the Saints* (University of Chicago Press, 1981), and *Society and the Holy in Late Antiquity* (University of California Press, 1983).

ROBERT L. COHN, Philip and Muriel Berman Scholar in Jewish Studies at Lafayette College, teaches courses in Hebrew Bible, Judaism, and comparative religion. He is the author of *The Shape of Sacred Space: Four Biblical Studies* (Scholars Press, 1981), as well as numerous articles on biblical narrative and the essay "Sainthood" in *The Encyclopedia of Religion* (Macmillan, 1987).

JOHN A. COLEMAN, S. J., is Associate Professor of Religion and Sociology at the Graduate Theological Union, Berkeley. He is the author of three books — *Sociology: An Introduction* (Bruce Publishing, 1968), *The Evolution of Dutch Catholicism*

(University of California Press, 1978), and *An American Strategic Theology* (Paulist, 1982) — and has edited six other works, including *The New Religious Movements* (Seabury, 1982). He is on the board of editors of *Concilium,* the international Catholic journal, and serves as editor-in-chief for the Paulist Press series on American culture and religion.

HESTER GOODENOUGH GELBER is Assistant Professor of Religious Studies at Stanford University. Her interests include religious thought and theology in the European Middle Ages and their connections with philosophy and psychology. She is the author of a book, *Exploring the Boundaries of Reason: Three Questions on the Nature of God by Robert Holcot, OP* (Pontifical Institute of Mediaeval Studies, 1983), and of articles on the Dominicans teaching at fourteenth-century Oxford.

JOHN STRATTON HAWLEY is Professor of Religion at Barnard College, Columbia University. He is the author of *At Play with Krishna* (with Shrivatsa Goswami, Princeton University Press, 1981), *Krishna, the Butter Thief* (Princeton University Press, 1983), and *Sūr Dās: Poet, Singer, Saint* (University of Washington Press and Oxford University Press, 1984). An earlier edited volume, *The Divine Consort* (Berkeley Religious Studies Series, 1982; Beacon, 1986), concerned Rādhā and the goddesses of India and was prepared in collaboration with Donna M. Wulff.

MARK JUERGENSMEYER is Professor of Ethics and the Phenomenology of Religions at the Graduate Theological Union, where he serves as Director of the Office of Programs in Comparative Religion. He also coordinates the Program in Religious Studies at the University of California, Berkeley. His books include *Fighting with Gandhi* (Harper and Row, 1984; paperback title: *Fighting Fair*), *Religion as Social Vision* (University of California Press, 1982), and a forthcoming study called *Radhasoami Reality: The Logic of a Modern Faith.*

LAMIN SANNEH is Associate Professor of History of Religion at Harvard Divinity School. He is the author of two books — *The Jakhanke: The History of an Islamic Clerical People of Senegambia* (International African Institute, 1979), and *West African Christianity: The Religious Impact* (Orbis, 1983) — and of a forthcoming study entitled *Mission, Translation and Cultural Change.* He has written over thirty articles on aspects of Islam and Christianity, many of them dealing with his special interest: the cultural basis for the assimilation of Islam and Christianity through history.

STANLEY J. TAMBIAH, a Fellow of the American Academy of Arts and Sciences, is Professor and Chairman in the Department of Anthropology at Harvard University. His theoretical concerns range widely over the fields of religion and ritual, politics and economy, and their interrelationships; regionally, he has a strong interest in South and Southeast Asia. His most recent publications are *The Buddhist Saints of the Forest and the Cult of Amulets* (Cambridge University Press, 1984), *Culture, Thought and Social Action* (Harvard University Press, 1985), and *Sri Lanka: Ethnic Fratricide and the Dismantling of Democracy* (University of Chicago Press, 1986).

TU WEI-MING, Professor of Chinese History and Philosophy at Harvard University, is Chair of Harvard's Committee on the Study of Religion. Among his publications are *Neo-Confucian Thought in Action: Wang Yang-ming's Youth* (University of California Press, 1976), *Centrality and Commonality* (University Press of Hawaii, 1976), *Humanity and Self-Cultivation* (Asian Humanities Press, 1976), *Confucian Ethics Today: The Singapore Challenge* (Singapore: Federal Publications, 1984), and *Confucian Thought: Selfhood as Creative Transformation* (SUNY Press, 1986).

INDEX